President McKinley

"I Done My Duty"

The Complete Story of the Assassination of President McKinley

By:
Jeffrey W. Seibert

Heritage Books, Inc.

Published 2002 by

HERITAGE BOOKS, INC.
1540E Pointer Ridge Place
Bowie, Maryland 20716

1-800-398-7709
www.heritagebooks.com

ISBN 0-7884-2118-2

A Complete Catalog Listing Hundreds of Titles
On History, Genealogy, and Americana
Available Free Upon Request

Dedication

To Mom, Dad, Stacey, Brad, Jill and Ralph

Table of Contents

Acknowledgements

This book has been a three-year project and as such, there are many people who have been of assistance.

In the beginning I did much of my research at the Cincinnati Hamilton County Public Library. The staff of the periodical department was very helpful in supplying me with assistance in researching the *New York Times* and *Washington Post*, as well as the Cincinnati newspapers. They also helped tremendously in running down various publications, including magazines and reports. Special thanks to Myron Neal in the Literature Department for his help in securing some of photographs for publication.

The staff of the Clermont County Library indoctrinated me in getting inter-library loans and were very helpful also in helping me obtain hard to find books and articles. They always helped with a smile and friendly word.

I also did some work in the Kenton County Library in Covington, Kentucky, mainly on the microfilm machines.

I looked through many of the Buffalo newspapers originally at the Library of Congress in Washington, D.C., and as one would expect, discovered the staff to be professional, helpful and friendly. I particularly would like to remember Jeff in the manuscript room for his assistance in helping me locate the Cortelyou papers.

I spent three long days in the Buffalo Erie County Public Library, in the Special Collections room. Their collection of resources relating to the assassination was amazing and helpful. I constantly bothered the librarian on duty, at least I felt like I was bothering her, with my endless requests for assistance. But she never made me feel like I was a bother, and I very much appreciate all the help that Varney Greene gave me, as well as the rest of the Special Collections staff. Whoever put the scrapbooks in this collection together years ago was also a huge help. What an impressive job that was. It made my life much easier those few days.

I also spent a day at the Buffalo Erie County Historical Society. I feel reluctant to complain about the treatment I, and other researchers while I was there, received at the hands of the staff. I was able to look at a few things I have included in this work, but not without feeling like I was trying to get away with something. Apparently, from talking to other researchers and librarians from other places, this is common and not the exception. I had received the same treatment on the telephone. I would like to remind the historical society that they should be there to serve the people who show interest, not guard there precious possessions to the point where people are made to feel like criminals for asking to view them. The administration seems to be much more interested in making a buck than providing help to researchers. Enough said on that score. But at least, I got to see Czolgosz's gun and handkerchief, which are on public display there.

Thanks to the helpful staff at the library of Cleveland State University. They helped me track down the little information I could find on what became of the family of Leon Czolgosz.

Mark H. Lozo, the Chief of Interpretation and Education Director at the Theodore Roosevelt Inaugural National Historical Site, gave me a personal tour of the Wilcox mansion and was of help in locating some of the local sites. I also very much enjoyed our conversation in the gift shop of the site.

Thanks to Dr. Jack C. Fisher, author of *Stolen Glory: The McKinley Assassination,* for generously providing me with copies of the Secret Service agent's reports and for giving me some pointers in running down the photos used in this work.

Thanks to Joseph Boyd of Albert Whitman and Company, Morton Grove, Illinois, for giving me permission to reprint some quotes from the book *Theodore Roosevelt Takes Charge* by Nancy Whitelaw. That made it much easier for me, preventing me from having to run down some of the original quotes of President Roosevelt.

Thanks to James W. Clarke, of the University of Arizona, for permitting me to use some quotes from his book, *American Assassins.*

Thanks to Michael Greaves of Random House for his quick response concerning the copyright of Emma Goldman's book, *Living My Life.*

Special thanks to Laird Towle for sending me one of the most exciting letters I have ever received, telling me that Heritage Books was interested in publishing this book. After all the work I had put in, it was such a boost to see that it would all come to pass.

I would also like to thank a few of my personal friends who encouraged and helped me. Thanks to Michelle Robinson, who talked to me into buying a laptop. (How did people write books before laptops? Was it possible?) She also accompanied me to the Cincinnati library on occasion and offered encouragement.

Thanks to Karen Walsh, who started to read the first draft of my book, had some very encouraging comments, and was going to help edit it for me, until she lost it. Some might say she didn't miss anything. Nice try, anyway.

Thanks to my mom, Marilyn Seibert, who actually did read it and help edit it for me. She told me that she got caught up in the story at times and forgot to look for the mistakes. Aren't mom's great?

Rick Riley was of assistance in locating information regarding McKinley's Civil War career, in particular the first names of obscure union officers.

Eric Johns was invaluable with his technical assistance in preparing the photographs for this book. He also designed the book's cover.

Also, thanks to all the folks who, when I told them I was writing this book, thought to themselves, "Yeah, right," but did not let on to me that they did not think it would ever get done.

And finally, a special thanks to Valerie Anderson, who as always, gave me tremendous moral support and unmeasured personal inspiration.

Introduction

America at the turn of the twentieth century was a country in transition. Old was becoming new, and the American landscape was changing forever. With the advent of such wonders as the telephone, electricity, and the automobile, America was evolving into the nation that would lead the world throughout the new century. City streets were mixed with horse drawn buggies and horseless carriages. As a part of the celebration of the new century, the Pan American Exposition in Buffalo would provide an ideal opportunity for America to showcase its technological advances, and provide citizens of the world with a glimpse of what was to come. Sadly, a part of that glimpse would include assassination.

At the time of his death, William McKinley was perhaps, with the exception of Washington, the most popular sitting President in history. Some disagreed with his policies, but nearly everyone liked the amiable President personally. Unlike his two martyred predecessors, Lincoln and Garfield, William McKinley was struck down for reasons that even today are difficult to fathom. Lincoln was killed in the angry setting of the Civil War by a vengeful southern sympathizer. A man disappointed at not securing a political appointment and who wished to clear the way for his fellow 'Stalwart,' Chester A. Arthur, assassinated Garfield. But McKinley was a target simply because he was the President. His assassin admitted that he had nothing against McKinley, the man. It was the office at which Leon Czolgosz struck. For most Americans, it was difficult to understand the abstract political beliefs that led to the murder of their likable President.

McKinley, like Lincoln and Garfield before him, was struck down by pistol shots, a distinctly American method of assassination. In Europe, the weapons of choice were daggers, poison and bombs.

In the age before truly mass media, the McKinley assassination was the last prior to the invention of radio and television. While viewers tuned in by the millions to watch the drama of the Kennedy assassination unfold 62 years later, Americans in 1901 relied solely on newspaper and magazine coverage. As happens today, too much of what they read was not completely accurate.

Part of the reason for the inaccuracies of these accounts are the inadequacies of the human mind. On the slightly raised dais where the shooting occurred, there was enacted a tragedy so dramatic in character, so thrilling in its intensity, that few who looked on would ever be able to give a succinct account of what really did transpire. Even the actors playing the principal roles came out of it with blanched faces, trembling limbs, and beating hearts, while their brains throbbed with a tumult of conflicting emotions, which left behind only a chaotic jumble of impressions which could not be clarified into a lucid narrative of the drama.

During the research for the writing of this book, I reviewed newspaper accounts of the events, but caution must be exercised when judging for accuracy from those sources. Still, they are the first impressions given by the participants and in that regard, due to their spontaneity, they must be viewed as untainted accounts. First hand quotes and observations, published in various newspapers, magazines, books and publications are the primary sources I tried to use in the telling of this story. But these accounts are often self-serving and some are remembered long after the fact. In many instances, versions of the same event or statement vary in different sources. I have tried to include some of the different versions for historical accuracy. Unfortunately, most of these minor inconsistencies can no longer be reconciled, with the passage of time and people.

In particular, the quotes from the courtroom during the trail of Leon Czolgosz were reported differently in the various sources. For the most part, I decided to use the quotes from the *Buffalo Courier* and *Buffalo Express*. These newspapers had teams of reporters writing down, verbatim, all that was said during the trial. They also included other observations, and I thought these accounts were probably the best possible overall representation of the events. *American State Trials* has an edited version of the official trial transcript.

There are many quotes during this work, which are attributed to the assassin. These came from various newspaper sources. The police maintained that very few people saw Leon Czolgosz during his stay in Buffalo after the shooting. But many reporters print versions of conversations they had with him while he was his cell. In some cases, I feel some of these are fabrications. In others they seem more credible. It is possible that police officials publicly said no one was seeing the prisoner, while occasionally, they would let a friendly reporter have a few minutes with the accused, both as a favor to the reporter, and as an effort to learn more from the tight lipped Czolgosz. I have included these conversations in this work, but skepticism must be exercised when determining complete accuracy.

For biographical information about Leon Czolgosz, I relied heavily, as anyone who looks into his background must, on the writings of Walter Channing and L. Vernon Briggs, alienists (the old name for psychiatrists) who investigated Czolgosz and interviewed many of his family members and associates shortly after the assassination. They conducted the only such research and without their work, much less would be known about the private life and background of the assassin. With the exception of a very few cooperative moments in the short time he had to tell any details of his life after the shooting, Leon Czolgosz himself was of little help.

When I began the research, I was amazed at how little information there really was in print about the McKinley assassination. After nearly three decades of interest in the Kennedy assassination, I assumed that there would be dozens of books on the topic. I was wrong. In fact, I had to do my first of many inter-library loans to get the only book that I could find in existence dealing with only that topic. There were composite books about various assassinations, some about William McKinley himself and his administration, but only one specifically about the McKinley Assassination, and it dealt primarily with the assassin. I reasoned that, with the one hundredth anniversary of the event coming up, telling the story from start to finish was something that needed to be done.

Later, I was able to locate a number of books about the McKinley assassination printed as tributes and souvenirs in 1901, and these provided a good overview of the events, and additional details which I included in this work.

I visited Buffalo in August of 2001 for the first time. Arriving from Cincinnati at four o'clock in the morning, I was immediately drawn to Delaware Avenue, the scene of so much of this story. In the dark, I saw the Wilcox mansion and made the brisk mile and a half walk to the corner of Ferry and Delaware, where the Milburn mansion once stood. In the place of the house in which the President died is a newly paved parking lot on the grounds of Canisius High School. There was no plaque, no statue. No reminder that this piece of ground, for one brief week a hundred years ago, was the center of world attention and the center of the United States government.

That morning, I tried to locate the other places with which I have become so familiar in my mind. There was Seneca Street, Erie Boulevard, Main Street, Exchange Street, and Franklin Street. All of them played a small part of this drama. I drove up Broadway, to the intersection of Fillmore, where Czolgosz had had a trivial conversation that was later remembered. And I found 1078 Broadway, or more accurately the original site of John Nowak's boardinghouse, where Czolgosz had stayed just prior to the shooting. Of course, it was long gone. I ate at the Burger King at 1066 Broadway, next door. The best I could determine; the boarding house was located on the current site of a branch of the Erie County Library. On up the street, I noticed that the Amvets Post 45 was named in honor of Hank Nowak. The name jumped out at me. And I noticed the Polish names of many of the neighborhood streets. For one morning, I walked were Leon Czolgosz had walked.

Old City Hall is still there. As one enters from Franklin Street, there is a flag and floor display, which marks the spot where President McKinley lied in state. Up on the second floor is the courtroom in which Leon Czolgosz was tried. It is still in use. As I entered, a police officer and judge were the only ones in the room. I marveled at the room, the mahogany woodwork, and what it must have been like during those two exciting days in 1901 when a presidential assassin was tried and convicted. I wanted to walk through the "tunnel of sobs" where Czolgosz was led from the jail, but the officer told me no one was permitted there except them. Maybe someday.

In front of New City Hall is Niagara Square. In the square, a large Buffalo Nickel has the inscription, "In Roswell Park We Trust." This is, of course, a reference to the Roswell Park Cancer Institute, named in honor of the President's primary doctor. I could not help but think of the trust Dr. Park enjoyed in 1901, when almost everyone thought he alone could save the President.

I looked for the old police precinct one, where Czolgosz was taken after the shooting. I found it, but it was a new building. The old one was gone. Alas, time marches on.

After I left Buffalo, I stopped in Canton and visited the McKinley memorial. An impressive structure, I climbed the steps and stood within five feet of President and Mrs. McKinley; as close as I will ever come to the twenty-fifth President of the United States.

Few events change American history more than Presidential assassinations. At least, few events are more dramatic. But of the four murders of United States Presidents, the killing of William McKinley was the most senseless. McKinley was the third President killed in only thirty-six years. As a result of his assassination, security was tightened and eventually made permanent. Only one more President would be lost during the next hundred years.

One hundred years ago, the citizens of Buffalo had looked forward to the Pan American Exposition and to the day the President would visit their city and attend the event. An earlier scheduled appearance had been cancelled due to the President's heavy schedule. The rescheduled "President's Day" celebration would indeed be forever remembered, but not for the reasons the Buffalo citizens had hoped.

Jeff Seibert
Goshen, Ohio
December 25, 2001

1. The President

"In the long line of Presidents who have held this high office, no one of them was so popular as Mr. McKinley is," wrote *Harper's Weekly* shortly after the shooting. "There are Presidents in the list, some of whom we look back to with a feeling of reverence for their greatness, or of admiration for their astuteness, or of sincere regard for their courage and independence, but not one of them all, especially during his term of office, has enjoyed so completely the affection of his fellow-countrymen. Whether they believed with him or opposed his views, they liked him personally."[1]

At the time of his assassination, and after some trying times as President, William McKinley was very much enjoying the good will of the country he led.

In 1898, McKinley had annexed the Hawaiian Islands. Later that year, with the sinking of the *Maine,* he had entered into the Spanish American War, and quickly came out victorious. As a result of the war, the United States had taken control of the Philippine Islands. The future Panama Canal was high on President McKinley's list of priorities. Mr. McKinley had to dispatch troops to deal with insurrection in the Philippines and to protect American interests in China during the Boxer Rebellion.

The President and his new dynamic Vice Presidential candidate, Theodore Roosevelt, had swept to re-election over William Jennings Bryan in November of 1900, and during his second term McKinley was at his best. The country as a whole was tranquil, the economy had come out of a severe depression and the divisions and sectionalism of the Civil War were fading with the coming of the new century. All in all, at the time of his shooting, William McKinley had much to feel good about.

William McKinley was born in Niles, Ohio in Trumbull County on January 29, 1843. Of Scottish-Irish ancestry, his great-great grandfather had immigrated to America in 1743, settling in Pennsylvania. His grandfather, James McKinley, moved to Ohio in about 1830 where he became manager of a charcoal furnace. His parents, William and Nancy Allison McKinley had nine children, of which William was the seventh. William Sr. managed the iron foundry in Niles and his mother was remembered for her work with the poor and sick in Niles.

---

[1] *Harper's Weekly*, 14 September 1901, pg. 900.

Allison McKinley noticed that young William was quieter than most, watching everything intently.

"William was naturally a good boy, but he was not particularly a good baby. He began to take notice of things when he was very young," she remembered. "My ideas of education were wholly practical, not theoretical. I put my children in school just as early as they could go alone to the teacher, and kept them at it. I did not allow them to stay away."[2]

"We lived in a village and he had plenty of outdoor air and exercise," she continued. "He was a good boy in school and his teachers always said he was very bright. He had his little squabbles with his brothers and sisters, like all other children do. I guess I never paid attention to that. He was always obedient, however, affectionate and very fond of his home."

"We were Methodists, though we never went to the extent of curbing the innocent sports of children," 'Mother' McKinley explained. "William was taken to Sunday school about the same time that he began his studies in the village school house. He continued a faithful attendant every Sunday till he went away to the war. I brought up all my children to understand that they must study and improve their minds."[3]

One writer, while doing research for *Campaign Life of William McKinley,* which was printed in 1896, found a number of men who knew McKinley when he was a boy.

"Was he ever in mischief—like robbing orchards, or stealing watermelons, or carrying away gates at 'Hallowe'en?'" one was asked.

"I don't remember that William ever was in any scrape of that kind," answered the old man. Then after thinking a bit he added, "And if I did, I wouldn't tell it."[4]

At the age of nine, McKinley attended a private school, the Poland Seminary, in Poland, Ohio. The entire family had moved to Poland in 1852 to get the children a better education, but William's father had to remain in Niles to work in his iron manufacturing business.

---

[2] Murat Halstead, *The Illustrious Life of William McKinley* (Privately Published, 1901) 109.

[3] Murat Halstead, *The Illustrious Life of William McKinley* (Privately Published, 1901) 109.

[4] Marshall Everett, *The Complete Life of William McKinley* (Privately Published, 1901) 128.

One childhood friend remembered that McKinley was always studying. Another said that it was seldom that his head was not in a book.[5]

While in Poland, McKinley belonged to a notable literary society. He often served as the judge of debates. At school, he was president of another literary society and debate club.[6]

One of the books that greatly influenced McKinley's thinking was *Uncle Tom's Cabin*, by Harriett Beecher Stowe. It came during his formative years and did much to fill his soul with hatred for the institution of slavery. He was sure that the horrors of slavery were fairly depicted in the book.

Another book that also influenced him was *Noble Deeds of American Women*. This book taught him about the struggles and sacrifices of the nineteenth century women.[7]

"Mrs. Morse, who was his teacher, said that he excelled in the study of languages, although he was fairly 'good at figures,'" said Mrs. McKinley.

"I know that he was a constant reader, and by the time he was fifteen he began to read poetry, being especially fond of Longfellow and Whittier, and, I believe, Byron' Mrs. Morse said. "From this time of his boyhood he gave up most of his sports except ball playing, swimming and skating. The boys played ball on the common behind the seminary."[8]

"William had a great hand for marbles, and he was very fond of his bows and arrows," remembered his mother. "He got so that he was a very good shot with the arrow and could hit almost anything he aimed at. The thing he loved best of all was a kite. It seems to me I never went into the kitchen without seeing a paste pot or a ball of string waiting to be made into a kite. He never cared much for pets. I don't believe he ever had one."[9]

---

[5] Zachary Kent, *William McKinley* (Chicago: Children's Press, 1988) 14.

[6] Alexander K. McClure, *The Authentic Life of William McKinley* (W. E. Skull, 1901) 54.

[7] Marshall Everett, *The Complete Life of William McKinley* (Privately Published, 1901) 127.

[8] Murat Halstead, *The Illustrious Life of William McKinley* (Privately Published, 1901) 113.

[9] Murat Halstead, *The Illustrious Life of William McKinley* (Privately Published, 1901) 110.

"I declare I never thought Bill would be President," said Joe Fisher, a boyhood friend. "Little did I suppose as I sat fishing with him on Mosquito Creek with our legs dangling from the edge of the bridge, or as we caught angle worms to bait our hooks, that I was with a coming President. I well remember his patience with a hook and line. The rest of the boys would get disgusted at not getting a bite and would go in bathing, but Bill would keep on fishing. When it came time to go home he would carry a string of fish, while the rest had to be content with their baths."[10]

When McKinley was about fourteen, after a series of meetings, he officially joined the Methodist Church. According to Rev. A. D. Morton, one evening at a meeting of younger parishioners, William stood up and said, "I have not done my duty; I have sinned; I want to be a Christian; I believe religion to be the best thing in all the world. I give myself to the Savior who has done so much for me." A few nights later, he said, "I have found the pearl of great price. I love God."[11]

He immediately began to study the doctrines of the Bible and religion in earnest. Without making a display of his deep beliefs, they were to be his guiding light for the remainder of his life.

In 1860, when he was seventeen, McKinley attended Allegheny College in Meadville, Pennsylvania, enrolling as a member of the junior class. But he developed a severe illness and because of that illness and because of money problems, was forced to return home. There he got a job as a clerk in the Poland Post Office. Soon after that he took a job as a teacher in a district near Poland for $25 a month salary. He walked several miles from home to the school each day. His intentions were to save enough money to return to college in a year or two.[12] But before he could complete his plans, events changed his life.

William McKinley was the first in his hometown to volunteer when the Civil War broke out. When President Lincoln called for volunteers, McKinley and friends from school went to a tavern built in 1804, the Sparrow House. There, amidst a packed crowd, they listened to the recruiters.

---

[10] Alexander K. McClure, *The Authentic Life of William McKinley* (W. E. Skull, 1901) 53.

[11] Murat Halstead, *The Illustrious Life of William McKinley* (Privately Published, 1901) 422.

[12] Alexander K. McClure, *The Authentic Life of William McKinley* (W. E. Skull, 1901) 56.

One speaker exclaimed, "Our country's flag has been shot at. And for what? That this free government may keep a race in the bondage of slavery. Who will be the first to defend it?"

McKinley was the first to step forward, followed by many of his friends.[13]

The boy volunteers assembled on the village green where they said their good-byes, and were soon marching toward Columbus as Poland Company E of the 23rd Regiment of Ohio volunteers, where they would train at Camp Chase.[14]

"I always look back with pleasure on those fourteen months of soldiering," McKinley later remembered. "They taught me a great deal. I was only a schoolboy when I entered the ranks, and that year was the formative period of my life, during which I learned much of men and affairs. I have always been glad I entered the service as a private."[15]

He served first under Colonel William S. Rosecrans, who would soon become a general, then under another future President, Major Rutherford B. Hayes. By then, a commissary sergeant, McKinley left the security of his rear post and, at great peril to himself, carried food and water to front line soldiers during the battle of Antietam and used the opportunity to distinguish himself.

Hayes had been wounded in the battle, went home to recuperate, and told Ohio Governor David Tod what McKinley had done on his own.

"Let McKinley be promoted from Sergeant to Lieutenant," Tod told Hayes. [16] When Hayes returned to the field, he put McKinley on his staff.

McKinley also saw action at Kernstown and Cedar Creek.

At the battle of Kernstown, near Winchester, Virginia, McKinley was ordered by Major Hayes to go into the thick of the fight and bring out a regiment that was so hard pressed that it was doubted that any of its members where even alive at the time of the order. He accomplished the mission and was publicly cheered by the entire brigade.[17]

---

[13] Murat Halstead, *The Illustrious Life of William McKinley* (Privately Published, 1901) 418.

[14] Marshall Everett, *The Complete Life of William McKinley* (Privately Published, 1901) 130.

[15] G. Townsend, *Memorial Life of William McKinley* (Washington: Memorial Publishing Co., 1901) 37.

[16] Marshall Everett, *The Complete Life of William McKinley* (Privately Published, 1901) 131.

[17] *New York Times*, 14 September 1901, pg. 2, col. 1.

"A sad look came over Hayes' face as he saw the young, gallant boy pushing rapidly forward to meet almost certain death," wrote General Russell Hastings, who witnessed the event. "None of us expected to see him again, as we watched him push his horse through the open fields, over fences, through ditches, while a well directed fire from the enemy poured upon him, with shells exploding around about and over him.

"Once he was completely enveloped in the smoke of an exploded shell, and we thought he had gone down, but no, he was saved for better work for his country in the future years," Hastings continued. "Out of this smoke emerged his wiry little horse, with McKinley still firmly seated, and as erect as a hussar."[18]

"As McKinley rode up beside Hayes to make his report, I heard Hayes say: 'I never expected to see you in life again,'" wrote another witness, Whitelaw Reid, in his book *Ohio in the War*. "McKinley was greeted by us all with a happy contented smile—no effusion, no gushing palaver of words, though all of us felt and knew one of the most gallant acts of the war had been performed."[19]

"Young as he was, we soon found that in business, in executive ability, young McKinley was a man of rare capacity, of unusual and unsurpassed capacity, especially for a boy of his age," remembered Rutherford B. Hayes. "When I became commander of the regiment he soon came to be upon my staff, and he remained upon my staff for one or two years, so that I did literally and in fact know him like a book and loved him like a brother."[20]

Hayes was impressed with McKinley and said so in his war diary.

"Our new second lieutenant, McKinley, returned today," wrote Hayes, "an exceedingly bright, intelligent, and gentlemanly young officer. He promises to be one of the best." [21]

The day after Kernstown, on July 24, 1864, McKinley was promoted to Captain at the age of twenty-one.

McKinley also had a horse shot out from under him at Berryville, and he distinguished himself again and again in many other places. He

[18] Murat Halstead, *The Illustrious Life of William McKinley* (Privately Published, 1901) 31-32.

[19] Alexander K. McClure, *The Authentic Life of William McKinley* (W. E. Skull, 1901) 81.

[20] Alexander K. McClure, *The Authentic Life of William McKinley* (W. E. Skull, 1901) 65.

[21] Alexander K. McClure, *The Authentic Life of William McKinley* (W. E. Skull, 1901) 66.

served on General William H. Crook's staff after his service to Hayes was completed. It was under Crook that he participated in General Philip Sheridan's valley campaign.

Young McKinley was an eyewitness to the famous ride to rally the troops of Gen. Philip Sheridan at Winchester, later immortalized by Thomas Buchanan Read in the poem *Sheridan's Ride*.

"I had been across the pike to put in position Colonel Dupont's battery, by order of General Crook, and as I returned I met Sheridan dashing up, and he asked me where Crook was," McKinley wrote in a letter to Murat Halstead in 1895. "I took Sheridan to Crook, and they and the staff went back of the red barn. It was there determined by Sheridan to make the charge. Then it was suggested that Sheridan should ride down the lines of the disheartened troops. His overcoat was pulled off him, and somebody took his epaulettes out of a box. The epaulettes where placed upon his shoulders—and my recollection is that this was done by Colonel Forsythe and another officer. Then Sheridan rode down the lines. He was dressed in a new uniform."[22]

At the battle of Opequan, near Winchester on September 19, 1864, it was Captain McKinley's assignment to communicate a verbal order from General Crook to Colonel Isaac H. Deval, commanding him to move his troops up a certain road to quickly take a position. McKinley took the route to Deval and found the road to be blocked with broken wagons, dead horses and fallen trees. He delivered his order to Deval, and added, "But General, I have come over that road and it is so obstructed that an army could not move that way quickly enough to be of any service. There is another route by which I am sure you could reach the place assigned to you and I suggest you take that one."

Deval, a trained soldier, knew he must follow the order precisely. He asked McKinley what the exact order was. McKinley lied, and told him that Crook had instructed to take the route McKinley thought best.

Later, McKinley told Crook what he had done.

"Did you fully understand the risk you took in changing the order you were in-trusted to deliver to General Deval?" Crook asked him. McKinley said that he did.

"Did you know that you were liable to be court-martialed and dismissed from the service, and, had it led to disaster, shot as a traitor?"

"I did, General, but I was willing to take that risk to save the battle," was the Captain's reply.

---

[22] Murat Halstead, *The Illustrious Life of William McKinley* (Privately Published, 1901) 123.

After some thought, Crook told him, "Captain, you have saved the battle, and you are a brave man; but I would advise you not to take such risks again, as, in case of failure, even the officer who received the command, to do his duty in light of your knowledge, the blame would rest upon you alone."[23]

On March 13, 1865, McKinley received another promotion and without seeing any more fighting, was mustered out of the United States service on July 26. By this time he was a Brevet Major, awarded the rank by President Lincoln himself only a month before Lincoln's assassination. It read in part, "for gallant and meritorious services at the battle of Opequan, Cedar Creek, and Fisher's Hill."[24]

After the war, McKinley decided to study law and obtained admission to study in the office of Judge Charles E. Glidden, the leading lawyer in the area. McKinley felt he had some catching up to do. Other young men his age were already practicing law. He submerged himself in his studies, devouring his law books at a rapid rate. More than once the thought of quitting and going into the business world must have entered his mind. But he stuck with it and was admitted to the Ohio Bar Association in March of 1867.[25]

He settled in Canton, Ohio. McKinley chose Canton in which to practice law because it was the county seat of Stark County. Also, his sister Anna, with whom he had a very close relationship and who had been very supportive of his law study, was a teacher in the town. Canton was not large, having only 5,000 inhabitants. But McKinley immediately took an active interest in the affairs of the town and soon became one of its leading young men. And his powers as an orator were developing.[26]

It was Judge Glidden who gave McKinley his first case. The young lawyer sat up all night studying it, argued the case the next day, and won. A few days later Glidden dropped by McKinley's office with his pay for

[23] Murat Halstead, *The Illustrious Life of William McKinley* (Privately Published, 1901) 426-427.

[24] Alexander K. McClure, *The Authentic Life of William McKinley* (W. E. Skull, 1901) 94.

[25] Alexander K. McClure, *The Authentic Life of William McKinley* (W. E. Skull, 1901) 96.

[26] Alexander K. McClure, *The Authentic Life of William McKinley* (W. E. Skull, 1901) 96.

the case, twenty-five dollars. McKinley refused it saying, "It is too much for a days work."

"Don't let that worry you," smiled Glidden. "I charged them $100 for the case, and I can well afford a quarter of it to you."[27]

Another story of his law experience told of a case in which he was defending a surgeon for mending the broken leg of a man in a crooked fashion. John Sweeney, considered one of the most brilliant attorneys in the Ohio bar, had his client show his bowed leg to the jury. McKinley carefully viewed the healthy leg and at the end of the display asked that the healthy leg be displayed as well. Over the objection of Mr. Sweeney, this was done. It appeared to the jury that the other leg was even more crooked than the first.

"My client seems to have done better by this man than nature itself did," mused McKinley, "and I move that the suit be dismissed with the recommendation to the plaintiff that he have the other leg broken and then set by the surgeon who set the first one."[28]

As successful of an attorney as William McKinley could have become, it soon became apparent that he was a natural politician. In the autumn of 1867, during a hotly contested Gubernatorial race in Ohio, McKinley made his first political speech. It was in favor of the negro right to vote in New Berlin. At 24 years old, he spoke from the top of a dry goods box in front of the village tavern to an audience that was strongly opposed to him. He spoke in the place of an older judge who could not make the trip.

"Could he speak? Well, I should say he could," remarked Michael Bitzer, who introduced the young man. "Everybody was simply dumbfounded. For nearly an hour he talked as never a young man in Stark County had talked before. I told Judge Linderhill, who accompanied him, after the meeting, that McKinley did a blamed sight better than he did, and the Judge, too, pronounced him a coming politician."[29]

Later, as Governor, Bitzer would visit McKinley. "This is the man who first introduced me into politics," McKinley told a group of a dozen men, while a beaming Bitzer looked on.[30]

---

[27] Alexander K. McClure, *The Authentic Life of William McKinley* (W. E. Skull, 1901) 101.

[28] Murat Halstead, *The Illustrious Life of William McKinley* (Privately Published, 1901) 431.

[29] Alexander K. McClure, *The Authentic Life of William McKinley* (W. E. Skull, 1901) 103.

[30] Alexander K. McClure, *The Authentic Life of William McKinley* (W. E. Skull, 1901) 104.

In 1869, McKinley was elected to his first public office as Prosecutor of Stark County. By then he was known throughout the county as a rising young lawyer and an accomplished speaker. No one expected the young major to win. But McKinley worked hard and canvassed the county and made speech after speech. In spite of his being a Republican in a heavily Democratic county, at twenty-six his personal appeal won him the election. Though the office did not have a big salary, it would be a stepping stone to future success.

Two years later, the Republicans ran McKinley for re-election. This time the Democrats had been awakened and they were wary of McKinley's rising star. They put against him the best man they could find and ample resources. They were successful in their effort, but defeated McKinley by only 45 votes, instead of the usual hundreds. Though McKinley lost the election, he gained in prestige.

On January 25, 1871, fours days before his twenty-eighth birthday, McKinley married Ida Saxton. McKinley had first met Ida during a visit to see his sister in Canton at Meyer's Lake, about two miles from town. Her grandfather, James Saxton, had founded the first newspaper in Canton and was a close personal friend of Horace Greeley, the famous newspaper publisher. Ida had been working as a cashier in her father's bank, where she was the Belle of Canton and attracted the attentions of many suitors. Her father guarded her jealousy, but it was the handsome Major McKinley, who had just gotten a good start in his law practice when they began seeing each other, who stood head and shoulders above the others in Ida's eyes. As a testament of his trust, James Saxton told his future son-in-law, "You are the only man I have ever known to whom I would entrust my daughter."[31]

The McKinleys were married in the Presbyterian Church to which Ida belonged. William's brother Abner was the best man and Ida's sister Mary Saxton, or Pina as she was known in the family, was the maid of honor. Later, Mary was to marry John Barber, one of McKinley's ushers.[32]

The newlyweds took a honeymoon trip in which they saw many of the United States' eastern cities and then went back to settle in Canton. After Ida's mother died, they eventually settled into the Saxton estate, which was to be their home, the remainder of their lives.[33]

---

[31] Murat Halstead, *The Illustrious Life of William McKinley* (Privately Published, 1901) 419.
[32] Alexander K. McClure, *The Authentic Life of William McKinley* (W. E. Skull, 1901) 111.
[33] Alexander K. McClure, *The Authentic Life of William McKinley* (W. E. Skull, 1901) 112.

The couple had two children, both daughters. The first, Katherine was born on Christmas day in 1871. The younger one, Ida, died when she was only four months old in 1873. Shortly after, in 1873 little Katherine, or Kate as the family called her, died at the age of four. During that brief period, Mrs. McKinley also lost her mother. Mrs. McKinley had a physical breakdown due to her grief and never recovered from the loss and depression that followed, remaining in poor health for the rest of her life.[34]

One of Mrs. McKinley's medical problems, developed after the birth of Ida, could possibly have been phlebitis, as she had difficulty walking unassisted. She also suffered from seizures resembling epilepsy, but it was not referred to in any of the contemporary newspapers, being a much misunderstood disease in the early 1900's. In fact, it was seldom discussed even in the McKinley household. Her niece said after her death that she had first heard the term "epilepsy" to describe her aunt during a political campaign and had thought it was merely an attempt of political opponents to discredit McKinley.[35]

While Mrs. McKinley was struggling with depression and her health, her husband was beginning his career in national politics. McKinley ran for Congress in 1876 with the same vigor he had exhibited when running for prosecutor. He ran against a field of more experienced men who looked at him as somewhat of an upstart. His hard work paid off and he was nominated to run for the Republicans on the first ballot. He then defeated the Democratic candidate, a man named Sanborn, in the general election by over three thousand votes. McKinley served in Congress, with the exception of ten months, until 1891. As a Congressman, he won fame for his support of high tariffs to help American industry better compete against foreign interests.

"Home competition will always bring prices to a fair and reasonable level and prevent extortion and robbery," he said in his first speech to Congress on tariffs on April 15, 1871. "Success, or even apparent success, in any business or enterprise, will incite others to engage in like enterprises, and then follows healthful strife, the life of business, which inevitably results in cheapening the articles produced."[36]

---

[34] Alexander K. McClure, *The Authentic Life of William McKinley* (W. E. Skull, 1901) 112.

[35] Betty Boyd Caroli, *First Ladies* (New York: Oxford University Press, 1987) 109.

[36] Alexander K. McClure, *The Authentic Life of William McKinley* (W. E. Skull, 1901) 117.

His speech so impressed his fellow Congressmen that afterward McKinley was looked at as one of the chief defenders of protectionism and often led the debates.

Congressman McKinley also strongly supported the expansion of silver currency and voted for several bills providing for purchases of silver coinage.

Entering Congress while his old Colonel and friend Rutherford B. Hayes was President; McKinley gained prominence more quickly among the other members than he otherwise would have. But he also stood on his own, winning distinction and building a reputation as an excellent speaker and exhibiting his ability as a worker in committees. He was also considered one of the ablest debaters in Congress and as the acknowledged champion of the policy of protectionism. His debates with Democratic opponents on this issue were memorable and often humorous. [37]

The Democrats watched McKinley become a leading proponent of protectionism, much to their dismay. They decided to gerrymander him out of Congress. The Democrats controlled the Ohio legislature, and they redrew the district lines, throwing Stark County into a heavily Democratic district. McKinley was forced to run against Aquila Wiley of Wooster, himself an impressive war hero. But the Democratic ploy failed. McKinley's hard work of canvassing the district and his popularity gave him the victory, defeating Wiley 15,489 to 14,255. [38]

With the Republicans regaining control of the Government in 1889, McKinley was appointed chairman of the House Ways and Means Committee. As chairman, McKinley was instrumental in crafting new tariff legislation, dubbed the McKinley Tariff Bill.

"I was chairman of the Committee and I performed my duties as best I could," he remembered. "Some of the strongest men in Congress were on the Committee, and the eight of us heard everybody, considered everything, and made up the best tariff law we knew how to frame." [39]

Authoring the bill made McKinley famous nationally, and the Democrats targeted him in a smear campaign, saying among other things, that he had not even, in fact, authored the bill.

---

[37] Murat Halstead, *The Illustrious Life of William McKinley* (Privately Published, 1901) 132.

[38] Alexander K. McClure, *The Authentic Life of William McKinley* (W. E. Skull, 1901) 118.

[39] G. Townsend, *Memorial Life of William McKinley* (Washington: Memorial Publishing Co., 1901) 127.

Up for reelection in 1890, his stand on tariffs proved unpopular, and his district had again been redrawn to give advantage to his Democratic opponent in the heavily Democratic county. Some said it was the most outrageous partitioning of a state for partisan ends that had ever occurred. McKinley lost his bid for an eighth term in the United States Congress. McKinley characteristically fought hard, and lost by only about 300 votes.

But William McKinley bounced back big, accepting in 1891 the Republican nomination to run for Governor of Ohio. Ohio newspapers had begun to call for his nomination after his Congressional defeat and McKinley let it be known that he would accept it if it came spontaneously, but he would not enter into a contest. The Republicans held their convention in June of 1891, with McKinley being the only real candidate for governor. He was nominated by acclamation.[40]

During the Gubernatorial campaign, which was one of the most memorable ever waged in the Buckeye State, McKinley worked tirelessly. He campaigned in every corner of the state, often speaking several times a day. He believed that every citizen should be educated about the economic issues facing the country and he made it his business to try to educate them. He spoke in 86 of Ohio's 88 counties, making an estimated 130 speeches.[41] His efforts paid off as he defeated the Democratic candidate, former Governor James Campbell, by over 21,000 votes.

McKinley took the oath of office as Ohio's new governor on January 11, 1892, promising in his inaugural speech to cooperate with the legislature in every endeavor to secure a wise, economical and honorable administration.[42]

As governor, McKinley worked tirelessly to ensure better safety in factories for Ohio workers and allow them to join labor organizations to improve their working conditions, even supporting their right to peaceably strike. The workers for his efforts praised Governor McKinley. In addition, the Governor secured passage of an excise tax on corporations, which helped take the tax burden off Ohio's working people.

---

[40] Marshall Everett, *The Complete Life of William McKinley* (Privately Published, 1901) 169.

[41] Marshall Everett, *The Complete Life of William McKinley* (Privately Published, 1901) 169.

[42] Zachary Kent, *William McKinley* (Chicago: Children's Press, 1988) 43.

But these accomplishments did not come easily. Fifteen times during Governor McKinley's two terms in office, he was forced to call out the Ohio state troops to restore order after outbreaks of violence, usually in connection with these strikes and labor disputes. In all cases the Governor called out an ample force that was in each case able to end the disruption without the troops behaving in bad fashion.[43]

While McKinley was governor, a bank robbery occurred in Columbus Grove, in which the perpetrator shot and killed an innocent bystander. He was convicted and sentenced to death. The case went to Governor McKinley for a possible pardon. The Governor reviewed the case, convinced himself of the man's guilt and refused to intercede. The day before the execution he took a trip to Toledo to get away from the pressures of men trying to save their friend. McKinley's emotion was intense as he read wires from the prison. Finally word came that the man had confessed and McKinley breathed a sigh of relief, knowing that justice had been served.[44]

During his governorship, McKinley's devotion to his wife became legendary. One example was his habit of waving to her at precisely three o'clock every afternoon from the state house in Columbus to their comfortable lodging across the street. No matter what business was being conducted, the Governor would step to the window and wave with his white handkerchief.

Later, while President, McKinley would excuse himself from important meetings to pay a brief visit to Ida. When she was feeling poorly, he would do this as many as a dozen times per day. No matter how busy he was, he would even take an active part in the running of the household staff to save his wife the trouble, and her health.

While governor, McKinley wrote a daily letter, no matter how brief, to his mother. This practice continued upon his ascent to the White House. Every day, the Canton post office would receive a small White House envelope with a tender message from her "William at Washington," which was the way she often referred to her son, the President.[45]

---

[43] Alexander K. McClure, *The Authentic Life of William McKinley* (W. E. Skull, 1901) 161.

[44] G. Townsend, *Memorial Life of William McKinley* (Washington: Memorial Publishing Co., 1901) 431-432.

[45] Murat Halstead, *The Illustrious Life of William McKinley* (Privately Published, 1901) 420.

It was also during his tenure as governor that McKinley came into contact with the man who would help to shape his destiny; Cleveland millionaire and future senator Marcus A. Hanna. Hanna opened a "McKinley for President" headquarters at the Republican national convention in Minneapolis in 1892, and McKinley, thanks in no small part to Hanna's backing, wound up second in the balloting with 192 votes, behind only the nominee Benjamin Harrison. His fellow delegates had named McKinley as the convention chairman, partly because of his well-known fairness. His strong showing against Benjamin Harrison, though McKinley himself did not campaign for the job, served to encourage the McKinley movement of 1896.

But William McKinley's plans for high office were almost over before they even began, in 1893. He had cosigned for a loan to help a long time friend, Robert L. Walker of Youngstown, enter into the manufacturing business. McKinley had known Walker since boyhood. Several times over the years, McKinley had been aided by loans from Walker to help payoff campaign debts. By 1893, McKinley had accumulated about $20,000, and his wife had inherited $75,000 from her father's estate.

Walker asked McKinley for assistance, having him sign about $15,000 worth of paper notes, the Governor being assured that Walker was simply low on ready cash, and that they would be soon paid off. But soon, these notes started to come due and Walker asked McKinley to sign more notes with the understanding that these would pay off the original ones. McKinley had no reason to think that Robert Walker would not be able to pay them off. Walker was then one of the more prominent businessmen in the state. He was president of a national bank and a savings bank, owned a stamping mill company and a stove and range company. He also had interests in many coal mines in Ohio and Pennsylvania. Credited with a fortune in excess of $250,000 and as a childhood friend, McKinley trusted him.

On the day that the notes failed, a deeply concerned Governor McKinley went to Youngstown to find that he was personally liable for $100,000-130,000, rather than the $15,000 he thought. The amount wiped out his entire savings and then some. [46]

McKinley commented on the affair, saying that he had avoided entanglements his entire life and wondering aloud why it would happen as he prepared to run for President.[47]

---

[46] Alexander K. McClure, *The Authentic Life of William McKinley* (W. E. Skull, 1901) 162.

[47] Zachary Kent, *William McKinley* (Chicago: Children's Press, 1988) 45.

Many people sympathized with the Governor's plight. One Ohio newspaper wrote, "The financial troubles of Governor McKinley will be learned with deep regret not only in Ohio but all over the country. He has been a liberal, kind hearted man and has always done more for others than for himself."

A popular fund was started by sympathetic Ohioans to try to help the Governor. McKinley, refusing such help, returned all the money, declining to accept it.

But Mark Hanna and some businessmen friends came to the Governor's rescue. Hanna established a trust fund and industrialists who had approved of McKinley's tariff policies kicked in huge sums of money. Many others donated to the debt, including old Civil War friends and complete strangers alike. Thanks to Mark Hanna's efforts, the debt was paid in full.

McKinley again tried to decline the money, but his friends explained that most of it was donated anonymously and could not be returned. To his last day, McKinley never knew precisely who had helped him, with the exception of four or five donors. The treasurer of the fund paid off all the outstanding notes, Mrs. McKinley's fortune was returned to her and the Governor was returned his $20,000 with a small amount more. More importantly, McKinley's political future remained intact.[48]

With the scandal behind him, McKinley was elected to a second term as governor in a landslide of 80,000 votes after a campaign that took him to every one of Ohio's 88 counties. During the campaign, McKinley often wore a red carnation in his lapel. Later, the Ohio legislature voted to make the red carnation the official state flower.

McKinley remained devoutly religious, being a member of the Canton Methodist Episcopal church. His soft manner often disarmed angry visitors to his office, sending them away fifteen minutes later beaming and wearing a red carnation he had put in their lapels.[49]

McKinley's second term as governor was filled with turmoil. Thousands of Ohio's miners went on strike and in some places rioted, stopping trains and throwing rocks at lawmen. McKinley ordered out the National Guard, saying at one point that he did not care if his political career was not twenty-four hours long, but that the outrages would stop if it took every soldier in Ohio.[50]

---

[48] Alexander K. McClure, *The Authentic Life of William McKinley* (W. E. Skull, 1901) 163.

[49] G. J. A. O'Toole, *The Spanish War: An American Epic 1898* (New York: W. W. Norton & Co., 1984) 84.

[50] Zachary Kent, *William McKinley* (Chicago: Children's Press, 1988) 46.

Showing his compassion, though, McKinley also arranged for trainloads of emergency supplies to be delivered to starving mining families in the Hocking Valley.

McKinley was an early champion of eight hour work days and of arbitration as a means of settling labor disputes, and successfully ended strikes in 15 of 28 cases during his tenure as governor, using the State Board of Arbitration he had earlier established, which found solutions acceptable to both parties. Certainly, throughout his career, McKinley was conscience of the problems of American labor.[51]

Meanwhile, Mark Hanna had continued to work hard on securing for his friend the presidential nomination of 1896. McKinley became a private citizen by refusing to run for reelection and devoted all of his time to running for President. As 1896 opened, the presidential race was on every politician's mind and many states began to select delegates and declare their choice for president. Oregon was the first state to endorse the popular McKinley and others followed quickly. By the time the convention in St. Louis arrived, Hanna had secured for McKinley two-thirds of the vote on the first ballot. Another friend of Hanna's, Garret A. Hobart, a State Senator from Paterson, New Jersey and member of the Republican National Committee was nominated Vice President.

At the convention, McKinley's likeness was everywhere; on pamphlets, posters, telephone poles. Theodore Roosevelt was heard to say that Hanna had advertised McKinley as if he were a patent medicine.[52]

But McKinley had earned his way into the hearts of the voters with his honesty, hard work, and his persistent advocacy of the protectionism doctrine. And this fact was reflected in the convention vote totals.

McKinley, who did not attend the convention, waited at his home in Canton for word of his nomination. John Russell Young, a former Ambassador to China was with McKinley as they waited and finally learned that Ohio and Pennsylvania's delegates had assured his nomination.

The chairman of the convention announced that McKinley had obtained 661 1/2 votes and before he could say another word, the convention erupted in a wild frenzied demonstration. It was some time before the rest of the tallies could be read. McKinley's closest

---

[51] G. Townsend, *Memorial Life of William McKinley* (Washington: Memorial Publishing Co., 1901) 46.

[52] Zachary Kent, *William McKinley* (Chicago: Children's Press, 1988) 47.

competitor was House Speaker Thomas B. Reed of Maine with 84 1/2, then came Senator Matthew S. Quay of Pennsylvania with 61 1/2, followed by Levi Morton with 58, Senator William B. Allison of Iowa with 35 1/2 and Don Cameron with 1.[53]

On that Thursday evening, Mrs. McKinley was in the parlor of their Canton home surrounded by friends and family, including Mother McKinley. Her husband was in his office listening to the returns, as he heard, "Ohio-McKinley." Without a word, he rose from his seat and hurried across the hall to his wife, kissed her and said, "Ida, Ohio's vote has just nominated me."[54]

"There was just a faint touch of color on the face of McKinley as some friends spoke a word of congratulations to him on this the moment of his career," wrote Young. "He talked of some personal matters of minor import; showed no emotion and expressed no feeling, but when Pennsylvania was passed he calmly took up his convention form and continued to note the vote.

"But in the meantime the gun was fired, the bells were rung and Canton knew that the bolt had at last come out of the heavens, and all the town turned out. So I came from the Governor's house. The streets filled with people—men, women, children, all rushing in a double-quick to the McKinley home, everybody smiling and many cheering. The crowd was so large that it was necessary to walk in the street."[55]

The Democrats nominated Nebraska congressman William Jennings Bryan for their candidate for president at their convention in Chicago in July.

Mark Hanna raised three and a half million dollars for McKinley in that campaign, an astonishing amount of money in 1896. Mrs. McKinley was too ill to travel and McKinley refused to leave her in Canton. So Mark Hanna arranged for thousands of visitors to travel to Canton to meet McKinley. It became famous as the "front porch campaign," so named after the hundreds of speeches McKinley gave for thousands of delegates and visitors while standing on his own front porch.

While McKinley talked on his porch, William Jennings Bryan crisscrossed the country speaking. In the end, the voters were uneasy

---

[53] Alexander K. McClure, *The Authentic Life of William McKinley* (W. E. Skull, 1901) 183.
[54] Alexander K. McClure, *The Authentic Life of William McKinley* (W. E. Skull, 1901) 185.
[55] G. Townsend, *Memorial Life of William McKinley* (Washington: Memorial Publishing Co., 1901) 121.

with many of Bryan's radical economic ideas, as McKinley campaigned on sound money policies. One popular slogan was "McKinley and the Full Dinner Pail." By election day, it was estimated that 750,00 people had traveled to Canton to visit the Ohio candidate.

McKinley won the election by 600,000 votes, becoming the nation's twenty-fifth president. The McKinley-Hobart ticket received 7,101,401 popular votes with 271 electoral votes. Bryan-Sewall received 6,470,656 popular votes and 176 electoral votes, giving McKinley a 95 electoral vote victory.[56]

Hanna sent McKinley a telegram telling the President-elect that people who had always loved and trusted him had elected him to the highest office in the land.[57]

Upon his election, an old friend had been confused as to what to call the President-elect. He had been called a succession of names, Major McKinley, Lawyer McKinley, Congressman McKinley, Governor McKinley, and now he would be President McKinley. But he had not yet taken office.

McKinley laughed, and said, "John, I won't have a friend of mine, such as you are, address me by any prouder title than that of major. That rank belongs to me. I am not governor any more and I am not President yet. So you just call me plain major, which I like to be to all my friends."[58]

But McKinley had been very confident about his prospects of becoming President.

"I have never been in doubt since I was old enough to think intelligently that I would someday be made president," he once said.

McKinley's election can be said to have been a counter-revolution to one the Democrats had engineered in 1892, which swept Grover Cleveland into office. That year the people had elected Democrats to the House of Representatives, 219-127. There had been a severe depression from 1893-1896, and it was gradually easing as the election approached. In 1894, the tide had turned with the House being comprised of 245

---

[56] Alexander K. McClure, *The Authentic Life of William McKinley* (W. E. Skull, 1901) 186.

[57] Zachary Kent, *William McKinley* (Chicago: Children's Press, 1988) 53.

[58] Murat Halstead, *The Illustrious Life of William McKinley* (Privately Published, 1901) 420.

Republicans compared to 100 Democrats.[59] McKinley's candidacy and election gave new impetus to industrial interests and he was looked to by the general public to help solve the nation's economic woes. During his presidency, partly due to his tariff policies, the economy experienced an upturn and enjoyed very good times indeed.[60]

During William McKinley's rise to the Presidency, Ida McKinley was already developing a reputation of her own; one that would make her be known as one of the most demanding First Ladies in history. While many other First Ladies had been in poor health and generally used it as a reason to avoid some of the duties of the position, Ida McKinley craved the attention. She thought nothing of calling her husband out of an important meeting to solicit his opinion about the color of ribbons and the like.

In the White House, she always took a prominent place next to her husband at official dinners. McKinley would carry a handkerchief in his pocket and use it to cover her face in the event of an epileptic seizure. Future President William Howard Taft witnessed one of these seizures. He heard a hissing sound and before he realized what was happening, McKinley had placed the handkerchief over his wife's face. Mrs. McKinley sat rigid in her chair and the President continued talking as if nothing unusual was happening. When the seizure stopped, Mrs. McKinley removed the handkerchief and resumed her conversation. [61]

Mrs. McKinley was very persistent in taking her place next to her husband and was wary of any other woman who she perceived as moving in on her territory. She tried to appear unaware of the embarrassment her frequent seizures caused, or at any rate, seemed to ignore it. Mrs. McKinley, in spite of her health, was determined to receive all the accolades that went along with being First Lady.

During the McKinleys' first term, Ida struck up a very intimate friendship with Jennie Hobart, the wife of the Vice President. Mrs. Hobart would visit Mrs. McKinley at the White House almost daily, and the President grew to rely on her at state functions to help keep an eye on Mrs. McKinley whenever he was forced to leave. Mrs. Hobart, in spite

---

[59] Alexander K. McClure, *The Authentic Life of William McKinley* (W. E. Skull, 1901) 172.

[60] Alexander K. McClure, *The Authentic Life of William McKinley* (W. E. Skull, 1901) 24.

[61] Betty Boyd Caroli, *First Ladies* (New York: Oxford University Press, 1987) 110-111.

the attention paid her by the President, seemed to always remain in Ida's good graces.

Mrs. McKinley's health had made it impossible for her to assume the heavy social burdens of First Lady, Mrs. Hobart claimed later. She explained that President McKinley constantly turned to her to help whenever she could, not so much because she was the Vice President's wife, but because she was their good friend.[62]

Both McKinleys genuinely enjoyed the company of children and little ones were frequently guests in the White House. But they sometimes witnessed Mrs. McKinley's seizures as well.

Mrs. Joseph Stanley-Brown, formerly Molly Garfield, who herself had been a White House favorite as a child, brought her son Rudy to visit Mrs. McKinley. Soon after their arrival, Mrs. McKinley had one of her spells and the handkerchief was quickly placed over her face. Young Rudy was very frightened and wanted to know what was wrong with her. He was calmly told that she was not well. Soon, the fit passed, and Mrs. McKinley picked up the conversation right where she had left off. Rudy never forgot the visit.[63]

On October 7, 1898, tragedy again struck Mrs. McKinley as her brother, George Saxton, was murdered in Canton. On that evening, he had taken his bicycle to the home of an attractive widow he had been courting, Eva Althouse. Mrs. Althouse, as it turned out, was not home, and as George approached her front door, according to witnesses, a woman jumped out of the bushes and amid a volley of shots, delivered a mortal wound into George's belly. Police quickly found and arrested Anna George, another woman whom George Saxton had been seeing. George Saxton had broken up her marriage, promising to marry her. When the divorce was finalized, Saxton had then backed out and Anna George told friends that if he continued to see Mrs. Althouse she would shoot him.

The murder became somewhat of a controversy for the President, having his brother-in-law involved in such a matter. Eventually, in spite of the evidence, the Canton jury took pity on the pretty and well-mannered Anna George and found her not guilty. Anna George then disappeared from history.[64]

---

[62] Margaret Leech, *In the Days of McKinley* (New York: Harper and Brothers, 1959) 435.

[63] Margaret Leech, *In the Days of McKinley* (New York: Harper and Brothers, 1959) 437.

[64] Margaret Leech, *In the Days of McKinley* (New York: Harper and Brothers, 1959) 452-454.

President McKinley developed a reputation as a man of compassion and that of a devoted husband, seeming to have no pleasures other than the constant care and attention he showered on his wife. He enjoyed smoking cigars, but never did so in the presence of Ida, as she did not like the odor.

Some felt sympathy for the President, reminiscent of Lincoln's trials with his wife Mary. Ida McKinley was often given to fits of temper, once pointing a finger at an embarrassed guest saying, "There's somebody who would like to be in my place and I know who it is."[65]

President McKinley's caring and compassion was known nationwide, and many stories can be found to assert the fact.

"I remember one afternoon in Canton, when his library and parlors were crowded with men of national prominence," wrote Charles M. Pepper, a newspaper correspondent friend of McKinley's who spent a good deal of time with him. "There were three or four United States Senators, half a dozen Representatives in Congress, two or three Governors, and several party leaders.

"A poor woman, with her daughter, asked an interview. She had with her a number of papers, and she told the secretary that it was a pension case. The President-elect saw her at once. He looked over the papers, explained very patiently how the case would have to be sent to the Pension Office in Washington, and what course it would have to follow there. He also promised her that it should receive prompt attention. Whether it would be allowed or not, of course he could not say, but he called a stenographer and dictated a letter which at least would ensure it for an early hearing. All this took ten or fifteen minutes, but Major McKinley manifested no annoyance, and by his own patient forbearance he rebuked the distinguished visitors who showed signs of impatience because their business was not given preference over the poor woman with the pension case."[66]

One night, Vice President Hobart, who would not survive his term of office, dying after a lengthy illness on November 21, 1899, became sick in the White House and decided to walk back to his residence. His home was located in Lafayette Square, only a few steps from the White House, and it was President McKinley himself who insisted on accompanying him.[67]

---

[65] Margaret Leech, *In the Days of McKinley* (New York: Harper and Brothers, 1959) 456.

[66] Murat Halstead, *The Illustrious Life of William McKinley* (Privately Published, 1901) 387.

[67] Murat Halstead, *The Illustrious Life of William McKinley* (Privately Published, 1901) 412.

McKinley was also good at accepting criticism. Once a senator declared that McKinley was becoming a dictator much to the detriment of the country. The very next day, the same Democrat came calling at the White House to attempt to secure an appointment for a constituent to a small consulship. He left with the appointment in his pocket.[68]

The President usually spent his evenings in the White House playing cards with Ida or his personal secretary, George B. Cortelyou. Sometimes he answered letters or took walks and carriage rides. He enjoyed smoking cigars, usually only in private, and he occasionally chewed them as well. Just before retiring for the night, he liked to take a drink of whiskey.

William McKinley took office as President on March 4, 1897, escorted by a troop of handsomely dressed Ohio cavalry to the White House. There he entered a carriage with President Grover Cleveland for the ride down Pennsylvania Avenue to the Capital. McKinley was fifty-four years old.

During the McKinley inaugural speech, the new President exclaimed that he wanted no wars of conquest. The United States must avoid the temptation of territorial aggression, he said. War should never be entered upon until every effort at peace had failed.[69]

McKinley took office while a widespread commercial and industrial depression prevailed, not having fully passed away when McKinley took his seat. He thought something needed to be done immediately to help this problem and as one of his first official acts, called Congress into special session.

"It is conceded that its current expenditures are greater than its receipts and that such a condition has existed for now more than three years," the President told Congress on March 15, 1897. "With unlimited means at our command, we are presenting the remarkable spectacle of increasing our public debt by borrowing money to meet the ordinary outlays incident upon even an economical and prudent administration of the Government. An examination of the subject discloses this fact in every detail, and leads inevitably to the conclusion that the condition of the revenue which allows it is unjustifiable and should be corrected."[70]

[68] Alexander K. McClure, *The Authentic Life of William McKinley* (W. E. Skull, 1901) 424.

[69] Zachary Kent, *William McKinley* (Chicago: Children's Press, 1988) 56-57.

[70] Alexander K. McClure, *The Authentic Life of William McKinley* (W. E. Skull, 1901) 209.

"Congress should promptly correct the existing condition," concluded the President. "Ample revenues must be supplied, not only for the ordinary expenses of the Government, but for the prompt payment of liberal pensions and the liquidation of the principal and interest of the public debt. In raising revenue, duties should be so levied upon foreign products as to preserve the home market, so far as possible, to our own producers; to revive and increase manufacturers; to relieve and encourage agriculture; to increase our domestic and foreign commerce; to aid and develop mining and building, and to render to labor in every field of useful occupation the liberal wages and adequate rewards to which skill and industry are justly entitled. The necessity of the passage of a tariff law, which shall provide ample revenue, need not be further urged. The imperative demand of the hour is the prompt enactment of such a measure, and to this object I earnestly recommend that Congress should make every endeavor. Before other business is transacted let us first provide sufficient revenue to faithfully administer the Government without the contracting of further debt or the continued disturbance of our finances."[71]

"The best way for the Government to maintain its credit is to pay as it goes—not by resorting to loans, but by keeping out of debt—through an adequate income secured by a system of taxation, external or internal, or both," he said on another occasion.

McKinley's tariff bill provided fifty or sixty million dollars more than the Wilson-Gorman tariff then in effect. Various internal revenue duties brought in approximately $145 million—alcohol taxes earned $114.5 million, tobacco taxes brought in another $30.7 million, and stamp taxes garnered $260,000. The bill became known as the Dingley Tariff, after its sponsor, Nelson Dingley, chairman of the House Ways and Means Committee, who had worked to get it ready for passage, even before McKinley's election. The bill became law on July 24, 1897, with its features being close with McKinley's own views on the subject.[72]

But it was not until the Gold Standards Act was passed on March 14, 1900, that McKinley's financial reforms were completed. The law was designed to provide for a more stable currency by putting the country officially on a gold standard and stated, "when any of the United States notes are presented for redemption in gold and are redeemed in gold,

---

[71] Alexander K. McClure, *The Authentic Life of William McKinley* (W. E. Skull, 1901) 211.
[72] Alexander K. McClure, *The Authentic Life of William McKinley* (W. E. Skull, 1901) 211-212.

such notes shall be kept and set apart and only paid out in exchange for gold."[73] All currency was now fully backed by gold, with a fixed price at $20.67 an ounce.

President McKinley's first address to Congress had two aims. First was to place national finances in a more healthy condition than they had been in the preceding four years under Cleveland, especially receipts compared to expenditures. Second was to overcome the depression which had so long existed and to restore commerce and industrial confidence which would provide orders for manufacturers and fair wages to idle mechanics. [74]

Both of these aims were achieved in magnificent fashion. The new tariff proved to be the start of good times. Soon after came an industrial boom and a wave of prosperity almost unequalled in the United States to that time. The United States saw an extraordinary increase in commerce. The balance of trade in the favor of the United States became much greater, and by the opening of the new century, had become greater than any nation had ever known before.[75]

"And this striking phenomenon belonged almost solely to the McKinley administration and was mainly, perhaps wholly, due to it's commercial and fiscal policy," wrote one contemporary author.[76]

In June 1900, a group of Chinese nationalists, members of the I-ho Tuan (Righteous and Harmonious Society), massacred numerous Western missionaries and Chinese converts to Christianity. Popularly known as the Boxers for their pugilistic-like ritual of battle preparation, the group also held the foreign community of diplomats in Peking hostage. President McKinley was forced to quickly dispatch 2,500 troops, without seeking congressional approval, along with several gunboats to assist a European military force in the liberation of the foreign delegation. The Open Door policy, issued in the midst of the Boxer Rebellion was especially aimed at the other Western powers— letting them know in clear terms that the U.S. would not support further action by the liberation forces aimed at the dividing China.[77]

---

[73] G. Townsend, *Memorial Life of William McKinley* (Washington: Memorial Publishing Co., 1901) 80.

[74] Alexander K. McClure, *The Authentic Life of William McKinley* (W. E. Skull, 1901) 214-215.

[75] Alexander K. McClure, *The Authentic Life of William McKinley* (W. E. Skull, 1901) 215-216.

[76] Alexander K. McClure, *The Authentic Life of William McKinley* (W. E. Skull, 1901) 216.

[77] Marshall Everett, *The Complete Life of William McKinley* (Privately Published, 1901) 271.

The Open Door policy expressed the United States' desire to have all commercial nations on an equal footing in China, unencumbered by unfair tariffs or other restrictions. It declared U.S. support for a non-colonized and independent China. This new policy called for free trade in China, and it became one of the most important foreign policy statements issued by the U.S. State Department.

Also in 1897, gold was discovered in the Alaskan frontier, and the rush to the mines over the next five years resulted in a considerable addition to the world's gold supply as well as having the effect of greatly increasing the white population in Alaska.

Simultaneously with William McKinley taking office, the Cubans had begun a revolt against Spanish rule. This situation had been a long time coming. For years, Cuba had been loyal to Spain, even while other islands in the region revolted. But in spite of this and the fact that she poured money into the Spanish treasury, Cuba began to feel mistreated. Finally, enough was enough and uprisings began to occur across the small island. Spain decided to put them down and sent in Governor-General Valeriano Weyler to accomplish the mission. Weyler spread destruction and ruin across Cuba, collecting bands of non-combatants and herding them into camps where nearly one hundred thousand starved to death. Americans became aware of the atrocities when Congressmen began to tour the island and they reported with horror what they saw. The cries of international protest reached a fever pitch and world opinion, in particular American opinion, caused Spain to recall Weyler and replace him with General Ramon Blanco. But the change had little effect as conditions continued to be horrendous.

Despite public pressure to help the Cuban revolutionaries, McKinley tried to maintain neutrality. Into this delicate climate sailed the *U. S. S. Maine,* arriving in Havana Harbor, to be ready in case hostilities broke out between the United States and Spain.

On February 15, 1898, the American battleship was rocked and destroyed by an enormous explosion, which killed 266 officers and men.[78] Spain denied that she had attacked the ship.

Highly skeptical, William Randolph Hearst began a vicious attack on the President in his newspapers, urging him to declare war. So did Secretary of the Navy Theodore Roosevelt. President McKinley found it harder and harder to remain neutral; in fact he was coming to the

---

[78] Alexander K. McClure, *The Authentic Life of William McKinley* (W. E. Skull, 1901) 228-229.

conclusion that war would be inevitable. He waited patiently while an investigation was conducted to determine the cause of the explosion. Finally the investigation concluded that an outside explosion had destroyed the *Maine*.

Meanwhile, Congress had been preparing for war, appropriating $50 million dollars for "national defense" against Spain. Many Americans wanted to use the incident as an excuse for America to come to the aid of the Cuban revolutionaries. Patient and cautious to the last, President McKinley waited, while on April 18, Congress passed a resolution saying in part that Cuba should be free and that it was the duty of the United States to demand that Spain relinquish its authority on the island. The resolution empowered the President use the full force and power of the Untied States military to accomplish the purpose, while also stating that the United States had no intention of claiming or taking over the island. McKinley signed the resolution two days later, on April 20.

Events now began to move quickly. On April 22, the American naval fleet blockaded Havana. Two days later Spain declared war on the United States, which reciprocated the following day on April 25. President McKinley called for 200,000 volunteers and within a month America was mobilized. War ships were purchased, ocean passenger vessels were converted into transports and attack plans were formulated on a number of fronts. By July 1, 40,000 troops had been sent to Cuba and the Philippines.

The Spanish-American War lasted only 113 days, but it had the effect of ending American isolationism. As a war president, McKinley was hands on. He was commander in chief in fact, as well as in name, rarely leaving the office during this period before 1 or 2 o'clock in the morning. He personally supervised preparations and gathered the Cabinet in pursuit of the latest information.

Whenever he had been forced to use troops in Ohio as Governor, he tried to use an excessive amount so as to show that he meant business. He felt that an over abundance of soldiers and a superior show of strength would better keep the peace. But during the Spanish-American War, the President was flexible enough to immediately allow an attack, without waiting the necessary interval to allow the United States to build up an overwhelming force in the region. This quick, decisive action led to a speedy end of the war and saved countless lives and resources.

Quick and decisive hardly describes the victory. For the first time in naval history, the victor in two separate engagements destroyed every vessel in an enemy fleet, even though the United States was inferior in numbers and position.[79]

The Treaty of Paris, signed with Spain on December 10, 1898, marked the official end of the war. On January 3, Secretary of State John Hay forwarded the treaty to President McKinley, who sent it to Congress the next day. After careful consideration, the treaty was ratified.

As a result of winning the war, the United States acquired Guam, the Philippines, and the entire West Indies except Cuba and including Puerto Rico. Some Democrats and even members of the President's own party, opposed the United States taking possession of these territories.[80] They opposed expansionism in favor of isolationism. But in the coming years, the tide could not be stopped.

The new American expansionism soon extended to business as well. About that same time, Congress annexed Hawaii. McKinley had urged this annexation since early in his administration.

"We need Hawaii just as much as, and a good deal more, than we did California," he had said.[81]

Soon Tutuila and other islands in the Samoan group also came under United States control.

But in the Philippines, there was unrest as Filipinos revolted against the new American presence. Filipinos had been unhappy with Spanish rule and Emilio Aguinaldo had led a revolt against them. When the Spanish-American War broke out, Filipinos had fought along side of the Americans against the Spanish. When the war ended, by the terms of the treaty, the Philippines were ceded to the Untied States. This angered Aguinaldo, as he claimed that the United States had promised to make the Philippines independent immediately. Aguinaldo declared the establishment of the Philippine Republic on Jan 23, 1899 and fighting broke out on the island between his troops and Americans on February 4. In March of 1901, Aguinaldo was captured and signed an oath of

---

[79] Alexander K. McClure, *The Authentic Life of William McKinley* (W. E. Skull, 1901) 25.

[80] Alexander K. McClure, *The Authentic Life of William McKinley* (W. E. Skull, 1901) 25.

[81] Alexander K. McClure, *The Authentic Life of William McKinley* (W. E. Skull, 1901) 191.

allegiance to the United States, and soon after the fighting stopped as the United States extended its rule throughout the islands. The war lasted until early 1902, and before it was over, more than 5,000 Americans and some 200,000 Filipinos lay dead.

As the century closed, America was fighting to end the sectionalism that had existed since prior to the Civil War. President McKinley visited the battlefield of his youth, Antietam, and addressed a crowd of former soldiers.

"Standing here to-day, one reflection only has crowded my mind—the difference between this scene and that of thirty-eight years ago," said the President. "Then the men who wore the blue and the men who wore the gray greeted each other with shot and shell, and visited death upon their respective ranks. We meet, after all these intervening years, with but one sentiment—that of loyalty to the Government of the United States, love of our flag and our free institutions, and determined men of the North and men of the South, to make any sacrifice for the honor and perpetuity of the American nation."[82]

Once at such a ceremony, a Confederate badge was pinned on the President. He allowed it to remain all day and on another occasion recommended that the federal government join the southern states in the care of Confederate graves.[83]

President McKinley also took part in the removal of the remains of General Grant to his final resting place in a tomb erected on Morning Heights, overlooking the Hudson River.

"With Washington and Lincoln, Grant had an exalted place in the history and the affections of the people," McKinley said. "To-day his memory is held in equal esteem by those who he led to victory, and by those who accepted his generous terms of peace. The veteran leaders of the Blue and Gray here meet not only to honor the name of Grant, but to testify to the living reality of a fraternal national spirit which has triumphed over the differences of the past and transcends the limitations of sectional lines. Its completion—which we pray God to speed—will be the nation's greatest glory."[84]

When it came time for re-election in 1900, the Republican convention was held in Philadelphia and it named him the nominee by acclamation; no other name was even put to the convention. There was a

---

[82] Alexander K. McClure, *The Authentic Life of William McKinley* (W. E. Skull, 1901) 193.

[83] Alexander K. McClure, *The Authentic Life of William McKinley* (W. E. Skull, 1901) 427.

[84] Alexander K. McClure, *The Authentic Life of William McKinley* (W. E. Skull, 1901) 222.

small effort put forth by Roosevelt volunteers, but the delegates were firmly devoted to McKinley. His supporters claimed that they were living in an America with "prosperity more general and more abundant than we have ever known."[85]

Congressman Joe Cannon claimed that McKinley kept his political ear so close to the ground that it was full of grasshoppers much of the time.[86]

For Vice President, the Republicans nominated Theodore Roosevelt, who had returned from the Spanish-American War a hero. Again the Democratic opponent was William Jennings Bryan, with Adlai Stevenson as his running mate. They campaigned for the silver standard and against American imperialism.

William Jennings Bryan campaigned under a disadvantage. The general prosperity of the country, the high employment rate at fair wages, played no small part in the decision making of Americans as they went to the polls.

McKinley did little campaigning but Theodore Roosevelt logged 21,000 miles, making speeches on behalf of the ticket. McKinley won reelection 292-155, an impressive victory in the electoral college. It was the largest popular majority ever given to a national candidate up to that time.[87]

McKinley told a friend that he could no longer be called the President of a party and that he was now the President of the whole people.[88]

On March 4, 1901, McKinley was inaugurated for his second term as President. McKinley was so popular that people began to talk of him running for un unprecedented third term. The President had been reluctant to run for a second term, but he put an end to such rumors in a letter dated June 10, 1901.

"I will say now, once and for all, expressing a long-settled conviction, that I not only am not and will not be a candidate for a third term, but would not accept a nomination for it if it were tendered me," he wrote.[89]

---

[85] Murat Halstead, *The Illustrious Life of William McKinley* (Privately Published, 1901) 150.

[86] Zachary Kent, *William McKinley* (Chicago: Children's Press, 1988) 58.

[87] Alexander K. McClure, *The Authentic Life of William McKinley* (W. E. Skull, 1901) 27.

[88] Zachary Kent, *William McKinley* (Chicago: Children's Press, 1988) 77.

[89] Murat Halstead, *The Illustrious Life of William McKinley* (Privately Published, 1901) 33.

About the only important event of McKinley's short and incomplete second term was when the President took a six-week tour across the country immediately following his inauguration. He and Mrs. McKinley whistle-stopped across the south and west on a special train. It was planned to go into the heart of all sections of the country. The train stopped at every major city along the way and the journey became one continuous ovation for the President. But in San Francisco, the trip was called short when Mrs. McKinley fell seriously ill. In fact, there was much fear for her life. McKinley stayed with her until she was well enough to return to Canton. The train was then speeded along to the President's hometown and popular demonstrations were avoided wherever possible.[90]

As the fall of 1901 approached, there were events of significance unfolding. Congress, with confirmation by the Supreme Court, could impose tariffs on the newly acquired dependencies, and the Court ruled that the people of these dependencies did not have the rights of citizens. The United States began free trade with Puerto Rico, after setting up a government there. Cuba added to its constitution an amendment that permitted the United States to intervene in Cuban affairs in certain circumstances. William Howard Taft was appointed civil governor in the Philippines, which paved the way for peace.

With the nation at peace and the economy strong, while still in Canton, the President decided he could now accept an invitation he had put off to attend the Pan American Exposition in Buffalo. It would be a nice trip, a vacation of sorts. Mrs. McKinley was feeling better. It would be a pleasant distraction from the daily routine and pressures of the Presidency.

When President McKinley had left the White House on July 5, 1901, for his trip through the west that would eventually take him to Canton and ultimately to Buffalo, some of his aides had assembled on the portico to bid him farewell and a safe journey. As the President got into his carriage, he told them, "Take good care of yourselves, boys, until I come back in the fall."[91]

It was the last time President McKinley would see the White House.

---

[90] Alexander K. McClure, *The Authentic Life of William McKinley* (W. E. Skull, 1901) 27.

[91] Marshall Everett, *The Complete Life of William McKinley* (Privately Published, 1901) 349.

President McKinley
The picture on the left was taken while Governor of Ohio

President & First Lady, Ida McKinley

The McKinley Home In Canton, OH.

Secretary of State Day signing the peace treaty with Spain while President McKinley and others look on.

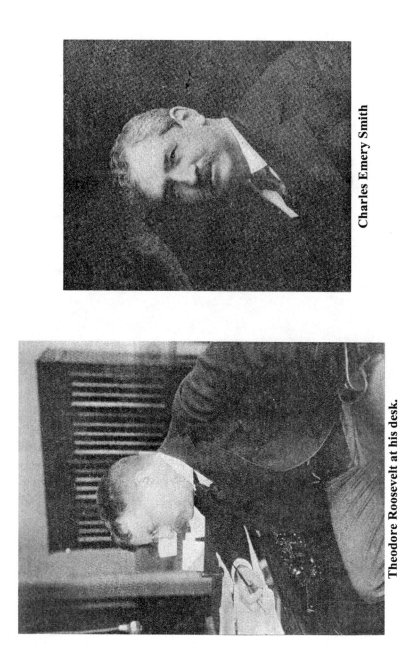

Charles Emery Smith

Theodore Roosevelt at his desk.

2. The Shooting

Buffalo was radiant. It was the center of world attention. The Pan American Exposition had already drawn millions of visitors; eventually eight million people would come; but this would be the crowning moment of the fair. The immensely popular President of the United States and his wife would add importance and grandeur to the event on "President's Day."

The McKinleys arrived in Buffalo for their visit at about 6:30 p.m. on September 4, aboard a special Presidential train on the Lake Shore and Michigan Southern Railway, which brought them right onto the Pan American Exposition grounds.[1] They had particularly been looking forward to the trip with cheerful anticipation and were met by an enormous crowd of enthusiastic supporters.

As part of the official welcome to Buffalo, artillery sounded a salute to the President. But an inexperienced soldier had placed the cannons too close to the railroad tracks, and when the big guns were shot, the concussion blew out windows on the presidential train, knocked down the only two men in the car, and frightened everyone. Ida McKinley, in poor health, fainted. Dr. Presley M. Rixey, the President's personal physician, attended to the First Lady. The cannonade continued, even as the President's personal secretary, George B. Cortelyou, frantically waved his arms from the train platform in an effort to get them to stop. After recovering, Mrs. McKinley seemed to feel well for the remainder of the next two days' activities. But it was a strange start to what was to be an eventful visit.[2]

After catching a brief glimpse of the Exposition, the McKinleys were quickly driven out the Lincoln Parkway gate to the home of Exposition President John G. Milburn, where they would be staying during their visit.

For twenty years, John Milburn had been known as one of the ablest lawyers in western New York. As a respected businessman in Buffalo, he was chosen as head of the Pan American Exposition because of his intellect, honesty and gentleness. Born in northern England, he had been a mechanical engineer, the occupation of his father. But Milburn had always wanted to be an attorney, and he suddenly left home and sailed

---

[1] Robert J. Donovan, *The Assassins* (New York: Harper & Brothers, 1952)100.

[2] *Buffalo Courier*, 5 September 1901, pg. 1.

for America in 1869, finding an opportunity to study law in the office of Wakeman & Watson in Batavia, New York. He passed the bar in 1873, but was not permitted to practice law because he had not yet become a citizen. He was granted a waiver and given citizenship by influential friends in the New York legislature in 1874. He had worked in his own law firm for the fifteen years prior, Rogers, Locke & Milburn. Coming to America as a poor boy, Milburn was truly an example of the American dream.[3]

The Milburn Residence, located at 1168 Delaware, on the west side of the street, was the second house north of Ferry Street. The spacious, wide three-story gabled brick house was dark green in color, set about sixty feet from the road, with a well-kept lawn, which sloped to the sidewalk. A number of shade trees were in the yard and ivy climbed over the porch and walls of the brownish gray brick exterior, hiding much of it from view. The McKinleys occupied a guestroom in the rear of the second floor.

The Pan American Exposition displayed all of the trends, developments, innovations, and attitudes of the McKinley years. The colorful buildings along the Grand Canal, built in ersatz Spanish colonial style, symbolized American influence over the Western Hemisphere.

While on a smaller scale than the World's Fairs of Chicago and Philadelphia, it surpassed them in architectural beauty. The Exposition centerpiece, the amazing 375-foot Electric Tower, announced to the world the United States' technological superiority with its dazzling electric display.

In memory of the fading frontier, there was a Wild West show, complete with an American Indian village. The aged Apache Chief Geronimo, accompanied by a U. S. Army guard, was displayed as a side show exhibit. The Indian Wars, now just a memory, were turned into spectacle and mock Indian vs. cavalry skirmishes were staged three times daily for Exposition visitors. Buffalo Bill Cody was a part of the show.

President McKinley had been scheduled to open the Exposition in the spring of 1901, but had been unable to attend due to an illness of Mrs. McKinley. Instead, Vice President Theodore Roosevelt had opened the event, and President's Day was postponed until McKinley himself could be present. September was the first chance the President had to attend the Exposition. President's Day would be the grandest of the entire fair.

---

[3] Murat Halstead, *The Illustrious Life of William McKinley* (Privately Published, 1901) 64-65.

The next morning, September 5th, the President and First Lady crossed the Triumphal Causeway that entered the fair grounds in an open horse-drawn carriage preceded by troops, military bands, and a mounted honor guard. The President was to give a major address on trade policy to a large crowd gathered on the esplanade. A crowd, estimated in excess of 50,000, waited to hear President McKinley speak.[4]

The excited fair patrons watched as the President and First Lady approached the Triumphal Causeway and the crowd began to cheer as they came into view. Behind an escort of horsemen, the President and his wife rode in the open carriage. Mr. McKinley stood upon arrival and helped his gray gowned wife from the carriage, after which they walked to the speakers platform. After a short introduction by John Milburn, and after a huge ovation, the President began his speech.

That same morning, another man arrived at the gates of the Pan American Exposition. That morning he had dressed into the best clothes he had with him, stuffed a bundle of papers he had in his pocket.[5] He breakfasted cheaply at a restaurant near his boardinghouse. On the way to the Exposition, he quietly dropped his papers into a sewer.[6] He bought his ticket for the "Grandest of all the World's Fairs." Just as he was going through the gate, a guard holding a club met Leon Czolgosz. Czolgosz panicked, turned to run, but before he could get more than a few steps, he was grabbed by the guard who knocked him into the dust. He thought he would be taken away, but just then a train whistle blew, followed by others and the guards moved toward the railroad tracks. Czolgosz picked himself up and to his great relief, blended in with the crowd nicely.[7]

After passing through the gates, Czolgosz was met with the sights of the Exposition grounds with its crowd of people, over 100,000 strong. Having already been to the Exposition on several occasions, he began a deliberate survey of the grounds, noticing the layout of the walkways, possible escape routes, and especially the security guards. Then he saw his objective. An enormous crowd had already gathered to hear the speech to be delivered by President McKinley.

---

[4] Robert J. Donovan, *The Assassins* (New York: Harper & Brothers, 1952)100-101

[5] Richard H. Barry, *The True Story of the Assassination of President McKinley at Buffalo* (Buffalo: Robert Allan Reid, 1901) 17.

[6] Richard H. Barry, *The True Story of the Assassination of President McKinley at Buffalo* (Buffalo: Robert Allan Reid, 1901) 18.

[7] A. Wesley Johns, *The Man Who Shot McKinley* (New York: A. S. Barnes & Co., Inc., 1970) 50.

Shortly before 9:00 a.m., Czolgosz moved with determination through the crowd that was waiting for the speech, trying to get as close to where the President would speak as possible, in hopes of doing his evil deed then. He did manage to get near enough to hear the President, but the crush of the crowd hemmed him in on all sides. He could not even move his arms. He made his way to near the front, and stood silently listening, yet not hearing.

The speech at the Exposition on September 5, turned out to be not only McKinley's last, but also one of his most notable, as he changed his long held view on high tariffs.

"Expositions are the timekeepers of progress," the President began. "They record the world's advancement. They stimulate the energy, enterprise, and intellect of the people, and quicken human genius. They go into the home. They broaden and brighten the daily life of the people. They open mighty storehouses of information to the student. Every exposition, great or small, has helped to some onward step.

"The Pan-American Exposition has done its work thoroughly," he continued, "presenting in its exhibits evidences of the highest skill, and illustrating the progress of the human family in the western hemisphere. This portion of the earth has no cause for humiliation for the part it has performed in the march of civilization. It has not accomplished everything; far from it. It has simply done its best; and without vanity or boastfulness, and recognizing the manifold achievements of others, it invites the friendly rivalry of all the powers in the peaceful pursuits of trade and commerce, and will cooperate with all in advancing the highest and best interests of humanity. The wisdom and energy of all the nations are none too great for the world's work. The success of art, science, industry, and invention is an international asset, and a common glory."

"My fellow-citizens: Trade statistics indicate that this country is in a state of unexampled prosperity," he explained as he began the meat of his speech. "The figures are almost appalling. They show that we are utilizing our fields and forests and mines, and that we are furnishing profitable employment to the millions of workingmen throughout the United States, bringing comfort and happiness to their homes, and making it possible to lay by savings for old age and disability. That all the people are participating in this great prosperity is seen in every American community, and shown by the enormous and unprecedented deposits in our savings banks. Our duty is the care and security of these deposits, and their safe investment demands the highest integrity and the best business capacity of those in charge of these depositories of the people's earnings.

"Our capacity to produce has developed so enormously, and our products have so multiplied, that the problem of more markets requires our urgent and immediate attention. Only a broad and enlightened policy will keep what we have. No other policy will get more. In these times of marvelous business energy and gain we ought to be looking to the future, strengthening the weak places in our industrial and commercial systems, that we may be ready for any storm or strain.

"By sensible trade arrangements which will not interrupt our home production, we shall extend the outlets for our increasing surplus. A system, which provides a mutual exchange of commodities, is manifestly essential to the continued and healthful growth of our export trade. We must not repose in fancied security that we can forever sell everything and buy little or nothing. If such a thing were possible, it would not be best for us or for those with whom we deal. We should take from our customers such of their products as we can use without harm to our industries and labor. Reciprocity is the natural outgrowth of our wonderful industrial development under the domestic policy now firmly established. What we produce beyond our domestic consumption must have a vent abroad. The excess must be relieved through a foreign outlet, and we should sell everywhere we can and buy wherever the buying will enlarge our sales and productions, and thereby make a greater demand for home labor.

"The period of exclusiveness is past. The expansion of our trade and commerce is the pressing problem. Commercial wars are unprofitable. A policy of good will and friendly trade relations will prevent reprisals. Reciprocity treaties are in harmony with the spirit of the times; measures of retaliation are not.

"If perchance some of our tariffs are no longer needed for revenue or to encourage and protect our industries at home, why should they not be employed to extend and promote our markets abroad? Then, too, we have inadequate steamship service. New lines of steamers have already been put in commission between the Pacific coast ports of the United States and those on the western coasts of Mexico and Central and South America. These should be followed up with direct steamship lines between the eastern coast of the United States and South American ports. One of the needs of the times is direct commercial lines from our vast fields of production to the fields of consumption that we have but barely touched."[8]

---

[8] Murat Halstead, *The Illustrious Life of William McKinley* (Privately Published, 1901) 222-227.

These lines reversed McKinley's long held views on protective tariffs and recognized the changing world environment and the role America would play. It also recognized the need for the United States to realize that it could no longer afford to remain isolated economically. After years of promoting policies of protectionism, it was a vast change for the President and showed the growth he had undergone while in office. He said that the only way to continue America's prosperity was to open the markets of the world to American products. He called for reciprocal treaties. He spoke extensively about the world's trade conditions of the time.

After the speech, hundreds of admirers broke through the security lines around the stand and the President held an impromptu reception, shaking the hands of hundreds. The carriages were then brought to the steps of the stand and the President and his specially invited guests prepared for a short trip to the Exposition stadium for the next event.[9]

The next day's news reports were very favorable in regard to the President's speech. One reported, "...never during his entire political career had he spoken with more assured wisdom or courage."[10]

"There will be some dispute as to what were the exact words last spoken by the President..." later reported the *Philadelphia Times*, a Democratic newspaper. "But it may be taken to be a small matter so long as we remember the hopeful, prophetic message, which he delivered to the American people only the day before he was stricken down by the assassin's bullet. This speech has become a dying message. It should linger with us to guide or future policy."[11]

"Mr. McKinley, always felicitous in his public addresses, has never appeared to better advantage either as an orator or a leader than he does in his admirable speech at the Pan American Exposition," commented the *New York World*.[12]

After the speech, Czolgosz tried, along with hundreds of other people, to get close to the President. As he quickly approached, he suddenly saw two men, dressed remarkably alike, climbing into the

---

[9] Murat Halstead, *The Illustrious Life of William McKinley* (Privately Published, 1901) 228.

[10] *Literary Digest*, 14 September 1901, pg.1.

[11] Alexander K. McClure, *The Authentic Life of William McKinley* (W. E. Skull, 1901) 312.

[12] Alexander K. McClure, *The Authentic Life of William McKinley* (W. E. Skull, 1901) 312.

President's carriage. It was President McKinley accompanied by Exposition President Milburn, but for a crucial moment Czolgosz was not sure which was McKinley. His brief hesitation gave the President just enough time to escape with his life. Czolgosz was forced to watch as the President was driven away.[13]

Czolgosz stayed at the Exposition until about six, wandered back into downtown Buffalo until ten, then returned to his rented room.[14]

Immediately following the speech, President McKinley reviewed troops in the packed Pan American Stadium, numerous times being loudly applauded. For fifteen minutes the troops performed intricate drills for the President. Afterwards, McKinley was driven to the Canadian Building, where he met with Canadian officials and viewed the exhibits. He next visited the Agricultural Building and its exhibits, which included meeting with many foreign commissioners who had exhibits in the building. From there he visited the buildings of Honduras, Cuba, Chile, Mexico, the Dominican Republic, Puerto Rico, and Ecuador, where he was again received by the commissioners of the respective countries. That night he watched a fireworks display and illumination. It was indeed a festive day. [15]

The next day, in the early morning of September 6, President and Mrs. McKinley, with the rest of the presidential cavalcade, including about a hundred invited guests,[16] traveled in the President's special train from Buffalo to Niagara Falls. The train left at 9 a.m., reaching Lewiston at 10:05, where many of the country people turned out to greet the President, and throughout the morning McKinley was in an unusually happy mood. Three trolley cars then transported the presidential party up the gorge, while the President chatted happily. At the Falls, McKinley visited all the points of interest, occasionally leaving his carriage for short walks with his personal secretary George Cortelyou and exposition official W. I. Buchanan. During the morning, Mrs. McKinley felt tired and was taken to the International Hotel, avoiding the trip to Goat Island, while the President continued the tour.[17]

---

[13] A. Wesley Johns, *The Man Who Shot McKinley* (New York: A. S. Barnes & Co., Inc., 1970) 60-61.

[14] Robert J. Donovan, *The Assassins* (New York: Harper & Brothers, 1952)101.

[15] Murat Halstead, *The Illustrious Life of William McKinley* (Privately Published, 1901) 228.

[16] *New York Times,* 7 September 1901, pg. 1, col. 2.

[17] *Buffalo Courier*, 8 September 1901, pg. 23, col. 5.

"I wish you could have seen them together, as they viewed the Falls," said one woman who was there. "Mrs. McKinley pointed out the places she had seen and gloried in, on her former trip, and the President, well his face as he looked down the gorge was beyond description. Awe, reverence and joy lit up is countenance until it was radiant.

"With all one hears about the thought and tenderness of Mr. President for his wife," she continued, "no one can realize his care and attention until she has been with them."[18]

Three young boys ran up to the carriage of the President as it traveled down Main Street and took off their hats and gave three cheers, which were quickly followed by the entire crowd which lined the street. The President and Mrs. McKinley were delighted at the boys, and Mrs. McKinley spoke of them afterwards, they seeming so happy to be so close to the President and having him notice them.[19]

Much had been made in the press about the possibility of the President leaving American soil and venturing into Canada. Up to that time, no sitting United States President had ever stepped foot outside of the country. But McKinley did not put this to a constitutional test. A few feet from the Canadian border, the President and his party turned around.

The President inspected the Niagara Falls Power Company plant and showed keen interest in it and the electrical power it could produce. He was particularly pleased that it did not detract from the natural beauty of the Falls.[20]

The presidential party lunched at Niagara Falls and stayed until 2:45 when they began the trip back, arriving in Buffalo at 3:30 p.m. Mrs. McKinley, still feeling fatigued, took a carriage back to the Milburn home. The President, accompanied by Milburn, Cortelyou and the Secret Service men, was then driven to the Temple of Music, where he prepared for a public reception where he would greet and shake hands for about ten minutes beginning at 4 p.m.

For security reasons, George Cortelyou had thought the trip to Niagara Falls would be more than enough for one day. The President's personal secretary and other members of the President's staff had repeatedly advised against doing the reception at the Temple of Music.

---

[18] *Buffalo Enquirer*, 9 September, 1901.

[19] *Buffalo Enquirer*, 9 September, 1901.

[20] *Buffalo Courier*, 8 September 1901, pg. 23, col. 5.

Twice they had taken the reception off the President's schedule, only to have McKinley put it back on.[21]

The day before, the President had expressed regret that he would not have the opportunity to greet more Buffalo citizens personally. He had noticed their efforts to get close to him and shake his hand after his speech, and said he was sorry that a public reception had not been planned.

"It's not too late yet," he told Milburn. "Why should we not have a public reception tomorrow after our return from Niagara Falls?"

"...it is a strange fact that the President himself, through the goodness of his heart, should have been responsible for his appearance in the throng with which the murderous Czolgosz mingled," later commented one Exposition official.[22]

Cortelyou felt McKinley had already visited the Exposition and made a major speech the day before and there seemed to be no need to return. He was also somewhat worried about rumors of an anarchist plot. There had already been at least two rumored plots to kill President McKinley.

On March 14, 1899, a former Civil War private who had served in the New York Regiment named Henry Muller was arrested in Montreal because of threats he had made against the President. Muller, who had been wounded in the head during the Civil War and had occasional bouts with insanity, had come to the conclusion that McKinley was an enemy of the German people and made threats of traveling to Washington to kill him. After he was arrested and investigated, his threats were not taken seriously.

Then on July 11, 1900, there had been a published report of a plot to kill McKinley by a group of Spanish and Cuban conspirators. After an investigation by authorities, the rumors of the plot, which was supposedly being hatched out of a cigar store on Broadway, were determined to be unfounded.[23]

Later, New York Police Commissioner Murphy would remember an incident, which occurred on March 3, 1900 regarding his department's protection of President McKinley. A drunken spectator had approached the presidential carriage and had to be driven away twice by New York Detective Funston for wanting to shake hands with the President. He had actually tried the driver side door to the carriage and then, after

---

[21] Robert J. Donovan, *The Assassins* (New York: Harper & Brothers, 1952)104.

[22] *New York Times*, 9 September 1901, pg. 1, col. 4.

[23] *New York Times,* 7 September 1901, pg. 6, col. 1.

being chased, had gone to the other side to try again. The gentleman persisted and appealed to Secretary Cortelyou who was seated in another carriage. Cortelyou had been successful in quieting the man down. The President, for his part, never seemed alarmed in the least.

Murphy later would contend that if New York detectives had been protecting the President, Czolgosz would never have gotten so close with his hand wrapped in a handkerchief. This act, he said, would have caused any New York detective to suspect him being a pick pocket at the very least, as it was a favorite method of stealing small items such as jewelry by such thieves. [24]

An additional consideration adding to Secretary Cortelyou's concern were the large number of recent plots and assassinations of European leaders, including the assassinations of Czar Alexander II of Russia, Empress Elizabeth of Austria and of King Humbert of Italy. Even King Edward of England had faced an attempt on his life in Brussels while he was still the Prince of Wales.

In August of 1900, Comptroller of Currency Charles G. Dawes, a young, close political advisor of the President, had received a report of an assassination plot by a group in Paterson, New Jersey. The most recent killing of a foreign leader had been that of King Humbert of Italy on July 30, 1900. The King was distributing prizes at a gymnastics competition when he was shot. His murderer was an anarchist named Angelo Bresci, who at one time had been a resident of Paterson.

King Humbert had just entered his carriage with an aide when Bresci shot him three times in quick succession with a revolver. Humbert died within minutes, as one of the bullets pierced his heart.

With no capital punishment in Italy, Bresci was sentenced to solitary life imprisonment, where some reports say he committed suicide. Other reports, however, suggested that his guards had murdered him.[25]

Because of the assassination of Humbert, Dawes took the anarchist rumor much more seriously than most such threats.

"I received a personal letter from Senator Hanna, enclosing a statement of a detective relative to a plot to assassinate the President," Dawes wrote. "Though not usually disturbed by the many vague warnings of this nature so often received, this was surrounded by so many evidences of reliability as compared with the others that I was much worried and saw the President and showed him the papers and insisted with all my power on less indifference on his part to his personal

---

[24] *New York Times*, 8 September 1901, pg. 4, col. 5.
[25] *New York Times*, 7 September 1901, pg. 6, col. 1.

safety. Saw Cortelyou about it and saw Chief Wilkie in connection with the matter. The guard was increased. The detective claims that the plot includes the assassination of all the leading rulers of the world and originates at Paterson, N. J., where Bresci, the assassin of Humbert came from."[26]

Hanna had enclosed for Dawes' inspection a memorandum from a secret service agent, saying that the government had information about the Paterson group. From an informant, they had learned that a group of leaders were indeed targeted, the first two of which had already been assassinated.

"The Anarchists or Socialists through their various organizations planned to rid the earth of a number of its rulers and the following selections were made; first the Empress Eugene of Austria was to be dispatched, then the King of Italy, then the Czar of Russia, then the Prince of Wales, or his mother, the Queen, then the President of the United States and lastly the Emperor of Germany, and as the first two calls made by this information have come to pass as predicted, this informant impressed with the possibilities of the situation, asks that the information by him to the government two years ago be gone over with a view of corroborating it," the memorandum read.

"Appreciating that the President and his best friends do not feel apprehensive for his safety, the party responsible for this statement of facts, prompted only by what he *knows* to be *true* as far as the informant's part is concerned, believes that proper and prompt steps should be taken to protect the person of the President and that purpose suggests that his secretary, Mr. Cortelyou be communicated with and requested to triple the guard now surrounding the President. There is but one man now doing the duty," the report concluded.[27]

Concerning the other recently assassinated leaders; an Italian anarchist named Luigini in Geneva, Switzerland on September 10, 1898 killed Empress Elizabeth of Austria. The Empress had been staying at the Hotel Beaurivage for several days and was walking from the hotel to a pier of lake steamers. Just before reaching the pier, a man ran up behind her and plunged a sharp file into her back. She was rushed back into the hotel, but never regained consciousness, and despite frantic efforts to save her, she died.

---

[26] Charles W. Dawes, *A Journal of the McKinley Years* (Chicago: R. R. Donnelley & Sons Co., 1950) 239.

[27] Charles W. Dawes, *A Journal of the McKinley Years* (Chicago: R. R Donnelley & Sons Co., 1950) 240-241.

Luigini made no effort to escape and was arrested. Later, he said that he had come to Geneva to kill Duc d'Orleans, but killed the Empress instead when he found his original target had left.[28]

Czar Alexander II of Russia, had been killed on March 13, 1881, the same year as President Garfield, and was also still vividly remembered in 1901. Even after a couple attempts on the Czar's life, the latest being a year earlier when an enormous explosion ripped apart the Winter Palace in St. Petersburg and failed to take his life, the killing of Alexander II was surprisingly unexpected.

The Czar had been publicly targeted for death by a group of Russian revolutionaries known as Nihilists. After the two unsuccessful attempts, the third try was not accompanied by the usual threats and proclamations. As the Czar was being driven in a carriage, and as it reached the Catherine Canal, an anarchist named Ryssakoff threw the first bomb. It landed beneath the carriage and did not injure the Czar. It did however badly wound two accompanying Cossacks.

Instead of leaving immediately, the Czar got out of his carriage to check on his men. His compassion cost him his life. After stepping from the carriage, a second bomb thrown by another anarchist named Grevevitsky, exploded at the Czar's feet, breaking both legs and penetrating his abdomen. The Czar died in agony two hours later. Grevevitsky was also killed in the explosion.[29]

Yet another leader, French President Carnot, had been assassinated at an exposition, coincidentally enough, on June 24, 1894. He was killed by a young baker while driving through the streets of Lyon, which was hosting the event.

President Carnot had ordered his special guard away and the assassin had no trouble leaping onto the step of the landeau in which the President sat. Concealing a poniard in a newspaper, with a vicious blow, the assassin was able to drive the poniard's point into the President's liver. Carnot died that night.

The assassin was taken prisoner by bystanders and was barely saved from a lynching on the spot by police. He was not to avoid his fate, however. He was guillotined at Lyon on August 16.[30]

And of course, the assassination of an American President was not far from consciousness. About four months after to the assassination of Alexander II, and only seventeen years after Lincoln, President James

---

[28] *New York Times*, 7 September 1901, pg. 6, col. 2.

[29] *New York Times*, 7 September 1901, pg. 6, col. 2.

[30] *New York Times*, 7 September 1901, pg. 6, col. 1.

Garfield was shot in the back on July 2, 1881 while at the old Union Terminal in Washington, D.C. The President was beginning a trip to New York and New England with many of his Cabinet members. As he was walking with Secretary of State James G. Blaine and passing through a ladies waiting room, he was shot twice by Charles J. Guiteau. One of the bullets hit him in the back and he slumped to the floor, bleeding badly. He lost consciousness for a moment and then commenced to vomit. He was rushed back to the Executive Mansion.

Guiteau was taken into custody and turned out to be a disappointed petitioner for a Presidential appointment to office. He had first applied to be U.S. Minister to Austria, and had been rejected. He then tried for Consul General to Paris, and was again disappointed.

On his person, Guiteau carried a letter stating that the death of the President was a "sad necessity" that would unite the Republican party and save the republic.

President Garfield's condition worsened, improved, then worsened again. After a long fight, the President finally died of blood poisoning on September 19, seventy-nine days after the attack.[31]

With all these recent plots, threats and murders on his mind, Cortelyou again requested the President skip the reception and McKinley asked him why he should? He said that no one would want to hurt him. Besides, Cortelyou argued, there was no chance the President could shake all of the hands that were going to be there. McKinley's answer to his secretary was simply, that they would know he had tried.[32]

The exact movements of Leon Czolgosz in the morning and early afternoon of September 6 are impossible to confirm. He said that he awoke early, bought a cigar in the hotel saloon, left the hotel with a bundle of old newspapers which he threw into the sewer, went to breakfast in a small restaurant, then went to a barbershop for a shave.[33] Some reports say he followed McKinley to Niagara Falls, but never catching up to the President, returned early once he realized that he could not get a good shot. But Czolgosz stated that he had already decided to kill McKinley at the Temple of Music, and he arrived at the Exposition about an hour ahead of McKinley, at 2:30.[34]

---

[31] *New York Times*, 7 September 1901, pg. 6, col. 1.

[32] Robert J. Donovan, *The Assassins* (New York: Harper & Brothers, 1952) 102.

[33] Robert J. Donovan, *The Assassins* (New York: Harper & Brothers, 1952) 101.

[34] Robert J. Donovan, *The Assassins* (New York: Harper & Brothers, 1952) 101.

Czolgosz later always denied going to the Falls in pursuit of the President, saying he had, by that time, already decided to kill him in the Temple of Music. When is was said during the trial that he had gone to the Falls, Czolgosz told his guards during his transfer to Auburn Prison the testimony in that regard was erroneous.

While it is highly doubtful that Czolgosz went to Niagara Falls, one thing that is absolutely certain about his actions that morning is that Czolgosz had a good place in line when the doors to the Temple of Music were opened.

The Temple of Music was a beautiful auditorium, which housed a large stage and a gigantic organ. The meeting between the President and his public would take place on the stage with the seating area empty. People would be herded through two large doors on the right side of the stage. They would be funneled into a single file line, which would pass through a line of soldiers from the 73rd Sea Coast Artillery, Exposition police, detectives, and Secret Service. A total of about fifty security guards of one form or another guarded the President.[35] The crowd would move toward a display of potted bay trees and palms with a backdrop of American flags, where President McKinley would be standing.

From a security stand point; there would be enough room to see each person before they reached the President. More soldiers outside controlled the vast throng that was waiting to see Mr. McKinley.

Waiting in line behind Leon Czolgosz, was a recently laid off, six-foot-six black waiter in his early thirties named James Benjamin Parker. "Big Jim," as he was known to friends, stood six foot six, was born in Atlanta on July 31, 1857, but had lived in New York and had received a job as a waiter in the Plaza restaurant (the Bailey restaurant in at least one other report) just a week earlier. He had attended the University of Atlanta, studying there for a little over three years. Parker had lived in Philadelphia and Savannah, becoming somewhat of a politician among the blacks of that city. He had worked, after that, as a waiter in Chicago, before going back to Atlanta, then to Buffalo.[36] Parker had gotten a half hour leave from work to be able to shake hands with the President.[37]

---

[35] Robert J. Donovan, *The Assassins* (New York: Harper & Brothers, 1952) 102.

[36] *Buffalo Times*, 12 September, 1901.

[37] *Buffalo Commercial*, 7 September 1901.

"I was in line waiting to shake hands with the President," Parker told the *Buffalo Evening News*. "This fellow (Czolgosz) when I left the door crowded in front of me. I was next to a little girl, 12 years old, and wanted to keep there, but he kept along beside me and crowded in. I tried to keep him out, but at last I said 'You go on then.'"[38]

Parker had been waiting to see the President for a long time and while in line, he tried to strike up a conversation with Czolgosz. Czolgosz made no effort to become engaged in the banter and Parker gave up. Czolgosz was moving too slowly in front of him and Parker was getting impatient.[39]

"What is the --- is the matter with you?" Parker asked him. "If you want to get ahead of me, get ahead."[40]

Shortly before 4 p.m., the President's carriage, also containing Milburn and Cortelyou, pulled up to the side entrance of the Temple, with the Secret Service carriage right behind. Inside, Exposition Grounds Director General W. I. Buchanan met the Presidential party and the President was taken inside and directed where to stand.[41]

On his way into the building, as the President climbed the steps, photographer Jimmy Hare took a quick snapshot of the President. Hare, having heard many of McKinley's speeches before, decided not to enter the Temple of Music, but instead decided to seek out his friend, official Exposition photographer C. D. Arnold. Hare's photograph was to be the last of President McKinley alive.[42]

The President took off his hat, smiled to those around him and said, "It's much cooler in here, isn't it?"[43] Another witness thought he had said, "It's nice and cool in here. Where shall we stand?"[44]

Both sides of the aisle in which the public would pass were covered with purple bunting, the color to mark the majesty of the occasion. As McKinley waited for the doors to open, he rubbed his hands together in anticipation, adjusted his coat and chatted amiably with Milburn and Cortelyou.[45]

---

[38] *Buffalo Evening News*, 8 September 1901, pg. 4, col. 4.
[39] A. Wesley Johns, *The Man Who Shot McKinley* (New York: A. S. Barnes & Co., Inc., 1970) 92.
[40] *Buffalo Commercial,* 13 September 1901.
[41] *Cincinnati Enquirer*, 7 September 1901, pg. 1.
[42] Cecil Carnes, *Jimmy Hare: News Photographer* (New York: MacMillan Co., 1940) 119.
[43] G. Townsend, *Memorial Life of William McKinley* (Washington: Memorial Publishing Co., 1901) 189.
[44] *Buffalo Express*, 7 September 1901.
[45] *Cincinnati Enquirer*, 7 September 1901, pg. 1.

As the President began the reception, he was reportedly in high spirits, rarely having been in a better mood. When he had arrived back from his Niagara Falls excursion, one of the hosts, J. B. Olmstead had said, "I am glad to see you back in Buffalo." McKinley replied, "Yes, and I don't know if I'll ever be able to get away."[46]

It is strange how often small comments take on added importance after events and how it seems that there are unconscious premonitions to disaster. Major Louis L. Babcock, a prominent Buffalo attorney and Grand Marshall of the Exposition, was lunching on sandwiches and imported beer with James L. Quackenbush, a member of the committee on ceremonies. Quackenbush made an ominous off-hand comment that it would be Roosevelt's luck if someone shot the President.[47]

During the President's luncheon at the New York Building the day before, McKinley had asked Harry Winder, who had waited on him during the 1896 Republican convention in St. Louis and had been chosen to wait on the President, "What's on the other side of that door, my boy?"

Winder told him a pool and garden and asked the President if he would like to see. McKinley declined, saying he was only curious. Winder thought, in light of later events, that McKinley perhaps had experienced a premonition and some apprehension of what was to come.[48]

Secretary of Agriculture James Wilson also had a premonition of sorts the night before during the fireworks display; "Last Thursday night, when the President witnessed the grand illumination at the Exposition, I was impressed with the ease with which some evil-disposed person might have crept up in the darkness between the flashes of the pyrotechnics and have done the President bodily harm.

"Secretary Cortelyou was similarly impressed and we talked the matter over at great length as we sat on the benches watching the display. I confess that much of my pleasure was destroyed by the dread of what might happen. Secretary Cortelyou and I went over carefully the precautions, which are always taken with the public appearance of the President. He said that if any other precautions could be suggested or devised he would employ them. We spoke of the reception at the

[46] *Buffalo Express*, 7 September 1901.

[47] Robert J. Donovan, *The Assassins* (New York: Harper & Brothers, 1952) 102.

[48] A. Wesley Johns, *The Man Who Shot McKinley* (New York: A. S. Barnes and Co, Inc., 1970) 64.

Temple of Music, which had been arranged for the next day, and agreed that the only danger that might exist would be from organized Anarchists or someone actually demented and irresponsible. The possibility of just such a tragedy as occurred we could not but admit.

"We realized that it would not do to dissuade the President from holding the reception. With the memory of this conversation in his mind, Secretary Cortelyou yesterday took special precautions."[49]

Former Attorney General John W. Griggs related, "I warned him against this very thing time and again. I asked him for the country's sake, if not for his own, to have a bodyguard when he went out. He refused. He laughed at me. He insisted on going about almost as freely as if he was not liable to attack. He insisted the American people were too intelligent and too loyal to their country to do any harm to their Chief Executive. He had supreme confidence in the people. He was right, perhaps, but the irresponsible individual has done what I feared would be done."[50]

B. H. Warner told of a talk he had with Secret Service Agent George Foster, the Wednesday prior to the assassination.

"Why is it, George, that the President will go into such a crowd as this when personal danger to him cannot be avoided," Warner told him. "He ought to stop accepting such invitations."

"Oh, nobody would want to harm President McKinley," said Foster in reply. "Everybody loves him too well."[51]

"He (the President) was smiling from the moment he stepped into the building, and when he announced that he was ready for the doors to be thrown open, he appeared as though the coming on-slaught of handshaking was to be a long-looked-for pleasure," reported the *Buffalo Courier.*[52]

By 4 p. m., the President had taken his position under the bower of palms. He nodded to Babcock to open the door. "Let them come," he said. W. J. Gomph began to play the huge pipe organ and the sounds of Bach filled the room. [53]

"Excellent," exclaimed the President at the sounds of the music.[54]

---

[49] *New York Times*, 8 September 1901, pg. 2, col. 4.

[50] *New York Times*, 7 September 1901, pg. 5, col. 4.

[51] *Washington Post*, 7 September 1901, pg. 2, col. 4.

[52] *Buffalo Courier*, 7 September 1901, pg. 1.

[53] *Cincinnati Enquirer*, 7 September 1901, pg. 1.

[54] *Buffalo Express*, 7 September 1901.

The first man in line was a silver haired gentleman with a little girl on his shoulders, whom the President greeted warmly. It was Dr. Clinton Colegrove of Holland, New York, and as he shook the President's hand, he compared McKinley to Washington and Lincoln. The smiling President thanked him as he moved him along.[55]

One young boy broke from his mother and bolted up to the President. His mother quickly apologized, but the President simply complimented him on his brightness.[56]

John D. Wells, an eyewitness, watched, saying later that to every child, the President bent over, shook hands warmly and said some kind words. Wells also noted that as each person passed, the Secret Service men watched closely. [57]

While the security of President McKinley could not compare by today's standards, with a guard force of fifty plus, he was relatively well protected. Twelve Exposition police officers stood guard outside the Temple of Music. Inside were 18 more Exposition officers and another eleven soldiers from the United States Coast Artillery. There were also four Buffalo police detectives stationed near the President, with one directly behind him. Two Secret Service agents, George F. Foster and Samuel R. Ireland stood at arms length. Another, Albert L. Gallaher, stood nearby. President McKinley was flanked by Cortelyou and Milburn.[58]

Private Francis P. O'Brien was stationed close to the reception area, near the President. Private Brooks was on O'Brien's left. Private Ivey Fenenbaugh was across the aisle directly in front of the President. Privates Maximilian R. Kubatz and William Heiser were about fifteen feet from the reception area.[59]

Normally, Secret Service Security Chief Foster would stand next to the President on such occasions, but in this case Milburn wanted to be

---

[55] A. Wesley Johns, *The Man Who Shot McKinley* (New York: A. S. Barnes and Co, Inc, 1970) 91.

[56] A. Wesley Johns, *The Man Who Shot McKinley* (New York: A. S. Barnes and Co, Inc, 1970) 92.

[57] A. Wesley Johns, *The Man Who Shot McKinley* (New York: A. S. Barnes and Co, Inc, 1970) 93.

[58] Robert J. Donovan, *The Assassins* (New York: Harper & Brothers, 1952)102.

[59] A. Wesley Johns, *The Man Who Shot McKinley* (New York: A. S. Barnes and Co, Inc, 1970) 89.

next to McKinley so he could point out local dignitaries as they met the President. Foster accordingly took a position directly behind the President and Milburn. Agent Ireland was likewise moved from his normal position.

Foster was a favorite guard of the President's and had accompanied McKinley on every trip. Often he was specifically requested by McKinley and had arrested a number of cranks on the recent western trip for trying to get at the President.[60]

"It has been my custom to stand back of the President and just to his left, so that I could see every person approaching, but yesterday Secretary Cortelyou requested that I stand opposite the President, so that Mr. Milburn could stand to his left and introduce the people who approached. In that way, I was unable to get a good look at everyone's hand," he later said in a newspaper interview.[61]

Still, with so much protection, it would seem that a close up assassination attempt would be futile. But as often happens, luck and circumstance played into the hands of the assassin.

Many factors made it easier for twenty-eight year old Leon Czolgosz to escape suspicion as he moved closer to the President. Being a hot day, many people had handkerchiefs out to wipe their hands and faces, so a handkerchief covered right hand did not arouse as much suspicion as it normally may have, being only one of many. Before Czolgosz reached McKinley, another man had even approached the President with an injured right hand in a handkerchief, shook hands with his left and harmlessly moved on.[62] In fact, because of the heat, the President himself even carried three extra handkerchiefs that day.[63]

Still, it has never been fully explained why a major rule of security, that of watching very closely everyone's hands, was overlooked that day. Normally, the hands of everyone must be plainly visible and empty upon approaching. For whatever reason, this procedure was ignored, with tragic results.[64]

---

[60] *Cincinnati Post*, 7 September 1901, pg. 4, col. 3.

[61] *New York Times*, 8 September 1901, pg. 2, col.4.

[62] Robert J. Donovan, *The Assassins* (New York: Harper & Brothers, 1952) 103.

[63] A. Wesley Johns, *The Man Who Shot McKinley* (New York: A. S. Barnes and Co, Inc., 1970) 90.

[64] Margaret Leech, *In the Days of McKinley* (New York: Harper & Brothers, 1959) 591.

Also, Czolgosz himself, by his appearance and manner, did nothing to attract the attention of the President's security force. A good deal of criticism was directed at the President's guards after the fact about how a man of Czolgosz's appearance could have been permitted to approach the President with his hand wrapped in a bandage large enough to conceal a revolver. The most common response was that almost every one of those entering the Temple of Music to greet the President was carrying some type of lunch box or parcel. For this reason, it did not arouse particular suspicion, as there was nothing peculiar in Czolgosz's over all appearance.[65] Finally, the President's own security force, even though they were vigilant that day in their protection, did not think that an attack was at all probable.

"It is incorrect, as has been stated, that the least fear of an assault was entertained by the Presidential Party," explained Samuel R. Ireland, the Secret Service agent nearest the President. "Since the Spanish War, the President has traveled all over the country and has met people everywhere. In Canton, he walks to church and down town without the sign of a Secret Service man or any kind of an escort. In Washington, he walks about the White House grounds, drives out freely and has enjoyed much freedom from the presence of detectives."[66]

As for Czolgosz and his appearance, Ireland pointed out that he never thought for even a moment that Czolgosz had a revolver with him. Even the bandage did not raise particular suspicions.

"It was nothing out of the ordinary," Ireland explained. "We see men with bandages almost every time the President has a public reception. Of course, we watch these fellows just as we watch everyone else who approaches Mr. McKinley, but we never thought for a moment that he had a revolver with him. His face was in his favor. He didn't look like a man who would attempt to take the life of another unprovoked. If there had been anything about his appearance to arouse our suspicions, we certainly would have stopped him, but there wasn't. As I said before, he was the last man in the world we would picked out of a crowd as dangerous" [67]

Another security factor was that the crowd was not checked as they entered the building to make certain that they were not carrying weapons, as they would be in later times. In addition, the soldiers who were helping to provide security were not trained in that area. They

[65] *New York Times*, 8 September 1901, pg.2, col. 1.
[66] *New York Times*, 8 September 1901, pg.2, col. 1.
[67] *Buffalo Express*, 8 September 1901.

tended to obstruct the view of patrons from the Secret Service. Finally, no large clear area was left open in front of and to the sides of the President, as was customary.[68]

In hindsight, however, it is easy to blame the assassination on the President's security. But even the best plans can fail in one careless, luckless instant. But by most reports, the President's security force was alert to all possible dangers.

"When we saw the bandage on Czolgosz' hand we gained the impression that he had received a bad burn," said Ireland. "He extended his left hand to the President and the President was ready to grasp it. Instead of taking the President's hand he steadied the revolver, which he was holding in the right hand with his left hand and then fired. He had been careful to ward off the President's hand so that the bullet would be sure to reach its destination.

"Another thing too, is that he was foxy," Ireland concluded. "He didn't aim for the heart. He knew that if he attempted any game like that the revolver would probably have been knocked from his hand before he got a chance to fire at all."[69]

McKinley continued to shake with his right hand and politely, with the help of Secret Service Agent Ireland, move the people along with his left. Over half were women and children. He generally just smiled or said one or two brief words, bending down and shake hands with the children and have a couple words. After about five minutes, Cortelyou was becoming fidgety. He called for Edward R. Rice, an Exposition Committee member and told him, "See Babcock and have him end the reception in five minutes."

Rice quickly told Babcock to speed up the line, that Cortelyou wanted the reception to end in five minutes. Babcock did as he was instructed, and waited for Cortelyou's signal. [70]

At about this same time, Leon Czolgosz entered the room, approximately 64 feet from the President. Two lines of security guards funneled the visitors into the single file line about 15 feet or so from the President. Outside, Czolgosz had reached into his pocket with his right hand and wrapped a handkerchief to conceal a .32 caliber Iver Johnson

---

[68] Margaret Leech, *In the Days of McKinley* (New York: Harper & Brothers, 1959) 591.

[69] *Buffalo Express*, 8 September 1901.

[70] A. Wesley Johns, *The Man Who Shot McKinley* (New York: A. S. Barnes and Co, Inc., 1970) 92.

revolver. He knew that once he was inside, he would be watched more closely. Once inside the Temple, Czolgosz drifted out of line to the left and was ordered by a security guard to get back in line. He quietly did as he was told.[71]

Secret Service Agent Foster, who was standing near the President with Ireland, remembered specifically looking the assassin dead in the eye. Czolgosz calmly returned the gaze in a manner that did not arouse any suspicion in Foster, who was looking for the tell tale sign in his eyes.[72]

"I thought him a mechanic out to see the Exposition, anxious to shake hands with the President," Foster later said of Czolgosz.[73]

Instead, a short Italian man with a thick mustache in front of Czolgosz in line caught Foster's eye. Something about him made Foster and other guards suspicious. Foster quickly grabbed the man, who was shocked, but harmless. Foster allowed him to remain in line. This incident distracted Foster and the other guards at a critical time, just as Czolgosz approached the President.

John D. Wells said that his attention was drawn to a short, heavy, and dark man with a heavy black mustache. This was obviously the man who Foster permitted to shake the hand of the President.[74]

"A few moments before Czolgosz approached, a man had come along with three fingers of his right hand tied in a bandage and he had shaken hands with his left," said Ireland. "When Czolgosz came up I noticed that he was a boyish-looking fellow with an innocent face, perfectly calm, and I also noticed that his right hand was wrapped in what appeared to be a bandage. I watched him closely, but was interrupted by the man in front of him, who held onto the President's hand an unusually long time. This man, who appeared to be an Italian, and who had a short cropped, heavy black moustache, was persistent and it was necessary for me to push him along so that the others could reach the President."[75]

---

[71] Robert J. Donovan, *The Assassins* (New York: Harper & Brothers, 1952) 104.

[72] Robert J. Donovan, *The Assassins* (New York: Harper & Brothers, 1952) 104.

[73] *Buffalo Courier,* 25 September 1901, pg. 8, col. 3.

[74] A. Wesley Johns, *The Man Who Shot McKinley* (New York: A. S. Barnes and Co, Inc., 1970) 93.

[75] *New York Times*, 8 September 1901, pg.2, col. 4.

"I believe now the man in front of Czolgosz was an associate or friend of the assassin and was there to make way for him and keep his ruse from being discovered until it was too late," Ireland said in an interview the next day. "The man with the black moustache is being sought for."[76] Later, the man was found and cleared of any complicity.

Ireland placed his hand on Czolgosz's shoulder and intended to guide him away after the handshake. But the handshake never happened.[77]

"The actual shooting of President McKinley was done so quickly there was no time to do anything until the two shots had been fired," explained Ireland. "The President turned from the fellow with the black moustache and as I shoved him along and made a move to extend his hand to Czolgosz when the sound of the two shots came."[78]

"The noise was like that made by firecrackers, which have been softened by dampness" explained Secret Service Agent Albert Gallaher. "It was not enough to attract attention a dozen yards away."[79]

Two hundred people had not made it through the line when Czolgosz stepped forward and with his "injured" right hand, fired two shots at close range.

Wells described what he saw, saying Czolgosz withdrew his right hand, and before anyone knew what was happening, two shots were fired, one quickly following the other.[80]

"The President shook hands with the little girl and then reached out his hand to this fellow," was how Big Jim Parker described the scene. "Bang! bang! went a revolver which the fellow had in his right hand near his waist. He had his hat in his left hand."[81]

"I was stationed about 10 feet to the right of the President and near me was Detective John J. Geary," Albert Gallaher wrote in his official Secret Service report. "I was keeping the crowd moving on after they met the President so as not to delay the ceremonies or give anyone a chance to turn back; the reception had been on about 8 or 10 minutes when I heard two shots fired, in rapid succession and standing in front of the President and close to him was a young fellow with a handkerchief in

---

[76] *Buffalo Evening News*, 7 September 1901, pg. 4, col. 2.

[77] *Cincinnati Enquirer*, 7 September 1901, pg. 1.

[78] *New York Times*, 8 September 1901, pg. 2, col. 4.

[79] *Cincinnati Enquirer*, 8 September 1901, pg. 1, col. 3.

[80] A. Wesley Johns, *The Man Who Shot McKinley* (New York: A. S. Barnes and Co, Inc., 1970) 94.

[81] *Buffalo Evening News*, 8 September 1901, pg. 4, col. 4-5.

his hand concealing the revolver from which he had shot the President."[82]

"I was merely sizing up the looks of the people coming to the reception," said Charles J. Close, the Exposition Superintendent of Buildings, who was an eyewitness. "I saw the President pat the head of a child on the arms of an old man, then a few others came, and then the man that did the shooting. He carried his right hand wrapped in a handkerchief, and against his chest as if in a sling. He extended his left hand to greet the President and then two shots were fired."[83]

"It all happened so quickly and the man was so close to the President I thought he had handed the President a bomb, and that it had exploded in his hands," said H. F. Henshaw, another witness.[84]

Gomph was playing background music during the reception on the great pipe organ, which was a major attraction at the Temple of Music. He had reached the highest notes in one of Bach's masterpieces, and as he stopped at the height to let the strains reverberate through the auditorium the two shots sounded.

A white puff of smoke drifted into the air and the handkerchief that had covered the gun in Czolgosz's hand burst into flames, falling to the floor. The shots left powder burns on the President's vest; one deflected by a button and McKinley's breastbone, did not penetrate. But the other shot pierced directly through the President's stomach, finally lodging somewhere in his back muscles.

The President straightened up, looked at Czolgosz astonished, drew his right hand quickly to his chest, his eyes looked upward and rolled back. He reeled a little and was caught by Cortelyou to his right. As he staggered, McKinley caught himself for a brief second and his face had turned pale.

"The President stood erect and seemingly did not realize he had been shot," wrote Gallaher.[85]

Supported by Milburn and Cortelyou, the President looked at his assailant and supposedly said, "May God forgive him."[86]

Later, the *Washington Post* reported that it was "conceded that the President did not say 'May God forgive him' after he was shot," and agreed that his first audible speech was a reference to his wife, "I trust

---

[82] Albert L. Gallaher, *Official Secret Service Report*, 6 September 1901.

[83] *Buffalo Evening News*, 7 September 1901, pg. 8, col. 6.

[84] *Buffalo Commercial*, 7 September 1901.

[85] Albert L. Gallaher, *Official Secret Service Report*, 6 September 1901.

[86] *Cincinnati Enquirer*, 7 September 1901, pg. 1.

Mrs. McKinley will not be informed of this; at least I hope it will not be exaggerated."[87]

"I stood about ten feet behind the President and saw Czolgosz approach him," said a reporter who witnessed the shooting. "The latter had his right hand drawn up close to his breast and a white linen handkerchief wrapped about it. It bore the appearance of a bandage. He extended his left hand, and I am quite sure the President thought he was injured, for he leaned forward and looked at him in a sympathetic way. When directly in front of the President, Czolgosz threw his hand forward and fired. I saw the flash and smoke followed by the report, and then heard the second shot."[88]

Secret Service Agent Samuel Ireland was quoted describing the moment; "As the President was reaching for the hand of the assassin, there were two quick shots. Startled for a moment, I looked and saw the President draw his right hand under his coat, straighten up and, pressing his lips together, give Czolgosz the most scornful and contemptuous look possible to imagine."[89]

"Not seeing the flash of any metal, there being very little or no smoke escape from the handkerchief at moment of firing, and the President standing so erect and showing no blood on his person, it was difficult to take in, in an instant, from the muffled sound alone, what had really happened," Ireland later reported.[90]

The next day's newspapers said that the shots were fired "as quick as a flash, as though trained by long practice." Another witness said that the "President stood stock still, a look of hesitancy, almost of bewilderment on his face. Then he retreated a step while a pallor began to steal over his features."[91]

Charles J. Close described it; "I saw the President clasp both hands over his abdomen. He turned a little and Milburn, Cortelyou and Detective John W. Geary caught him. He never reeled or flinched."[92]

Even before the shouts of the angry crowd filled the room, the Secret Service reacted immediately, but it was Private Frank O'Brien who reacted by diving at the shooter, knocking him to the ground. Jim

---

[87] *Washington Post*, 8 September 1901, pg. 5, col. 2.

[88] *Washington Post*, 8 September 1901, pg. 5, col. 2.

[89] *New York Times*, 8 September 1901, pg. 2, col. 4.

[90] Samuel R. Ireland, *Official Secret Service Report*, 6 September 1901.

[91] *New York Times*, 7 September 1901, pg. 1, col. 2.

[92] *Buffalo Evening News*, 7 September 1901, pg. 8, col. 6.

Parker, the man who had tried to talk to Czolgosz in line, hit Czolgosz in the face with his fist, resulting in Czolgosz hitting the hard wood floor. Private Brooks and Private Louis Neff also leaped in to help O'Brien.[93]

"When I heard the shots I grabbed him..." Parker explained. "'You son of a bitch! You've shot the President!' I shouted."[94]

"At the same time I reached for the young man and caught his left arm," said Ireland. "The big negro (Parker) standing just back of him, and who would have been next to take the President's hand, struck the assassin in the neck with one hand and with the other reached for the revolver, which had been discharged through the handkerchief, and the shots from which had set fire to the linen."[95]

In the confusion, Agent Foster shouted to Secret Service Agent Albert L. Gallaher, "Get the gun! Al, get the gun!"[96]

"I sprang into the crowd, grabbed the assassin by the throat in my right hand and took from his right hand, by my left, the revolver and the handkerchief," recalled Agent Gallaher, "it being on fire as the shots had been fired through it; as the handkerchief was blazing my hand was slightly burned."[97]

"The hold I had on his throat caused him to throw up the hand and the revolver," explained Parker. "If it hadn't been for that action he would have fired the other three shots. As soon as his hand went up, Foster grabbed the revolver."[98]

"Someone, I don't know who it was, got me by the throat and choked me and while they were choking me the revolver was taken from me but I held onto the handkerchief and still have it in my possession properly marked for identification," Gallaher described.[99]

"Instantly, Jim Parker, the colored man, and Secret Agent Foster were upon Czolgosz and they bore him to the floor," said the reporter witness. "Czolgosz, lying prostrate, still retained a hold on his revolver, and seemed to be trying to get his arm free to fire again."[100]

---

[93] A. Wesley Johns, *The Man Who Shot McKinley* (New York: A. S. Barnes and Co, Inc., 1970) 94.

[94] *Buffalo Evening News*, 8 September 1901, pg. 4, col. 5.

[95] *New York Times*, 8 September 1901, pg.2, col. 4.

[96] *Buffalo Courier,* 25 September 1901, pg. 7, col. 2.

[97] Albert L. Gallaher, *Official Secret Service Report*, 6 September 1901.

[98] *Buffalo Evening News*, 8 September 1901, pg. 4, col. 5.

[99] Albert L. Gallaher, *Official Secret Service Report*, 6 September 1901.

[100] *Washington Post*, 8 September 1901, pg. 5, col. 2.

"After we had the fellow on the floor, I kneeling with one knee on each arm, he made a desperate effort to shoot again, and, struggling fiercely, he raised one hand and tried to pull the trigger," Agent George Foster remembered. [101]

Foster quickly checked to see if Czolgosz had any other weapons.

"He's got no more guns, boys," someone heard him say.[102]

Charles J. Close also verified Parker's involvement in the apprehension of the prisoner, saying, "A colored man hit the murderer a smash in the nose and he went down."[103]

"Oh, for only ten seconds more!' another heard Parker cry in rage.[104]

Yet another witness said, "The Secret Service men, Foster and Ireland, at one bound seized the assassin, before the smoke had cleared away, and, in fact, before the sound of the second shot was heard. The negro, Parker, also turned instantly and confronted Czolgosz, whose right hand was being tightly held behind him by the Detectives and whose face was thrust forward. Parker, with his clenched fist, smashed the assassin three times squarely in the face, and was apparently wild to kill the creature, while all the crowd of artillerymen, policemen, and other, also set upon the object of their wrath."[105]

"The printed pictures of the anarchist give no correct idea of the man as he appeared in the Temple of Music, said Samuel Ireland, describing Czolgosz. "I had a good look at him as he passed in line, handkerchief in hand. He was not ill dressed or ill looking: his hair, a light wavy brown, was parted almost in the middle. I noticed his light blue eyes. He seemed innocent rather than vicious. Immediately after the shooting, however, his appearance was completely transformed."[106]

The soldiers rushed at Czolgosz and began to beat him with their rifles and their fists. Private Neff grabbed at Czolgosz's hand while Private O'Brien wrestled the revolver away, apparently from Secret Service Agent Gallaher,[107] as others tried to beat the assailant.

---

[101] *Cincinnati Post*, 7 September 1901, pg. 2, col. 3.

[102] *Buffalo Commercial*, 7 September 1901.

[103] *Buffalo Evening News,* 7 September 1901, pg. 8, col. 6.

[104] Samuel Fallows, *Life of William McKinley: Our Martyred President* (Chicago: Regan Printing House, 1901) 16.

[105] Marshall Everett, *The Complete Life of William McKinley* (Privately Published, 1901) 39.

[106] *Washington Post*, 10 September 1901, pg. 1, col. 2.

[107] A. Wesley Johns, *The Man Who Shot McKinley* (New York: A. S. Barnes and Co, Inc., 1970) 95.

"As soon as I got to my feet I demanded the revolver," said Gallaher. "One of the Coast Artillery Corp informed me he had the revolver and intended to keep it."[108]

Most of their punches hit each other in the confusion, but some found their mark. Secret Service Agent Foster was able to land one good punch to the face, driving Czolgosz to the floor again. Agent Ireland had to step in to prevent one of the soldiers from bayoneting Czolgosz on the spot.[109] In short order, Czolgosz was beaten bloody.

"Immediately a dozen men fell upon the assassin and was borne to the floor," Ireland described. "While on the floor, Czolgosz again tried to discharge the revolver, but before he could get it to the President it was knocked from his hand by the negro. As it went across the floor, one of the artillerymen picked it up and put it in his pocket."[110]

"An artilleryman grabbed the weapon out of Secret Service Officer Foster's hand and drew a big knife on him," was how Parker remembered it. "He must have thought Foster looked like an Anarchist. He did look more like one than the other one did, because he had glasses and a three-day's growth of beard."[111]

Agent Foster, who had traveled almost everywhere with the President, was enraged and tried again to get at the assassin, but was restrained, even as he protested that he knew what he was doing.[112]

"Just then a big fleshy officer struck the man that fired the shot a heavy blow in the face," continued Parker. "It knocked us both down. The murderer tried to get up, but I held him down by that elbow clasp of his throat. If he had got up he would have escaped because the struggle was all about Foster, who kept crying: 'It ain't me who shot the President. There he is, there.' In spite of that he got pummeled by the artillerymen and the guards."[113]

Confusion reigned. The crowd surged forward, men shouted and fought, women screamed and children cried. Some began to flee for the nearest exit, in fear of a stampede, while hundreds of those outside frantically pushed forward in an effort to discover the source of the growing commotion.[114]

---

[108] Albert L. Gallaher, *Official Secret Service Report*, 6 September 1901.

[109] Robert J. Donovan, *The Assassins* (New York: Harper & Brothers, 1952) 104.

[110] *New York Times*, 8 September 1901, pg. 2, col. 4.

[111] *Buffalo Evening News*, 8 September 1901, pg. 4, col. 5.

[112] G. Townsend, *Memorial Life of William McKinley* (Washington: Memorial Publishing Co., 1901) 195.

[113] *Buffalo Evening News*, 8 September 1901, pg. 4, col. 5.

[114] *New York Times*, 7 September 1901, pg. 1, col. 2.

"The women in the vast audience were hysterical, and the men were little less than crazy," said one eyewitness. "The transformation of the scene of smiles and gladness of a moment before, to the wild, rushing, mighty roar of an infuriated crowd, was simply awful. The police and military at once set about the task of clearing the building, which they accomplished with amazing celerity and good judgment, considering the fact that a crowd of 50,000 at the outside was pressing into the entrance."[115]

"At the report of the shots somebody cried: 'Close the doors; don't let anybody in or out,'" said Close.

The President was led first one-way and then another as Cortelyou, Milburn and others tried to decide what to do. Quackenbush immediately rushed for the telephone to call the doctors at the Exposition Hospital.[116]

Finally, the President was helped inside the purple edged aisle to a chair. In passing over the bunting, the President's foot was momentarily caught and an alert reporter helped get him untangled. The President, for his part, was able to walk, but leaned heavily on his escort of Cortelyou and Milburn. As he was being led, he whispered to Cortelyou, telling him, "Be careful about my wife—do not tell her." Half a dozen men stood around McKinley and vigorously began to fan him.[117]

"The President did not fall," explained a reporter. "He raised his right hand and felt his breast, and seemed to be maintaining his upright position only by a wonderful effort. I am sure he did not speak at that moment. He gazed fixedly at his assailant with a look which I cannot describe, but which I shall never forget, and in a moment reeled back into the arms of Secretary Cortelyou."[118]

"The President was led forward, walking with great composure, supported by Mr. Cortelyou and Mr. Foster," said another witness, F. D. Owen, probably mistaking Milburn for Foster. "As he approached the settee I assisted in placing him on it. The President sat there with entire self-possession. I began fanning him with my straw hat. Others then began to gather. The President was but slightly pale, and showed no signs whatever of nervousness."[119]

---

[115] Marshall Everett, *The Complete Life of William McKinley* (Privately Published, 1901) 39-40.

[116] A. Wesley Johns, *The Man Who Shot McKinley* (New York: A. S. Barnes and Co, Inc., 1970) 95.

[117] *Cincinnati Enquirer*, 7 September 1901, pg. 1.

[118] *Washington Post*, 8 September 1901, pg. 5, col. 2.

[119] *Washington Post*, 9 September 1901, pg. 10, col. 1.

"Am I shot?" the President asked Detective Geary.

"I fear you are, Mr. President," was Geary's response. [120]

Meanwhile, Foster had pulled Czolgosz to his feet, shouting at him, then punched him hard, knocking Czolgosz back to the floor.[121] As the President fought the pain, he noticed the beating his men were giving his attacker. He told his guards, "Be easy with him, boys."[122] Some thought that the President's exact words were, "Let no one hurt him."[123] In any event, it was the President's words that probably saved his assassin's life at that moment. The President, in terrible pain, then reached up for Milburn and again implored, "My wife, be careful about her. Don't let her know."

"After seeing the man was captured, I turned to the President and assisted Mr. Cortelyou and Mr. Milburn in taking the President to a seat," said Ireland. "While on the way, the President said he hoped that his wife would not hear of the matter and then added that if she must hear it, the fact must not be exaggerated."[124]

Having his waistcoat opened, McKinley admonished those around him to remain calm and refrain from becoming alarmed.[125] At first, according to some witnesses, the President did not think himself badly hurt. As Cortelyou tried to open his vest, the President protested.

"But you are wounded," Cortelyou told him. "Let me examine."

"No, I think not," McKinley answered. "I am not badly hurt, I assure you."[126]

Cortelyou asked him, "Do you feel much pain?" White and trembling, the President slipped his hand into the opening of his shirt and said, "This wound pains me greatly." As he withdrew his hand, it was covered in blood, and he dropped it to his side and began to faint. His chin sunk to his chest and those around him looked away.[127]

---

[120] Samuel Fallows, *Life of William McKinley: Our Martyred President* (Chicago: Regan Printing House, 1901) 14.

[121] A. Wesley Johns, *The Man Who Shot McKinley* (New York: A. S. Barnes and Co, Inc., 1970) 96.

[122] *Buffalo Courier,* 25 September 1901, pg. 8, col. 3.

[123] *New York Times*, 8 September 1901, pg. 1, col. 3.

[124] *New York Times*, 8 September 1901, pg. 2, col. 4.

[125] *New York Times*, 7 September 1901, pg. 1, col. 3.

[126] *New York Times*, 7 September 1901, pg. 1, col. 3.

[127] *Cincinnati Enquirer*, 7 September 1901, pg. 1.

"He seemed to be fairly easy as he rested in the chair and some of the color came back to his face," explained the reporter witness. "He reached his right hand inside of his shirt and when he withdrew it his fingers were tipped with blood. He paled again at the sight of the blood and I think he fainted."[128]

Suddenly, through the crowd came a Mexican diplomat, Minister Aspiroz. He reached the President and his words seemed to bring McKinley out of his faint. Aspiroz asked, "Oh, my God, Mr. President. Are you shot?" As Aspiroz was restrained from getting too close to McKinley, the President, gasping between each word said, "Yes, I believe I am."[129]

As he sat in the chair, awaiting medical attention, McKinley again started to faint and his head drifted back. Milburn added support with his hand behind the President's head. Seeming to help, the President remained conscience with his legs spread out and his lips clinched firmly together fighting off the pain.[130]

Meanwhile, the assailant was forced into a small room off the stage by Patrolmen James and McCauley and thrown onto a table. Bleeding from the lip and his face swollen from the blows he had sustained, the assault on Czolgosz continued.

In a few seconds, the artillerymen and guards cleared the building of those who just moments before waited happily to greet President McKinley. But to do this, according the newspaper accounts, "it was necessary to draw their saber bayonets and use extreme force."[131]

Outside the room, there was confusion as the crowd pressed toward to door. Some officials tried to conceal the assassin's presence for his protection, but others loudly announced he was there. One excited Exposition official went so far as to invite the crowd to go in and get him.[132]

Czolgosz sat on the table, looking at the floor, and occasionally mopping his cut lip with his shirtsleeve. He rubbed the soles of shoes together, keeping his feet close and sometimes nervously took deeps breaths. He remained silent.[133]

---

[128] *Washington Post*, 8 September 1901, pg. 5, col. 2.
[129] *Washington Post*, 8 September 1901, pg. 5, col. 2.
[130] *Cincinnati Enquirer*, 7 September 1901, pg. 1.
[131] *Cincinnati Enquirer*, 7 September 1901, pg. 1.
[132] *Cincinnati Enquirer*, 7 September 1901, pg. 1.
[133] *Cincinnati Enquirer*, 7 September 1901, pg. 1.

"The blows that felled him brought the blood from his nose, his collar was torn loose, and his rather long heavy hair became rumpled" explained Ireland. "He fought desperately for a moment, but when thrown on a table ceased to struggle. He then assumed a rigid position on his back and refused to open his eyes or mouth. We finally forced his eyes open to get a better look at him. As I was searching him, someone called for a wet towel to wash the blood from his face. this was brought and his countenance was scrubbed rather roughly, but completely. All the time he refused to speak, but there were no convulsive movements of the body and he seemed free from excitement. We noted his pulse too, and found it beating regularly."[134]

Back in the reception area, Private O'Brien had handed Czolgosz's revolver to his immediate supervisor, Corporal Louis Bertschey. When Cortelyou asked to see it, Bertschey refused to surrender the weapon without Captain John P. Wisser's expressed order. Reminded that it was Babcock who was in charge, Bertschey finally showed the weapon to Cortelyou, but also dispatched Private Heiser to find Wisser. When he arrived on the scene, Wisser examined the weapon, noting, "the next chamber being opposite the barrel was not visible." All other chambers were loaded.

"Secretary Cortelyou came to me and inquired for the revolver," wrote Gallaher. "I took him to the man who had it, Corporal Louis Bertschey, of the 73rd Artillery Corpse, who denied having it saying he had given it to his Captain. I told him I knew he had it, and who Mr. Cortelyou was, when he took the gun from his pocket and "broke" it so as Mr. Cortelyou could see what caliber it was; it was a 32 short, 5 shot and two of the cartridges had been fired (I kept the revolver and the cartridges)."[135]

The gun, which bore the serial number 463344, was manufactured by the Johnson Arms & Cycle Works at Fitchburg, Massachusetts. Later, Wisser placed it in a box, which he tacked and sealed for evidence.[136]

It was eventually determined that the revolver had been purchased at Walbridge's Main Street Store in Buffalo. John F. Suor, a clerk at the store, had come to Police Headquarters, as had half a dozen other area businessmen, to try to identify the makings on the box police had in their possession. Suor was satisfied that the markings were from his store, but could not positively identify Czolgosz.

---

[134] *Washington Post*, 10 September 1901, pg. 1, col. 2.

[135] Albert L. Gallaher, *Official Secret Service Report*, 6 September 1901.

[136] A. Wesley Johns, *The Man Who Shot McKinley* (New York: A. S. Barnes and Co, Inc., 1970) 97.

"I never saw that man before," he said when he was taken to Czolgosz. "At least, I'm not positive."[137]

As it never had before in Buffalo, news spread quickly across the city and the grounds of the Pan American Exposition. The entire event came to a standstill. At first, many who heard the news thought it was only a hoax. As often happens upon receiving bad news, people tried not to believe. Many felt shame for what had happened to the President in their city, the Rainbow City. That feeling added to the frustration and grief.

Representative Bailey Avery went to the Mexico exhibit were a bullfight was taking place to announce the news. The crowd was told the bullfight was canceled and Avery addressed the crowd.

"Ladies and Gentlemen," he began, "it is my sad duty to inform you that our kindly President has been seriously shot by an assassin. There will be no more entertainment in this concession tonight."

A woman near the president of the bullfight's box fainted and was taken out. The crowd was quiet. Then suddenly a cowboy shouted, "And what are we going to do, boys?" No one responded as they sat in shocked silence trying to comprehend the news.[138]

The effect of the news on the Midway was immediate, the mood shifting from gayety to disbelief to horror. All performances were stopped and signs went up announcing the suspension of business for the day. Within five minutes, by one estimate, everyone on the grounds knew of the shooting.[139]

"Deeper and denser the shadow of pain and sorrow drew itself across the faces of those down town who heard rumor after rumor, and their hearts beat more violently. With trembling voices many rushed up and down inquiring of all they met for further particulars. Like a fire spreading across dry grass, the news spread through every street, along every highway, out into the East Side, down in the south section, over in the West Side and doubly quick through the northern section of the city." Thus reported a Buffalo newspaper.

There had not been more shocking and terrible news in Buffalo since perhaps the Lincoln assassination. The Exposition, which was to showcase the city, suddenly took on a different, infamous meaning. In the days before instant news, rumors sped through the city. Many hoped that the President had merely been wounded, and not killed. There were

---

[137] *Buffalo Express*, 8 September 1901.

[138] *Buffalo Courier*, 7 September 1901, pg. 3, col. 6.

[139] *Buffalo Courier*, 7 September 1901, pg. 3, col. 6.

rumors to that effect. But there were also rumors that the President was indeed dead. No one seemed to know for sure and the question of the President's condition was on all lips.

In Washington, the news was being heard with disbelief and horror as well. The city was virtually abandoned of high-ranking officials. Not a single Cabinet member, Supreme Court Justice or member of the Diplomatic Corps was in town. Clerks and heads of departments were the only ones there to receive the news.[140] Telegraph offices were swamped and many who had telephones could not secure service for hours after the shooting. In the War Department, Acting Secretary of War George L. Gillespie and Acting Adjutant General Aaron Ward were in their offices when news came from Colonel Wisser, commandant of Fort Porter, of the shooting. His dispatch read, "President shot at reception in Temple of Music about 4 p.m. Corporal Bertschey and detail of men of my company caught the assassin at once and held him down till the Secret Service men overpowered him and took the prisoner out of their hands, my men being unarmed. Condition of the President is not known. Revolver in my possession."[141]

Secretary of War Elihu Root and Assistant Secretary William C. Sanger were immediately contacted at their homes in New York and instructions were sent back to Colonel Wisser to take a detachment of men and guard the President. At the White House, requests for official information began to pour in by the hundreds over the telephone and telegraph to the besieged clerks and telegraph operators. Colonel Benjamin F. Montgomery, the chief of White House operators, gave out official bulletins as fast as they were received from Buffalo.[142]

As visitors arrived at the White House, many simply sent their calling cards upstairs and left. Other waited for official word to come from Secretary Cortelyou. The halls and rooms were filled with groups of serious-faced men who were slowly beginning to realize that attack had indeed happened.[143]

The first news of the shooting was actually taken to the White House by an Associated Press reporter, as the phone lines in the city were jammed. This news reached the Executive Mansion at 4:24. Inside, few were there to receive the news, most having gone home for the day.[144]

---

[140] *Cincinnati Enquirer*, 7 September 1901, pg. 4, col. 2.

[141] *Buffalo Express*, 7 September 1901.

[142] G. Townsend, *Memorial Life of William McKinley* (Washington: Memorial Publishing Co., 1901) 211.

[143] *Washington Post*, 7 September 1901, pg. 3, col. 2.

[144] G. Townsend, *Memorial Life of William McKinley* (Washington: Memorial Publishing Co., 1901) 215.

Official word of the shooting was not relayed to the White House until three hours later, when Cortelyou telephoned Montgomery telling him of the operation and that, "So far everything is favorable." Later he gave him more information on the operation and told him the President had been taken to the Milburn house.[145]

Colonel W. H. Crooks had served on the White House staff since the days of Lincoln. It was Crooks who thought it strange when President Lincoln, on the evening of his assassination, told him, "Goodbye, Crooks," rather than his usual way of parting; a more final way of putting it. Later that night Crooks' apprehension was proven justified.

Crooks was the most noticeably affected by the McKinley shooting, unable to maintain his composure and allowing tears to stream down his face. Like Secretary of State John Hay, he had personally been through all three presidential assassinations.

"Yes, it is the third affair of the kind since I came into the White House," Crooks said. "How could anyone do it? How could anyone want to hurt him? He is so big and good and kind"

At the time, Crooks was in Assistant Secretary to the President O. L. Pruden's office and his grief affected all who saw it.[146]

The news spread quickly around Washington. About 8 p.m., the hopeful news of the doctors was received and a cheer went up along Pennsylvania Avenue.[147]

It was decided that every member of the Cabinet was to speed to Buffalo immediately where there would be held a counsel to determine the course the government would take during the President's expected long convalescence.

Senator Hanna learned of the shooting at the Union Club in Cleveland.

"I have just received a message from the Associated Press and I am forced to believe that the rumor is true," he commented. "I cannot say anything about it. It is too horrible to even contemplate. To think that such a thing could happen to so splendid a man as McKinley, and at this time and upon such an occasion. It is horrible, awful."[148]

The Senator too, made plans for a speedy trip to Buffalo.

---

[145] *Cincinnati Enquirer*, 7 September 1901, pg. 4, col. 4.

[146] *Washington Post*, 7 September 1901, pg. 3, col. 2.

[147] *Cincinnati Enquirer*, 7 September 1901, pg. 4, col. 2.

[148] G. Townsend, *Memorial Life of William McKinley* (Washington: Memorial Publishing Co., 1901) 218.

In the President's hometown of Canton, news of the events in Buffalo arrived and after the first bulletin, all was at a standstill as the anxious citizens awaited more information. As elsewhere, at first the news was disbelieved. But confirmation was soon to follow. The Stark County Fair, which the President had attended the preceding week, was just closing as the awful news spread. People deserted the fairgrounds to rush to the city, where it was hoped news would arrive faster. Others hurried to the McKinley house, but no news reached there until the evening.

Mrs. McKinley's sister, Mrs. Mary C. Barber, was the only relative living in Canton. She was extremely anxious about the condition of her sister, as well as that of the President.[149]

Former President Grover Cleveland was fishing in Darling Lake near Tyringham, Massachusetts when he heard the awful news. He immediately started for shore to hear more details.

"With all American citizens, I am greatly shocked at this news," he said. "I cannot conceive of a motive. It must have been the act of a crazy man."[150]

William Jennings Bryan, President McKinley's two time rival for the Presidency, declared, "The attempted assassination of the President is a shock to the entire country, and he and his wife are the recipients of universal sympathy. The dispatches say that the shots were fired by an insane man, and it is hoped that this is true, for while it is a terrible thing for a President to be the victim of the act of a maniac, it would be even worse for him to be fired upon by a sane person prompted by malice or revenge."[151]

King Edward VII and Queen Alexandra of England were traveling in Germany when they heard the news. Police guards on the train and along the route were immediately increased, lest it be a worldwide plot.[152]

---

[149] G. Townsend, *Memorial Life of William McKinley* (Washington: Memorial Publishing Co., 1901) 223.

[150] Marshall Everett, *The Complete Life of William McKinley* (Privately Published, 1901) 109.

[151] Marshall Everett, *The Complete Life of William McKinley* (Privately Published, 1901) 109.

[152] Marshall Everett, *The Complete Life of William McKinley* (Privately Published, 1901) 111.

"McKinley and I are enemies," declared Senator George L. Wellington of Maryland. "I have nothing good to say about him, and under the circumstances do not care to say anything bad. I am indifferent to the whole matter."

Later, when asked if he had said such a thing, the Senator refused to comment. This was universally taken to mean that he had said it. *The Atlanta Journal* quickly called on the United States Senate to expel him for his utterances. [153] Wellington did not seek re-election.

Immediately following the shooting, a crowd had formed outside the Temple of Music and began shouting death threats to the unknown assassin. One yelled to "take him to the arch and burn him." Some pounded on the walls and windows in frustration, trying to get at Czolgosz. A marine detachment and fifteen police officers guarded the door. As officials tried to decide what to do with the assailant, the crowd surged forward. In an effort to discourage them, Captain Leonard shouted a loud command to "load rifles." As the sound of the steel reverberated and the soldiers lowered the bayonets to charge position, it had the effect of making the crowd fall back. [154]

"The breeches clicked and the men held up to plain view the hard steel and the encasing brass as they filled their Lee-Mitfords with cartridges. The effect was obvious, for the women started the movement to draw back. Men and women who had been dry-eyed began to cry. The lips of the policemen and soldiers were twitching."[155]

Czolgosz would have to be taken to police headquarters. In preparation for moving the prisoner, Colonel Byrne, Commandant of the Exposition Police, instructed his men to "rope off the south approaches so we can get the wagon in here."

"You will never get the wagon with him in it forty feet away," replied Ireland. "We must have a carriage and horses. The people can stop an automobile better than they can horses."

Some feet way sat the carriage that had carried some members of the committee to the Temple.

"Get that carriage over there, oh, here, never mind, I will," said John N. Scatcherd, a Buffalo businessman and an Exposition official, to the Sergeant of Police at the southwest door. Scatchard went to get it himself.

---

[153] Marshall Everett, *The Complete Life of William McKinley* (Privately Published, 1901) 112.

[154] *Cincinnati Enquirer*, 7 September 1901, pg. 1.

[155] *Buffalo Enquirer,* 7 September 1901, pg. 1.

As the mob grew more blood thirsty, Ireland suggested to Colonel Byrne that he send for another platoon of police, preferably from the second precinct.

"Gentlemen, every minute of this delay is making the task all the more dangerous," instructed Ireland. "This crowd is getting more and more worked up and it is getting bigger. It reaches way out over the esplanade now. Give this man to me and I give you my word I will get him to Buffalo. Here are two Buffalo officers who will go with me."

"The best plan is to jump him right into this carriage and get right out of here," he continued, within earshot of a reporter.[156]

Captain Demer and Colonel Byrne directed the exterior security force, and the carriage was directed into the roped off area. As the carriage had been pulled up, some in the crowd alerted others by yelling, "Here he comes, this door." When all was secure and ready, Colonel Byrne gave the signal.[157]

The southwest door opened and out popped Czolgosz and his escort; guards James and McCauley on either side with Captain James F. Vallely, Chief of Exposition Detectives, leading the way, and Buffalo Police Detectives Albert Solomon and John W. Geary just behind. Czolgosz was quite literally hurled into the carriage. As the prisoner was quickly hustled out the door, the crowd shouted, "kill him" and urged each other to stop the carriage. Foster slammed the door of the carriage closed, and it began its mad dash for the Triumphal Causeway and the Lincoln Park gateway beyond. Vallely leaped onto the carriage, up next to the driver, as it started to move away.[158]

The driver whipped the horses to push through the crowd, the whip occasionally hitting those close to the horses. At one point, the mob tried to flip the wagon to get to Czolgosz. The police and service men beat, whipped, and threatened the rioters. With great difficulty, the carriage made it to the causeway, and from then on, all was clear. People continued to chase the carriage but soon gave up as it pulled away on the downhill slope.[159]

The carriage carrying the President's assailant sped straight down Delaware with about four bicyclists in hot pursuit, spreading the news.[160] Cyclist Dick Carr, a postal telegraph messenger, for years recalled the

---

[156] *Cincinnati Enquirer*, 7 September 1901, pg. 1.

[157] *Cincinnati Enquirer*, 7 September 1901, pg. 1.

[158] *Cincinnati Enquirer*, 7 September 1901, pg. 1.

[159] *Cincinnati Enquirer*, 7 September 1901, pg. 1.

[160] *Cincinnati Enquirer*, 7 September 1901, pg. 1.

three gray uniformed Pan American police officers guarding the prisoner while the driver and another Exposition guard were on the high front seat.[161]

During the ride, Czolgosz, cowering in the rear left, occasionally looked out the windows. He had heard the crowd shout for his head and his eyes showed fear and he wet his lips constantly with his tongue.

As the carriage passed the Milburn residence, where Mrs. McKinley slept in an upstairs room, the detective who was seated beside Czolgosz looked up at the front of the house, then gave Czolgosz a mean look that cowered him deeper into his seat.[162]

Near Utica Street, the carriage was met by the Superintendent of Buffalo Police William S. Bull's carriage, which was on its way to the Exposition. Bull turned around and followed the carriage to the Buffalo Police First Precinct Headquarters, located at the intersection of Terrace, Erie and Seneca.[163]

The carriage pulled up sharply just before five o'clock and the prisoner was quickly taken inside. Onlookers and pedestrians barely noticed. Moments later, bikers came with the news of the President being shot and that the man just taken into the building had done it.[164]

From that moment, another mob began to quickly form outside. The police were kept busy all during the night dispersing them. Fearing the worst might come and in a show of force to control the mob, the militia was ordered into readiness. New York Governor Benjamin B. Odell arrived at the scene and the 65th Regiment was placed under waiting orders. [165]

Shortly before five o'clock, wild rumors with seemingly more credence circulated that the President had died. Many flags on Main Street were lowered to half-mast. But later, editions of the *Buffalo Enquirer* hit the street to inform anxious readers about details of the shooting and the official bulletin announcing the President's true condition. The people of Buffalo eagerly absorbed the news and just as eagerly, wanted additional information. As they learned the details of

---

[161] A. Wesley Johns, *The Man Who Shot McKinley* (New York: A. S. Barnes and Co, Inc., 1970) 103.

[162] *Cincinnati Enquirer*, 7 September 1901, pg. 1.

[163] *Cincinnati Enquirer*, 7 September 1901, pg. 1.

[164] *Cincinnati Enquirer*, 7 September 1901, pg. 1.

[165] *Cincinnati Enquirer*, 7 September 1901, pg. 1.

the cold-blooded nature of the shooting, their attention and indignation began to be directed at the assailant.

Some in the crowd that began to line Main Street and other busy roads began to yell, "Lynch him! Lynch him!" More and more people began to assemble on Main Street in search of information and excitement. Soon, there were hundreds in the streets.

News spread primarily by word of mouth. Carried outside the Exposition grounds by pedestrians and streetcars, Buffalo came alive. Many yelled the news, others hollered questions. In no time at all, everyone knew. And the mood of some of the people reached a fervent pitch.

Crowds began gathering in front of the *Courier* and *Enquirer* offices as people eagerly read the latest bulletins as soon as they could be gathered and posted. At the Iroquois Hotel, the Ellicott Square, the Tifft House, the Genesee, and others, especially on Main Street, great masses of people waited for the extras, while the whole length of Main Street, from Seneca to Tupper Street was literally jammed with hundreds, if not thousands, of people; estimates varied widely.

The crowd compared in numbers with those of the most exciting Presidential campaigns. One report guessed that at its peak, the crowd may have reached 50,000 people.[166]

There were no festive activities however, no bursts of enthusiasm. The crowd instead was very quiet. As the full details of the shooting became known, the threats of lynching cropped up again. Orders were issued to the policemen to demand that everyone preserve law and order. Every effort was made to preclude the possibility of a lynch mob. But the despair and anger increased in some pockets, and when the news came that the assassin Czolgosz had been removed to the First Precinct, a group formed at the corner of Main and Erie Streets.

By 9:00 p.m., the Main Street crowd had grown to a thousand, and instigators did their best by hurriedly suggesting their own form of justice. Then suddenly, the crowd surged toward police headquarters. Above the clamor of the crowd could be heard such things as "Hang him! Lynch him!" and other violent oaths. Ropes were stretched around the station, and many officers were stationed around the Precinct to prevent an out right attack, while other officers who passed through the crowd cautioned and reasoned against violence.[167]

---

[166] *Washington Post*, 7 September 1901, pg. 1, col. 4.

[167] *Cincinnati Enquirer*, 7 September 1901, pg. 1.

An hour later, fully 10,000 people had gathered in the streets between Main, Erie and Niagara Streets and Delaware Avenue. One man began a speech in front of the Columbia Bank in the Prudential Building at Pearl and Church Streets and the crowd went wild, many bursting into applause, but the speaker's remarks could often not be heard above the roar of the crowds.

"To number one and lynch him," was one cry he made, referring to Buffalo Precinct One, where Czolgosz was being held. The shouts of approval could be heard for blocks, each time with a more maddening frenzy. Then the speaker shouted, "This way," and turned toward Niagara Street, leading part of the crowd. A large group charged down Pearl to Erie Street and down toward Police Headquarters.

"To number one and lynch him," they shouted, shoving the police aside and crowding nearer the station house. As is usually the case in such instances, some persistent disturbers were causing most of the trouble, and the biggest part of the crowd was simply following curiously. The police jumped into patrol wagons and started to force the crowd back. They did not hesitate to perform their duties and the reluctant crowd fell back to Franklin Street, where several patrolmen and two mounted officers kept them in restraint.

"We do not propose to allow our prisoner to be taken from us," commented Buffalo Police Chief Bull to reporters. "We are able to protect him, and we have the Sixty-fifth and Seventy-fourth Regiments under arms if we need them. No matter how dastardly this man's crime is, we intend for the good name of American people to keep him safe for the vengeance of the law."[168]

Back at the Temple of Music, the crowd remained, and did serious damage to the ledges and walls as hundreds climbed to see inside. Rumors began to circulate that the prisoner was still inside. Guards who were left in place to guarantee the buildings security, only fed the rumors and made the crowd certain that the assailant was indeed still there.

Outside, one man in the crowd made the statement, "Well, this is the result of Bryan's doctrine." Another answered, "Bryan is not so far wrong, after all, neighbor." Another by-stander heard the exchange and shouted, "Here's an anarchist!" That was about all it took. Very soon, the unfortunate man who stood up for William Jennings Bryan, the man McKinley had defeated twice for the presidency, was driven from the crowd under the threat of violence.

---

[168] Marshall Everett, *The Complete Life of William McKinley* (Privately Published, 1901) 100.

Only many hours later, when the guards were dismissed, did the final angry throngs head for home.

Long before the angry crowds had amassed, the Exposition's electric ambulance had arrived at the Temple of Music, and Dr. Zittell and Dr. Kenerson rushed to attend the President, who remained seated in the chair. They looked at him in his white powder and bloodstained vest, opened the shirt and examined the wound. After seeing the wound and hearing that another bullet had entered the President's abdomen, they quickly called for a stretcher. On it they placed a row of pillows. Milburn, Cortelyou and the ambulance attendees placed McKinley on the stretcher.

One report said that the President was asked if he was badly hurt by Secret Service Agent Foster. "I think not, George," was the President's reply. [169]

When the President saw the stretcher, he tried to get up and go to it but his strength failed. He had to be helped onto the litter.

A reporter who witnessed it stated that there was no moaning, outcry, or other sign of suffering except some spasmodic twitching, expressions of pain and an occasional quivering of the shoulders.[170]

Another account told of McKinley groaning slightly as he was being placed on the stretcher, as if in tremendous pain, but soon recovering and resuming pressing his lips together. At least twenty men helped get the President's stretcher up the three or four stairs leading out of the Temple of Music. As he was taken to the ambulance, the crowd parted and those who saw the President's ashen face were struck with emotion. At 4:14 p.m., he was carried out of the Temple.[171]

"After the President had been comfortably adjusted in the electric ambulance, Secretary Cortelyou desired to ride on the front seat with the driver, but the latter objected," remembered F. D. Owen. "I said to him: 'This is the President's secretary and must go.' As the ambulance started, finding no guard on the rear step, I jumped on myself to prevent the door from flying open. There were two hospital attendants on the ambulance, one with the driver on the box, the other riding inside with George Foster. The only government officials accompanying the ambulance were Secretary Cortelyou and myself."[172]

---

[169] *Washington Post*, 7 September 1901, pg. 1, col. 2.
[170] A. Wesley Johns, *The Man Who Shot McKinley* (New York: A. S. Barnes and Co, Inc., 1970) 99.
[171] A. Wesley Johns, *The Man Who Shot McKinley* (New York: A. S. Barnes and Co, Inc., 1970) 99.
[172] *Washington Post*, 9 September 1901, pg. 10, col. 1.

A call had already gone out for all area doctors. The President's personal physician, Dr. Presley Rixey was the first called. He had gone back to the Milburn house with Mrs. McKinley. Messengers were sent to all parts of the city in search of Buffalo's most eminent physicians. Rixey was the first to arrive at the emergency Exposition hospital by steam automobile with two trained nurses. The car tore through the crowded grounds to reach the President.

"Mr. T. F. Ellis, who was driving the motor vehicle, handled the steering bar with the utmost skill," wrote Dr. Nelson Wilson. "No chauffeur however skillful, however expert, ever drove an automobile with more speed and more wisdom through dangerous places than did Ellis, who is a third year medical student at the University of Buffalo. The crowd was dense all along the route to the hospital and yet, although the machine was driven at top speed, there were no accidents."[173]

The crowd cleared a pathway for the ambulance with many shouting for people to get out of the way. A band of Indians adorned in head-dresses and war paint galloped to the Temple crying that Big White Feathers, as they called him, had been killed.[174]

The President's head rested on Foster's knee inside the ambulance. Dr. G. McK. Hall and Edward C. "Ned" Mann, a medical student on the staff of the Exposition Hospital and the son of the doctor who would soon perform the operation on McKinley, attended the President during the ride.[175] Near the Amherst Gate, the President was touching his chest. As Foster leaned closer, McKinley asked, "Foster, does that feel like a bullet?"

Foster felt for himself and said, "Yes it does, Mr. President."

"Well, we have got one of them anyway," McKinley said as he smiled slightly and closed his eyes.[176]

Another account said that the President commented during the ride, "I am sorry to have been the cause of trouble at the Exposition."[177]

---

[173] Nelson W. Wilson, M.D. "Details of the McKinley Case" (*Buffalo Medical Journal, 41-57*) 207-208.

[174] A. Wesley Johns, *The Man Who Shot McKinley* (New York: A. S. Barnes and Co, Inc., 1970) 98.

[175] Nelson W. Wilson, M.D. "Details of the McKinley Case" (*Buffalo Medical Journal, 41-57*) 208.

[176] *Cincinnati Post*, 7 September 1901, pg. 2, col. 3.

[177] Marshall Everett, *The Complete Life of William McKinley* (Privately Published, 1901) 36.

While the President was receiving care, W. I. Buchanan went directly to the Milburn residence in an attempt to stop the information of the shooting from reaching Mrs. McKinley prematurely by phone or otherwise. Other reports say the house was notified before Buchanan's arrival by telephone. The block from Ferry Street to Delaware Avenue had already closed to traffic by Captain Cable of the Buffalo Police by five o'clock.[178] Fortunately, Mrs. McKinley was still unaware of the news when Buchanan arrived."[179]

Buchanan immediately disabled all the telephone communications to the house for fear that the frequent calls that were beginning to come in would arouse the suspicions of Mrs. McKinley.[180] The President's wife was still asleep when he arrived. Buchanan broke the news gently to Mrs. McKinley's nieces, who had made the trip, and then consulted with Mrs. Milburn to decide on the best course to take in informing the First Lady. It was decided that Dr. Rixey should tell her, and if she awoke and Dr. Rixey had not yet arrived, Buchanan would tell her, as best he could. All were concerned about Mrs. McKinley's health and her reaction.[181]

Mrs. McKinley awoke at about 5:30 p.m., feeling well. She began to crotchet, one of her favorite hobbies.[182] There was no clock in her room and as darkness began to fall, she became more and more concerned about her husband, who had been expected to return about 6 p.m.[183] When at dusk, the President had still not arrived, she worriedly remarked to her niece, "I wonder why he does not come."[184]

Finally, at 7 p.m., undoubtedly to the relief of Buchanan, Dr. Rixey arrived. He had been quickly driven to the house in an open carriage along Delaware Avenue. When he arrived Buchanan met him on the lawn.

"Do you know," Buchanan told him, "I had a sort of premonition of this? Since early morning I had been extremely nervous and feared that something might go wrong. Our trip to the Falls was uneventful, but what an awful sad ending to our day."[185]

---

[178] *Buffalo Evening News*, 7 September 1901, pg. 8, col. 3.

[179] *New York Times*, 7 September 1901, pg. 1, col. 4.

[180] *New York Times*, 7 September 1901, pg. 1, col. 4.

[181] *Cincinnati Enquirer*, 7 September 1901, pg. 1.

[182] *New York Times*, 7 September 1901, pg. 1, col. 4.

[183] *New York Times*, 7 September 1901, pg. 1, col. 4.

[184] *Washington Post*, 7 September 1901, pg. 1, col. 4.

[185] G. Townsend, *Memorial Life of William McKinley* (Washington: Memorial Publishing Co., 1901) 222.

So it was indeed Dr. Rixey who broke the news of the President's shooting to his wife. Buchanan later said that Rixey broke the news "in a most gentle manner."

When Mrs. McKinley saw Dr. Rixey, alarmed, she asked, "Where is Mr. McKinley? Why does he not come?

"I have bad news for you, Mrs. McKinley," Dr. Rixey told her.

She dropped her needlework, stood up and said, "What is it? Is there anything wrong with him? Has he been hurt?"

"Yes, he has been hurt," Dr. Rixey replied. "He has been shot."

"Then I must go to him at once."

"No, we are going to bring him to you," Dr. Rixey continued. "and everything depends upon you. We look to you to help us. It is your bravery that will do everything."[186]

Mrs. McKinley took it bravely, yet she was clearly affected, as she paled. The *Buffalo Enquirer* happily reported that anyone who had expected a scene or the collapse of Mrs. McKinley were most agreeably disappointed.[187] Dr. Rixey assured her that the President could safely be brought to the house and that he was going back to the Exposition to complete the arrangements for his return. Meanwhile, a large police force was assigned to guard the Milburn House.[188]

Rixey left at 7:20 p.m., accompanied by Webb Hayes, a son of President Rutherford B. Hayes.[189] They entered a carriage and returned to the Exposition Hospital.

"On the way down to the police station, Czolgosz would not say a word, but seemed greatly agitated," said Ireland. "When searched at the station, on him was found a card of the Regal Hotel, on Ferry Street, and a card showing that he was a member in good standing in a Cleveland lodge of the Knights of the Golden Eagle. This was dated August 3rd last."

Inside police headquarters, Czolgosz was being questioned. He first gave police his name as Fred C. Nieman, an alias he had used while working at a wire mill near Cleveland. When arrested he had on him $1.54 cash, a rubber nipple from a baby bottle, and a letter certifying his paid membership in the Knights of the Golden Eagle. The police

---

[186] *Buffalo Express*, 12 September 1901.

[187] A. Wesley Johns, *The Man Who Shot McKinley* (New York: A. S. Barnes and Co, Inc., 1970) 116.

[188] *Cincinnati Enquirer*, 7 September 1901, pg. 1.

[189] *New York Times*, 7 September 1901, pg. 1, col. 4.

speculated that the nipple might have been used as a protective nuzzle for the revolver.[190]

Czolgosz was questioned from about 5:30 until shortly after midnight and according to Buffalo Police Chief Bull, refused to answer questions until he had been given something to eat. After that, he became pleasant and cooperative.[191] Assistant District Attorney Frederick Haller wrote down in longhand what Czolgosz told them.

As Czolgosz was being questioned, he must have heard the crowd amassing on the street below. The shades in the room were drawn and the scene was dark as the police officials tried to wrangle a confession out of the suspect.[192]

"In reply to questions, he said that he had been born in Detroit, but had been living in Cleveland, coming to Buffalo last Saturday," Ireland later explained. "Besides some keys and trinkets, he had a little over a dollar in his pockets. When asked why he had shot the President, he simply replied, 'I have done my duty.'"

"This is taken to indicate that he is the one chosen by the Anarchistic group to kill the President, and on this line, much work is being done," Buffalo District Attorney Thomas Penney told the *Buffalo Courier* later that evening. "We are looking for the man with the black moustache and the Italian appearance who preceded the assassin to the President and who made way for him. A description of him has been sent out, and he may be brought in."

As for a motive, Czolgosz told detectives, "I am a disciple of Emma Goldman"[193] and that, "I killed President McKinley because I done my duty. I don't believe in one man having so much service, and another man should have none."[194] Czolgosz also supposedly said that he was well known in the west as a socialist, but this was most likely said by others. Bull thought that Czolgosz was "rather haughty," and that it was plain to see that Czolgosz was in love with Goldman.[195]

---

[190] A. Wesley Johns, *The Man Who Shot McKinley* (New York: A. S. Barnes and Co, Inc., 1970) 97.

[191] L. Vernon Briggs, *The Manner of Man That Kills* (Boston: R. G. Badger, Gorham Press, 1921) 266.

[192] *Buffalo Evening News*, 7 September 1901, pg. 8, col. 3.

[193] *Buffalo Evening News*, 7 September 1901, pg. 9, col. 4.

[194] Dr. Walter Channing, *The Mental Status of Czolgosz* (Brookline, Mass: American Journal of Insanity, Vol. LIX, No. 2, 1902) 23.

[195] L. Vernon Briggs, *The Manner of Man That Kills* (Boston: R. G. Badger, Gorham Press, 1921) 266.

Chief Bull asked Czolgosz if he understood the enormity of his crime, and Czolgosz said that he did, but that he knew that sometimes people did escape from being hung and he might also. He knew at that time that the President had survived for the moment. Afterwards, the President's condition was always kept from him.[196]

At about nine o'clock, Czolgosz was taken to his cell, but he was very indignant because he was not permitted wash up. At about 10:00 p.m., District Attorney Penney arrived at Police Headquarters, with Haller, who had previously taken Czolgosz's confession. Czolgosz was brought back in, and the District Attorney read over the confession, asking Czolgosz to sign each page. Czolgosz read each page carefully, lining out things he claimed he did not say. In fact, he denied a great deal of what Haller had written down earlier, but he signed each page, after corrections, in a very fair hand, writing quickly.[197]

The press reports of the confession were less than reliable, at best. While based in truth, much of it was guess work. By one account, the assassin told them that he had come to Buffalo from his home in Cleveland three days ago with the express intention of assassinating the President. But Czolgosz was at times less than candid with the authorities. Another account had him saying, "Not until Tuesday morning did the resolution to shoot the President take hold of me. It was in my heart; there was no escape for me. I could not have conquered it had my life been at stake."[198]

Penney himself questioned Czolgosz, asking him if he had intended to kill the President, to which Czolgosz replied, "Yes, I did." When asked why, he responded, "I am an Anarchist. I am a disciple of Emma Goldman. Her words set me on fire."[199]

He said he had been a student of anarchist Emma Goldman, and had approved of her doctrines and did not believe in the American form of government. He described with seeming pride the preparations he had made to kill the President, how he had practiced in folding the handkerchief about his hand so as to conceal the revolver, and described how he had shot the President.

In a report in the *Buffalo Courier*, District Attorney Penney gave the substance of Czolgosz's confession:

---

[196] L. Vernon Briggs, *The Manner of Man That Kills* (Boston: R. G. Badger, Gorham Press, 1921) 266.

[197] L. Vernon Briggs, *The Manner of Man That Kills* (Boston: R. G. Badger, Gorham Press, 1921) 268-269.

[198] *New York Times*, 8 September 1901, pg. 1, col. 7.

[199] *New York Times*, 8 September 1901, pg. 1, col. 7.

"This man has admitted shooting the President. He says he intended to kill; that he has been planning to do it for the last three days since he came here. He went into the Temple of Music with murder in his heart, intending to shoot to kill. He fixed up his hand by tying a handkerchief around it and waited his turn to get near the President, just as the newspapers have described. When he got directly in front of the President he fired. He says he had no confederates, that he was entirely alone in the planning and execution of his diabolical act."[200]

This report was about all the information the public received at that early stage. A full copy of the confession of Czolgosz began to circulate, but it was reported to be a phony. The text of the true confession, which covered twelve typewritten pages, was kept secret, with District Attorney Thomas Penney disclosing only those essential elements.[201]

Still, the "full confession" found its way into print. One version appeared in various newspapers on September 8. Leon Czolgosz's "confession," originating from Buffalo, was reported as saying:

"I was born in Detroit nearly twenty-nine years ago. My parents were Russian Poles. They came here forty-two years ago. I got my education in the public schools of Detroit and then went to Cleveland, where I got work. In Cleveland I read books on Socialism and met a great many Socialists. I was pretty well known as a Socialist in the West. After being in Cleveland for several years, I went to Chicago where I remained for several months, after which I went to Newburg, on the outskirts of Cleveland, and went to work in the Newburg wire mills.

"During the last five years, I have had as friends Anarchists in Chicago, Cleveland, Detroit and other Western cities, and I suppose I became more or less bitter. I never had much luck at anything, and this prayed upon me. It made me morose and envious, but what started the craze to kill was a lecture I heard some time ago by Emma Goldman. She was in Cleveland, and I and other Anarchists went to hear her. She set me on fire.

"Her doctrine that all rulers should be exterminated was what set me to thinking so that my head nearly split with the pain. Miss Goldman's words went right through me, and when I left the lecture I made up my mind that I would have to do something heroic for the caused I loved.

"Eight days ago, while I was in Chicago, I read in a Chicago newspaper of President McKinley's visit to the Pan-American

---

[200] *Cincinnati Enquirer*, 7 September 1901, pg. 1.
[201] *New York Times*, 8 September 1901, pg. 2, col. 1.

Exposition at Buffalo. That day I bought a ticket for Buffalo and got here with the determination to do something, but I did not know just what. I thought of shooting the President, but I had not formed a plan.

"I went to live at 1078 Broadway, which is a saloon and hotel. John Nowak, a Pole, a sort of politician, who has led his people here for years, owns it. I told Nowak that I came to see the Fair. He knew nothing about what was setting me crazy. I went to the Exposition grounds a couple of times a day.

"Not until Tuesday morning did the resolution to shoot the President take a hold of me. It was in my heart; there was no escape for me. I could not have conquered it had my life been at stake. There were thousands of people in town on Tuesday. I heard it was President's Day. All those people seemed bowing to the great ruler. I bought a 32-calibre revolver and loaded it.

"On Tuesday night I went to the fairgrounds and was near the railroad gate when the Presidential party arrived. I tried to get near him, but the police forced me back. They forced everybody back, so the great ruler could pass. I was close to the President when he got into the grounds, but was afraid to attempt the assassination because there were so many men in the bodyguard that watched him. I was not afraid of them or that I should get hurt, but was afraid I might be seized and that my chance would be gone forever.

"Well, he went away that time and I went home. On Wednesday I went to the fairgrounds and stood right near the President, right under him near the stand from which he spoke.

"I thought half a dozen times of shooting him while he was speaking, but I could not get close enough. I was afraid I might miss and then the great crowd was always jostling, and I was afraid lest my aim fail. I waited until Wednesday and the President got into his carriage again, and a lot of men were about him and formed a cordon that I could not get through. I was tossed about by the crowd, and my spirits was getting pretty low. I was almost hopeless that night as I went home.

"Yesterday morning I went again to the Exposition grounds. Emma Goldman's speech was still burning me up. I waited near the central entrance for the President, who was to board his special train from the gate, but the police allowed no one but the President's party to pass out while the train waited. So I staid at the grounds all day waiting.

"During yesterday I first thought of hiding my pistol under my handkerchief. I was afraid if I had to draw it from my pocket I would be seized by the guards. I got to the Temple of Music the first one, and waited at the spot where the reception was to be held.

"Then he came, the President—the ruler—and I got in line and trembled and trembled until I got right up to him, and then I shot him twice through my white handkerchief. I would have fired more, but I was stunned by a blow in the face—a frightful blow that knocked me down—and then everybody jumped on me. I thought I would be killed, and was surprised the way they treated me."[202]

When asked his motive, he told District Attorney Penney, according to the account, "I am an Anarchist. I am a disciple of Emma Goldman. Her words set me on fire."

"I deny that I have had an accomplice at any time," he was quoted as saying. "I don't regret my act, because I was doing what I could for the great cause. I am not connected with the Paterson group, or with those Anarchists that sent Bresci to Italy to kill Humbert. I had no confidants, no one to help me. I was alone absolutely."[203]

While this report was probably not the actual original written confession verbatim, it did agree in substance with what Czolgosz had been telling the police. Other newspapers embellished on the confession of Czolgosz.

"I am an anarchist," read one. "I do not believe in the American form of government. My faith in this government was destroyed by Emma Goldman, whom I heard deliver lectures in New York a few years ago, and with whom I have since been in correspondence. I believe that any man that accepts the Presidency is a foe to the common people. He represents only the class of oppressors.

"I did my duty. I am sorry that Mr. McKinley has suffered. I intended to kill him, and I regret that I did not succeed.

"I hope that no one will mistake my position. I am not a common assassin. Personally, I had little to gain as a result of this act. The shot that I fired was for the benefit of all mankind. I intended to kill the President of the United States. Against President McKinley the man I could have no feeling. I have been told that he is a good man. I did not wish to inflict suffering on his family, but in accomplishing my purpose could not consider them. I say again that I did not assassinate the man. I intended to kill the President, because I believe it would have a good effect upon this country and upon all mankind."[204]

---

[202] *New York Times*, 8 September 1901, pg. 1, col. 7.

[203] *New York Times*, 8 September 1901, pg. 1, col. 7.

[204] *Literary Digest*, 14 September 1901, pg.2.

It is certain, however, that Czolgosz, at the urging of James Quackenbush, signed a brief one sentence confession that he supposed would be given to reporters. He thought Quackenbush was a newsman as he began to try to write it himself. But he was shaking and a stenographer wrote it out and Czolgosz signed it. It read, "I killed President McKinley because I done my duty. I don't believe one man should have so much service and another man none."[205]

In many newspaper accounts, Czolgosz had been quoted as saying this. In all likelihood, those quotes came from this written statement. But even with it in writing, some papers still managed get it wrong.

"I killed the President because it was duty and I did not believe one man should have such services and all the rest should be glad only to stand by and cheer," was how the statement appeared in the *Buffalo Express*.[206]

At 7 p.m. that night, the President's attending physicians issued the following bulletin to a waiting public: "The President was shot about 4 o'clock. One bullet struck him on the upper portion of the breast bone, glancing and not penetrating; the second bullet penetrated the abdomen five inches below the left nipple, and one and a half inches to the left of the median line."

"The abdomen was opened through the line of the bullet wound. It was found that the bullet had penetrated the stomach. The opening in the front wall of the stomach was careful closed with silk sutures, after which a search was made for a hole in the back wall of the stomach. This was found, and also closed in the same way."

"The further course of the bullet could not be discovered, although careful search was made. The abdominal wound was closed without drainage. No injury to the intestines or other abdominal organ was discovered."

"The patient stood the operation well, pulse of good quality, rate of 130. Condition at the conclusion of the operation was gratifying. The result cannot be foretold. His condition at present justifies hope of recovery"

Signed— P.M. Rixey, Mathew D. Mann, Eugene Wasdin, Roswell Park, Herman Mynter[207]

---

[205] Dr. Walter Channing, *The Mental Status of Czolgosz* (Brookline, Mass: American Journal of Insanity, Vol. LIX, No. 2, 1902) 126.
[206] *Buffalo Express*, 8 September 1901.
[207] *New York Times*, 7 September 1901, pg. 1, col. 1.

At 7:30, Secretary of Agriculture James Wilson and his daughter arrived and were admitted into the Milburn house. Soon hundreds of telegrams began to pour into the home, and George Cortelyou spent much of his time answering them. The volume was so heavy that two White House stenographers set up shop with typewriters in the parlor and soon the room was bustling as they banged out responses to the anxious correspondence. The world was beginning to learn the dreadful details of what had transpired in Buffalo.

Back at the exposition, the illuminations went out and all was dark. Ironically, there had been a power failure caused by a freak accident. The remaining patrons sadly headed for home.[208]

---

[208] *Buffalo Courier*, 7 September 1901, pg. 3, col. 7.

George B. Cortelyou

Marcus Hanna, Senator from Ohio

Lyman C. Gage

Elihu Root

Grover Cleveland

Charles Dawes

Judge Emery

The President giving his September 5 speech at the Exposition.

McKinley in the reviewing stand at the stadium the day before the shooting.

The President and Mrs. McKinley leave the Milburn house for their trip to Niagara Falls the morning of the shooting.

**McKinley at Niagara Falls, September 6, 1901.
The morning of the shooting.**

**Arriving back in Buffalo from the falls with Mrs. McKinley.
This is the last photograph of Mr. & Mrs. McKinley together.**

President McKinley Being Transported to Events in Buffalo, NY.

President McKinley Reviews Troops at the Stadium at the Pan-American Exposition-September 5, 1901 the day before the shooting.

President McKinley leaves New York Building after appearance on September 5, 1901.

The Temple of Music at the Pan American Exposition where President McKinley was Shot.

Another View of the Temple of Music With Fairgoers in Foreground

**The Ambulance that Transported the Wounded President
to the Hospital.**

**The Pan American Hospital Where The Operation on
President McKinley was Performed.**

Another View of the Pan American Hospital

3. The Assassin

Leon F. Czolgosz (no middle name, just the initial and pronounced Chol-gosh) was born in 1873 in Detroit, Michigan. His parents were Polish immigrants, of German-Polish decent, who had ten children, all of who lived in Cleveland, Ohio, where they had moved in 1881. Leon was the fourth child.

Leon was born at 141 Benton Street, one of a very few brick houses in the Parish. They had occupied the first floor, a family named Smith the second. Mrs. Mincel, who owned the house with her mother, lived on the third floor.

Mrs. Mincel remembered the family very well, "Leo" being born about the year she had married. They were a law-abiding family with four children at the time. The mother took in washing.[1]

Leon's real mother died in 1885 when he was 12. She had given birth to a child in Posen, Michigan after which she became ill. Leon's father, Paul Czolgosz, took her to his brother's house in Alpena to be closer to doctors, but she died about six weeks after giving birth. During her final illness, Paul remembered her saying, "My children, the time will come when you will have greater understanding and be more learned." She would also get up and walk the floor during her illness.[2] At his age, this must have been traumatic for young Leon.

At the time of the assassination, the family of Leon Czolgosz included his father Paul, 59, and his stepmother. His father had remarried a woman named Catarina (Katren Metzfaltr, according to Leon's sister Victoria)[3]. Paul Czolgosz lived in America for over thirty years but never learned English, and was a city worker.

Paul Czolgosz had earlier been involved in an incident at a Polish settlement in Posen, Michigan, although other reports placed it in Rogers City. A German priest named Henry Moliter, an illegitimate son of the crazy King Louis of Wurtemburg, had founded the settlement and was said to have ruled with an iron hand, making those under him work like

---

[1] L. Vernon Briggs, *The Manner of Man That Kills* (Boston: R. G. Badger, Gorham Press, 1921) 281.
[2] L. Vernon Briggs, *The Manner of Man That Kills* (Boston: R. G. Badger, Gorham Press, 1921) 289-290.
[3] L. Vernon Briggs, *The Manner of Man That Kills* (Boston: R. G. Badger, Gorham Press, 1921) 286.

slaves in his lumber company. One day, the people finally rebelled, killing the priest. Paul Czolgosz was supposed to have been involved as a member of a 'jury' who sentenced the death, but he was never arrested.[4] About fifteen years later, Czolgosz was said to have been one of a group of men who turned States evidence and five of the chief actors were sentenced to life imprisonment in Jackson, Czolgosz escaping that fate.[5] A son, Waldek, denied that his father had even been in the city when Moliter was killed, saying the real killer was a business competitor.[6]

A neighbor of the Czolgoszes on Benton Street, Jacob J. Lorkowski, remembered Paul Czolgosz as a good storyteller, who played cards and gambled, but did not drink in excess. In all, he was a hard working laborer. He only remembered that there had been children in the family, and thought that Leon had been baptized under the name of Czolcholski at the Parish of St. Alberta. An extensive search of church records produced no name close to that or to Czolgosz.

Leon had five brothers. Waldek, 34, was a mill hand and was unmarried. Frank, 32, was married and also a mill hand. Jacob, 23, was drawing a $30 dollar per month government pension due to injuries to his right hand and forearm received while in federal service at Sandy Hook in 1899 during the Spanish-American War and was married to a girl who had been a friend of the family. Leon also had two younger unmarried brothers: Joseph, 22, worked as a meat packer; Michael, 21, was a farmer. Czolgosz also had two sisters. Ceceli, age unknown, was a married housekeeper; Victoria, 21, an unmarried waitress.[7]

As a small child, his father described Leon as quiet and retired. He thought he had the appearance of thinking more than most children, and when angry, tended not to say anything. He seemed to have a difficult time making the acquaintance of other children, possibly due to his bashfulness, which seemed to increase with age. He sometimes failed to do as he was told, but possibly no more than other children. Paul Czolgosz could not remember any childhood chums of either sex, and said he had never seen his son in the company of a girl.[8] Likewise, he

[4] L. Vernon Briggs, *The Manner of Man That Kills* (Boston: R. G. Badger, Gorham Press, 1921) 280.

[5] *New York Times,* 18 September 1901, pg. 3, col. 2.

[6] L. Vernon Briggs, *The Manner of Man That Kills* (Boston: R. G. Badger, Gorham Press, 1921) 302.

[7] Dr. Walter Channing, *The Mental Status of Czolgosz* (Brookline, Mass: American Journal of Insanity, Vol. LIX, No. 2, 1902) 4.

[8] Dr. Walter Channing, *The Mental Status of Czolgosz* (Brookline, Mass: American Journal of Insanity, Vol. LIX, No. 2, 1902) 6.

could not remember any childhood diseases or illnesses and could not remember ever having called a doctor for Leon.[9]

Joseph, a younger brother who was quite well respected in his community, thought Leon was "a nice boy." Joseph said that Leon lived by himself, did not care to be around strangers and never talked to girls. In fact, when Leon saw girls he knew coming toward him on the street, he would actually cross the street to avoid talking to them. Joseph said that Leon was "always awful bashful."[10]

"He never had anything to do with women and acted as though he was afraid of them," confirmed his father.[11]

Years later, after his arrest, according to Buffalo Assistant District Attorney Frederick Haller, Leon would tell that he had been in love with a girl once, and that she had gone back on him and that since then he had nothing to do with women. Paul Czolgosz upon being told of that statement, said that Leon had gone into the city from the farm for several days at a time, usually from one to five days. They never knew where he went but the family did not think it strange because of Leon's secretive nature. During this time, it is at least possible that Leon had become romantically involved.[12]

Leon attended parochial school in Alpena under a priest named Sklizek, after which he attended a public school for a short time, when the family left for Netronia (Natrona), near Pittsburgh. [13]

One friend of the family, Valentine Misgalski, said he never witnessed any viciousness in the family. He remembered Leon when he was questioned by a reporter after the assassination and remembered him as a perfectly normal boy who attended parochial school and was devoted to his church.[14]

---

[9] L. Vernon Briggs, *The Manner of Man That Kills* (Boston: R. G. Badger, Gorham Press, 1921) 290.

[10] Dr. Walter Channing, *The Mental Status of Czolgosz* (Brookline, Mass: American Journal of Insanity, Vol. LIX, No. 2, 1902) 10.

[11] *Cleveland Plain Dealer*, 13 September 1901, pg. 12, col. 3.

[12] L. Vernon Briggs, *The Manner of Man That Kills* (Boston: R. G. Badger, Gorham Press, 1921) 291.

[13] L. Vernon Briggs, *The Manner of Man That Kills* (Boston: R. G. Badger, Gorham Press, 1921) 287.

[14] Marshall Everett, *The Complete Life of William McKinley* (Privately Published, 1901) 73.

However, Leon's home life was at times, less than pleasant. His family noticed that he often withdrew and would shy away from them. He took long naps, which is a possible sign of clinical depression.

His sister-in-law, Jacob's wife, who had been a family friend for years, thought Leon was unlike other boys and that he acted queerly.[15] She said Leon was a sickly boy at times, and that if you said anything to Leon about his illness, he would get angry.

Part of his depression could have stemmed from his relationship with his stepmother. She took to calling him crazy to his face. Their relationship was very strained.

"Leon was a regular devil," said a family friend, Albert Lemanski. "He gave his father no end of trouble. The old folks licked Leon with a strap all the time. The mother thought her son crazy."[16]

Outside of an aunt who was reportedly "out of her head," there was no evidence of insanity in the family. The Czolgosz family were hard working people who eventually owned a small farm and a combination store-saloon, built by Paul in about 1892, which he ran for four or five months. Afterwards it was rented to the Findlay Beer Company.[17] Arriving in America a few months before Leon was born, they had worked to get what they owned, although never really prospering. After living in Detroit for about seven years, they moved north to Rogers City, Michigan, briefly, then to Posen and Alpine. These areas were all heavily Polish and it was there that Leon fine-tuned his mastery of the Polish language.

In 1889, the Czolgoszes arrived in Natrona, and Leon acquired a job working in a glass bottle factory, carrying hot bottles with a fork from the ovens to a cooling area. In this job, he eventually earned a dollar a day.

A year and nine months later, in 1891, the family finally made its last move, to Cleveland, Ohio. There Leon got a job in the Newburg Wire Mills, where he worked until 1897. He started by winding wire, and was a good enough worker that he eventually was promoted and was placed in charge of some heavy machinery. Earning ten dollars a week, he was

[15] Dr. Walter Channing, *The Mental Status of Czolgosz* (Brookline, Mass: American Journal of Insanity, Vol. LIX, No. 2, 1902) 9.

[16] *Cincinnati Post*, 10 September 1901, pg. 3, col. 1.

[17] L. Vernon Briggs, *The Manner of Man That Kills* (Boston: R. G. Badger, Gorham Press, 1921) 303.

able to put some money away, and even chipped in four hundred dollars to enable his family to purchase a fifty-five acre farm near Cleveland in Warrensville, Ohio. He also attended night school with his brother Waldek for about three months one winter.[18]

Czolgosz worked in the mill for seven years. The foreman under whom Leon had worked, a Mr. Page, said that he was a very reliable worker who never got into trouble, quarreled or otherwise became involved in disputes and that he was quiet and cheerful. He usually brought in his dinner, as did most of the men. While he was not quick to join in conversations, neither did he try to avoid the other men. He was by all accounts a good worker and had fewer disciplinary fines than most of the other workers.[19]

Foreman Frank Dalzer of Consolidated Mill told the newspapers, "I know Leon Czolgosz very well.... Leon at one time was employed as a blacksmith in the Consolidated Mill. Later he kept a saloon at the corner of Third Avenue and Tod Street. He sold the saloon and went to live on the farm with his father."[20] Actually, this had been his father's saloon.

"I know that Leon is, or was, an Anarchist," he continued. "He attended Socialist and Anarchist meetings very frequently. He is a man of rather small stature, about twenty-six years of age. The last time I saw him he had a light brown mustache."[21]

A couple that became quite familiar with Leon Czolgosz while he was employed in the factory was Mr. and Mrs. Dryer. Mr. Dryer had bought the saloon from Paul Czolgosz, and Leon was a frequent visitor. He would come in after work, wash up, and read the paper, often falling asleep in the process. Neither Mr. nor Mrs. Dryer ever saw Leon lose his temper, use profane language or talk to girls, whom he appeared not to have the nerve to approach.

Mrs. Dryer could hardly believe that Leon could later commit such a violent act as the shooting of the President. She told that while he was in the saloon, he would never even kill a fly, literally. He would swipe them away, or catch and release them, but never kill them.

---

[18] L. Vernon Briggs, *The Manner of Man That Kills* (Boston: R. G. Badger, Gorham Press, 1921) 303.

[19] Dr. Walter Channing, *The Mental Status of Czolgosz* (Brookline, Mass: American Journal of Insanity, Vol. LIX, No. 2, 1902) 13.

[20] *New York Times*, 8 September 1901, pg. 4, col. 1.

[21] *New York Times*, 8 September 1901, pg. 4, col. 1.

She said he was very thrifty with his money and would not drink heavily, saying "No, I have use for my money."

Mr. Dryer could only remember one "chum" of Leon's, that being a co-worker named Jugnatz Lapka, with whom he walked back and forth to work. [22]

Leon Czolgosz never appeared happy to Mr. and Mrs. Dryer. Mr. Dryer called him "stupid and dull-like." Mrs. Dryer described him as "kind of broke-down like."

The Dryers noticed Leon taking his medicine from a bottle and a box of pills he always seemed to carry. He rarely talked to any stranger, never really saying much to anyone. On off days from work, he would sometimes spend all day lounging in the saloon, reading and sleeping. He would rarely take part in card games, doing so only when urged to take a fourth hand.[23]

On many occasions, Mrs. Dryer tried to talk Leon into eating with them. She was successful but once, and on that occasion, Leon sat at the table and ate very little.[24]

Mr. Dryer said that Leon would not become involved in a fight and would not become involved even for his own brother. One night, Jacob was returning from a dance and was across the street in the middle of a crowd where someone was trying to knife him. Leon would do nothing, saying, "If he will associate with those Polaks, he will have to take the consequences."[25]

After Leon had worked at the mill for about two years, an event happened which apparently had a profound impact on his thinking. In 1893, the workers at the mill went on strike. At issue were the poor wages they received. As a result of this strike, Leon Czolgosz, along with many other workers, lost his job. His brother and co-worker Waldek later remembered that Leon "got quiet and not so happy" during this time. Waldek did not remember his brother reading any abnormal amount during this period, and said that Leon would get quite angry if teased about his lack of drinking or girls.[26]

---

[22] L. Vernon Briggs, *The Manner of Man That Kills* (Boston: R. G. Badger, Gorham Press, 1921) 298.

[23] L. Vernon Briggs, *The Manner of Man That Kills* (Boston: R. G. Badger, Gorham Press, 1921) 298.

[24] Dr. Walter Channing, *The Mental Status of Czolgosz* (Brookline, Mass: American Journal of Insanity, Vol. LIX, No. 2, 1902) 11-12.

[25] L. Vernon Briggs, *The Manner of Man That Kills* (Boston: R. G. Badger, Gorham Press, 1921) 299.

[26] Dr. Walter Channing, *The Mental Status of Czolgosz* (Brookline, Mass: American Journal of Insanity, Vol. LIX, No. 2, 1902) 7.

When Leon returned to the mill to work, after a new manager was hired, he did so under an assumed name; Fred C. Nieman. According to Waldek, some of the workers had been blacklisted, and when Leon applied again six months after the strike, he did so under the assumed name and he was hired. Waldek thought the foreman knew some of the new hires were working under assumed names and were strikers, but the mill was short of workers so they were hired anyway.[27]

There has been much speculation as to why Czolgosz used the name Nieman as an alias. He said he chose that particular name because it was his mother's maiden name. Actually, her name was Nebrock, which Czolgosz contended was German for Nieman. The reason for the alias, Leon also claimed, was that he had gone on strike under his real name at the wire mill, and that he changed it in order to secure employment afterward. [28]

It was during the strike that Leon lost faith in either God, the Catholic Church, or both. He and his brother Waldek, who also worked at the mill, had prayed feverishly during the strike. Leon felt the prayers were not answered, he and his brother confronted a priest about prayer. They were told to pray more and harder, which they did. They also purchased a Polish Bible and Leon read it four or five times. Leon, after reading his Bible, decided, according to Waldek, that the priests "told it their own way and kept back most of what was in the book," He remembered Leon comparing the priest trade as "the same as the shoemakers or any other."

The brothers began what could be described as a serious study of the religious issue. In addition to the Bible, they read other pamphlets and books they could accumulate. They read the books together for about a year and a half, when Leon began to prefer to read alone and began to spend more and more time with his books. Waldek also remembered Leon reading *Looking Backward* and *Peruna Almanac*. He said Leon liked the latter because it told him of his lucky days.[29]

In 1896, disillusioned and after much reading, Leon completely broke ties with the Catholic Church, although he continued to believe in God. Reverend Benedict Rosinski of St. Stanislaus Church in Cleveland told of an encounter he had with Czolgosz after this break.

---

[27] L. Vernon Briggs, *The Manner of Man That Kills* (Boston: R. G. Badger, Gorham Press, 1921) 303-304.

[28] Dr. Walter Channing, *The Mental Status of Czolgosz* (Brookline, Mass: American Journal of Insanity, Vol. LIX, No. 2, 1902) 27.

[29] Dr. Walter Channing, *The Mental Status of Czolgosz* (Brookline, Mass: American Journal of Insanity, Vol. LIX, No. 2, 1902) 7.

"About four years ago, I asked Czolgosz for a contribution for the church," he said. "He surprised me very much by refusing to give it. I asked him why he would not contribute, and he said that he was an Anarchist. I always supposed that he was a Catholic, and that was why I had approached him on the subject of contributions. He told me that he had no religion and that he did not wish to help churches. He said that Anarchy was his religion. I tried to argue with him and drive the Anarchistic principles from his head, but it was to no purpose. I believe that he was mentally unbalanced, because he acted and talked so strangely to me."[30]

Leon was becoming more and more interested in education and reading and he began thinking in earnest about politics. He joined a Polish education circle in which socialism and anarchy were often discussed. Coming on the heels of his factory strike experience, Leon soaked up the doctrine. A Cleveland man who he had met in 1894, Anton Zwolinski, had introduced Leon to the group, and Leon faithfully attended meetings for over seven years, right up to the time of the assassination. In fact, he later credited Zwolinski with opening his eyes to the evils of American government, and he said that it was at these meetings that he obtained his anarchist ideas. But after his arrest, Czolgosz said that at no time during the meetings was presidential assassination discussed. That idea came to Leon on his own. Czolgosz had come to see American social injustice and rebelled against it by embracing the anarchist doctrine. He viewed all leaders as enemies of the state and thus felt justified killing them. He thought it right and that it was his duty.

"Czolgosz made no secret of the fact that he was an Anarchist," said Zwolinski. "He was always talking about and trying to force Anarchistic principles on everyone whom he talked with. He was a great coward, however, and I am surprised that he had the nerve to do as he did. It would not surprise me to learn that he is merely the tool of some other persons. When the Sila club broke up, Czolgosz joined another one, the name of which I have forgotten."[31]

"It was no secret that Czolgosz was an Anarchist," Zwolinski said in another interview. "He was a rattle-brained fool, always talking about Anarchy when he could find anybody to listen to him. I really think he was a tool. He was nothing more than the instrument of some smarter and even more cowardly man than himself. When the police and

---

[30] *New York Times*, 8 September 1901, pg. 4, col. 2.
[31] *New York Times*, 8 September 1901, pg. 4, col. 2.

newspapers get to the bottom they will find he was picked out by some Anarchist society to do the job. I am certain of it."[32]

When asked who he thought had sent Czolgosz, Zwolinski replied, "Oh, I don't know that but I am sure he was sent. He did not have brains enough to plan the deed himself."[33]

"Sila," meaning, "force," was an Anarchist organization, which met at the corner of Tod Street and Third Avenue in Cleveland. The *New York Times* reported that it had learned "without a doubt" that Czolgosz was a member of the organization.[34]

"The papers state that this man Czolgosz was an Anarchist and that the idea of getting rid of all authority was put into his head by reading Emma Goldman's writings and listening to her address here in Memorial Hall about four months ago," said another self-proclaimed Cleveland anarchist, A. B. Eberhardt. "That statement you can brand for me as an infamous lie. He was never seen at any of our meetings in Cleveland and is unknown to us as a co-worker or even as a co-thinker."

"If he is the tool of any organization, which I doubt very much," continued Eberhardt, "it is of the Revolutionary Communists, a secret band of what I believe to be downright fools."[35]

While there has never been any direct evidence linking Czolgosz as a true member of any anarchist group other than attending some meetings, there is one association to which he undoubtedly belonged. And the Order of Knights of the Golden Eagle was anything but an anarchist organization.

The society was formed to "Promote the principles of true benevolence by associating its members together for the purpose of mutual relief against the trials and difficulties attending sickness, distress and death; to care for and assist the widows and orphans; to assist those out of employment and encourage each other in business" and otherwise lend each other support. The group was based on the Bible and patriotism and its motto was "fidelity, valor and humanity."

This organization of such high and political aims, Leon Czolgosz, through his association with his co-workers, entered into; this in spite of his Polish immigrant status and the fact that he was a Catholic, and looked upon as somewhat inferior.

---

[32] *Cincinnati Post*, 7 September 1901, pg. 5, col. 3.

[33] *Cleveland Plain Dealer*, 7 September 1901, pg. 4, col. 3.

[34] *New York Times*, 8 September 1901, pg. 4, col. 2.

[35] *Cleveland Plain Dealer*, 7 September 1901, pg. 1, col. 6.

But his co-workers elected Leon for membership anyway and this was truly an honor. It also says a great deal about how well he was accepted among them.[36] Czolgosz did not regularly attend the Golden Eagle meetings, but did go occasionally. He was not only a member in good standing but was also thought of by the members quite highly.[37] When he did attend, Waldek said he generally took a seat near the back and just listened, never having spoken to his knowledge.[38]

His lodge associates, when interviewed by a reporter, said that he was a queer man and was known to have a most violent temper, even though there seems to be little evidence of it. It was said that he was a strong infidel and a red-hot socialist. They said they had last seen him around the spring before the shooting. [39]

Very soon after the shooting of the President, members of the Golden Eagle organization were questioned by police in Cleveland. The investigators were satisfied with what they heard and were totally convinced of the group's non-involvement.

When his father bought the saloon-grocery in 1895, Leon joined the socialist club, which met upstairs. His brother-in-law, Frank Bandowski, was the secretary. There Leon quietly listened to the plight of the working man, of which he knew, and of socialist doctrine, of which he was becoming more and more familiar. He also began reading on the subject and among the books was *Looking Backward* by Edward Bellamy, which was a glamorous portrayal of socialism.

"When I kept the saloon on Third Avenue, an organization called the Social Labor party held meetings in the hall above," remembered Paul Czolgosz. "I attended several meetings but nothing extraordinary ever happened. The speakers confined themselves to the subject of Socialism. Leon belonged to the organization, but never delivered any speeches because he was not capable of doing so. I never heard Leon speak against the government or the President nor did I ever hear him mention Emma Goldman or any other Anarchist. I never saw any Anarchist

---

[36] Dr. Walter Channing, *The Mental Status of Czolgosz* (Brookline, Mass: American Journal of Insanity, Vol. LIX, No. 2, 1902) 13-14.
[37] Dr. Walter Channing, *The Mental Status of Czolgosz* (Brookline, Mass: American Journal of Insanity, Vol. LIX, No. 2, 1902) 15.
[38] L. Vernon Briggs, *The Manner of Man That Kills* (Boston: R. G. Badger, Gorham Press, 1921) 311.
[39] Marshall Everett, *The Complete Life of William McKinley* (Privately Published, 1901) 75.

literature in his possession. His reading was confined to the Cleveland newspapers. He did not attend many meetings."[40]

Leon was reading more and more of the socialist and anarchist newspapers that were appearing across the country. In the years just prior to the Soviet Revolution, he took an avid interest in labor issues. And he quietly cheered news of any anarchist victory.

When King Humbert I of Italy was assassinated on July 29, 1900 at his summer palace in Monza by the anarchist Gaetano (Angelo) Bresci, Leon cut out the newspaper stories and supposedly read them over and over again, memorizing the entire incident. Bresci was praised in anarchistic publications around the world. To Leon Czolgosz, Bresci was a hero, and someday soon he too would achieve something as great. No one can know for sure if this was when Czolgosz decided to kill the President. Later, he said that he did not think of killing McKinley until three or fours days before he did it. But this event, and Czolgosz's intense interest in it, could very well have been the seed of an American assassination.

During this period, Leon was very quiet, sluggish, and remote; withdrawn and unsociable, yet not conformational. But he was also very gentle, and those who knew him where shocked at his later actions in Buffalo. He smoked and drank moderately, but never swore. He gambled only sparingly. And it appeared that he began to develop the symptoms of a hypochondriac.

Then suddenly, seemingly without cause or warning, in about 1898, Leon had what appeared to be some type of a mental breakdown. Dr. Walter Channing, an alienist and Professor of Mental Diseases at Tufts University, investigated quite thoroughly the background of Czolgosz and wrote an important early analysis, *The Mental State of Czolgosz*, which was published in 1902. He concluded that during this period Czolgosz changed from "being an industrious and apparently fairly normal young man into a sickly, unhealthy and abnormal one."

Channing further wrote, "While in this physical and mental condition of sickliness and abnormality, it is probable that he conceived the idea of performing some great act for the benefit of the common and working people. This finally developed into a true delusion that it was his duty to kill the President, because he was an enemy of the people, and resulted in the assassination."[41]

---

[40] *Cleveland Plain Dealer*, 13 September 1901, pg. 12, col. 3.
[41] Dr. Walter Channing, *The Mental Status of Czolgosz* (Brookline, Mass: American Journal of Insanity, Vol. LIX, No. 2, 1902) 46.

But could this sudden change in mental attitude have bee rooted in something as simple as the failed love affair that Leon vaguely alluded to in a later talk with the Assistant District Attorney in Buffalo? Could he have gone into a mental depression over a woman? It is something that will never be known.

During this "illness", Czolgosz, who had been employed virtually his entire life, on August 29, 1898, suddenly quit his job. When he quit, Foreman Page said that he just came up to him and told him that he was going to quit, telling him he was going to the country for health reasons. After seven years at the mill, it came as a surprise to everyone. Leon Czolgosz was never again in his life to be fully employed. [42]

As his mental condition deteriorated, his temperament became extremely cranky. He hung around the family farm, napping under trees for abnormally long hours, waking up to read, then going back to sleep. Occasionally he would hunt rabbits with his breech-loading shotgun. According to Waldek, he also occasionally shot them with his revolver if they strayed close enough. His brother Waldek thought him quite skillful with his revolver. [43]

"He would frequently take his revolver and go into the woods to shoot birds," remembered his father. "While his actions were queer, there was noting to indicate that his mind was unbalanced."[44]

Waldek was also concerned enough with his brother's attitude and appearance that he suggested to Leon that he check into a hospital. Waldek thought he looked like he had "gone to pieces like" and looked pale. Perhaps Leon's socialist leanings influenced his judgment of hospitals, because he told Waldek, "There is no place in the hospital for poor people. If you have lots of money you get well taken care of."

While Leon would occasionally visit a doctor, he never did check himself into a hospital, perhaps to save his family and himself the burden of the cost.[45]

Leon began to lounge around for hours at a time reading and sleeping. His reading comprised of mostly newspapers of the anarchist variety, including *Free Society*. His father thought him not well, and did

[42] L. Vernon Briggs, *The Manner of Man That Kills* (Boston: R. G. Badger, Gorham Press, 1921) 314.

[43] Dr. Walter Channing, *The Mental Status of Czolgosz* (Brookline, Mass: American Journal of Insanity, Vol. LIX, No. 2, 1902) 8.

[44] *Cleveland Plain Dealer*, 13 September 1901, pg. 12, col. 3.

[45] Dr. Walter Channing, *The Mental Status of Czolgosz* (Brookline, Mass: American Journal of Insanity, Vol. LIX, No. 2, 1902) 6.

not think it wise for Leon to work at a regular job. He was pale and did almost nothing, except to do an occasional odd job around the farm, and was even more withdrawn than usual.

He told Jacob's wife that he was sick, but she could see no outward signs other than a cough he had in which he "would spit out great chunks." She thought he was more likely just lazy. But she explained, "If you said anything to him about his sickness he would get mad." And she recalled him always talking about going west, in order to improve his health.[46]

Leon's brother Joseph also remembered his nasty cough while on the farm. He knew he took medicine for it and at one point even sent off for an inhaler, which he used about two months.

Joseph confirmed what many others said; that Leon slept "a great deal of the time. It seemed like all of the time." He said Leon would fall asleep while reading the newspaper, awaken, and begin reading again.[47]

Leon's uncle Michael and his aunt would tease him about being an "old woman" or "grandmother" because of his habit of falling asleep at odd times and for appearing rather stupid at others.[48] Jacob told of how Leon was more given to keeping to himself and less inclined to talk after his illness. He told of him frequently dropping off to sleep in the middle of the day with no explanation whatever and said that he never got excited. But he did not notice a physical change in Leon as a result of the illness. He said that his brother was fond of reading and that he was the best-educated member of the family. Jacob told of Leon's mechanical aptitude, and of the time he once took a clock apart and put it back together again so that it ran perfectly.[49]

His sister Victoria described Leon as "a rather lazy but a nice boy." She too echoed the descriptions of his sleeping and eating habits, his fondness of hunting, and his refusal to use bad language. She confirmed that he and his stepmother could not get along and were always bickering. If he was ever close to using bad language, she thought, those were the times.[50]

---

[46] L. Vernon Briggs, *The Manner of Man That Kills* (Boston: R. G. Badger, Gorham Press, 1921) 293.

[47] Dr. Walter Channing, *The Mental Status of Czolgosz* (Brookline, Mass: American Journal of Insanity, Vol. LIX, No. 2, 1902) 10.

[48] L. Vernon Briggs, *The Manner of Man That Kills* (Boston: R. G. Badger, Gorham Press, 1921) 292.

[49] L. Vernon Briggs, *The Manner of Man That Kills* (Boston: R. G. Badger, Gorham Press, 1921) 296.

[50] Dr. Walter Channing, *The Mental Status of Czolgosz* (Brookline, Mass: American Journal of Insanity, Vol. LIX, No. 2, 1902) 11.

Leon had never gotten along particularly well with his stepmother and now they were quarreling openly. She did not believe him to be sick and would try to get him to work, but was unsuccessful. She thought he was lazy.[51]

Czolgosz began to refuse to eat with the family, eating in his room instead, and he became even more withdrawn. Dinner would usually consist of milk from the barn, bread and sometimes cake. He usually drank two quarts of milk a day, sometimes more.[52]

In the winter of 1900-01, when Leon's stepmother left the farm for a city visit, during her absence, Leon cooked for himself and for the family. According to his brother Joseph, when she returned he went back to eating by himself and would not even enter the house if she was there. He would get his milk and bread and either eat it in his room, or go outside and eat it beneath a tree.

Occasionally, Leon would fish in a small pond near the house. He would keep the fish until his stepmother left the house, and then would rush in to cook and eat his catch. If she came back in too quickly or if strangers came, he would just let the fish burn or throw them away.[53]

Waldek was asked later if Leon would have gotten violent with her had he stayed on the farm. Waldek said yes, and that he thought that was the reason Leon left.[54]

Leon, by nature, seemed to prefer not to talk to anyone.

"He never talked much and did not like it if you talked to him too much," said Jacob's wife. She added that he did not dress well on the farm, but was "all ragged out."[55]

This appears to be in sharp contrast with his behavior after his arrest and stories told by acquaintances about Leon's constant attention and preoccupation to his personal appearance.

[51] Dr. Walter Channing, *The Mental Status of Czolgosz* (Brookline, Mass: American Journal of Insanity, Vol. LIX, No. 2, 1902) 9.

[52] Dr. Walter Channing, *The Mental Status of Czolgosz* (Brookline, Mass: American Journal of Insanity, Vol. LIX, No. 2, 1902) 10.

[53] Dr. Walter Channing, *The Mental Status of Czolgosz* (Brookline, Mass: American Journal of Insanity, Vol. LIX, No. 2, 1902) 11.

[54] L. Vernon Briggs, *The Manner of Man That Kills* (Boston: R. G. Badger, Gorham Press, 1921) 311.

[55] Dr. Walter Channing, *The Mental Status of Czolgosz* (Brookline, Mass: American Journal of Insanity, Vol. LIX, No. 2, 1902) 10.

She also remembered Leon playing with the children, of whom he seemed quite fond. He would talk childish talk with them, but if anyone came around he would talk differently. His sister-in-law thought the way he behaved was crazy, he did such childish things.[56]

On May 6, 1901, five months to the day before he would assassinate the President of the United States, Leon traveled to Cleveland to witness a speech by the "Queen of Anarchists," Emma Goldman. That night at the Franklin Liberal Club at 170 Superior Street, the famous woman spoke with fire to Czolgosz, though others called the speech only mediocre for Goldman. The talk would not have enticed anyone to commit an assassination, however after the shooting, the *New York Times* reported, "Some days ago he attended a lecture by Emma Goldman in Cleveland. He accepted her doctrine that all rulers should be exterminated. He went away from the lecture determined to do something heroic for the cause."[57]

Emma Goldman claimed that she did not encourage violence of any kind and said that she did not like the fact that many thought anarchists, as a rule, did. But the tone of her speech and her glamorization of the motives of other anarchist assassins, in effect characterizing them as men of action, at best sent mixed signals, even if she stated that she opposed violence. She seemed to be saying that while she herself would not commit a violent act, others who did so exercised the highest of nobility.

Goldman had given two speeches on May 5 in Cleveland. One was on "anarchism," the other on "the cause and effect of vice." It is not known whether Czolgosz heard both speeches, but it seems clear that he heard the one on anarchism.

Far from openly encouraging violence, *The Cleveland Plain Dealer*, the only record of the speech, reported that Goldman "deprecated the idea that all anarchists were in favor of violence and bomb throwing. She declared that nothing was further from the principles they support."

Had she stopped there, in light of later events, history may have been different.

The Plain Dealer further reported, "She then went on however into a detailed explanation of the different crimes committed by anarchists lately, declaring that the motive was good in each case, and that these actions were merely a matter of temperament. 'Some men are so

---

[56] L. Vernon Briggs, *The Manner of Man That Kills* (Boston: R. G. Badger, Gorham Press, 1921) 293-294.
[57] *New York Times*, 8 September 1901, pg. 2, col. 1.

constituted,' she said, 'that they are unable to stand idly by and see the wrongs that were being endured by their fellow mortals.'"[58]

Czolgosz apparently did not envision himself as standing idly by and these words must have stirred him.

"She herself did not believe in these methods but she did not think that they should be too severely condemned in view of the high and noble motives, which prompted their perpetration," the account continued. "'We must have education before we can have power,' declared Miss Goldman. 'Some believe that we should first obtain the force and let the intelligence and education come afterwards. Nothing could be more fallacious. If we get the education and intelligence first among the people the power will come to us without a struggle.'"[59]

Upon reading the complete account of Goldman's speech, it is difficult to say that she was not condoning, and by inference, encouraging, illegal acts, even violence. On the one hand, she said she was not in favor of violence; on the other, she said such acts had the "highest and noble motives."

It also must be considered that Goldman was under some pressure during the speech and unable to fully articulate her positions, for fear of action by official authorities.

"Miss Goldman did not hesitate to put forward a number of sentiments far more radical and sensational than any ever publicly advanced here," reported the *Chicago Daily Tribune*. "During Miss Goldman's lecture a strong detail of police was in the hall to keep her from uttering sentiments which were regarded as too radical. This accounts for the fact that the speaker did not give free rein to her thoughts on this occasion. By reason of anarchistic uprisings elsewhere it was thought best by the city officials to curb the utterances of the woman."[60]

But regardless of what her intended message was that day in Cleveland, what is important is how Czolgosz received it. He himself stated that the speech was a motivating factor in his decision to kill the President. And in reading the account, one can easily understand that acting rather than "idly standing by" would appeal to someone who so desperately wanted to do something noble for the cause, whatever he may have perceived that to be.

---

[58] *Cleveland Plain Dealer*, 7 May 1901.

[59] *Cleveland Plain Dealer*, 7 May 1901.

[60] *Chicago Daily Tribune,* 8 September 1901.

One thing that is also clear; Emma Goldman did not intentionally become a component in a plot to assassinate President McKinley. While she was certainly acquainted with Czolgosz, it could not be said that she knew him.

Later, in a letter, Goldman wrote, "I do not know whether Czolgosz was an anarchist, nor have I the right to say he was not. I have not known him sufficiently to be acquainted with his political views."[61]

After her speech, Leon worked his way through the crowd and met Goldman. She remembered seeing Czolgosz at the speech in her autobiography, *Living My Life.*

"The subject of my lecture in Cleveland, early in May of that year, was Anarchism, delivered before the Franklin Liberal Club, a radical organization," she wrote. "During the intermission before the discussion I noticed a man looking over the titles of the pamphlets and books on sale near the platform. Presently he came over to me with the question: 'Will you suggest something for me to read?' He was working in Akron, he explained, and he would have to leave before the close of the meeting."[62]

Czolgosz must have made a strong impression on Goldman, as she would remember him months later.

"He was a very young man, a mere youth, of medium height, well built, and carrying himself very erect," She wrote. "But it was his face that held me, a most sensitive face, with a delicate pink complexion; a handsome face, made doubly so by his curly golden hair. Strength showed in his large blue eyes. I made a selection of some books for him, remarking that I hoped he would find in them what he was seeking. I returned to the platform to open the discussion and I did not see the young man again that evening, but his striking face remained in my memory."[63]

During the evening, other high-ranking Anarchists started to talk to Czolgosz, trying to find out about him, and if they could use him or not.

On May 19, Czolgosz approached Emil Schilling, who was treasurer for a Cleveland based anarchist group called the Liberty Club, saying a friend named Hauser sent him. He used his alias, Fred Nieman.

---

[61] Dr. Walter Channing, *The Mental Status of Czolgosz* (Brookline, Mass: American Journal of Insanity, Vol. LIX, No. 2, 1902) 20.

[62] Emma Goldman, *Living My Life* (New York: Alfred Knopf, Inc.,1931) 289.

[63] Emma Goldman, *Living My Life* (New York: Alfred Knopf, Inc.,1931) 290.

Schilling met with him and gave him some printed material, including the book *Chicago Martyrs*.

Schilling later said that Czolgosz was seeking out anarchists and that his views seemed somewhat revolutionary. He told Schilling he had belonged to the 'Sila Club,' apparently a socialist organization, but that they had quarreled and he no longer belonged.

Schilling took Czolgosz home for dinner where he seemed like one of the family and sat down to eat like the rest, although he was characteristically very quiet.

"I thought he was all right this time when he called on me," Schilling said. "He did not talk German but English. Talked about his farm and said he lived in Bedford on a farm with his brother."[64]

About three weeks later, Czolgosz returned and asked Schilling if he knew of any secret societies, and that he had read in some capitalist papers that there were plots in the works, much as that of Gaetano Bresci.

"I said we do not do any plotting," explained Schilling. "He then asked if anarchists did not organize to act; that is if anybody do something against a king or officer and you was an anarchist, would you say you were an anarchist. I told him yes, for everyone knew I was an anarchist. When I answered him he was always laughing at my answers as if he either felt superior or had formed a plan and was putting out a feeler."[65]

Schilling, becoming suspicious that Czolgosz was a spy of some type, assured him that he did not read that in any of this literature. In fact, Schilling did not think that Czolgosz had even read the literature, based on future discussions with him.

"I think that Nieman wanted to be smart enough to find out something as a secret detective and I think that he was not smart enough to do what he wanted," said Schilling. "I think he was very ignorant. He asked his questions in a very quick way, such as 'say, have you any secret societies. I hear the anarchists are plotting something like Bresci; the man was selected by comrades to do the deed that was done.' I asked him, 'where did you read that?' He answered, 'in some capitalist paper,' 'well,' I said, 'you did not read it in any anarchist paper.'"[66]

---

[64] Dr. Walter Channing, *The Mental Status of Czolgosz* (Brookline, Mass: American Journal of Insanity, Vol. LIX, No. 2, 1902) 15.

[65] Dr. Walter Channing, *The Mental Status of Czolgosz* (Brookline, Mass: American Journal of Insanity, Vol. LIX, No. 2, 1902) 15.

[66] Dr. Walter Channing, *The Mental Status of Czolgosz* (Brookline, Mass: American Journal of Insanity, Vol. LIX, No. 2, 1902) 15-16.

During his second visit to Emil Schilling, Leon Czolgosz came during dinner and waited for Schilling to finish. He returned the book Schilling had loaned him and when Schilling asked how he had liked it, Leon told him that he had not had the time to read it.

"This made me mad and I was suspicious of him," Schilling said.

After dinner, the two men went out and Czolgosz refused to drink beer. He finally consented to a soft drink when they returned to Schilling's home.

"After his second visit, I visited Hauser and asked him about Nieman," explained Schilling. "He told me he was a good and active member of the Polish Socialist Society of the labor party but that his name was not Fred Nieman and he had forgotten his real name. I then told him my suspicions and Hauser said to watch out if I thought so."[67]

A week later, Czolgosz made another appearance at Schilling's home and talked to him about being tired of life. He talked about the abuse of his step-mother and when Schilling asked if his father would not step in, Czolgosz told him that he was "not of his own will, but was bound by the will of his stepmother." Schilling did not yet tell Czolgosz of his suspicions.[68]

Schilling described Czolgosz and the way he dressed, saying that he was "awful particular about the care for his body; his clothes always nice and clean. He had a red complexion; was healthy looking; a round face. I see on his hands he did not work much."[69]

On his third visit, Czolgosz asked Schilling to provide a letter of introduction to Emma Goldman, whom he said he had heard speak in Cleveland in May. Schilling, reluctant to do that, told Czolgosz that Goldman was currently in Chicago and that he could go there and meet her himself. Czolgosz gave Schilling the impression that he was very taken with Goldman and very much wanted an introduction. He went away, however, without a letter from Schilling.[70]

Leon Czolgosz visited Emil Schilling for the final time in August. Schilling was, at the time, reading a letter from Abraham Isaak of

---

[67] Dr. Walter Channing, *The Mental Status of Czolgosz* (Brookline, Mass: American Journal of Insanity, Vol. LIX, No. 2, 1902) 16.

[68] Dr. Walter Channing, *The Mental Status of Czolgosz* (Brookline, Mass: American Journal of Insanity, Vol. LIX, No. 2, 1902) 16.

[69] Dr. Walter Channing, *The Mental Status of Czolgosz* (Brookline, Mass: American Journal of Insanity, Vol. LIX, No. 2, 1902) 16.

[70] Dr. Walter Channing, *The Mental Status of Czolgosz* (Brookline, Mass: American Journal of Insanity, Vol. LIX, No. 2, 1902) 17.

Chicago, the editor of the anarchist paper *Free Society*, asking about a man named Nieman who had said he was a friend of his, when Czolgosz coincidentally suddenly appeared at his door.

"I was then suspicious and thought that the letter might have been opened in the post," commented Schilling. "I asked him where he had been all these two months. He said he was working in Akron in a cheese factory and then laughed. I thought as I catched him in a lie I would give him a chance once or twice more."

They took a walk with one of Schilling's friends and did not talk business and Czolgosz was very quiet. When they returned and as Czolgosz was preparing to leave, Schilling asked him where he would be going. Czolgosz told him maybe Detroit or Buffalo.[71]

During the spring of 1901, Czolgosz had badly wanted to get away from the farm and began demanding repayment of the four hundred dollars he had contributed to purchase it. He pressed for quite some time for the money and told Waldek, "If I cannot get my money now, I want it in the summer." He repeated this statement in July. Waldek asked him, "What do you want the money for?" They were standing in the street near a dying tree."

"Look," said Leon, "it is just the same as a tree that commences dying. You can see it isn't going to live long." Waldek understood that Leon was referring to himself.

Waldek pointed out that even if he went west, he would not be able to stay for long, as he did not have that much money. Leon told his brother that he could get a job as a conductor, binding wheat, fixing machines or doing something else. Waldek remembered that Leon had applied for a job as a conductor. This was the last time Waldek ever knew Leon to look for work.

Just before Leon finally left the family farm forever, he told Waldek he "had got to go away and must have the money."

Waldek answered, "Why you got to go so far? What is the matter with you?"

"I can't stand it any longer," was Leon's reply.[72]

It was Jacob's wife who advanced Leon a first payment of seventy dollars for his much anticipated and talked about "western trip." She

[71] Dr. Walter Channing, *The Mental Status of Czolgosz* (Brookline, Mass: American Journal of Insanity, Vol. LIX, No. 2, 1902) 16-17.
[72] Dr. Walter Channing, *The Mental Status of Czolgosz* (Brookline, Mass: American Journal of Insanity, Vol. LIX, No. 2, 1902) 9.

later recalled that he seemed very happy on that day and that he went upstairs, dressed in his best clothes and left with only the clothes on his back. He did not want his parents to know that he was leaving. He told his sister-in-law that he was off for Kansas. But he told his sister he was going to California for his health. Leon actually wrote his sister Victoria from Fort Wayne, Indiana about five days later, saying that he did not know where he would be going, that he hoped they were in good health and that he would write more later. Victoria destroyed the letter, thinking she would hear from him again. But she never did and was worried that he had died when she received the news he had shot the President of the United States.[73]

"Early in the summer he several times tried to borrow money from his brothers, and on July 1 my son Jake loaned him $70, which Leon claimed he wanted in order to pay his expenses to go out west," Paul Czolgosz said later through an interpreter. "The day after that Jake went on the farm to milk the cows and when he came back Leon was gone and none of us have seen him since. He had not said he was going away and we were at a loss to account for his disappearance. I do not know whether he received any letter or telegram asking him to leave."[74]

"A neighbor, Joseph Klima, received a postal card a few days afterwards from Leon, in which he stated he was on his way to the west," Leon's father continued. "Two of my sons received similar postcards. I do not remember where they were postmarked. After the receipt of the postals none of us received any further word, and Mr. Klima and the rest of us concluded that he was dead."[75]

From Ft. Wayne, Czolgosz went on to Chicago to see Emma Goldman again, who was working as the visiting editor of the *Free Society*. Czolgosz caught Goldman in Isaak's apartment on July 12, when she was literally on her way out of town, and had a train to catch.

"On the day of our departure the Isaaks gave me a farewell luncheon," Goldman later explained in her autobiography. "Afterwards, while I was busy packing my things, someone rang the bell. Mary Isaak came in to tell me that a young man, who gave his name as Nieman, was urgently asking to see me, I knew nobody by that name and I was in a hurry, about to leave for the station. Rather impatiently I requested Mary

---

[73] L. Vernon Briggs, *The Manner of Man That Kills* (Boston: R. G. Badger, Gorham Press, 1921) 294.

[74] *Cleveland Plain Dealer*, 8 September 1901, pg. 4, col. 2.

[75] *Cleveland Plain Dealer*, 8 September 1901, pg. 4, col. 3.

to inform the caller that I had no time at the moment, but that he could talk to me on my way to the station. As I left the house, I saw the visitor, recognizing him as the handsome chap of the golden hair who had asked me to recommend him reading-matter at the Cleveland meeting."[76]

She also later described the meeting to Police Chief O'Neill in Chicago, saying that she saw Czolgosz as she was getting ready to board the train. She he traveled with them as far as the Rock Island Depot, but that nothing else happened. She denied knowingly saying anything to him that would have led him to act. She said that she could not help what some "crack brain" person thought of what she said.[77]

On the way to the train station aboard Chicago's celebrated "elevated train," Czolgosz spoke to Goldman.

"Hanging on to the straps on the elevated train, Nieman told me that he had belonged to a Socialist local in Cleveland, that he had found its members dull, lacking in vision and enthusiasm," Goldman wrote. "He could not bear to be with them and he had left Cleveland and was now working in Chicago and eager to get in touch with anarchists."[78]

"Isaak and some other comrades were there to bid her goodbye," Schilling later related. "He introduced himself to Emma as a socialist from Cleveland; he had heard her speak and he was a friend of mine. Then Emma turned around and introduced him to Isaak and asked him if he was an anarchist. He said no, he was a socialist. Then he said he had not read any anarchist literature but *Free Society*."[79]

Goldman remembered it slightly differently when she wrote, "At the station I found my friends awaiting me, among them Max. I wanted to spend a few minutes with him and I begged Hippolyte to take care of Nieman and introduce him to the comrades."[80]

Abraham Isaak stated that on this occasion Emma Goldman "was simply introduced to Czolgosz without having any conversation with

---

[76] Emma Goldman, *Living My Life* (New York: Alfred Knopf, Inc.,1931) 290-291.

[77] A. Wesley Johns, The Man Who Shot McKinley (New York: A. S. Barnes and Co., Inc., 1970) 150.

[78] Emma Goldman, *Living My Life* (New York: Alfred Knopf, Inc., 1931) 290-291.

[79] Dr. Walter Channing, *The Mental Status of Czolgosz* (Brookline, Mass: American Journal of Insanity, Vol. LIX, No. 2, 1902) 18.

[80] Emma Goldman, *Living My Life* (New York: Alfred Knopf, Inc., 1931) 290-291.

him." After the train left with Goldman aboard, Isaak talked with Czolgosz for about forty minutes.

Czolgosz immediately asked Isaak about any "secret meetings" and addressed him as "comrade." As it did with Schilling, the question aroused Isaak's suspicions.

"After having told him that anarchists have no secret meetings, I asked him whether he call himself an anarchist and whether he had read anarchist literature," said Isaak.

Czolgosz told him that he knew nothing of anarchism other than the speech he had heard Goldman give in Cleveland and that he was a socialist.

"Altho' being suspicious I could not help thinking that his eyes and words expressed sincerity," remembered Isaak. "He was rather quiet. But the 'outrage committed by the American government in the Philippine Islands' seemed to trouble his mind. 'It does not harmonize with the teachings in our public schools about our flag,' he said."[81]

Far from being a confidant, Czolgosz was arousing suspicions among almost every anarchist with which he made contact, so much so that it prompted Isaak to write to Schilling asking about him. Isaak had his reservations about Czolgosz and he told Schilling this in his letter. Schilling himself already doubted Czolgosz's honesty and he told Isaak as much. Since both men seemed to have the same gut instinct, Schilling suggested Isaak warn other anarchists publicly about Czolgosz in *Free Society*.[82]

Later while in Chicago, Czolgosz visited Abraham Isaak and wanted money, explaining that was the only way he could stay, as his family was very poor. He was offered food but no money. Apparently disgusted, he immediately went away.

"Two comrades wanted to take him home for the night and turn his pockets taking any papers or information that they could get as to whether he was a spy or not," explained Schilling.[83]

"Czolgosz seemed to be normal and sound as the average man," commented Schilling upon reflection. "He might be excused as ignorant—not educated, or, as I had thought, a spy, a bad person. He

---

[81] Dr. Walter Channing, *The Mental Status of Czolgosz* (Brookline, Mass: American Journal of Insanity, Vol. LIX, No. 2, 1902) 18-19.

[82] Dr. Walter Channing, *The Mental Status of Czolgosz* (Brookline, Mass: American Journal of Insanity, Vol. LIX, No. 2, 1902) 18.

[83] Dr. Walter Channing, *The Mental Status of Czolgosz* (Brookline, Mass: American Journal of Insanity, Vol. LIX, No. 2, 1902) 17.

was consistent in his tactics; he did not give himself away. He was not against the President, but against the party, as he said the last minutes, and we thought from his education that he thought he could not leave the world without doing anything. After he done it, I assume he planned to do it some months before he done it, and only waited a good chance and hoped to get some help from friends."[84]

"During the past few years he has gained quite a reputation in Chicago, Cleveland, Detroit and other western cities as an Anarchist of the most bitter type," reported the *New York Times* a couple days after the shooting.[85] But Leon, by their own post assassination account, was obviously not accepted among the anarchists and he had only scant knowledge of anarchistic ideas.

After discovering that Czolgosz was using an alias, on September 1, 1901, only five days before the assassination, and at the urging of Schilling, Abraham Isaak did indeed issue a warning in *Free Society* regarding the strange character:

ATTENTION!
The attention of the comrades is called to another spy. He is well dressed, of medium height; rather narrow shouldered, blond, and about 25 years of age. Up to the present he has made his appearance in Chicago and Cleveland. In the former place he remained a short time, while in Cleveland he disappeared when the comrades had confirmed themselves of his identity and were on the point of exposing him. His demeanor is of the usual sort, pretending to be greatly interested in the cause, asking for names, or soliciting aid for acts of contemplated violence. If this individual makes his appearance elsewhere, the comrades are warned in advance and can act accordingly.

Emma Goldman was not at all pleased when she saw the warning in print.

"My holiday in Rochester was somewhat marred by a notice in *Free Society* containing a warning against Nieman," she wrote. "It was written by A. Isaak, editor of the paper, and it stated that news had been received from Cleveland that the man had been asking questions that aroused suspicion, and that he was trying to get into the anarchist circles.

[84] L. Vernon Briggs, *The Manner of Man That Kills* (Boston: R. G. Badger, Gorham Press, 1921) 320-321.
[85] *New York Times,* 8 September 1901, pg. 2, col. 1.

The comrades in Cleveland had concluded that he must be a spy.

"I was very angry. To make such a charge, on such flimsy ground! I wrote Isaak at once, demanding more convincing proofs. He replied that, while he had no other evidence, he still felt that Nieman was untrustworthy because he constantly talked about acts of violence. I wrote another protest. The next issue of *Free Society* contained a retraction."[86]

Later, Goldman wondered if that very warning in Free Society had unwittingly spurred Czolgosz to act more then her own words could have.

"Czolgosz must have read the charge," she wrote, "It must have hurt him to the quick to be so cruelly misjudged by the very people to whom he had come for inspiration. I recalled his eagerness to secure the right kind of books. It was apparent that he had sought in anarchism a solution of the wrongs he saw everywhere about him. No doubt it was that which had induced him to call on me and later on the Isaaks. Instead of finding help, the poor youth saw himself attacked. Was it that experience, fearfully wounding his spirit that had led to his act? There must also have been other causes, but perhaps his great urge had been to prove that he was sincere, that he felt with the oppressed, that he was no spy."[87]

Although it has been generally believed that Goldman was Czolgosz' sole influence for killing the President, she appeared, by Czolgosz' own statements, to be only part of that influence. Her importance to Czolgosz's reasons for committing the crime should not be over emphasized, notwithstanding what the assassin himself said.

"I know other men who believe what I do, that it would be a good thing to kill the President and to have no rulers," Czolgosz said in his first interview with police on September 7, hinting at these other influences. "I have heard that at the meetings in public halls. I heard quite a lot of people talk like that. Emma Goldman was the last one I heard. She said she did not believe in government or rulers. She said a good deal more. I don't remember all she said."[88]

---

[86] Emma Goldman, *Living My Life* (New York: Alfred Knopf, Inc., 1931) 291.

[87] Emma Goldman, *Living My Life* (New York: Alfred Knopf, Inc., 1931) 291.

[88] Dr. Walter Channing, *The Mental Status of Czolgosz* (Brookline, Mass: American Journal of Insanity, Vol. LIX, No. 2, 1902) 22-23.

His brother Joseph, when he later heard the news, did not at first believe that Leon had shot the President. During the time that Leon would leave the farm for two or three days at a time, Joseph did not know where he went, but he did not believe it was to be with anarchists.[89]

Regardless, many people in an organization to which he wanted so badly to become a part did now not trust Leon Czolgosz. They thought he was attempting to solicit their help in a plot of some kind which he had brewing. However, soon enough he realized he did not need anyone's help. Perhaps Czolgosz was already thinking about forming his own plan of action.

Schilling said that Czolgosz had told him that things were getting worse and worse; more and more strikes, which were being put down by increasing brutality. Czolgosz, watching closely the new American labor movement and its impact, said something had to be done.

"Then I did not think he had a plan," said Schilling. "Afterwards, I did."[90]

After his encounter with Goldman in Chicago, and after sending his family a letter from Fort Wayne, Indiana, Czolgosz landed in West Seneca, New York, a small town in the suburbs of Buffalo. He lived there in a boardinghouse that was connected to downtown by a trolley line with the family of Antoine Kazmarek, a track worker for Lake Shore Railroad.[91] He stayed until late August, unemployed the entire time.

Exactly why Czolgosz decided to move to Buffalo has always been a matter of interest and speculation. He could not have found out about McKinley's visit until early August when it was announced in the local Buffalo newspapers. However, the Presidential visit to the Exposition was common knowledge to anyone who read the papers. The exact date was the only thing not known.

There was a heavy concentration of Poles in the area, but that was not uncommon almost anywhere in the Midwest. If it was a job he was looking for, he apparently made no effort to find one, even though his money supply presumably could not last forever. It is more likely that he

---

[89] Dr. Walter Channing, *The Mental Status of Czolgosz* (Brookline, Mass: American Journal of Insanity, Vol. LIX, No. 2, 1902) 11.

[90] L. Vernon Briggs, *The Manner of Man That Kills* (Boston: R. G. Badger, Gorham Press, 1921) 321.

[91] A. Wesley Johns, *The Man Who Shot McKinley* (New York: A. S. Barnes and Co., Inc., 1970) 42.

chose the Buffalo area on a whim. Possibly the Pan American Exposition that was going on in the city had something to do with his decision.

At the boardinghouse in West Seneca, Czolgosz again used his alias of Fred C. Nieman and rented the room from Kazmarek, including laundry services, for three dollars a month, providing that he sleep with another tenant, a Pole who spoke no English. Later the man said that Czolgosz slept well, occasionally getting up in the night and immediately returning. Apparently, Czolgosz slept normally.[92]

Czolgosz continued his custom of living primarily on milk and crackers and always ate alone, usually in the front of the house at a counter. Even when invited, he refused to join the others for dinner, at one time saying he did not wish to eat with "those fellows," referring to the other borders. Characteristically, he avoided conversation with the family and stayed to himself.

Kazmarek said that Czolgosz "washed very carefully, dressed neatly— would come downstairs, stand before the glass for a minute or two, looking at himself first on one side then on the other." He said he normally took a walk in the mornings, and upon returning would sit on the piazza, chair tipped back, reading pamphlets and papers. In the afternoon he would hire a boy to bring him another paper, which he would then read very carefully, retiring about ten in the evening.[93]

While in West Seneca on July 30, Leon sent a note to John Ginder, a brother in his lodge. It read, "Inclosed you will find $1 to pay my lodge dues. I paid $1 to Brother George Coonish to pay the assessment sent out on account of the death of Brother David Jones. Brother Ginder, please send my book to me at my cost, and also send password if you can do so. I left Cleveland Thursday, July 11. I am working here and will stay for some time. The fare from here to Buffalo is $5.15. Hoping this finds you well, as it leaves me, I remain—Fred C. Nieman"[94]

The statement about Buffalo seems strangely out of place. But it is known that two or three times a week, Czolgosz dressed up in his best clothes and made the trip to Buffalo, he said to attend meetings. He would leave early in the morning and return about ten or ten-thirty at night.

---

[92] L. Vernon Briggs, *The Manner of Man That Kills* (Boston: R. G. Badger, Gorham Press, 1921) 245-275-276.

[93] L. Vernon Briggs, *The Manner of Man That Kills* (Boston: R. G. Badger, Gorham Press, 1921) 276.

[94] Marshall Everett, *The Complete Life of William McKinley* (Privately Published, 1901) 75.

On August 29, Czolgosz suddenly left West Seneca, seemingly in good spirits, hiring a little boy to carry his trunk and claiming that he was unable to pay the $1.75 rent he owed. To make restitution to the landlord, he gave him a broken revolver.[95] Kazmarek asked Czolgosz where he would be going, and was told Detroit, Toledo, Cleveland or Baltimore—maybe Pittsburgh.[96] When or where Leon had obtained his gun is a mystery. But he was not broke, as later he purchased the revolver he would use in the assassination at a shop on Main Street in Buffalo for four dollars and fifty cents.

Kazmarek thought Leon a rather strange man and wondered how he got along without having to work. Leon had told him he worked in the winter and lived the rest of the time on what he had earned. The Kazmarek family had never expected Leon to leave so suddenly, as he never said anything that would indicate he was contemplating a move.[97]

Another report had Czolgosz living at the house of Joe Martin in West Seneca. This report says that he often had "money to settle" and the last three weeks he stayed there, he began to go into Buffalo almost every day.

Mr. Hoener, a hotel proprietor, and a young man who worked in the hotel barbershop said that Czolgosz hung around the hotel and that he had at least two different men visit him. One was a man about 5-8 who wore a long black coat and soft hat. The other, who saw Czolgosz at least twice, was about 5-9, heavy set and wore a heavy black mustache. He called at least twice. No one could remember seeing Czolgosz with any women.

Before Czolgosz supposedly left Martin's place, he went to a Pole who ran a boarding house in a section of West Seneca called "the lots." He tried to get a room there but the boarding house was full.[98]

The above account is from the fast and loose *Buffalo Courier*. The account also claims that Czolgosz gave "Martin" the revolver to pay the rent he owed when he left. It seems probable that this was Kazmarek, but it is not known where the name "Martin" came from or if indeed these were two different men. The newspaper also claimed to have found another Czolgosz alias; Frank Snider.

[95] Dr. Walter Channing, *The Mental Status of Czolgosz* (Brookline, Mass: American Journal of Insanity, Vol. LIX, No. 2, 1902) 21.

[96] L. Vernon Briggs, *The Manner of Man That Kills* (Boston: R. G. Badger, Gorham Press, 1921) 277.

[97] L. Vernon Briggs, *The Manner of Man That Kills* (Boston: R. G. Badger, Gorham Press, 1921) 278.

[98] *Buffalo Courier*, 20 September 1901, pg. 7, col. 2.

The night he left West Seneca, Czolgosz took a boat to Cleveland, where he stayed for a day, supposedly sight seeing and reading the newspapers. He returned to Buffalo on August 31. He may have visited Schilling during this trip, but that is far from certain. It has been speculated that he may have returned to Cleveland to secure funds. If he did not have the money to pay his rent in West Seneca, he suddenly came into some money by the time he arrived in Buffalo.

One person came forward to shed light on one place Czolgosz could have gotten some money. Cecil Hooke, a member of the Pan American Exposition Exhibitors Center, said that Czolgosz had worked for him that summer. Hooke said that he found out very quickly that Czolgosz was no carpenter. He stated that his young son had identified Czolgosz from a photograph in the newspaper. He said that Czolgosz was the man who had worked for him for two or three weeks and then disappeared.[99]

When Czolgosz arrived in Buffalo, he rented a two-dollar a week room over John Nowak's Station, at 1078 Broadway, a Raines Law Hotel in the downtown area. The owner, John Nowak, was a politician and a known leader of the Polish people in the area.[100] One account has Czolgosz oddly using the alias of John Doe.[101] Another said he used his usual alias of Fred C. Nieman and even provided a reference to Nowak upon request.[102] Actually, Czolgosz used both, signing in at the desk and telling John Nowak he was John Doe, then explaining to hotel clerk Frank Walkowiak, when asked his real name, that it was Fred Nieman.

Walkowiak said later that he had asked Czolgosz about the use of John Doe. He related Czolgosz's response, claiming Leon had told him that he had used it to avoid discrimination because he was Polish. He feared he would not be able to rent a room if it were known, he said. When asked his real name, he said it was Nieman. He told Walkowiak that he was going to make some money by selling souvenirs at the Exposition. He also said that he had been to church and that he had heard a sermon saying that if God did not care about the world for five minutes that everything would go to damnation, claimed Walkowiak.[103]

---

[99] A. Wesley Johns, *The Man Who Shot McKinley* (New York: A. S. Barnes and Co., Inc., 1970) 151.

[100] A. Wesley Johns, *The Man Who Shot McKinley* (New York: A. S. Barnes and Co., Inc., 1970) 122.

[101] Robert J. Donovan, *The Assassins* (New York: Harper & Brothers, 1952) 100.

[102] Dr. Walter Channing, *The Mental Status of Czolgosz* (Brookline, Mass: American Journal of Insanity, Vol. LIX, No. 2, 1902) 21.

[103] A. Wesley Johns, *The Man Who Shot McKinley* (New York: A. S. Barnes & Co., Inc., 1970) 136.

When Czolgosz had been asked for a reference, he had said that a Dalkowski of Toledo had told him me to come there. He said he had left the preceding night. Nowak knew that to be true and assumed Czolgosz was a friend of Dalkowski's. But when Nowak later wrote to Dalkowski about him, Dalkowski replied that he knew no Nieman or Czolgosz.[104]

While at Nowak's, Czolgosz talked little and was a model tenant, coming and going with little bother. He was somewhat of an enigma to the Nowaks, and Mrs. Nowak thought he must be a barber or a waiter because he dressed so neatly. Czolgosz kept regular hours, leaving at seven in the morning and returning about ten thirty, retiring immediately. They did not know where he ate. Only one time did he come home early and on that night, a Sunday, he sat in the hotel saloon. Czolgosz was drawn into a conversation about priests and said that he had been to St. Casimir's on Sunday and that "all the priests talked about was money."[105]

John Romantowski, a 31-year-old widower who lived at 144 Sycamore Street nearby and occasionally visited the saloon, had a conversation with Czolgosz in the vicinity of Fillmore and Broadway. Czolgosz asked Romantowski to have a drink and the pair went to Gressner's saloon, which was located on a corner. Romantowski claimed that Czolgosz showed him a roll of bills, at least one being a fifty.[106]

Czolgosz also talked to barber Joseph Rutkowski about Socialism while being shaved. Rutkowski described Czolgosz as being very quiet and rational; a cigar smoker who was always sober and spoke intelligently. Czolgosz never gave his name, Rutkowski claimed, but Leon asked him about Socialists in Buffalo. Czolgosz told Rutkowski that he didn't believe in Socialism.[107]

Czolgosz awoke another tenant, retired German army officer Alphonse Stutz, one morning in search of a pitcher of water. Stutz thought him a pest.[108]

---

[104] L. Vernon Briggs, *The Manner of Man That Kills* (Boston: R. G. Badger, Gorham Press, 1921) 278.

[105] L. Vernon Briggs, *The Manner of Man That Kills* (Boston: R. G. Badger, Gorham Press, 1921) 279.

[106] A. Wesley Johns, *The Man Who Shot McKinley* (New York: A. S. Barnes & Co., Inc., 1970) 136-137.

[107] A. Wesley Johns, *The Man Who Shot McKinley* (New York: A. S. Barnes & Co., Inc., 1970) 137.

[108] A. Wesley Johns, *The Man Who Shot McKinley* (New York: A. S. Barnes & Co., Inc., 1970) 30-31.

Later, Stutz was held in custody for three days for suspicion of complicity in the assassination attempt, and was released on September 8. He threatened to seek damages for false imprisonment. He said that he had told the truth and produced his credentials when he was first arrested, but the police had refused to believe him. He claimed to have seen Czolgosz at Nowak's but said he had not spoken with him.[109]

"We are satisfied the Stutz did not even know Czolgosz and that he had nothing to do with the crime," said Buffalo Police Chief Bull, after Stutz' release. "He arrived here the day Czolgosz did and roomed near him. We rounded him up with several others whom we believed might have been implicated. We found a pair of brass knuckles on him and as that was an offense we held him for it."[110]

One account said Czolgosz asked John Nowak the night before he went to the exposition about the President's visit, where exactly he would be and how long he would stay. Nowak, supposedly told him all he knew about it.[111]

News of Leon's deed reached the Czolgosz household on the morning of September 7. Jake ran to a local store for a copy of a newspaper. The entire family could not believe it.

"My God! That is my brother!," exclaimed Jake, after seeing the front page. "How could he do it?"

"I can't think it of Leon," was his father's reaction, as he paced the floor.[112]

Jake told the *Cleveland Plain Dealer*, "I don't know what to say—we have not seen Leon for several months. He always was a timid lad and we never would have suspected him of doing such a thing as this. I suppose the people think we had something to do with it, but they surely cannot blame us. Leon never acted like an Anarchist. He never talked to us about such things."[113]

Jake was asked if Leon was crazy.

"Oh, no! He was no more than I am," he replied. "He was peculiar in many ways, but he was not crazy. He never mingled with the rest of the family, or talked to us much so that we knew little of his doings."[114]

---

[109] *New York Times*, 11 September 1901, pg. 2, col. 4.

[110] *Buffalo Evening News*, 8 September 1901, pg. 3, col. 2.

[111] Marshall Everett, *The Complete Life of William McKinley* (Privately Published, 1901) 66.

[112] *Cleveland Plain Dealer,* 7 September 1901, pg. 4, col. 1.

[113] *Cleveland Plain Dealer,* 7 September 1901, pg. 4, col. 1.

[114] *Cleveland Plain Dealer,* 7 September 1901, pg. 4, col. 1.

Leon's stepmother Catarina, bitter to the end, told reporters, "I always thought Leon was crazy. He was never like an ordinary boy. He was timid, a regular coward. He must have been crazy or he never would have tried anything like this."[115]

"Now Paul will never get any work," she exclaimed. "People will point at him and say his son killed McKinley, and no one will have anything to do with him. Oh! It is awful!"[116]

Paul Czolgosz talked of the crime, saying his son should be hanged and that there was no excuse for the crime. At first, the enormity of the crime was not understood by the assassin's father, but once he understood what his son had done, he declared that he must have been mad.[117]

After his arrest, Czolgosz seemed to be more concerned about his personal appearance than with the plight in which he found himself. His guards thought him vain. When he asked for anything that first night in jail, it was only for a chance to clean himself up and get a change of clothes. His nose and face had been bruised and cut during the scuffle back at the Temple of Music, and blood had dripped down onto his torn clothing.[118]

Czolgosz conducted himself very calmly during his first night in captivity, even while authorities were soliciting his confession. In fact, he told detectives only what he wanted to tell them, and did so in a very cool, even braggadocio way.[119]

The morning of September 7, Czolgosz asked to see the newspapers. Denied this, he lay down on a bench and went to sleep.[120] Czolgosz was then submitted to about six hours of questioning and was reportedly tired out when he was finally returned to his cell for the night.[121]

Czolgosz had wanted a change of clothes, and finally he was told a guard could get him clean linen if he would pay for it. Czolgosz gave them all the money he had on him, about a dollar, and when given the clothes, disputed the change. He was then told the cost of each item and he finally gave up, saying, "Oh that's all right. Let it go." [122]

[115] *Cleveland Plain Dealer,* 7 September 1901, pg. 4, col. 1.

[116] *Cleveland Plain Dealer,* 7 September 1901, pg. 4, col. 3.

[117] Marshall Everett, *The Complete Life of William McKinley* (Privately Published, 1901) 73.

[118] *New York Times,* 8 September 1901, pg. 2, col. 1.

[119] *New York Times,* 8 September 1901, pg. 2, col. 1.

[120] *New York Times,* 8 September 1901, pg. 2, col. 1.

[121] *New York Times,* 8 September 1901, pg. 2, col. 1.

[122] L. Vernon Briggs, *The Manner of Man That Kills* (Boston: R. G. Badger, Gorham Press, 1921) 267.

Czolgosz told detectives during that first session that he did not believe in the Republican form of government and didn't believe the people should have rulers.

"It is right to kill them," he is quoted by detectives as saying. "I had that idea when I shot the President, and that is why I was there. I planned killing the President 3 or 4 days ago after I came to Buffalo. Something I read in *Free Society* suggested the idea. I thought it would be a good thing for the country to kill the President." [123]

Czolgosz then described the actual shooting: "My gun was in my right pocket with a handkerchief over it. I put my hand in my pocket after I got in the door, took out the gun and wrapped my handkerchief over my hand. I carried it in that way in the row until I got to the President; no one saw me do it. I did not shake hands with him. I shot twice. I don't know whether I would have shot again." [124]

Later in his cell, Czolgosz would often take his handkerchief out of his pocket and wrap it around his right hand, as he had done in the Temple of Music. He demonstrated his apparently well practiced technique to the detectives, and his guards would see him doing the same thing in his cell, apparently deep in thought. After he was arrested, Chief Bull asked him to demonstrate and Czolgosz refused until a clean handkerchief could be produced. He then demonstrated freely.[125]

Czolgosz also pointed out during questioning that he did not want to shoot McKinley at Niagara Falls, that "it was my plan from the beginning to shoot him at the Temple. I read in the paper that he would have a public reception.

"After I shot twice they knocked me down and trampled on me. Somebody hit me in the face. I said to the officer that brought me down, ' I done my duty.'

"I fully understood what I was doing when I shot the President," he explained. "I realized that I was sacrificing my life. I am willing to take the consequences.

[123] Dr. Walter Channing, *The Mental Status of Czolgosz* (Brookline, Mass: American Journal of Insanity, Vol. LIX, No. 2, 1902) 22.

[124] Dr. Walter Channing, *The Mental Status of Czolgosz* (Brookline, Mass: American Journal of Insanity, Vol. LIX, No. 2, 1902) 22.

[125] L. Vernon Briggs, *The Manner of Man That Kills* (Boston: R. G. Badger, Gorham Press, 1921) 267.

"I know what will happen to me," he continued, " If the President dies I will be hung. I want to say to be published—I killed President McKinley because I done my duty. I don't believe in one man having so much service, and another man should have none."[126]

Detectives also focused extensively on getting names of other co-conspirators whom they felt surely existed. They questioned him intensely about his time in Buffalo prior to the shooting, starting with his arrival. They also particularly tried to tie him to known Socialists living in the Buffalo area, but were unable to make any connection. By nightfall, they had pretty much given up on that angle. They also continued to maintain a theory that Czolgosz had an accomplice in line, preceding him on his approach to the President. In spite of Czolgosz's denial and the lack of evidence to support it, they refused to abandon that notion.

John F. von Muegge was a deputy U. S. Marshall from Chillicothe, Ohio, and happened to be visiting the Exposition at the time of the shooting. He was standing within ten yards of the President and prior to the shooting his attention had been gained by two individuals in line in behind Czolgosz. He thought they looked suspicious. After the shots were fired, he looked for the men. He could not find them. The Marshall thought these men were accomplices and that if Czolgosz had been unable to do the shooting, they were in reserve to carry it out.[127]

At least one other man claimed to have seen Czolgosz in the company of two other men at the Exposition. R. L. Munn, an employee in the Liberal Arts Building, said he saw Czolgosz and the two men in the stadium, the night before the President's appearance there. A police officer moved them along by waving his club. A moment later, the officer came over to where Munn was standing.

"It's a wonder you don't fire me out, too," Munn told him.

"I don't suppose I have any right to fire anybody out," confided the officer. "but those fellows are up to some devilment. They have been in here for twenty minutes and whenever I came near them they stopped talking."

Munn saw the men after he left the stadium and got a good look at them.

"Today and yesterday, I have seen many good pictures of Czolgosz and am perfectly positive that he was one of the three," said Munn. "I got a good square look at him and if he looks like his pictures it was

[126] Dr. Walter Channing, *The Mental Status of Czolgosz* (Brookline, Mass: American Journal of Insanity, Vol. LIX, No. 2, 1902) 23.

[127] *Buffalo Express,* 10 September 1901.

Czolgosz whom I saw. The others were shorter men, older and heavier set. The one had on a derby hat, had a black mustache and heavy eyebrows and looked as if he had been just fresh shaved and the powder left on his face. He was so white it made his hair and mustache look darker, I guess. The other was a dark, curly-haired fellow with a loose dirty coat over a dark shirt and a cap or a small hat on his head.

"I did not stop to see what they did or where they went, but now I wish I had," said Munn. "I did not hear anything they said."[128]

Strangely, the description of one of the men matched that of the man described by Ireland at the assassination scene. Still, it must be remembered that the description of the man had been published in the papers.

The consensus among the detectives was that Czolgosz was not shrewd enough to have properly planned the crime alone and that he had accomplices in the attack on the President. Never mind the fact that Czolgosz simply concealed the gun, walked right up to the President and fired before any security guard could do anything. It would not appear a lot of shrewdness would have been necessary. Still, the detectives concentrated heavily on all known associates, in particular those with any anarchistic leanings. The detectives felt certain that among these people, the co-conspirators, thus the planners of the crime, would be found.[129]

In an effort to connect Chicago anarchists with the assassin, Czolgosz's coat was sent there by the Secret Service to see if it had been made in a shop near Abraham Isaac.[130] (The Chicago anarchists will be discussed in Chapter 5).

The police looked for anything that could be perceived as evidence. Buffalo Detective Albert Solomon found a bottle of cod liver oil in Czolgosz' room. He thought it best to turn it over. Soon a theory emerged that Czolgosz has stolen it from a barbershop, thinking it was glycerin, which he could easily make into a bomb.[131] Much more likely, this was simply a remedy for one of Czolgosz' real or imagined ailments.

One enterprising reporter from the *Buffalo Evening News* was successful in getting into the basement of the jail where Czolgosz was being held in cell number 21.

---

[128] *Buffalo Courier*, 11 September, 1901.

[129] *New York Times,* 8 September 1901, pg. 2, col. 1.

[130] *Buffalo Commercial,* 10 September 1901.

[131] *Buffalo Commercial,* 10 September 1901.

"I am sorry I did not kill him," Czolgosz was reported to have said. "I intended to kill him. I thought of doing it in Cleveland during the G. A. R. encampment, but my mother lives there and I did not want the muss there."[132] Considering strained relationship with his stepmother, this account seems to be complete fantasy.

Another reporter said he saw Czolgosz lying in his cell. When the prisoner saw him he got up and stretched.

"How do you feel about it now?" asked the reporter.

"Well, they're pretty stiff yet but they'll get alright," Czolgosz replied, apparently misunderstanding the question.

"I mean how do you feel about the shooting?" the reporter pressed.

Czolgosz smiled and asked, "What's that?" The reporter repeated the question and Czolgosz only laughed. "Some other time," he said.[133]

"That man is by long odds the most unconcerned prisoner I have ever had behind bars," said Police Captain Regan. "He will talk, no doubt, of his crime, but I believe that he will never go to pieces physically. Why, there is a man about his age, who occupies a cell not fare from Czolgosz's, and who was arrested for stealing a bicycle. That bicycle thief is all broken up over his crime, while the man who tried to murder the President is as unconcerned as possible."[134]

Curious citizens would occasionally try to see the prisoner. One fellow with long hair came to the jail with his camera, wanting to take a photograph of Czolgosz. He was denied permission, to which he was incredulous.

"But I insist upon it," he told the officer. "I simply must have a picture of him to take back home with me. How strange that one can't see the prisoner and take a photograph."[135]

Many witnesses were paraded in to confront Czolgosz in Bull's office, but not much new was learned. Walter Nowak, a cigar manufacturer from Cleveland (other reports New York) who had known Czolgosz for four years, was brought in by Detective Frank Koehler to see Czolgosz.

[132] *Buffalo Evening News*, 9 September 1901.

[133] *Buffalo Express*, 8 September 1901.

[134] *Buffalo Commercial*, 9 September, 1901.

[135] *Buffalo Express*, 9 September 1901.

"I knew Czolgosz in Cleveland," Nowak said. "He belonged to several secret societies and one of them was Anarchistic. I think the idea of assassination had been turning in his mind for some time, as that sort of business is what is taught in the anarchistic society in which he belongs. He is well known in Cleveland, Chicago, and other Western cities, where he has talked his doctrine."[136]

Nowak told police he was staying on Broadway, near Fillmore, not far from where Czolgosz was boarding, but that he had not seen Czolgosz since he had been in Buffalo. He said that he had known Czolgosz in Cleveland and that Leon had formed a social organization that later developed into a socialist organization. Nowak said that he remembered many radical resolutions being proposed and he withdrew from the club. He added, perhaps conveniently, that Czolgosz, in his opinion, did not have the intelligence to plan the crime alone.[137]

"I believe Emma Goldman put Czolgosz up to this fearful act," Nowak said. "I know him well enough to believe that alone he was incapable of directing any such plot."[138]

Supposedly, upon coming face to face with his former friend, Nowak was reported to have refused to shake hands, called him a scoundrel and asked him who had planned the crime, saying he knew he did not do it alone. Czolgosz insisted again that he had indeed acted alone.[139]

"Who told you to commit this crime," asked Nowak angrily.

"No one: I conceived it myself. No on else is guilty," was Czolgosz' reply.

"I know better," Nowak challenged. "You were selected to do this by your organization."

"That is not so."

"Why did you shoot the President?" Nowak pressed.

"It was my duty," came the standard reply.[140]

Apart from the local police having Czolgosz in custody, they had little to do with the ascertaining of what instigated the crime, and what confederates, if any, he had in planning it. The War Department and Secret Service Bureau practically took the work right out of the local authorities hands and the investigation in both Buffalo and elsewhere, was placed under federal "supervision."[141]

---

[136] *Buffalo Evening News,* 7 September 1901, pg. 8, col. 4.

[137] *New York Times,* 8 September 1901, pg. 2, col. 2.

[138] *Buffalo Evening News,* 7 September 1901, pg. 8, col. 5.

[139] *New York Times,* 8 September 1901, pg. 2, col. 2.

[140] *Buffalo Commercial,* 7 September 1901.

[141] *New York Times,* 8 September 1901, pg. 2, col. 1.

Not until after the assassination of President Kennedy sixty-two years later was the killing of a President of the United States made a federal crime. Assaults on the President were still, legally, to be handled by local authorities in the jurisdiction in which the crime occurred. Thus, the trial of Czolgosz would be held in New York State.

Meanwhile, the press was clamoring for information about the investigation.

"In order that people will not be unduly and improperly excited, Secretary of War Root has asked that this matter be treated as quietly as possible," said District Attorney Penney. "The making of a hero of this man with certain classes or the bitter condemnation of him will tend to disturb the people and Mr. Root's idea is to curb that. We will therefore not make public the confession made by the prisoner, nor will we permit anyone other than officials or witnesses to see the prisoner. We fully appreciate the suggestion of Mr. Root and will do all we can to carry it out. There is always an inclination to overplay a man of the character of the prisoner, and we will do what we can to check it in this case."[142]

On September 8, the questioning continued with Czolgosz, described as "not nervous or excited," telling police of his trip to Cleveland "to look around and buy a paper."[143]

"During his examination; the prisoner was very indignant because his clothing was soiled at the time of his arrest; he had not had the opportunity to care for his clothing and person as he wished... He said he would have slept well last night but for the noise of people walking about. He heard several drunken people brought into the station at night. Said he felt no remorse for the crime he had committed. Said he supposed he would be punished, but that every man had a chance on trial; that perhaps he wouldn't be so badly punished after all."[144]

Again and again, officials made their way to Czolgosz's cell, but he would tell them little.

"He is an obstinate, sneering, supercilious sort of a wretch who now seems to glory more than ever in his heinous crime and resists all their blandishments," objectively reported the *New York Times*.[145]

---

[142] *Cleveland Plain Dealer*, 7 September 1901, pg. 2, col. 2.

[143] Dr. Walter Channing, *The Mental Status of Czolgosz* (Brookline, Mass: American Journal of Insanity, Vol. LIX, No. 2, 1902) 23.

[144] Dr. Walter Channing, *The Mental Status of Czolgosz* (Brookline, Mass: American Journal of Insanity, Vol. LIX, No. 2, 1902) 23.

[145] *New York Times*, 9 September 1901, pg. 1, col. 7.

Indeed, Buffalo police were having a difficult time getting any information from Czolgosz; or at least, it was not information to their liking. They had arrested almost everyone who had been unfortunate to even meet Czolgosz during his Buffalo stay. But they were slowly becoming convinced that Czolgosz had no local confederates. To get more from him, they even staged a tricky incident to extort more information.

The plumbing in Czolgosz's cell was deliberately broken so that a detective, disguised as a plumber, could have a few minutes alone with the assassin, in the hopes of getting more information. The detective told a suspicious Czolgosz that he too was an anarchist and that he gloried in the killing of the President. At this point, Czolgosz believed McKinley to be dead. The detective did seem to somewhat gain the confidence of Czolgosz, but while speaking of himself, Czolgosz did not implicate anyone else.

"No, I did it myself," he told the detective. "I simply did my duty. There was no conspiracy. I planned it and did it myself."[146]

On the next day of questioning, September 9, detectives noticed a sudden and marked change in Czolgosz's attitude towards the interrogation. He now denied that he killed McKinley or even meant to kill him. He refused to answer their questions and seemed decidedly more guarded.

"He persisted in this course until nearly the end of the interview, then he said, 'I'm glad I did it.'" [147]

During the early part of the questioning, Czolgosz repeated his story of Friday's events with the police concentrating on extracting from the prisoner a list of his accomplices. Czolgosz's story, however was unshakable. At times, Czolgosz would correct his statements as taken by police, so as to make them have the exact meaning he wished to express.

Czolgosz would never again discuss in depth the assassination, and generally refused to answer questions except for ones about his condition, food, sleep and other such topics. His guards reported that he had a good appetite, talked to them freely and enjoyed taking walks in the corridor of the jail outside his cell. He said he did not like lawyers and would not talk to his; that he did not believe in them and did not want them.[148]

---

[146] *New York Times*, 9 September 1901, pg. 1, col. 7.

[147] Dr. Walter Channing, *The Mental Status of Czolgosz* (Brookline, Mass: American Journal of Insanity, Vol. LIX, No. 2, 1902) 23.

[148] Dr. Walter Channing, *The Mental Status of Czolgosz* (Brookline, Mass: American Journal of Insanity, Vol. LIX, No. 2, 1902) 24.

He walked in his cell most of the morning, asking a guard to hang his coat and vest outside his cell. Czolgosz told one guard that he was a great smoker. He said that someone had offered him a cigarette, but that he didn't smoke them. The guard then asked him if he had heard from his family. He answered that he had not and that he thought they were probably afraid.[149]

A reporter from the *Buffalo Courier* claimed to have seen Czolgosz in his cell during this time. He asked Czolgosz if he knew that the President would live. Czolgosz did not answer. After a few questions, Czolgosz finally responded.

"The police appear to know more about this than I do," he said sarcastically. "Very well; let them go ahead. They have me, they know I tried to kill McKinley. Yes, I have told them all that, but now they want me to tell them more. Let them be satisfied with me."

"But they want to find those who forced you to shoot the President," said the reporter.

"No one forced me," he said curtly. "I shot him because I wanted to. But I won't say anymore."

As the reporter left, he asked him, "You know there will be another President if McKinley dies?"

"Yes," came the reply as Czolgosz turned to his questioner, "but there will be the same medicine for all of them. This form of government is wrong. All men should be equal, no better than the other. I have offered my life to the cause and I guess there are others who are just as willing."

The reporter found Czolgosz much better looking than his pictures indicated and thought that while Czolgosz was not particularly proud of what he had done, he did seem satisfied and had no real hope that the President should die.[150]

"On his miserable hard bench he lies all day and night, stretched his full length, his face down, his head buried in his uplifted and folded arms in the dark corner of the cell," was how the *Buffalo Courier* described the prisoner's behavior. "Now and then there is a sign of anguish, a moan as though remorse was his sole companion, and once in a long while he will raise his head, shift it to one side, and in one of the most agonizing tones, cry: 'Oh, my God.' His guards fear that unless some variety be injected in his cell life, he will become insane."[151]

---

[149] A. Wesley Johns, The Man Who Shot McKinley (New York: A. S. Barnes and Co., Inc., 1970) 150-151.

[150] *Buffalo Courier*, 9 September 1901, pg. 3, col. 1.

[151] *Buffalo Courier*, 12 September 1901, pg. 4, col. 1-2.

Yet, in the same newspaper, there is a contradictory report of mental state. Superintendent Bull was asked if Czolgosz was weakening.

"No, I don't think he is," replied Bull. "He seems to keep his nerve right up. He is a remarkable man in some ways. He is bright and shrewd and well versed in the political situation throughout the world."

While some reports were saying Czolgosz was refusing to eat, Bull had a different story.

"He seems to be having it (his appetite) right with him," Bull said. "We are feeding him well and there is no reason why we should not. We are giving him smoking tobacco, too. He seems to be a heavy smoker and I think he should have a cigar when he wants one. It would do no good to starve him or to keep smoking from him."[152]

"The police are amused at a statement in a morning paper that Czolgosz is a mental and physical wreck," commented the *Buffalo Evening News* concerning the *Courier* reports.

"The statement is absolutely absurd," one of Czolgosz's guards responded. "Why he eats like a prizefighter training for a battle. He talks as unconcernedly as one of the most sane men in Buffalo. He is in good physical condition, as any person can see who takes one glance at him.

"The long cross examinations that he has been subjected to by the District Attorney do not seem to worry him a bit, so far as we are able to learn," the official continued. "Every time he comes back to his cell after being subjected to an examination lasting an hour or two, he has a smile on his face. He is healthy, physically, as any man at Police Headquarters."[153]

Detective John Geary was asked by a reporter if he thought Czolgosz acted as if he was insane.

"He may be but from what I saw of him he is just an anarchist," Geary replied. "Not crazy to all outward appearances and his actions and speech show him to be sane, as far as I can see."[154]

"During his stay at Police Headquarters there was no time when he exhibited any symptom of insanity," Police Chief Bull agreed.[155]

In the evening hours, Dr. Floyd S. Crego and Dr. Joseph Fowler, two alienists who were brought in to determine whether Czolgosz was sane, interviewed the assassin. The doctors spent about a half-hour with

---

[152] *Buffalo Courier*, 11 September 1901, pg. 4, col. 2.

[153] *Buffalo Evening News*, 9 September 1901, pg. 4, col. 2.

[154] *Buffalo Express*, 7 September 1901.

[155] *Buffalo Courier*, 18 September 1901.

Czolgosz, after which they would make no statement to the public, other than to firmly assert that Czolgosz was sane.

In the evening, at about 11:00, Czolgosz developed a nosebleed, but after lying down, it seemed to get better.[156]

At this time, it must be remembered, the President was still very much alive. Authorities toyed with ideas of exactly how to prosecute Czolgosz and for what. Most felt that the worst thing Czolgosz could be charged with was assault in the first degree, which carried a maximum penalty of ten years. Some thought it could be said that Czolgosz assaulted the President twice, once with each bullet he fired. They added in supposed assaults upon those who pounced on him immediately after the shots. In that way, they hoped to pile up concurrent sentences, which would, in effect, amount to a life sentence. But in all probability, had McKinley survived, Czolgosz would have been charged with a single charge of assault and been sentenced to the full ten years.

Reporters continued to periodically interview the parents and relatives of Leon Czolgosz. His stepmother spoke freely to reporters, through an interpreter, since she herself did not speak English.

"Leon left home about sixty days ago," she related. "We heard from him a few weeks ago. He was then in Indiana and wrote to us that he was going away, stating that in all probability we would not see him again."[157]

His stepmother, Catarina, denied that Leon was a disciple of Emma Goldman or in any way interested in her doctrines. She claimed that he was not intelligent enough to understand them. She had always considered the boy partially demented.

"I cannot believe that Leon is the one," she said, referring to the one who shot the President. "He was such a timid boy, so afraid of everything. Why he was the biggest coward you ever saw in your life."[158]

As she spoke, the newspaper reported, she "failed to show any decided emotion when confronted with the account of Leon's horrible crime."[159] Little wonder, considering their strained relationship.

---

[156] L. Vernon Briggs, *The Manner of Man That Kills* (Boston: R. G. Badger, Gorham Press, 1921) 270.

[157] *New York Times,* 8 September 1901, pg.4, col.5.

[158] *New York Times,* 8 September 1901, pg.4, col.5.

[159] *New York Times,* 8 September 1901, pg.4, col. 5.

"He had no ill will against the rich or against the country's ruler," she elaborated to another reporter who tracked her down. "If such ideas came into his head, it was after he left home. I can't believe he ever became interested even in Anarchists. Why he always thought Mike (his brother) was a great man because he was a soldier, and I can't believe the poor man could so change that he would try to kill the President."

"His father will feel much pain," she said. "He liked Leon. He knew the boy was not right. We have had bad luck. Now my husband will not find work. Everybody will say 'His boy tried to kill the President.' We are not to blame, but it will be that way."[160]

" We did not for a moment entertain the idea of trying to get him out of his trouble, as we considered his crime an inexcusable one, and we do not propose to interfere with the government inflicting proper punishment," Paul Czolgosz said. "In fact, none of us had a great liking for Leon. From the time he came to the farm, about three years ago, he would not work and was entirely worthless. He continually claimed that he was sick and took some kind of herb tea as treatment. He thought that he had caught a bad cold by drinking a glass of beer when he was perspiring. Dr. Kohler, a physician on Broadway near Magnet Street, treated him."[161]

"During the last presidential campaign somebody gave Leon a free ticket to go on one of the campaign excursions to Canton. Some politician invited him to go on the trip," Paul Czolgosz remembered. "When he returned he did not say anything against President McKinley. In fact, I never heard him make any remarks against the president."[162]

"Leon's deed is giving us terrible worry and we feel that he is deserving of any punishment that may be inflicted," he concluded.[163]

"We will not do anything to help him," said Leon's brother Joseph. "He never confided in us and if he has gone and done such a terrible thing he can suffer the penalty."[164]

Andrew Czolgosz, an uncle of Leon's, was located by a reporter, but could not speak English. His sons acted as interpreters. Andrew told the reporter that he knew Paul lived in Cleveland, but that he did not know what had become of Leon. Later, when the interviewer returned, he asked Leon's cousins if they had heard that President McKinley had been shot.

---

[160] *Cincinnati Post*, 7 September 1901, pg. 5, col. 2.
[161] *Cleveland Plain Dealer*, 13 September 1901, pg. 12, col. 3.
[162] *Cleveland Plain Dealer*, 13 September 1901, pg. 12, col. 3.
[163] *Cleveland Plain Dealer*, 13 September 1901, pg. 12, col. 3.
[164] *Cleveland Plain Dealer*, 13 September 1901, pg. 12, col. 2.

"Did Leon shoot him?" one of them replied. Then they refused to answer any more questions or to translate for their father.[165]

Mary Czolgosz, Leon's aunt, added, "I have not kept track of Leon lately, and know little about him. He was a strange boy, not having many friends, and being very timid. He was such a coward that everybody knew it."[166]

"If Leon did it, I hope he swings for it," said his brother Jacob. When asked if Leon was insane, he replied, "I can't say that he was ever bright. He was a morose sort of a fellow—not at all sociable. He would not eat his meals with the family half the time, I have been told. That was a good thing for the family, too."[167]

"He was strange in some ways," Jacob told another reporter. "I never got along with him and had little to do with him. We always had rows when we were together. You see, he was a great deal older than I and he bullied me, or tried to, and when he did, I resisted. None of us boys could get along with him. Sometimes I used to think he was not sociable because we would rather he would keep away from us, for he was pretty gabby with other people."[168]

"Why it can hardly be possible," commented an elderly German lady who was a neighbor. "I knew Leon when he wore dresses. He was such a quiet, timid, bashful boy. I can't think he would do such a thing."[169]

On September 10, Cleveland police did a thorough search of the home of Paul Czolgosz at 306 Fleet Street in the hopes of finding letters or other evidence of the crime. Drawers and boxes were emptied of their contents, carpets lifted and pictures taken from walls. They were unable to find any evidence of the involvement of any members of the family in any plot nor where they able to find any evidence that any family member other than Leon was an anarchist.[170]

While at the Buffalo Police station, Czolgosz received no letters of consequence pertaining to the crime, but he did receive thousands of letters from all over the country offering advice and threatening him. All

---

[165] Marshall Everett, *The Complete Life of William McKinley* (Privately Published, 1901) 74.

[166] *Cincinnati Post*, 7 September 1901, pg. 5, col. 2.

[167] *Cincinnati Post*, 7 September 1901, pg. 5, col. 3.

[168] *Buffalo Enquirer*, 7 September 1901.

[169] *Cleveland Plain Dealer*, 8 September 1901, pg. 4, col. 2.

[170] *Cleveland Plain Dealer*, 11 September 1901, pg. 7, col. 2.

during his stay, Chief Bull noticed, Czolgosz was extremely particular about his dress and appearance, washing and fixing himself up a good deal of the time. He had a good appetite, would eat everything given him, and drank a little beer every day. He was also permitted two or three cigars a day. One reporter for the *Buffalo Commercial* told of a conversation he had with Czolgosz in his cell.

"Why did you shoot the President?" asked the reporter.

"Oh, I don't know," Czolgosz, responded in a barely audible voice.

"Don't you wish now that you had left the President alone? Wouldn't you rather have your liberty?"

Yes, I'd like to have my liberty," Czolgosz replied. "I'd like to be free again. Do you think they'll let me go?"

"That may depend on whether you tell them the truth about your confederates," was the reporter's reply.

"Do you think so?" was Czolgosz's hopeful reply.

"Are you sorry you shot the President?"

"I don't know."[171]

Another reporter asked Czolgosz why he had chosen the public reception at which to shoot the President, knowing full well that he could not escape capture.

"I'll tell you, I made an agreement with myself that I would either kill him here on in Cleveland," he replied. This was the last chance I had at him here. He was scheduled to leave last night. I did not want to kill him in Cleveland because my folks live there and yesterday afternoon was the last chance I would have at him in Buffalo."

"You mentioned Cleveland?"

"Yes," supposedly replied Czolgosz. "You know the G. A. R. encampment is to be in Cleveland next week and I would certainly have caught him there had I failed here."[172]

Few people saw Leon Czolgosz during his confinement in the Buffalo jail except a handful of police officials and examining physicians. Leon refused counsel on the apparent grounds that he did not believe in courts or law, as a part of his anarchistic philosophies.

He ate well enough. When Czolgosz was weighed upon arrest his weight was 138. When he checked in at Auburn Prison two weeks later, he was up three pounds to 141. Czolgosz was reportedly not permitted to shave and fives days after the shooting, one newspaper was reporting

---

[171] *Buffalo Commercial,* 8 September 1901.

[172] *Buffalo Enquirer,* 7 September 1901.

that he was even still wearing the same blood stained shirt he had on when he committed the crime. The *Buffalo Courier* reported that Czolgosz had not even combed his hair since Friday and that he had a full, brown, rather dark beard. The report said Czolgosz had been denied a comb. This report does not agree with most of the others at the time.[173]

"The treatment accorded Czolgosz was no different than that of any other prisoner held at police Headquarters," said Chief Bull. "Each day his meals consisted of meat, one vegetable, bread and butter, and coffee. The man had a healthy appetite and ate more than ordinary prisoners."[174]

Thomas Penney refused to help most investigators and never did release Czolgosz's confession or his notes. He explained that he thought Czolgosz was sane and that any writing or talking on the matter only kept it in the public mind. He did not even allow Dr. Carlos MacDonald to use the confession in the preparation of his official report. Penney was determined to suppress all that was possible.

Even though confessions were printed in the newspapers at the time, the *Buffalo Evening News* reported authoritatively that these were fakes, stating that the District Attorney's office had allowed them to be seen by no reporter, even though bribes had been offered.[175]

Some newspaper reports even seem to be outright fabrications. One stated that on his way to the shooting, Czolgosz was carrying with him a bundle of papers that without a doubt proved the conspiracy, complete with the names of the co-conspirators. Included in the bundle was a group of letters that Czolgosz did not want found. It seemed to be based enough in fact to have the local police search the area sewers, but in vain. Czolgosz had said they were only newspapers, but if that were truly the case, it seems improbable that Czolgosz would go through that much trouble to dispose of them in such a mysterious way. It is a mystery that can never be answered.

"Papers are in existence, which, if they can be discovered, will lay bare the entire conspiracy, and will result in wholesale arrests, followed by prosecutions," read the story, which appeared in the *Buffalo Courier*. Czolgosz supposedly told detectives that there had been no time to burn the incriminating documents, and he had been forced to gather them together at Nowak's, conceal them in his coat, and said he walked around the city and finally threw them in a sewer.[176]

---

[173] *Buffalo Commercial,* 11 September 1901.

[174] *Buffalo Courier,* 18 September 1901.

[175] *Buffalo Evening News*, 9 September 1901, pg. 7, col. 1.

[176] *Buffalo Courier*, 11 September 1901, pg. 1, col. 3.

The story claimed that Czolgosz confessed to police that he was part of a conspiracy. But no credible source confirms this. In fact, in every other report, Czolgosz always steadfastly maintained that he alone committed the crime.

Later, Czolgosz's confession was discovered missing from the District Attorney's files. The six original type written pages (twelve by some accounts) with Czolgosz's signatures and corrections have never been found, and were probably destroyed by Thomas Penney as he tried to erase from the world any evidence of the existence of Leon Czolgosz.

Later the once sentence written confession was found, apparently in the files of Czolgosz's legal council, and was eventually auctioned off by a large New York auction house, selling for a price in six figures in the 1980's. It was the dictated note that Czolgosz had signed as a statement for the press, described during the trial by James Quackenbush. It read: "I killed President McKinley because I done my duty. I didn't believe one man should have so much service and another man should have none."[177]

---

[177] Dr. Walter Channing, *The Mental Status of Czolgosz* (Brookline, Mass: American Journal of Insanity, Vol. LIX, No. 2, 1902) 126.

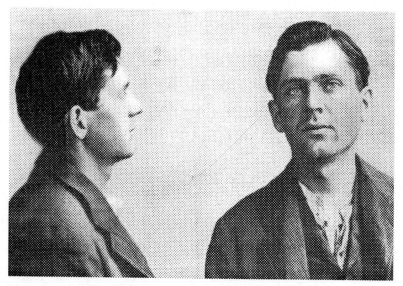

Buffalo Police photos of Leon Czolgosz

An earlier photo of Leon Czolgosz

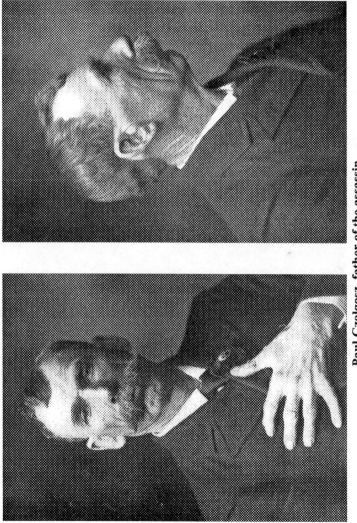

Paul Czolgosz, father of the assassin.

A letter penned by the assassin to a friend. This is one of the few examples of the signature of Leon F. Czolgosz.

Jacob Czolgosx, brother of the assassin.

Letter sent to lodge brother John Grinder by Czolgosz while he was staying in West Seneca, using his alias of Fred C. Nieman. Most co-workers and casual acquaintances knew Czolgosz by his alias, which he said he used to prevent discrimination.

4. The Fight for Life

Friday, September 6

The President arrived at the Exposition hospital at 4:18 in severe shock, but he was conscious, alert and composed. As he was being born up the steps into the hospital, he thought of the assailant.

"Good gracious, the poor fellow did not know what he was doing," he said.[1] The doctors immediately began to tend to the President's personal comfort, and gave him a hypodermic of morphine.[2]

A hurried search began for qualified physicians to treat the President. Dr. Roswell Park, the Exposition's Medical Director and one of the most renowned surgeons in the country, had gone to Niagara Falls for another operation that day. Dr. Edward J. Meyer was also summoned but he was out of the city.[3] One by one, doctors who could be found began to arrive.

Dr. Edgar Wallace Lee was visiting with Buffalo Bill Cody on the opposite side of the Exposition grounds from the Temple of Music when a friend who knew where he could be located arrived with news of the presidential shooting. Lee, who was former medical director of the Omaha Exposition, was one of the first to reach McKinley's bedside.[4] He voluntarily, some would later say forcibly, took charge until the Exposition resident staff relieved him.[5]

"The President had been undressed and was lying on the operating table when I entered the operating room," explained Dr. Lee. "There were no outsiders there."[6]

Dr. Peter W. Van Peyma, a Buffalo obstetrician, and J. N. Adam, a Buffalo businessman, heard the news as they were standing near the Temple and saw the ambulance rush by. They immediately went to the hospital. Adam went in, but Dr. Van Peyma waited outside. Adam soon

---

[1] *Buffalo Express*, 7 September 1901.

[2] Nelson W. Wilson, M.D. "Details of the McKinley Case" (*Buffalo Medical Journal*, *41-57*) 208.

[3] Nelson W. Wilson, M.D. "Details of the McKinley Case" (*Buffalo Medical Journal*, *41-57*) 208.

[4] A. Wesley Johns, *The Man Who Shot McKinley* (New York: A. S. Barnes and Co., Inc., 1970) 106.

[5] Nelson W. Wilson, M.D. "Details of the McKinley Case" (*Buffalo Medical Journal*, *41-57*) 208.

[6] Murat Halstead, *The Illustrious Life of William McKinley* (Privately Published, 1901) 47.

came back out, inviting Van Peyma in, saying that he may be able to provide some assistance.

Van Peyma later said that as he looked around for anyone he knew, a man who had been "looking at me fixedly and sternly for some time, inquired as to who I was. I informed him and returned the question, and I was informed that he was Mr. Cortelyou, private secretary to the President."[7]

Dr. Van Peyma was then asked to look at the President.

"I found him lying upon the operating table undressed and lightly covered," explained Dr. Van Peyma. "I was shown the wound and finding that it had been carefully and aseptically dressed, advised the reapplication of the dressing. At this time the only physician who had seen the President was Dr. McK. Hall, an interne."[8]

"As soon as I saw the President I was struck with his condition," said Dr. Lee. "There was a pallor in his face, and upon examination it was found his pulse was abnormally high. There was every indication that he was dangerously wounded and that an immediate operation was necessary."[9]

Van Peyma was impressed by President McKinley's "calm and dignified manner." He tried to reassure the President and McKinley asked him, "Poor fellow, why did he do it?"[10]

Van Peyma stayed with the President and introduced surgeons as they arrived.

It was not until about 4:45 p.m. that Dr. Herman Mynter, who was the first surgeon to examine the wounds of the President carefully and in detail, arrived, bringing with him Dr. Eugene Wasdin. Mynter, who had served in both the army and navy medical corps in his native Denmark before settling in Buffalo, knew immediately that the President's abdominal wound had the potential of being a fatal injury. Surgery would be imperative.[11]

---

[7] P. W. VanPeyma, M.D. "Last Hours of President McKinley" *The Daily Bazaar* (28 November 1902) 5.

[8] P. W. VanPeyma, M.D. "Last Hours of President McKinley" *The Daily Bazaar* (28 November 1902) 5.

[9] *Washington Post,* 9 September 1901, pg. 2, col. 4.

[10] P. W. VanPeyma, M.D. "Last Hours of President McKinley" *The Daily Bazaar* (28 November 1902) 5.

[11] Selig Adler, "The Operation on President McKinley," *Scientific American* (March, 1963) 121.

Mynter had seen the President at the reception at the Government Building only the day before and had said, "I am glad to meet you Mr. President. I am Dane and one of your most ardent admirers, but I have nothing to ask of you except to take your hand and say, 'God bless you.'"

"Doctor, I have had the pleasure of meeting you before," the President said upon seeing the doctor, remembering the exchange. "Then you said you wanted nothing from me. Now, I fear, I am in need of something from you."[12]

Dr. Van Peyma remembered the exchange, "One of these gentlemen spoke of having shaken hands with him at the reception the day before and reminded him of something he had said to the President. The President looked up and considerately said, 'Yes, I think I remember.'"[13]

As he examined the President, Dr. Mynter saw two wounds. The first was just below the nipple of the left breast, a flesh wound and relatively harmless. But the second had entered about four inches below the left nipple and four inches to the left of the naval, and about level with it.

"In the mean time, at Secretary Cortelyou's request, I stationed myself at one of the doors of the operating room, with George Foster at the other, with instructions not to permit any undesirable person to pass," remembered F. D. Owen. "By the rear entrance to the hospital, several physicians had entered, and were pressing their claims. This entrance was quickly barred and several policemen were stationed there.

"During the operation, Secretary Cortelyou was in and out of the room receiving numerous telegrams from all parts of the world and answering urgent calls at the main entrance."[14]

McKinley told Cortelyou to be careful about the doctors. He was leaving it all to him. Cortelyou, not knowing any of the doctors personally, turned to Milburn for assistance, wanting him to recommend who should take charge of the situation.

"You know these men," he told him. "When the right one arrives, tell me."

When he arrived after being summoned by John Milburn, Milburn immediately pointed out Dr. Matthew D. Mann as being the man for the operation.[15] Mann had been located in a barbershop with his haircut half-

---

[12] *Buffalo Express*, 12 September 1901.

[13] P. W. VanPeyma, M.D. "Last Hours of President McKinley" *The Daily Bazaar* (28 November 1902) 5.

[14] *Washington Post*, 9 September 1901, pg. 10, col. 1.

[15] Selig Adler, "The Operation on President McKinley, *Scientific American* (March, 1963) 121.

done. He had left immediately and it was to be many hours before the haircut would be completed.

Mann, 56 years old and at the height of his career, had a worldwide reputation in gynecology, even authoring a standard textbook on the subject. He had served on the staff at the Yale Medical School and was presently the chair of obstetrics and gynecology at the University of Buffalo. Dr. Mann was an expert in his own field, but had little experience with upper abdominal wounds, most likely never having operated on a gunshot wound. Dr. Mann's son, E. C. "Ned" Mann, had been in charge of the Exposition hospital. He had immediately sent for his father upon hearing the news of the presidential shooting. An extremely confident person, Mann did not insist that Mynter was the more experienced of the two, and performed the operation. But it was also Mann, to his credit, who insisted the operation be performed at once.[16]

The doctors were faced with basically two options. The first was to wait and take the President to Buffalo General Hospital and wait for Dr. Roswell Park's arrival. Park was the area's most renowned surgeon. The problem with that course was the possibility of a concealed hemorrhage and increased odds of post-operational peritonitis. There was also the fear of gastric or intestinal contents escaping into the peritoneal cavity.[17]

During the recent Spanish-American and Boer Wars, much had been learned about dealing with gunshot wounds. Rifle wounds could be treated more conservatively, but slower velocity gunshot wounds, such as those caused by revolvers, presented a more serious problem. Soft lead pistol projectiles produced tears and more irregular damage to the tissues as well as having a tendency to carry infectious material into the body. For these types of wounds, a more drastic and radical treatment was needed, even though only seventeen years before Dr. Emil Theodore Kocher had performed the first successful surgery for a gunshot wound of the stomach. Mann felt that any delay could result in the President's death.[18]

The other option was to operate immediately in conditions that were known to be inadequate. After consultation among themselves, this was the course that was chosen.

---

[16] Selig Adler, "The Operation on President McKinley, *Scientific American* (March, 1963) 122.

[17] "The Official Report on the Case of President McKinley (*Buffalo Medical Journal 41-57*) 272.

[18] Selig Adler, "The Operation on President McKinley, *Scientific American* (March, 1963) 122.

"The question of time is of the greatest importance in a case of this kind," said Dr. Charles McBurney later. "An operation could not have been performed too soon. It was performed in one of the quickest times on record. It will be famous in the history of surgery."[19]

Doctors Mann, Mynter, Lee, and Wasdin held a huddled conference. It was agreed that Dr. Mann would be in charge of the operation. He informed the President.

Dr. Van Peyma recalled the President's reaction. "Gentlemen, I am in your hands," he said calmly.[20]

Dr. Lee remembered the President saying, "Gentlemen, I want you to do whatever in your judgment you think is necessary."

"That was the last thing he said at the hospital," said Lee.[21]

Dr. Mann assigned the other participating doctors duties to perform during the President's operation. Dr. Mynter was to be Mann's chief assistant. Young Dr. Edward C. Mann and Dr. Simpson where in charge of sutures and instruments. Dr. Wasdin would administer the anesthetic, with Miss Catherine Simmons of Roosevelt Hospital in New York assisting him. Dr. Nelson Wilson would keep the records of the operation. The sterile nurses were Miss A. P. Barnes and Miss M. C. Morris, both from St. Luke's Hospital in New York. Rose Barron of the Long Island College Hospital, Mary A. Shannon of Cincinnati General Hospital and Miss L. E. Dorchester of Buffalo General Hospital were assigned as general assistants. Dr. Hall would assist Dr. Zittel in the general business of the hospital during the operation. Dr. Lee had a prominent place next to Dr. Mynter who was opposite Dr. Mann at the operating table. Dr. John Parmenter was next to Dr. Mann and acted as an advisor.[22]

"I had no idea it was the President who was to be operated upon, when Miss Walters told me to get a hypodermic of morphine and strychnine," said Nurse Morris. "I looked at the face of the man on the table and said to myself: 'That looks like the President,' but it was some little time before I was quite sure about it."[23]

---

[19] Marshall Everett, *The Complete Life of William McKinley* (Privately Published, 1901) 43.

[20] P. W. VanPeyma, M.D. "Last Hours of President McKinley" *The Daily Bazaar* (28 November 1902) 5.

[21] *Washington Post,* 9 September 1901, pg. 2, col. 4.

[22] Nelson W. Wilson, M.D. "Details of the McKinley Case" (*Buffalo Medical Journal, 41-57*) 210-211.

[23] *Buffalo Express,* 14 September 1901.

"The operation was performed calmly and deliberately," said Dr. Lee. "While we never forgot for an instant that the patient was a magnificent man and our President, our emotions did not in the least hamper our work."[24]

Dr. John Parmenter had arrived at the hospital to find Doctors Mann, Mynter, Wasdin and Lee already there and later wrote, "I am informed that a consultation had been held, at which it was decided that the President should receive the same general line of treatment which would be indicated and carried out in the case of a person of much less exalted position. In other words, the personality of the patient was not to weigh in the scientific treatment of the case. I was invited by Dr. Mann to participate in the operation which began as nearly as I can recollect about twenty minutes after five o'clock."[25]

Dr. Mathew D. Mann was ill prepared from an equipment standpoint to perform the most important operation of his life.

"Unfortunately, when called I was not told what I was wanted for, and went to the exposition grounds entirely unprepared," Dr. Mann later wrote. "Dr. Mynter had his large pocket case, the contents of which were of great use."[26]

Mann was unaware that Dr. Roswell Park's instruments, having been rushed to the hospital in preparation of Park's arrival, were waiting nearby. Also, due to the haste in getting the operation underway, no one in the operating room prepared properly. According to Dr. Park's notes, "I do not recall anyone in the room wore caps or gauze."[27]

"When I went to give the hypodermic he looked at it in a rather distrustful sort of way and asked me what it was," commented Nurse Morris. "When I told him what it was he said 'All right,' very quietly, but pleasantly."[28]

"He was the most admirable patient I ever saw," said Nurse Barnes. "We're Canadians, Miss Morris and I, and we don't have any of the patriotic enthusiasm that you have for him as President of the United States, but I can tell you that he was the finest man I ever saw."[29]

[24] Murat Halstead, *The Illustrious Life of William McKinley* (Privately Published, 1901) 47.

[25] John Parmenter, "The Surgery in President McKinley's Case," (*Buffalo Medical Journal*, 41-57) 205.

[26] "The Official Report on the Case of President McKinley (*Buffalo Medical Journal 41-57*) 275.

[27] *Buffalo Evening News*, 15 September, 1945.

[28] *Buffalo Express*, 14 September, 1901.

[29] *Buffalo Express*, 14 September, 1901.

"It is hard to wait so long," The President said as the surgeons prepared for the emergency surgery

Dr. Mann told him, "We have lost one President, and we don't mean to lose you."

"All right, doctor," replied the President. "Do whatever you think is necessary."[30]

"It was pathetic," remembered Nurse Morris. "When he was on the table before the anesthetic was given. He seemed to feel so badly that anyone should shoot him because of personal hatred. That seemed to be the thought that pained him most. He lay there, so white and still, never uttering a complaint and seemed to be trying to comprehend what prompted his assailant to the deed."[31]

The President was awake and in full control of his faculties. At about 5:20 p.m., as the President recited the *Lord's Prayer*, ether was administered by Dr. Wasdin. Ether was selected as an anesthetic because it was considered safer than other methods. In nine minutes, the President was under its effects.

At about 5:52, V. W. Cox of the Government Board of Exposition Managers arrived with Dr. and Mrs. Presley M. Rixey, the President's personal physician, and Mrs. Cortelyou. They had left the Milburn house where Mrs. McKinley slept, yet to be told of the events.[32]

President McKinley was operated on for an hour and thirty-one minutes, with Dr. Mann beginning the operation with an incision about three inches long near the entrance wound. The abdomen was carefully scrubbed with green soap and shaved, then washed with alcohol and ether and the bichlorid solution. Due to the layer of fat encasing the President's stomach, Mann was forced to lengthen the incision by another inch before he could reach the peritoneum. In the bullet wound, he discovered a small piece of cloth, presumably part of the President's undershirt that the bullet had carried inside, which he removed. [33]

Mann opened the peritoneum and found that the intestines had not been damaged. At first, upon seeing the wound, he had thought the intestines might have been lacerated, and at that point he had said, "My God—then nothing that can be done for him."[34]

---

[30] Franklin Matthews, "The President's Last Days". *Harper's Weekly*, 21 September 1901, pg. 943.

[31] *Buffalo Express*, 14 September 1901.

[32] G. Townsend, *Memorial Life of William McKinley* (Washington: Memorial Publishing Co., 1901) 209.

[33] Nelson W. Wilson, M.D. "Details of the McKinley Case" (*Buffalo Medical Journal, 41-57*) 212.

[34] Selig Adler, "The Operation on President McKinley, *Scientific American* (March, 1963) 123.

The stomach was drawn up and the perforation slightly enlarged. Dr. Mann then introduced his finger and the contents of the stomach were palpated. This was done to determine if the stomach contained any food and to see if the bullet could possibly be found in the stomach. The stomach was found to be half full of liquid food, but there was no evidence of the bullet. In pulling the stomach up, a small amount of the contents escaped, along with a good deal of gas. The tissues around the wound were carefully irrigated with a hot salt solution and dried with gauze pads. The perforation in the anterior wall was then closed.[35]

Mann sutured the jagged wound with a fine black silk thread. He then lengthened the incision by another two inches, to a total of about 15 centimeters, so he could examine the posterior wall of the President's stomach. The omentum and traverse colon were pulled well out of the abdomen, the omentum being enormously thickened with fat and rigid. In order to reach the back wall of the stomach, Dr. Mann found it necessary to divide by about four inches of the gastrocolic omentum, tying the cuts ends with strong black silk in two masses on each side. This wound was a bit larger and more jagged than the other one, and Mann closed it in the same manner as he had the anterior wound, finding it more difficult because the opening was near the bottom of a deep pocket. Little or no gastric contents appeared around this opening and after it had been closed, to be safe, the parts were irrigated with the salt solution.[36]

"The greatest difficulty was the great size of President McKinley's abdomen and the amount of fat present," explained Dr. Mann later. "This necessitated working at the bottom of a deep hole, especially when suturing the posterior wall of the stomach."[37]

During the operation, Dr. Rixey stood nearby and attempted to reflect the fading sunlight with a small hand mirror so that the surgeons could better see. When that was inadequate, he rigged up a dim electric light.

The surgeons were frustrated in their efforts to locate the bullet. Dr. Mann reached into the President and palpated carefully all the deep structures behind the stomach. No trace of the bullet could be found and since the effort had a negative effect on the President's pulse, Mann ceased that activity. The folds of the intestines below the stomach were

[35] "The Official Report on the Case of President McKinley (*Buffalo Medical Journal 41-57*) 273.

[36] "The Official Report on the Case of President McKinley" (*Buffalo Medical Journal 41-57*) 274.

[37] "The Official Report on the Case of President McKinley" (*Buffalo Medical Journal 41-57*) 275.

checked for injuries and none were found. The entire gut was not removed from the abdomen for inspection because the location of the wound seemed to exclude injury in that area. To make a thorough search of the President's back muscles for the bullet, it would have been necessary to completely eviscerate him. Given the fact that he was already suffering from shock, this was deemed inadvisable and might have caused the President's death right on the operating table.[38]

"We were often asked why, after the operation, we did not use the x-ray to find the bullet," wrote Dr. Mann. "There were several reasons for this. In the first place, there were, at no time any signs that the bullet was doing harm. To have used the x-ray simply to have satisfied our curiosity would not have been warrantable, as it would have greatly disturbed and annoyed the patient, and would have subjected him also to a certain risk. Had there been signs of abscess-formation, then the rays could and would have been used."[39]

Dr. Mann, probing the bullet path for quite some time, the President's size being a hindrance, thought that in his weakening condition, McKinley could not stand further exploration of the wound.

"The autopsy shows that it (the bullet) could not have been found, and that the injuries inflicted by the bullet after it passed through the stomach were of a nature as to render impossible and unnecessary any further surgical procedure," wrote Mann. "A bullet after it ceases to move does little harm."[40]

The last unfortunate sentence was one Dr. Mathew Mann would live to regret.

Meanwhile, Dr. Roswell Park, who had an extensive knowledge of gun shot wounds, had been performing a lymphoma operation on a Mr. Ransom of Ransomville in Niagara Falls. Charles W. Goodyear, an Exposition director, went to Dr. Park's house in an attempt to locate him. The maid informed him of his whereabouts and in an attempt to be helpful, gave Goodyear Park's medical instrument bag to take with him. They would be waiting at the hospital for his arrival.

Then, there was the problem of how to speed Dr. Park back to Buffalo. Harry Parry, New York Central's general agent, communicated

---

[38] "The Official Report on the Case of President McKinley" (*Buffalo Medical Journal 41-57*) 274.

[39] "The Official Report on the Case of President McKinley" (*Buffalo Medical Journal 41-57*) 274.

[40] "The Official Report on the Case of President McKinley" (*Buffalo Medical Journal 41-57*) 275-276.

with the Niagara Falls office and arranged for a special train for the transport of Dr. Park.[41]

It was during the most crucial stage of the operation that Dr. Park received his summons to Buffalo. Park replied, "Don't you see I can't leave—even for the President of the United States."

"It is for the President," was the astonishing reply.[42]

Park explained what happened next. "As soon as I recovered my equanimity, I turned to Doctor Campbell, who knew all the railroad people at the station, and asked him to go at once and make the necessary arrangements for a special engine or train, saying that Doctor Chapin and I would finish the operation and be at the station by the time things could be readied."[43]

"It had always seemed to me that the engine might have been speedily detached or furnished for the emergency," he continued, "but I was told that a Michigan Central through train would be along shortly, and that I should be sent up on that, while a special engine would be waiting at the Black Rock Junction to take me round on the Belt Line and down upon the special tracks which had been laid into the Exposition grounds."[44]

Through the efforts of many, Dr. Park arrived on the grounds at about 6 p.m.; only two hours after the President had been shot, and was rushed by automobile to the hospital. The crowd waiting outside the hospital recognized him as he was rushed inside. Dr. Park was quickly introduced to Cortelyou who informed him that the operation was already underway. Park hurriedly scrubbed up and entered the room.

Dr. Park described, "Just as I entered the operating room the first incident which attracted my attention was Dr. Mann rapping Dr. Mynter's fingers with one of the instruments because said fingers were apparently in his way. This was but a sample of Dr. Mann's petulance when excited during the operation, nevertheless it was an unfortunate time at which to make such an exhibition of annoyance."[45]

Park asked Mann what he wanted him to do and Mann responded that he was almost finished. Park, noticing Mann's complaints about the instruments, gave him his own, after they were sterilized. Dr. Park was then updated on the developments of the operation. Mann said that all

[41] A. Wesley Johns, *The Man Who Shot McKinley* (New York: A. S. Barnes and Co., Inc., 1970) 105.

[42] *Buffalo Evening News*, 15 September 1945, Magazine Section, pg. 1, col. 2.

[43] *Buffalo Evening News*, 15 September 1945, Magazine Section, pg. 1, col. 2.

[44] *Buffalo Evening News*, 15 September 1945, Magazine Section, pg. 1, col. 2.

[45] *Buffalo Evening News*, 15 September 1945, Magazine Section, pg. 1, col. 8.

was left to do was to flush the abdominal cavity with a saline solution, and then sew up the incision.[46]

"The operation had then lasted somewhat over an hour, and it was deemed inadvisable to prolong the search for the bullet, the belief being that it had passed into the muscles of the back and would there become encysted," explained Dr. Parmenter later.[47]

The abdominal cavity had been thoroughly irrigated with a salt solution two or three times during the operation.[48] Dr. Mynter emphatically advised drainage of the wound. This question was put to Dr. Park, but he deferred the decision to Dr. Mann, probably out of professional courtesy. Park remained silent in spite of the fact that for years he had lectured about gunshot wounds and had always advised the removal of injured or contaminated tissue and full drainage.[49] The other doctors out numbered Dr. Mynter about whether or not to drain the wound and it was closed without drainage.

The last step of the operation was to trim the tissues around the bullet track in the abdominal wall in order to remove any infected tissue. The abdominal wound was then closed. Where the bullet had entered there was a slight gaping of tissue, but it was not thought wise to close it tightly. The doctors thought it best to allow for some drainage. The wound was then washed with hydrogen dioxide and covered with aristol powder and dressed with sterilized gauze and cotton, which were held in place by adhesive straps. Over all of this was put an abdominal bandage.[50]

It was 6:50 p.m. when the operation ended. The President's pulse was 122 (it had been as low as 84), his respiration 32.[51]

Dr. Rixey told Dr. Park that he was the only one of the doctors that he knew anything about and even questioned the experience of Dr. Mann. In fact, he went as far as to tell Park that he wanted him to take

---

[46] A. Wesley Johns, *The Man Who Shot McKinley* (New York: A. S. Barnes and Co., Inc., 1970) 112.

[47] John Parmenter, "The Surgery in President McKinley's Case," (*Buffalo Medical Journal*, 41-57) 206.

[48] John Parmenter, "The Surgery in President McKinley's Case," (*Buffalo Medical Journal*, 41-57) 206.

[49] Selig Adler, "The Operation on President McKinley, *Scientific American* (March, 1963) 124.

[50] "The Official Report on the Case of President McKinley (*Buffalo Medical Journal 41-57*) 274.

[51] Nelson W. Wilson, M.D. "Details of the McKinley Case" (*Buffalo Medical Journal, 41-57*) 214..

over the case. But Park again, because of the stage of the operation, deferred to Dr. Mann, saying that it could be worked out later. After the operation, Park was officially placed in charge.[52]

The President's pulse was fairly good immediately following the operation, registering as high as 130, and he had taken the anesthetic well with no adverse symptoms, the credit for which was given Dr. Wasdin by Dr. Parmenter for his "skillful administration."[53]

In hindsight, after McKinley's death, several possible mistakes during that hurried operation were exposed. These mistakes could have accelerated the President's death. Had these mistakes been avoided, the President may have survived the ordeal.

First, it is argued, Mann should have drained the wound from the second bullet. Failing to do so helped to generate the gangrene that eventually killed McKinley. Secondly, it was said, the President could easily have been taken to Buffalo General Hospital, where a much better operating room, lighting and equipment were available. Immediately after the President was shot, his pulse rate was 84. This meant that he could have made the longer trip to Buffalo General and had the better operation, without the need to hurry at a frantic pace. But at the time, the doctors were faced with split second decisions, and since their patient was the President of the United States, this must have added to the pressure.

Dr. Park gathered the physicians together, before the President was removed, and told them in no uncertain terms that no information about the President's medical condition was to be given out unless it was cleared by Secretary Cortelyou. Dr. Mynter immediately had a problem with the President's removal to the Milburn house, thinking he should remain in the hospital. Park simply told him that plans were already being made. Park told the other doctors that he thought Dr. Rixey should make the decision as to who would be in charge of the case, and Rixey immediately, in front of the others, said he preferred Dr. Park. Delicately, Park replied that it was not fair to Dr. Mann, but that he was certain that everyone, including Dr. Mann, would provide any service that was needed. Dr. Rixey allowed Dr. Park to make all other decisions regarding the assignments of Drs. Mann, Mynter, and Wasdin. Others doctors were available as needed.[54]

---

[52] Selig Adler, "The Operation on President McKinley" , *Scientific American* (March, 1963) 126.

[53] John Parmenter, "The Surgery in President McKinley's Case," (*Buffalo Medical Journal*, 41-57) 206.

[54] A. Wesley Johns, *The Man Who Shot McKinley* (New York: A. S. Barnes and Co., Inc., 1970) 113.

At 7:30 p.m., the ambulance that had brought McKinley to the Exposition hospital backed up to the entrance, through the crowd, which seemed to sense what was about to happen.

Dr. Park came out first, followed by the President on a stretcher carried by four doctors. The President's face was ashen white and his eyes were open as he was carried out and put into the waiting ambulance. Dr. Park and Dr. Wasdin climbed into the back with the President, and Simpson leaped into the front seat with the driver Ellis for the ride to the Milburn house. Generals Welch and Chapin drew up their soldiers to guard the ambulance in route. Behind the ambulance followed two cars crowded with doctors and members of the presidential staff.

Dr. Park later remembered that the procession "passed no faster than men can easily walk, this partly because many of the escort were on foot, and because although the streets were very smooth, we did not want to jostle the patient any more than was necessary.

"The passage ... through the crowd and down Delaware Ave. was one of the most dramatic incidents I have ever witnessed. The fairgrounds were crowded that day, and it seemed as though the entire crowd had gathered to witness the event. Every man's hat was in his hands, and there were handkerchiefs at many eyes. I never saw a large crowd so quiet."[55]

McKinley bore the journey well, but at one point was given a small hypodermic of morphine during the ride, as he became very restless.[56]

Upon arrival at Milburn's house, Dr. Park and Ellis took out the stretcher and moved toward the door. The President's moans were audible and he was wrapped in a blanket with a white towel concealing his face from the crowd of onlookers. The men took the President to an upstairs room, which Dr. Park observed was a large room at the rear of the house, connecting with an equally large front room. Everything had been prepared down to the smallest detail.[57]

Ida McKinley had been anxiously waiting an hour for the arrival of her husband and she rushed to the street as she saw the ambulance arrive. As the President was being lifted from the ambulance, his wife bent close to him and witnesses heard her say, "My poor husband, how could they do this?"

[55] *Buffalo Evening News*, 15 September, 1945.

[56] "The Official Report on the Case of President McKinley" (*Buffalo Medical Journal 41-57*) 275.

[57] A. Wesley Johns, *The Man Who Shot McKinley* (New York: A. S. Barnes and Co., Inc., 1970) 117.

"Don't worry Ida," the President replied with a smile. "The doctors are making a fuss over me. I am not badly hurt."

Mrs. McKinley returned the smile and stroked the President's right hand, walking beside the litter as it moved into the house. After he was made comfortable, the President briefly saw his nieces.[58]

After conferring with Dr. Park, Miss A. M. Walters, the superintendent of nurses at the Exposition Hospital, had dispatched Miss K. R. Simmons and Miss A. D. Barnes to set up the medical equipment, including a surgical bed, in preparation for the President's arrival.[59]

"To illustrate the rapidity and perfection of the arrangements, Mr. Huntley, of the General Electric Co. had run a special wire, and installed electric fans, with possibilities for anything else needed in this direction and the fans were actually in operation by the time we reached the house," explained Dr. Park.[60]

The President was put to bed and was, for the most part, in satisfactory condition. His pulse improved and he slept at intervals throughout the evening. He was given brandy and morphine hypodermically. At 8:43, Dr. Rixey noted that the President rested peacefully, but eight minutes later, at 9:15, he vomited a bit of undigested food and a blood clot. The President vomited again at 9:40.[61] After midnight, the President slept a good deal, was free from pain and comfortable.[62]

"When we were taking care of him that first night, sick as he was, there was not the slightest service performed for him that he did not recognize in some way," remembered Nurse Barnes. "If he could not speak, he would just give a little 'umph-humph' just to let you know that he noticed what we were doing for him.

"We counted his pulse every five minutes all night and, of course, they kept us at his side almost continuously. And once," Miss Barnes told smiling, "the President of the United States had his arm around my waist and I didn't take it away. I just let it stay there! He was throwing his arms about as he came out from the influence of the anesthetic."[63]

---

[58] *Cincinnati Post*, 7 September 1901, pg. 4, col. 7.

[59] Nelson W. Wilson, M.D. "Details of the McKinley Case" (*Buffalo Medical Journal, 41-57*) 214.

[60] *Buffalo Evening News*, 15 September, 1945.

[61] *Buffalo Courier*, 27 October 1901, pg. 1, col. 5.

[62] "The Official Report on the Case of President McKinley" (*Buffalo Medical Journal 41-57*) 277.

[63] *Buffalo Express*, 14 September, 1901.

During the evening, Mrs. McKinley asked Dr. Rixey if her husband would die. Rixey replied that he hoped not and Mrs. McKinley became overcome with emotion and fainted. [64]

The clothes that President McKinley wore at the time of the shooting, as well as the contents of his pockets, were sent to the Milburn house. In his pocket was $1.80 in currency; a well-worn silver coin that appeared to be a pocket piece, three small penknives, and another battered coin. The President's well-worn wallet contained $45 dollars in cash and a number of business cards in one of the compartments. In his vest pocket, there was a silver-shell lead pencil and three cigars that had been given to him that day at Niagara Falls, two of which he had chewed on. The President also had been carrying his gold open faced watched attached to a gold chain. His shirt had been cut during the preparations for the operation and was covered in blood.[65]

Saturday, September 7

All through the night of September 6-7, members of the press arrived, setting up tents across from the Milburn house on the northeast corner of Ferry and Delaware. Guards began to intercept nearly everyone who came and went.

"The guard will be instructed to hold up everybody, even members of the President's Cabinet," said John Scatcherd. "We want to aid the President and his physicians by preserving absolute quiet."[66]

Before the week was up, more than 250 newsmen and correspondents would descend on Buffalo. It was the largest news corps ever assembled for a major event up until that time.[67]

A military presence was felt as sentries marched along the walk. The Milburn house was almost immediately turned into a virtual fortress. A large group of visitors came and went with the curious being drawn to the spot, and being kept at a safe distance by police and soldiers. Delaware Avenue was cordoned off with rope to stop the flow of traffic, and in a premonition of an era to come, diagonally across the street; the tents accommodated the press who maintained a twenty-four hour vigil.

---

[64] *Cincinnati Post*, 7 September 1901, pg. 4, col. 7.

[65] Murat Halstead, *The Illustrious Life of William McKinley* (Privately Published, 1901) 45.

[66] *Buffalo Commercial*, 7 September 1901.

[67] A. Wesley Johns, *The Man Who Shot McKinley* (New York: A. S. Barnes and Co., Inc., 1970) 132.

The President's chef and house servants were brought to the residence and began preparing and serving up to 140 meals per day for high government officials and other visitors.[68]

The room the President occupied was ideally situated for being a sick room. The Milburn house had been remodeled only the year before and the President was placed in a north bedroom in the newer section in the rear of the house. Mrs. McKinley was on the opposite side of the house, down a long hallway from the President.

As the crowd of onlookers and the press grew, the noise increased to the point where it was necessary for the President's physicians to issue an order for absolute quiet. The people cooperated to the point that one reporter claimed that a hummingbirds' wings could be heard nearby.[69]

As visitors arrived at the Milburn residence, they were usually met at the door by John Milburn and taken into the large downstairs library. Crowded in the room were also White House stenographers and messages from all over the world. They would soon be moved out of the main building. Secret Service Agent George Foster was organizing the security outside.[70]

At 6 a.m. the President's physicians issued a bulletin, "The President has passed a good night. Temperature 102, pulse 110, respiration 24."[71] Dr. Rixey and Dr. Mynter had kept the all night vigil at the President's bedside. At 9 a.m., the bulletin was updated for the waiting public, "The President passed a fairly comfortable night and no serious symptoms have developed. Pulse 146, temperature 102, respiration 24."[72]

The policy of the McKinley doctors that first full day of convalescence was to keep the President as quiet as possible. They did not allow even family members to visit him; only Mrs. McKinley and the President's brother, Abner, got a few minutes. Otherwise, it was only the doctors; two of them being by his bed constantly, with two trained nurses always on duty to help out.

The one hundred and two temperature was a cause of alarm among many. A report came from the house in the morning hours that the doctors would operate again to try to locate and remove the second

[68] Selig Adler, "The Operation on President McKinley, *Scientific American* (March, 1963) 126.

[69] A. Wesley Johns, *The Man Who Shot McKinley* (New York: A. S. Barnes and Co., Inc., 1970) 132.

[70] *Washington Post*, 8 September 1901, pg. 3, col. 2-3.

[71] *New York Times*, 8 September 1901, pg. 1, col. 3.

[72] *New York Times*, 8 September 1901, pg. 1, col. 3.

bullet. But by the afternoon, the doctors, with the help of Mr. Milburn, had quieted the rumor and made it clear that there would be no operation immediately and that efforts to locate the bullet would be abandoned until at least another day.[73]

One account said the President, on this morning, commented on his assailant.

"He must have been crazy," the President said. "I never saw the man until he approached me at the reception." When told Czolgosz was an anarchist, McKinley responded, "Too bad, too bad. I trust, though, that he will be treated with all fairness."[74]

News of the President's progress and condition was telegraphed across the country. Major Thomas W. Symons sent a message to General Gillespie in Washington telling him that the President was alive and resting comfortably except for the moments that he breathed deeply. He relayed to him the news of the doctor's optimism.[75]

At noon the medical bulletin was updated, "There is no decided change in the President's condition since last bulletin. Pulse 136, temperature 102, respiration 28."

High government officials quickly began to assemble. Agriculture Secretary James Wilson had been the only Cabinet member who had accompanied to President to Buffalo, but soon most of the others would arrive.

Vice President Theodore Roosevelt was tracked down on an island in Lake Champlain and arrived along with all the members of the President's Cabinet on Saturday, September 7, except for Secretary of State John Hay and Navy Secretary John D. Long, who remained in Washington.

When the Vice President heard the news, he was at Isle La Motte with John Barrett, an ex-minister to Siam and a young author named Winston Churchill. The news had reached him at about 5:30 p.m. on the sixth.

"I shall never forget the demeanor of the Vice President under the influence of this great shock," said John Barrett. "He was about changing his clothes when called to the telephone. As soon as he

---

[73] *New York Times*, 8 September 1901, pg. 1, col. 4.

[74] Samuel Fallows, *Life of William McKinley: Our Martyred President* (Chicago: Regan Printing House, 1901) 22.

[75] A. Wesley Johns, *The Man Who Shot McKinley* (New York: A. S. Barnes and Co., Inc., 1970) 131.

realized the meaning of the terrible news, a dazed expression followed by a look of unmistakable anguish came to his face, and tears immediately filled his eyes. He was plainly laboring under deep emotion, and asked Senator Proctor, likewise keenly affected, to make the sad announcement to the waiting crowd outside.

"The Vice President paced nervously, but not excitedly, up and down the room, passed a few appropriate remarks in conversation with us, dictated a telegram to Buffalo, and quietly waited for more news. When shortly the second bulletin followed saying that the President's wounds were not necessarily fatal, and that he might recover, the Vice President exclaimed with sincerest feeling: 'That's good—it is good. May it be every bit true,' and immediately he brushed aside those about him, hastened out on the veranda, and made the reassuring announcement himself."

"When the Vice Presidential party were en route back to Burlington we were all much impressed with the Vice President's calmness, sincere sorrow, and unselfishness. Although face to face with the significant possibility that he might receive word of the President's death when the boat reached Burlington, he betrayed no excitement, but seemed entirely wrapped in the one hope that the President would recover."

He was asked if he was anxious about arriving in Burlington to find out McKinley had died and he was President.

"Do not speak of that contingency," he snapped. "Our one thought and prayer is now for the President, and that he may be spared."

"He is such a lovable and gentle as well as great man that I cannot understand how any man could do this," he said of McKinley. "Of all the men I have known in public life he was the last to excite animosity."[76]

Roosevelt left aboard the yacht *Elfrida*, which was owned by W. Seward Webb, met up with a special train at Burlington, Vermont, and preceded on to Buffalo. President Clement of the Rutland Railroad made the train available. When arriving at the wharf, Roosevelt was asked for a statement.

"I am so inexpressibly grieved, shocked, and horrified that I can say nothing," he replied.[77]

Arriving at 1:00 p.m. on the eastbound New York Central railroad at the Exchange Street, the Vice President jumped from his car, the *Grand*

[76] *New York Times*, 8 September 1901, pg. 1, col. 6.
[77] *New York Times*, 7 September 1901, pg. 1, col. 5.

Isle, and literally ran through the station with reporters chasing and bounded into a waiting carriage. He only shouted back to reporters that he had nothing to say.[78]

Roosevelt first went to the Iroquois Hotel, where it had been planned that he would stay. As he drove from the station to the hotel, the crowd cheered him with cries of "Teddy." Roosevelt did his best not to acknowledge the cheering, looking very grave. At the Iroquois, he met an old friend of his from his days in the New York Assembly, Ansley Wilcox, who offered the Vice President the use of his house. Wilcox's family was on vacation and the house was empty. The Wilcox mansion was located about a mile and a half and on the opposite side of Delaware Avenue from the Milburn house, near North Street. Roosevelt readily accepted the invitation.

Roosevelt stopped at the mansion briefly before going on the Milburn house to listen to an encouraging physician's report. He was heard to express how glad he was to hear the news.[79]

Once at the house, he went into the library with Cortelyou and Dr. Rixey. Roosevelt demanded the very best information as to the true condition of the President, and Rixey left to consult with the other doctors. After about thirty minutes, Rixey returned with the news that in all probability the President would indeed recover.

With that news, Roosevelt began sending messages to party leaders across the country and abroad, telling them of the optimistic reports of the physicians.

After he left the Milburn residence, Roosevelt went to the Buffalo Club, where he updated the Cabinet members who were waiting there. He refused to talk to reporters, but did chat with an old New York friend, and his comments found their way into print.

"When I came here this morning I felt a hundred years old," he said. "I did not think there was any hope. The situation is still very grave, and we may lose our President within a few hours, but the best surgeons and physicians to be secured are at his bedside and they say he will get well. We must prepare for the worst, but we have got the best of reasons for hoping for the best."[80]

---

[78] A. Wesley Johns, *The Man Who Shot McKinley* (New York: A. S. Barnes and Co., Inc., 1970) 134.

[79] A. Wesley Johns, *The Man Who Shot McKinley* (New York: A. S. Barnes and Co., Inc., 1970) 135.

[80] *New York Times*, 8 September 1901, pg. 1, col. 6.

At 2 p.m., Roosevelt left the Milburn house with Secretary of War Elihu Root and strolled along Ferry Street. He told reporters who were following along, again informing them that he did not wish to make any statements.[81]

Soon close friends and family of the President also began to arrive. Among the first was McKinley's political financial sponsor, Senator Mark Hanna of Ohio. Charles G. Dawes, another close confidant of the President's official family, also arrived. Other friends, many teary eyed, rushed to be near the President's sick bed: Judge William R. Day, Senator Charles W. Fairbanks, Charles H. Grosvenor and others. Longtime friend Myron T. Herrick started for Buffalo in his private car, accompanied by Mr. and Mrs. William Duncan, the President's sister and brother-in-law. Cabinet members Elihu Root, Emory Smith and others had taken the train to Buffalo from Washington, DC.[82]

The President's other sister, Helen McKinley, came and his brother Abner McKinley and his wife left a Colorado vacation in Denver early for Buffalo. Friends of Ida McKinley came too, including Mary McWilliams, Pina Barber and Sue Rand. John Barber, the First Lady's nephew, also arrived.[83]

The second floor of the Milburn house was virtually turned into a hospital ward. Downstairs there was a never-ending reception for visiting dignitaries, doctors and other visitors. The stables were converted into a White House communications office complete with telegraph. Next door, White House clerks and stenographers who arrived from Washington helped to answer the large volume of mail, which began to pour into what was fast becoming the "Buffalo White House."

By 3:30 p.m., the press release on the President's condition was unchanged; "The President continues to rest quietly, no change for the worse. Pulse 140, temperature 102, respiration 24."

Around the country, there was much speculation about the information being issued and about the type of injury the President had suffered. According to Dr. John B. Walker, a well-known New York surgeon, "Any injury to the stomach similar to that which has been inflicted on President McKinley is serious. There have been cases of

---

[81] A. Wesley Johns, *The Man Who Shot McKinley* (New York: A. S. Barnes and Co., Inc., 1970) 135.

[82] A. Wesley Johns, *The Man Who Shot McKinley* (New York: A. S. Barnes and Co., Inc., 1970) 131-132.

[83] A. Wesley Johns, *The Man Who Shot McKinley* (New York: A. S. Barnes and Co., Inc., 1970) 132.

stomach perforation where the patients have recovered. The diagnosis of any perforated wound of the stomach in an adult is very serious. The trouble is that inflammation following such an injury is more acute to an older person than to one more youthful. The fear is that the contents of the stomach might ooze into the intestines and peritonitis will set in."[84]

Another short bulletin was issued at 6:30 p.m., saying, "There is no change for the worse since last bulletin. Pulse 130, temperature 102.5, respiration 29."[85]

Many of the prominent government officials spent their time waiting at the Buffalo Club, about a block closer to downtown on Delaware Avenue and on the opposite side of the street from the Wilcox Mansion. The Buffalo Club was to serve as a virtual Cabinet room during the weeklong ordeal.

"We are meeting at the club here informally talking over the misfortune of the President," Postmaster General Emory Smith told reporters. "State matters are not being discussed either formally or informally. Four of the Cabinet members are stopping at the club at present. These are Gage, Knox, Hitchcock and myself. Secretary Wilson is expected to join us soon. His daughter left for Washington today. Secretary Root is at the home of Carleton Sprague. Secretaries Hay and Long have not arrived from Washington yet.

We have great hopes for the President's recovery. The statements of the physicians have made us quite confident."[86]

Senator Hanna left the Buffalo Club at about seven o'clock that night to go to the Milburn house. Looking grave, he entered and came out about thirty minutes later with his spirits lifted.

"It is favorable news because it is not unfavorable news," he told a newsman. "I have just had a fifteen minute talk with Dr. Rixey in which he thoroughly went over the entire situation. I wanted to know just how things stood. Dr. Rixey, who has been the President's physician for three years, knows him thoroughly. The President's excellent constitution gives him the chances of a man twenty years younger. His blood is in good condition and his heart action is all right. His will, his equipoise, and his character all tend to aid him in this emergency."

"And then you know what a strong will can do for a man," continued the Senator. "When a man like the President makes up his mind and says: 'I will not die,' the old one himself cannot knock him out."

---

[84] *New York Times*, 7 September 1901, pg. 1, col. 6.
[85] *New York Times*, 8 September 1901, pg. 1, col. 3.
[86] *Buffalo Courier*, 8 September 1901, pg. 22, col. 1.

Hanna was asked about the bullet still lodged in the President's body, and whether or not it had been found. Hanna told the reporters it had not, and that there was no sign of peritonitis. He also assured them that the President's high pulse rate was not something to be alarmed about, because according to Dr. Rixey, it was common for the President to have a high pulse. He added that the doctors said they would be able to tell by the next night if the President would indeed recover.

Before he left, he assured the public that the President's family and friends knew that the authorities had done everything possible to protect the President and that nothing "could have been done by any one to have thwarted so ingenious a plot as the one planned by the would-be assassin." He also assured the newsmen that the official bulletins being issued by the doctors could be relied upon as factual and accurate.[87]

When asked if it were true that he had sent a letter to his son Daniel saying that the President was sinking and would not live, he responded, "Absolutely not. There is not a word of truth in it. I have sent no telegram of the kind nor is the condition of the President such to warrant it."[88]

"I am sorry to have been the cause of trouble to the Exposition or of inconvenience to its officials or the people," the President had said weakly, characteristically thinking only of others.[89]

The final bulletin from the doctors that first day after the shooting was released at 9:30 p.m., with not much new to report; "Conditions continue much the same. The President responds well to medication. Pulse 132, temperature 102.5, respiration 25. All temperatures reported are taken in the rectum. The physicians in attendance wish to say that they are too busily engaged to reply to individual telegrams."[90]

At 10:40 p.m., John Milburn walked across the street to the press tent and chatted with reporters.

"Everything is proceeding satisfactorily." he told them. "If the President maintains his strength for twenty hours more we feel that he will surely recover. I personally feel quite hopeful."[91]

---

[87] *New York Times*, 8 September 1901, pg. 1, col. 4.

[88] *Buffalo Courier*, 8 September 1901, pg. 22, col. 1.

[89] *Buffalo Express*, 7 September 1901.

[90] *New York Times*, 8 September 1901, pg. 1, col. 3.

[91] *New York Times*, 7 September 1901, pg. 1, col. 1.

Sunday, September 8

As Saturday turned to Sunday, at 1:45 a.m., Secretary George Cortelyou issued a statement saying there was no change in the President's condition, while Drs. Mynter and Rixey kept watch in an all night vigil, the other physicians having left the house. There was a great deal of tension and if the President's condition were to deteriorate, it was believed, it would be during these hours.[92]

In the morning, Vice President Roosevelt, after attending church, stopped by with Senator Hanna and was very encouraged by the progress of the President. He used the occasion to attempt to expel rumors that the President's doctors were not being truthful with the public over the President's condition.

"Let me put it this way," Roosevelt said. "The doctors' bulletins are made with a scrupulous understatement of the favorable conditions, a scrupulous understatement."

"That expresses it well," seconded Senator Hanna.

"Yes," continued Mr. Roosevelt. "If anything, the doctors understate the hopefulness of the situation."[93]

Shortly thereafter, echoing Roosevelt's words, Cortelyou issued an official statement to the public: "The public will be kept fully advised of the actual condition of the President. Each bulletin is carefully and conservatively prepared and is an authoritative statement of the most important features of the case at the hour it is issued. The people are entitled to the facts and shall have them."[94]

Robert Todd Lincoln, son of President Lincoln and an ex-Secretary of War, left the house shortly after Roosevelt, and expressed the same hopeful air as had the Vice President.[95]

During Sunday's early morning hours, McKinley slept a great deal, and was at times somewhat confused and chilly. He was described as clear and bright by 8:20 a.m., and his pulse was strong. The dressing was then changed and the wound was found to be in a very satisfactory condition with no indication of peritonitis. [96]

---

[92] *New York Times*, 8 September 1901, pg. 1, col. 1.

[93] *Buffalo Evening News*, 9 September 1901, pg. 3, col. 3.

[94] Nelson W. Wilson, M.D. "Details of the McKinley Case" (*Buffalo Medical Journal, 41-57*) 221.

[95] *New York Times*, 9 September 1901, pg. 1, col. 3.

[96] "The Official Report on the Case of President McKinley" (*Buffalo Medical Journal 41-57*) 278.

The President looked at a group of his doctors and asked good-naturedly, "Which one of you did the cutting?"

"There is the guilty man," replied Dr. Mynter, pointing at Dr. Park.

"Ah, so you are the man," smiled the President, and he added with a bright face, "I think we shall have to invite you down to breakfast pretty soon."[97]

At 9 a.m. a bulletin was issued saying that the President had "passed a good night and his condition this morning is quite encouraging. His mind is clear and he is resting well; wound dressed at 8:30 and found in a very satisfactory condition. There is no indication of peritonitis. Pulse, 132; temperature 102.8; respiration, 24."[98]

During the morning hours, Dr. Charles McBurney, having been summoned by the other physicians as a consultant, arrived from New York City and examined the President. "McBurney's point" of abdominal tenderness was a household medical word, and his celebrated small incision for appendicitis operations had been widely copied.[99]

"I am not able to find a single unfavorable symptom in the President's case," Dr. McBurney told reporters. "There is not the slightest indication of peritonitis. The promptness with which the physicians and surgeons at the Emergency Hospital on the Exposition grounds operated upon the President and dressed his wounds is undoubted the reason for the splendid condition we find now. Everything is progressing as well as could be wished, and in another twenty-four hours we may be able to state as a fact what we now have every reason to believe—that the President will fully recover."[100]

After consulting with Dr. McBurney, Dr. Park added, "I feel certain President McKinley will get well. This is not 1881, but 1901, and great strides have been made in surgery in the past twenty years."[101]

But other doctors were not so confident. Dr. Edgar Wallace Lee, who had been the first to reach the President after the shooting, thought the President's condition was far more serious than generally believed.

"I consider that President McKinley's condition is serious, very serious," Lee said. "It does not matter where that second bullet lodged. We did not ascertain where it was. It may be in the President's back, or

---

[97] *Buffalo Courier*, 9 September 1901, pg. 1, col. 2.

[98] Nelson W. Wilson, M.D. "Details of the McKinley Case" (*Buffalo Medical Journal, 41-57*) 221.

[99] Selig Adler, "The Operation on President McKinley, *Scientific American* (March, 1963) 126.

[100] *New York Times*, 9 September 1901, pg. 1, col. 2.

[101] *New York Times*, 9 September 1901, pg. 1, col. 2.

it may be loose in the abdominal cavity. That is not important at present. It has done its work."[102]

The President's improvement continued throughout the day and at 4 p.m., another bulletin was issued saying that he had slept about four hours since nine o'clock. By 9 p.m., he was reported as resting comfortably with no change since the last bulletin.[103]

While the President slept, at about 2:30 p.m., Mrs. McKinley went for a carriage ride, being markedly better in spirits than the previous day. As she entered the carriage, the crowd began to cheer, but was admonished to keep quiet, so they complied and simply removed their hats.[104]

Major and Mrs. Rand arrived. The Rands were intimate friends of the McKinleys and Mrs. Rand's presence was viewed as very positive for Mrs. McKinley.[105]

The four hours of natural sleep encouraged the physicians as well. The President was completely recovered from the ether, and was in need of the rest. His sleep, the doctors unofficially reported, had been "quiet and reposeful."[106]

In addition, liquid nourishment of whiskey, hot water and raw egg was injected, in order to avoid inflaming the stomach wounds, for the first time since the shooting.

Through much of Sunday, the Cabinet and Vice President waited, much as everyone waited for news, at the Buffalo Club for news of the President's condition. The entire Cabinet was in Buffalo, with the exception of Secretaries Hay and Long, and they were expected within twenty-four hours. However, no government business was conducted. They waited.

As he left the house in the evening hours, Senator Hanna expressed the expectation of the President's recovery.

"Of course I want to be conservative," he said. "If the present condition of affairs continues for the next twenty-four hours the surgeons at the President's bedside will be able to give us news as satisfactory as we could wish, and, of course, that means news of his full and complete

---

[102] Murat Halstead, *The Illustrious Life of William McKinley* (Privately Published, 1901) 46.

[103] Nelson W. Wilson, M.D. "Details of the McKinley Case" (*Buffalo Medical Journal, 41-57*) 221.

[104] *New York Times*, 9 September 1901, pg. 1, col. 3.

[105] *Buffalo Evening News*, 8 September 1901, pg. 1, col. 3.

[106] *New York Times*, 9 September 1901, pg. 1, col. 2.

recovery. So far as any human agency can predict, the present satisfactory state of affairs will continue. The four hours of sleep that the President had today is evidence of his almost natural condition. His mind is clear and his whole condition is most hopeful." [107]

Monday, September 9

The morning hours of Monday, September 9 were quiet around the Milburn house. Few of the occupants stirred early, and except for the reporters, police and sentries, the street was deserted. The first bulletin of the morning on Monday, September 9 came at 6 a.m., reporting the President sleeping a "somewhat restless night, sleeping fairly well." [108]

This bulletin caused some concern of all whom read it, dashing momentarily the optimism that had been felt the previous night. But all was better upon the issuance of the next bulletin. Shortly after 8 o'clock, the doctors who had not sat with the President during the night began to arrive.

The 9:20 a.m. bulletin reported his condition was "becoming more and more satisfactory. Untoward incidents are less likely to occur." [109]

Upon leaving the house, Dr. Park was asked if the first bulletin was any cause of alarm.

"Not in the least," he replied. "It is entirely natural that a patient in the President's condition should have some periods of restlessness. But he is receiving no anesthetics. He is fully conscience at all times when he is awake and his mind is clear." [110]

As the day unfolded, the cloud that had prevailed over much of the preceding days seemed lifted. The question did not seem to be if the President would fully recover, but how quickly. While all had a reluctance to categorically state that the President would definitely survive, which was most certainly the feeling.

Shortly after noon, Secretary Ethan Allen Hitchcock and Senator Hanna emerged from the house, and when asked if the President was talking, Hanna quipped, "As much as he's allowed to."

---

[107] *New York Times*, 9 September 1901, pg. 1, col. 2.
[108] Nelson W. Wilson, M.D. "Details of the McKinley Case" (*Buffalo Medical Journal, 41-57*) 222.
[109] Nelson W. Wilson, M.D. "Details of the McKinley Case" (*Buffalo Medical Journal, 41-57*) 222.
[110] *New York Times*, 10 September 1901, pg. 1, col. 7.

"Mrs. McKinley was with the President for some little time this morning," he added. "She is doing splendidly."[111]

Mrs. McKinley had been admitted to her husband's bedside and stayed a bit. By all accounts she was bearing up well. The worries about her health that cropped up shortly after the shooting were also subsiding. Her presence also seemed to help the President immensely, even though Mrs. McKinley, for the most part, observed the rule of no talking to aid in the President's recovery.

"We must bear up," the President had told her. "It will be better for both."[112]

"I'm feeling much better this morning and have very little pain," he said to her. "In a few days more, my dear, we can talk all we wish. Keep brave and cheerful for my sake."[113]

Abner McKinley, with his daughter Mabel, was also allowed a brief moment with his brother. "Thank God that it was no worse," was Abner's first remark.

"It might easily have been," replied the President, "but the doctors say I am doing every bit as well as could be expected and that I will pull through all right. I am confident of it."[114]

Cortelyou told the reporters at 12:30 p.m., "The President is brighter now than at any time since the shooting. He asked what the news was a moment ago. While not out of danger, he is nearing the safety line. Mrs. McKinley is also much better."[115]

McKinley asked for the daily papers and for food, but was denied these things. He joked with one of the doctors that it was hard enough to be shot without being starved to death. He spoke of his assailant, "He must have been crazy." When told that the man had been an anarchist, McKinley said only that he hoped that he would be treated fairly.[116] He was also told of the outpouring across the nation and he remarked that he thought he was being too highly honored.[117]

---

[111] *New York Times*, 10 September 1901, pg. 2, col. 1.

[112] *Buffalo Commercial*, 7 September 1901.

[113] *Buffalo Courier*, 10 September, 1901.

[114] *Buffalo Courier*, 10 September 1901, pg. 1, col. 5.

[115] *Cincinnati Post*, 9 September 1901, pg. 1, col. 1.

[116] G. Townsend, *Memorial Life of William McKinley* (Washington: Memorial Publishing Co., 1901) 237.

[117] G. Townsend, *Memorial Life of William McKinley* (Washington: Memorial Publishing Co., 1901) 239.

The President asked when he might be able to eat and Dr. Rixey told him that it would take a week to ten days for the stomach wound to heal and that during that time he would not be able to eat solid food. Not good news, but the President bore it well. [118]

During the day, the President grew tired of lying in one position and asked his doctors if he might change the position some. With their consent, the President then, under his own power, adjusted himself. This was looked upon as another sign of his improving condition.

"I'm feeling much better," the President said as he smiled at Dr. Mynter.[119]

Later, the President was cautioned to remain quiet and he was reminded not to excite himself and what he had been told about talking. "Yes, I know yesterday, but I am a great deal better now."[120]

By 2:30, the press corps was getting restless. There had been no official bulletin since the 9:30 report and it began to provoke comments. However, since the doctors where not called back to the house, it was assumed that things had not changed for the worse. When Mrs. McKinley left the house for a thirty-minute carriage ride with Mrs. Lafayette McWilliams, it had the effect of calming fears.

Finally, at 3 p.m., the news from an official bulletin remained encouraging: "The President's condition steadily improves and he is comfortable, without pain or unfavorable symptoms. Bowel and kidney functions normally performed."[121]

"God's contribution to the American people will be the sparing of the President's life," John Milburn told reporters.[122]

As the doctors left after the afternoon consultation, Dr. Wasdin cheerily called to reporters saying, "Nothing new, gentlemen. The examination was perfectly satisfactory, and the patient is improving."[123]

Vice President Roosevelt, throughout the day seemed quite sanguine. He resolved to stay in Buffalo until the physicians issued a report virtually guaranteeing the President's recovery.

"I came here because I believed my place was near the President and I will not leave until the situation has entirely cleared up," he said. "If I

---

[118] G. Townsend, *Memorial Life of William McKinley* (Washington: Memorial Publishing Co., 1901) 240.

[119] *Buffalo Commercial*, 10 September 1901.

[120] *Buffalo Courier*, 10 September, 1901.

[121] Nelson W. Wilson, M.D. "Details of the McKinley Case" (*Buffalo Medical Journal, 41-57*) 222.

[122] *Buffalo Express*, 8 September 1901.

[123] *New York Times*, 10 September 1901, pg. 2, col. 2.

were predicting when I shall leave here I would say tomorrow because I firmly believe that the physicians will announce tomorrow that there is absolutely no doubt that the President will recover. I have been twice to the President's temporary home today, and I have seen nothing but smiling, happy faces, including a host of physicians, that would not be so unless the bulletins did not tell the exact truth."[124]

At 9:30 p.m., the bulletin simply stated that the President's condition continued to be favorable.[125]

McKinley's condition seemed to improve steadily throughout the day, and there was no pain or pressure over the abdomen. He took hot water by mouth throughout the day. Codeia was substituted for morphia, as the pain was less.[126] Mrs. McKinley dropped in on her husband long enough to kiss him and say good night.[127]

The President's brother Abner accompanied his sister and nieces, Mary and Kate Barber, to the train station at about 9:45 p.m.

"The nearest relatives of the President are so confident of his recovery that they have no hesitation about leaving," Abner told reporters at the station.[128]

By the late evening hours, there was a relaxed feeling on Delaware Avenue. The officers who guarded the street were less particular about who traversed the street. Police did not stop wagons from going at top speed by the nearest corner. The many newspapermen did not seem as quiet as they had the previous three days. In the press tents, while the lights of the Milburn house, except for the sickroom, were extinguished, the reporters, police and guards settled down for a quiet night.

Tuesday, September 10

By Tuesday, September 10, the country was being reassured as to the President's impending recovery. His temperature was down and he had been given nourishment by an enema. He was getting stronger. The weather that had been so much in the President's favor took an

---

[124] *New York Times*, 10 September 1901, pg. 2, col. 2.

[125] Nelson W. Wilson, M.D. "Details of the McKinley Case" (*Buffalo Medical Journal, 41-57*) 222.

[126] "The Official Report on the Case of President McKinley" (*Buffalo Medical Journal 41-57*) 279.

[127] Marshall Everett, *The Complete Life of William McKinley* (Privately Published, 1901) 45.

[128] *New York Times*, 10 September 1901, pg. 1, col. 6.

unfavorable turn during the morning hours, with drizzling rain coming with a cold front.

The first bulletin of the day, at 6:20 a.m., said only that the President had spent a comfortable night.

President McKinley was somewhat restless in the morning and asked to see the morning papers. He also asked the doctors when he would be permitted to sit up. But the physicians were extremely cautious. Only Mrs. McKinley and Cortelyou were permitted to see him.[129]

Dr. Charles McBurney, the prominent surgeon from New York who had arrived and was acting as a consultant, joined the other physicians in assuring the public that all was well. McBurney had pioneered the diagnosis and cure for appendicitis.

At 7:30 a.m. a bulletin was issued from the President's physicians, including Dr. McBurney. "The President has passed the most comfortable night since the attempt on his life," it read. "Pulse, 118; temperature, 100.4; respiration, 28."[130]

An automobile arrived at the Milburn residence about 7:50, bringing Secretary of State John Hay. He met a Secret Service man who showed him the morning bulletin and was pleased to hear of the President's condition. After being told that no one had come out of their rooms yet that morning, he went on to the Buffalo Club, promising to return.

The doctors began arriving for their formal morning consultation at eight o'clock[131] and by nine, the press bulletin was even more optimistic, saying, "The President's condition this morning is eminently satisfactory to his physicians. If no complications arise a rapid convalescence may be expected. Pulse, 104; temperature, 99.8; respiration, 26. The temperature was taken by mouth and should be read about one degree higher by rectum."[132]

The doctors came out of the house at 9:00 a.m. and made the results of their morning consultation public. Dr. Roswell Park explained, "The condition of the President this morning is entirely satisfactory. The bulletin will state this and it sums up the situation. The President spent the most comfortable night he has had since the shooting. He slept well, and when he was awake he was cheery, and even chatty. He is not receiving any nourishment thus far, except by enema. This is an all together natural incident of the case at this stage."

---

[129] *New York Times*, 11 September 1901, pg. 2, col. 3.

[130] *New York Times*, 11 September 1901, pg. 1, col. 5.

[131] *New York Times*, 11 September 1901, pg. 1, col. 7.

[132] *New York Times*, 11 September 1901, pg. 1, col. 5.

When asked if he thought the President was out of danger, Park stated, "I do not want to go that far. What can be said is that unless there are unexpected complications, we expect him to recover."

As far as the removal of the President, "No, it is too early for that, but when he is moved, he will probably go to Washington."

Dr. Mynter emerged and agreed, "The President is doing splendidly, and he is out of the woods, if I may express it that way."

"Yes," Dr. Wasdin added. "And he has plenty of daylight behind him."

"I have never been really optimistic because I do not like to prejudice serious cases," explained Dr. Mynter. "But now I can say to you that everything in the President's condition warrants the statement that he on the road to quick recovery."

"I believed throughout that the President has a fair chance of recovery," agreed Dr. Wasdin. "Now I desire to say that the chances against recovery are very slight. His temperature is splendid and his pulse is getting normal."[133]

Dr. McBurney was in equally high spirits when he left a few minutes later.

"We believe he is practically out of danger," he said. "Of course there are still possibilities in the case, and we will all feel better when a week has gone by. But his improvement is so marked, his symptoms are so good, that we feel safe in assuring the public that he will recover. Blood poisoning might still develop. We could not give a guarantee now, but the chances are remote. As for peritonitis, I consider that the danger from inflammation of the peritoneum has passed."

McBurney was asked if an abscess might form around the missing bullet, to which he replied that it was possible, but if it happened, they would simply locate the bullet via x-ray and remove it. If the bullet did not give the President any trouble, Dr. McBurney told the reporters that there would not be any reason for a second operation to remove it.[134]

About the President's passing out of danger, McBurney said, "We have locked door after door against the grim monster. I am satisfied. I am going to Niagara Falls today and see the sights."[135]

Director General Buchanan of the Exposition said, "The outlook is so encouraging that the Exposition authorities expect to fix a day of thanksgiving, when the public can unite in thanks that the President's life has been spared. It will be held sometime between now and September

[133] *New York Times*, 11 September 1901, pg. 2, col. 1.

[134] *New York Times*, 11 September 1901, pg. 2, col. 1.

[135] *New York Times*, 11 September 1901, pg. 2, col. 2.

25. We have no doubt that the whole country will participate in the movement and that it will assume the dimensions of a National thanksgiving."[136]

Not long after the 9 a.m. bulletin, with Gen. Charles H. Grosvenor by his side, Senator Hanna announced, "There is continuous steady improvement. Conditions could not be better. I will probably leave this city tonight for Cleveland." Hanna left a bit later with Grosvenor and Senator Charles W. Fairbanks.[137]

Judge William R. Day of Canton, the former McKinley Secretary of State and one his closest friends, arrived and stayed for short time. He felt so reassured with the President's condition that he left in the afternoon to return to Canton. The rest of the Cabinet left the house at about 1:00 p.m.[138]

"The President asked to sit up again this morning," Dr. Rixey declared. "When I demurred he said: 'Oh, I am stronger; see, I can move easily.'

"Then he gave some orders about closing his home at Canton and suggested that they prepare to move him to Washington, besides asking about some state affairs. It will not be possible to move him for three weeks."[139]

The press concentrated on the Garfield ordeal in its speculation of McKinley's progress. Some also wondered if all the doctors treating the President were getting along.

"There has been no difficulty in the councils at any time; each has loyally seconded the efforts of the others; and all have joined in carrying out the masterly work done by Dr. Mann immediately after the shooting," reported the *New York Times.*[140]

In fact, the optimism was so great that the President's visitors started to go back to their respective locations. Secretaries Lyman Gage and Philander C. Knox returned to Washington. Colonel Herrick had taken the McKinley relatives' home to Ohio in his private train. In addition, Hanna, Dawes, Secretary Root and Postmaster General Smith were making preparations to leave. The local Buffalo doctors began taking up

---

[136] *New York Times*, 11 September 1901, pg. 2, col. 2.

[137] *New York Times*, 11 September 1901, pg. 2, col. 2.

[138] *New York Times*, 11 September 1901, pg. 2, col. 3.

[139] *Cincinnati Post*, 10 September 1901, pg. 1, col. 2.

[140] *New York Times*, 11 September 1901, pg. 1, col. 5.

their regular patients again. Dr. Park stated that he expected the President to be fully recovered in three to four weeks.[141]

Secretary of State John Hay, accompanied by F. Moberly Bell of the *London Times,* had been met at the Buffalo train station by Major Louis Babcock and was in a melancholy mood, to say the least. He said to Babcock that he was certain that the President would not survive and it was obvious that he felt he was partially to blame; that he had a cloud around him that cursed his presidential acquaintances.

Hay had been a personal secretary to Abraham Lincoln and a personal friend of President James Garfield; the first two assassinated American presidents. Even though he had been told of President McKinley's improving condition, he still thought that his personal bad luck, and perhaps a curse, would surely doom the President. This gloomy attitude of the Secretary of State was the minority opinion of those around the President, however.

But even in light of the tragedy, those around the President realized that the wheels of government still must be turned. The Cabinet, it was reported, would meet, around the President's bed on Friday at 3:00 p.m., and it was said that Secretary Hay planned to stay for the meeting.

Many of the President's relatives left, having been satisfied there was no further need for alarm and Mrs. McKinley went out driving again and seemed completely recovered from the shock of the event and was feeling well. She received many visitors at the Milburn house that day.[142]

One of those visitors was Charles Dawes. Mrs. McKinley, hearing he was in the house, sent for him.

"She broke into tears when I came in but soon recovered herself and I talked with her for some time," Dawes wrote that day in his journal. "She says that the 'Lord is with us' and that her husband will recover. She sent her love to Caro and the children, for I told her that now that the President was out of danger I was going to leave for Washington in the evening."[143]

Vice President Roosevelt stood and watched the telegraph machine click out the news from the Milburn house. When it was finished, he clapped his hands together and said to Ansley Wilcox, "There! Didn't I tell you God wouldn't let such a noble man die by an assassin's bullet?"

[141] *New York Times*, 11 September 1901, pg. 1, col. 6.

[142] *New York Times*, 11 September 1901, pg. 1, col. 6.

[143] Charles W. Dawes, *A Journal of the McKinley Years* (Chicago: R. R. Donnelley & Sons Co., 1950) 279.

After breakfast, Mr. Wilcox told reporters that the Vice President was being urged to use his last day in Buffalo touring the Exposition.

"I do not believe, even though I am assured of the President's convalescence, that it would be entirely proper for me to take part in any of the festivities. I studiously refrained from going out or being entertained during my visit and I will continue that policy until I leave. I came here absolutely as a matter of duty both to the President and the people and not for pleasure."[144]

When Roosevelt stepped out onto the sidewalk to head to the Milburn house, a Secret Service man approached him in order to provide protection.

"I do not need you to follow me," he said. "I don't need anyone, and I am not afraid."[145]

The Vice President stayed at the Milburn house for some time. When he came out he was even more encouraged.

"You may say that I am absolutely sure that the President will recover," he exclaimed, "so sure, in fact, that I leave here to-night."

There had been rumors of a Cabinet meeting having been held since so many members where at the house, but Roosevelt put the gossip to rest.

"It was purely accidental," he said. "The members happened to call at the same time. I assure you there is no consultation. As a matter of fact, the various Cabinet members are distributed in various parts of the house talking to different members of the family and to the physicians. The reason I staid in so long was that I had not seen Secretary of State Hay for some time, and he and I had a long personal talk. There is no reason why the Cabinet members should not leave to-day as far as the President's condition is concerned."[146]

Roosevelt, who had conducted himself with grace during the whole affair, felt so confident about the President's health that he planned to join his family in the Adirondacks, saying that he would not attend the scheduled Cabinet meeting and that he had duties elsewhere.

Newspapers reported good tidings and those who visited the President left the Milburn House much relieved. Mrs. McKinley went for her carriage ride and Dr. McBurney even made his excursion to Niagara Falls to see the sights. After all, the President was resting comfortably and seemed very much on the road to recovery.

---

[144] *New York Times*, 11 September 1901, pg. 2, col. 2.

[145] *New York Times*, 11 September 1901, pg. 2, col. 2.

[146] *New York Times*, 11 September 1901, pg. 2, col. 2-3.

As the day wore on, the President began to show more confidence in his condition as he regularly began to turn himself over in bed to gain a more restful position, this time without asking permission from his doctors, as he had the previous day. His nurses noticed this activity as proof of the patients growing strength.[147]

But even during this time of optimism, there was still the very real danger of the spread of infection in the President's wounds. In fact, this was the most dangerous aspect of the President's recovery, and the doctors were well aware of the risk. In the age before infection fighting antibiotics, infection, which could start small, could quickly turn deadly. And the President's wound was anything but small. Even as the newspapers, friends, family and public officials reveled in the optimism of recovery, the unfound bullet was at rest somewhere behind the President McKinley's stomach.

Doctors had guessed that the bullet had stopped somewhere in the President's back muscles and was not an immediate cause of danger. Besides, even if the bullet was located with the new x-ray machine, the President might be too weak to survive a second operation to remove it.

Secretary Cortelyou had telephoned Thomas Edison in his West Orange laboratory asking that an x-ray machine be sent to Buffalo to possibly help locate the bullet still in the President's body.

Edison had instructed his manager, William E. Gilmore, to attend to the matter without delay. Peter Weber, manager of the manufacturing department of Edison Works, went to work with the help of his assistants, and had the shipment ready within a few hours.

Edison telegraphed Cortelyou to tell him that the machine had been shipped and that he had arranged for Dr. H. A. Knoll, an expert on the operation of the machine, along with several Edison assistants, to accompany it to Buffalo.[148] Knoll, accompanied by two operators, had arrived at the Milburn house at 10:10 a.m. the previous day. All was ready except for the ability of the President to survive another operation.

"There is no intention at present of using the x-ray," Knoll said as he left the house. "The machine was brought on to be here in readiness for use if it should be deemed necessary. The idea was that if the presence of the bullet should give trouble means would be at hand to remove it. At present the second bullet is not giving any concern whatever."[149]

---

[147] *New York Times*, 11 September 1901, pg. 1, col. 7.

[148] *New York Times*, 8 September 1901, pg.1, col. 2.

[149] *Buffalo Evening News*, 8 September 1901, pg.4, col. 2.

Dr. McBurney was particularly optimistic and the White House continued to issue statements about the President's improving condition.

The bulletin, which was issued at 3:20 p.m., read, "There is no change since this morning's favorable bulletin. Pulse, 110; Temperature, 100; respiration 28."[150]

The country, which had held its collective breath during the first hours following the shooting, began to breathe a little easier.

Vice President Theodore Roosevelt was told confidentially that McKinley, while not quite out of the woods, was well on the way. He was told that the President was "coming along splendidly" and that he was "on the high road to recovery." Reassured, the Vice President left to join his family at a camp high in the Adirondacks, twelve miles from any telephone or telegraph.

It is not possible to over emphasize that by all outward indications the President was getting better. Only fifty-eight years old and robustly healthy and strong, his temperature was down, his pulse was strong, and he was awake and alert. His doctors thought the main thing he needed was rest, and for that reason, they insisted that people leave the President alone, even his own wife, much to her dismay. The President felt so well that he seemed to want visitors. Only Mrs. McKinley, the doctors and nurses and occasionally Cortelyou had been permitted to see the President.

"It's mighty lonesome in here," he complained to Cortelyou, asking for the newspapers. With his secretary, the President's mind now turned to politics. He wanted to know the reaction to his speech of September fifth at the Exposition, and was pleased when Cortelyou told him that it had been very well received, both home and abroad.

The doctors, with the exception of Dr. McBurney, who had gone to Niagara Falls, had their afternoon consultation at about 3 o'clock.

"The conditions remain as they were this morning," said Dr. Park as he emerged. "If the bulletin is not more favorable than the last one it is because that one was so entirely favorable that it is difficult to state the facts more specifically. The President has enjoyed some sleep this morning. He continues cheerful. He has not talked, as we continue to restrain him from that effort. Neither has the time come yet for taking

---

[150] Nelson W. Wilson, M.D. "Details of the McKinley Case" (*Buffalo Medical Journal, 41-57*) 222.

solid food into the stomach by the usual means. The question when it will be safe to remove him is for the future, as it is too soon to consider that."[151]

The President was feeling better. When told by one of his physicians that he was progressing better than expected, he told him, "Doctor, I told you I'd get well."[152]

A lengthy evening bulletin concerning the President's condition was released to a waiting public at 10:30:

"The condition of the President is unchanged in important particulars," it read. His temperature is 100.6, pulse 114, respiration 28.

"When the operation was done on Friday last it was noted that the bullet had carried with it a short distance beneath the skin a fragment of the President's coat. This foreign material was, of course, removed, but a slight irritation of the tissues was produced, the evidence of which has appeared only tonight.

"It has been necessary on account of this slight disturbance to remove a few stitches and partially open the skin wound. This incident cannot give rise to other complications, but it is communicated to the public as the surgeons in attendance wish to make their bulletins entirely frank. In consequence of this separation of the edges of the surface wound the healing of the same will be somewhat delayed. The President is now well enough to take nourishment by the mouth in the form of pure beef juice."[153]

The physicians gathered in the evening for consultation and did not leave until almost midnight. The length of the talk had been the source of yet more speculation. But when Dr. McBurney came out of the house, he did all he could to dispel the ever-present rumors.

McBurney also announced to the reporters that the President was taking nourishment that evening by mouth, the first time since the shooting. It had been planned for the next day, and Dr. McBurney used it as evidence of the President's fast progress. McBurney confirmed that the President was dining on beef extract.

The other doctors who had listened to Dr. McBurney's statement, confirmed the news, said that nothing unfavorable had appeared in the President's condition, all climbed into a waiting automobile and were driven away. [154]

---

[151] *New York Times*, 11 September 1901, pg. 2, col. 3.
[152] Franklin Matthews, "The President's Last Days", *Harper's Weekly*, 21 September 1901, pg. 943.
[153] *New York Times*, 11 September 1901, pg. 1, col. 5.
[154] *New York Times*, 11 September 1901, pg. 1, col. 5.

After the evening bulletin, Cortelyou and Milburn also made an appearance in the press tent to quiet any alarm that may have arisen, reasserting the unimportance of the procedure. Cortelyou announced that there would be no more consultations until morning. All was then quiet at the Milburn house. A thunderstorm that had been brewing for hours finally broke with the doctor's departure, and the rain came down in torrents.[155]

Wednesday, September 11

Shortly after midnight, in the first minutes of Wednesday, September 11, the President was given 4 c.c. of beef juice, which was the first food taken by stomach since the shooting. Later, at 2 a.m., a nutritive enema was given. Since the rectum was becoming irritated and did not take the enemas well, the President was given beef juice every one to two hours during the day.[156]

At six o'clock, the first morning bulletin was issued, saying, "The President has passed a very comfortable night."[157]

The physicians began to arrive that morning at about 8 o'clock, Dr. Mynter being the first. Doctors Park, McBurney, and Mann soon followed him. They had a consultation and issued a joint statement at 9 a.m., saying, "The President rested comfortably during the night. Decided benefit has followed the dressing of the wound made last night. His stomach tolerates the beef juice well and it is taken with great satisfaction. His condition this morning is excellent. Pulse, 116; temperature 100.2."[158]

The President was gaining so well that he was joking with his nurse. Miss Mohn was taking the President's temperature and he noticed her looking at her watch.

"One I had a watch too: yes, even a pocketbook," he chided. "I saw them taking my watch and my pocketbook and now I have nothing whatever."

---

[155] *New York Times*, 11 September 1901, pg. 1, col. 6.

[156] "The Official Report on the Case of President McKinley" (*Buffalo Medical Journal 41-57*) 280.

[157] "The Official Report on the Case of President McKinley" (*Buffalo Medical Journal 41-57*) 280.

[158] Nelson W. Wilson, M.D. "Details of the McKinley Case" (*Buffalo Medical Journal, 41-57*) 223.

Dr. Mynter joined in, "Oh, you are virtually convalescent, Mr. President. I don't know whether to ascribe it to your magnificent constitution or to the prayers of the whole nation."

"Undoubtedly, the prayers of the nation have had a very great deal to do with result," McKinley responded.

"A Catholic priest, a friend of mine, asked me to tell you that his whole congregation had prayed for your recovery," Mynter added.

"My Catholic friends have always been entirely kind to Mrs. McKinley and me," the President said. "Give your friend, the priest, my kind regards and tell him I am very grateful to him and his congregation."[159]

About 9:20, Mynter left the house telling the waiting reporters, "Everything is favorable and we have tripled the amount of nourishment, giving him now three teaspoonfuls of beef juice every hour instead of one. But the President's recovery will be slow. All talk of him sitting up in a few days and leaving Buffalo in a week is nonsense. I shall be satisfied if he can be moved in six weeks."[160]

Dr. Park emerged from the house a couple minutes later. He was very satisfied with the progress of the patient.

"It could not be better," he said. "The results have been excellent and this morning we have increased the quantity of beef juice fed by the mouth. The bowels have moved, showing that the natural digestive processes are operating and that the wounds in the side of the stomach are not interfering with the proper assimilation of food going into it."

Dr. Park then spent considerable time explaining the minor 'operation' that was performed the previous evening on the President's wound, insisting that the word 'operation' was not descriptive of the procedure and that it was a very minor thing. The doctors had simply been checking for contamination and had found none. He said this type of procedure was not unusual in gunshot cases were foreign matter is often carried inside the victim. He assured the reporters that "not a particle" was found.[161]

When he came out of the house with Dr. McBurney at 10:08 a.m., Dr. Mann found himself also explaining the previous evening's procedure.

"What was done last night was merely the usual dressing of the incision of the abdomen requisite to keep it in proper condition," Mann said. "The incision is about five inches in length, just above the naval,

[159] *Buffalo Express*, 11 September 1901.

[160] *New York Times*, 12 September 1901, pg. 1, col. 7.

[161] *New York Times*, 12 September 1901, pg. 1, col. 7.

horizontal and in line with the body. There is no cross incision. This cut was laid open carefully and some antiseptic gauze inserted. The results were entirely satisfactory and the President's condition this morning shows the benefit of what was done. He is cheerful and confident. In fact, he is doing so well that I would not be surprised if we let him have a cigar before long."

Mann told the reporters that moving the President was not being considered because the doctors felt he would be better off in Buffalo than in the Washington heat and he thought the President would remain in Buffalo until at least October.[162]

Dr. Mann was also asked if he thought the bullet might later cause problems for the President.

"Not at all," he replied. "There is no need of extracting the bullet. I have known a man who carried a bullet in the muscles of his heart. In this case the bullet in encysted by this time, and it is not a feature of the case to give further concern."[163]

Mann again repeated that the previous night's procedure had been routine.

"The incident of last night was insignificant," he said. "In an ordinary hospital it would not be mentioned in the history of the case. We debated the matter, however, and decided that as we had promised to be entirely frank with the public we would stand by our pledge."[164]

Dr. McBurney responded to questions about when the President could be moved to Washington by saying, "If it were necessary he could be moved today. He could be placed in an ambulance, taken to the train, placed on a lounge in a special car, and taken to Washington. This is, so far as his condition is concerned. But there is no reason why he should not enjoy every comfort and take his time about it. It will not hurt him to remain a few weeks in Buffalo."[165]

At about ten o'clock, the remaining stitches in the wound were removed, with the wound being separated and dressed. The doctors thought it appeared to be doing very well.[166]

During the day, Mrs. McKinley remained in good spirits, going for her usual carriage ride with Mrs. Lafayette McWilliams at 3:10 in the afternoon, appearing bright and cheerful, and not returning until 4:20.

[162] *New York Times*, 12 September 1901, pg. 2, col. 1.

[163] *New York Times*, 12 September 1901, pg. 2, col. 1.

[164] *New York Times*, 12 September 1901, pg. 2, col. 1.

[165] *New York Times*, 12 September 1901, pg. 2, col. 1.

[166] "The Official Report on the Case of President McKinley" (*Buffalo Medical Journal 41-57*) 280.

The Cabinet members who were in Buffalo, met in the Glenny house, which adjoined the Milburn mansion and was being pressed into service, but did no real business, spending time talking about the various legal phases of the case against the President's would-be assassin. After the meeting they crossed to the Sprague house for lunch.[167]

Shortly after the morning consultation, Consul Blanchetti called and brought a large floral arrangement on an easel featuring a flag six feet high. It was taken into the residence, but not to the President's room, as it was thought that it was not wise to have flowers in a sick room.[168]

The 3:30 p.m. bulletin read, "The President continues to gain and the wound is becoming more healthy. The nourishment taken into the stomach is being gradually increased."[169]

Dr. H. A. Knoll, the x-ray expert sent by Thomas Edison, left the house and was questioned by the reporters.

"The x-ray machine will positively not be used on the President within the next week or ten days," he told them.[170]

At ten o'clock the final bulletin of the day was issued, "The President's condition continues favorable. Blood count corroborates clinical evidence of the absence of any blood poisoning. He is able to take nourishment and relish it."[171]

The President slept throughout much of the day, and expressed himself as feeling comfortable. The only medicine given him was a hypodermic of strychnine. In the evening, the patient was changed to a fresh bed, and the enemas were resumed.[172]

Shortly before 11 p.m., Dr. Wasdin and Dr. Mynter left the house together. Immediately newspaper reporters besieged Mynter from all sides.

"Good news, good news, nothing but good news," he exclaimed. "We have washed and fed the President and moved him to another bed."

---

[167] *New York Times*, 12 September 1901, pg. 1, col. 6.

[168] *Buffalo Courier*, 12 September 1901, pg. 5, col. 1.

[169] Nelson W. Wilson, M.D. "Details of the McKinley Case" (*Buffalo Medical Journal, 41-57*) 223.

[170] *Buffalo Courier*, 12 September 1901, pg. 5, col. 2.

[171] Nelson W. Wilson, M.D. "Details of the McKinley Case" (*Buffalo Medical Journal, 41-57*) 223.

[172] "The Official Report on the Case of President McKinley" (*Buffalo Medical Journal 41-57*) 280.

When asked if the President was still improving he replied, "He is: and to prove it I desire to say that a count of his blood shows that it is in a normal condition, and we feel that we can announce definitely that there is not the least indication of blood poisoning."[173]

Dr. Wasdin then explained to the reporters present that a count of the blood was a microscopic determination of the relative number of white and red corpuscles in the blood to determine whether or not any inflammation existed. He said that if the number of white corpuscles increased, it might indicate the presence of inflammation and deterioration of the blood that might indicate peritonitis, which is a form of blood poisoning. Wasdin explained that in the morning hours, they had taken a blood sample from the lobe of the President's ear. Under his direction the white corpuscles were counted under a microscope.

"We found that the number of white corpuscles was just about normal, while the red cells were slightly below normal, due to insufficient nutrition since the operation," he told the reporters. "The count was not made to verify the fact that blood poisoning did not exist, of which we felt certain, but to remove every shade of doubt. The result is that we feel safe in announcing that not a trace of blood poisoning, peritonitis or inflammation exists. The test could not have been more satisfactory."[174]

Wasdin was asked if he thought the President was out of danger.

"No, I would not say that," he responded. "He is a very sick man, but his condition under the circumstances could not be better. That much I will say emphatically."[175]

Dr. McBurney left shortly after 11 p.m. and confirmed that no sign of blood poisoning or peritonitis was found. He confirmed that while the blood test was not undertaken to find peritonitis that it would have shown if it existed. The examination was a simply a way of testing the condition of President's blood, he said.

McBurney placed great emphasis upon the fact that the President was now taking up to an ounce of beef juice per hour and that his stomach was not rejecting it, and that the bullet wounds in the stomach were healing nicely. He felt it was vital to the recovery that the President be able to take nourishment in order to build his strength to fight possible infection. In addition, he said the wound was doing very well and it had been redressed. When asked if the President would recover, he simply smiled and said, "Oh, yes."[176]

[173] *New York Times*, 12 September 1901, pg. 1, col. 5.
[174] *New York Times*, 12 September 1901, pg. 1, col. 5.
[175] *New York Times*, 12 September 1901, pg. 1, col. 5.
[176] *New York Times*, 12 September 1901, pg. 1, col. 6.

"There is not the slightest sign of blood poisoning or any other complication," he told the reporters. "Altogether the conditions are all right. You may be sure of that."[177]

Dr. Mann, feeling his presence was not necessary did not go to the mansion and Dr. Park expressed his agreement with what the other doctors had said. Secretary of War Root, who had been given personal assurances by Dr. Park as to the President's improvement and condition, was comfortable enough to make plans to leave for New York City the following day. Secretary of State John Hay left Buffalo and returned to Washington.

Thursday, September 12

The President slept well through the night and awoke on the morning of September 12 feeling a good deal better. At about 7:20 a.m., Dr. Rixey, who had spent the night attending the President, reported that he had slept through the night. The President requested toast and coffee. After a consultation between the doctors, he ate a small quantity. He was apparently regaining his appetite, as later in the morning he asked for more beef juice. This he was given along with a little chicken broth, as well as some whiskey and water.[178]

A nurse later said that the President enjoyed it immensely and that he smacked his lips and asked if he could have more.[179]

"The President was not given solid food before he could stand it," explained Dr. Park later. "He was perfectly able to assimilate the food given him, had it not been that the impoverished blood affected the heart. The heart refused to act properly without strong blood food, and that was why the toast, soaked in hot beef juice, was given him. He was not given coffee. He relished the food and asked for a cigar, but this was denied. Everything known to medical science was done for him, and there was no mistake made."[180]

"At the time solid food was given him he was able to take it," agreed Dr. Mynter. "There can be no mistake about that. I do not believe that the food in his stomach had much effect on the heart."[181]

---

[177] *New York Times*, 12 September 1901, pg. 2, col. 1.

[178] "The Official Report on the Case of President McKinley" (*Buffalo Medical Journal 41-57*) 282.

[179] A. Wesley Johns, *The Man Who Shot McKinley* (New York: A. S. Barnes and Co., Inc., 1970) 154 .

[180] Alexander K. McClure, *The Authentic Life of William McKinley* (W. E. Skull, 1901) 332.

[181] Alexander K. McClure, *The Authentic Life of William McKinley* (W. E. Skull, 1901) 332.

At first denied, he was given more a bit later. Afterwards he seemed quiet and quite satisfied. He also was asking the nurse about how the press was reporting his case, but his doctors tried to discourage conversation. He seemed seeking information, thought the nurse, but his questions were ignored.[182]

At 9:30 a.m., the official statement, released by the doctors stated, "The President has spent a quiet and restful night and has taken much nourishment. He feels better this morning than at any time. He has taken a little solid food this morning and relished it."[183]

Indeed, the President had passed the time for peritonitis and sepsis. The bowels had moved and gas passed freely, indicating that there were no obstructions. His tongue was clear and his appetite was increasing, and he seemed to be able to digest what he ate. There was no pain in his abdomen and he was able to turn easily to sleep on his side. His spirits were good and his mind clear. His pulse was frequent but strong and his temperature had improved.[184]

The most important reason for feeding the President by mouth was his inability to retain any more "nutritive enemas" of egg and brandy. The surgeons, knowing that the President had not digested some chicken broth, beef extract and toast he had been given, subscribed to the theory of the day that the contents of the bowels were toxic and causing intestinal poisoning. Also, quite simply, the President wanted to eat.

To reporters, Dr. Mynter described the patient's progress as "Eminently satisfactory." Referring to his complaints of fatigue, he explained, "The President is feeling the strain of his long siege without food, no nourishment at all having been administered during the first three days and lying day and night practically in the same position is fatiguing and hard for even the most exemplary patient to bear without murmuring."[185]

Dr. Mann came out of the house and added, "The patient could not be doing better. Why he even asked for a cigar. But he will have to wait a while yet before we allow him to smoke."[186]

---

[182] A. Wesley Johns, *The Man Who Shot McKinley* (New York: A. S. Barnes and Co., Inc., 1970) 154.

[183] Nelson W. Wilson, M.D. "Details of the McKinley Case" (*Buffalo Medical Journal, 41-57*) 223.

[184] "The Official Report on the Case of President McKinley" (*Buffalo Medical Journal 41-57*) 282.

[185] *New York Times*, 13 September 1901, pg. 1, col. 7.

[186] *New York Times*, 13 September 1901, pg. 1, col. 7.

For his part, Dr. McBurney, as he came out to leave about 10:30, jokingly added, "If we can find a real hen's egg, fresh laid for invalids, we will give it to him soft boiled."[187]

McBurney also told of an exchange he had with the President.

"When he had finished his meal this morning, he told me he would like a mild cigar," Dr. McBurney related. "I replied: 'Well, Mr. President, you cannot have one but I can.' The President smiled and told me I could find all I desired downstairs."

When asked when the President may be able to sit up in bed, McBurney replied, "It is merely a manner of mechanics. So far as his general condition is concerned he would be able to sit up long before we will allow him to do so. The wound must heal tight. He is like a man with his vest open."[188]

"He could see a visitor now and then without injury," McBurney said in response to questions about if the President was well enough for visitors, "but we want to put off the beginning as long as we can. If one of his friends had been admitted three days ago, three would see him today. The longer we are able to keep the first visitor away, the better it will be."

As he turned to leave, McBurney advised the reporters, "Now, don't make it too strong. Say his condition is perfectly satisfactory to his physicians."[189]

Shortly after noon, McBurney left for Albany aboard the Empire State Express, along with Secretary of War Elihu Root, who was en route to New York City.[190] Root's son was very sick with typhoid fever, so the President's health was not the only thing on his mind that day.

Before Root left for New York, a Cabinet conference was held at the Buffalo Club. The secretaries present, who included Root, Wilson, Smith and Hitchcock, all agreed not to visit the President for at least a week, in order to give him time to fully recuperate. They resolved to try to keep the President's mind free from the affairs of state as long as they could. Dr. McBurney had advised them not to move the President until he was able to walk out under his own power, without assistance. [191]

---

[187] *New York Times*, 13 September 1901, pg. 1, col. 7.

[188] *New York Times*, 13 September 1901, pg. 1, col. 7.

[189] *New York Times*, 13 September 1901, pg. 1, col. 7.

[190] A. Wesley Johns, *The Man Who Shot McKinley* (New York: A. S. Barnes and Co., Inc., 1970) 155.

[191] *New York Times*, 13 September 1901, pg. 2, col. 1.

Upon arriving in New York, Secretary Root told waiting newsmen, "When I left Buffalo at 1 o'clock this afternoon the President was resting comfortably and a general air of optimism seemed to pervade all quarters. I was assured by Dr. McBurney that the President's recovery was but a question of a few weeks and that there was every reason for believing that the recovery would be complete."

Root said that some members of the Cabinet would remain in Buffalo but that the entire Cabinet would not be back in Buffalo unless summoned. The virtual capital of the nation would be Buffalo, until the President returned to Washington. Secretaries Smith and Hitchcock would remain indefinitely.[192]

Back in Buffalo, at almost that very moment, it was noticed that the President's pulse was not quite so good. The President was given an infusion of digitalis and strychnine. The doctors thought that in all probability the patient was suffering from some intestinal toxemia, as there had been no free movement from the bowels since the introduction of food. Gradually the pulse went to 130, and then grew weaker.[193]

The 3 p.m. bulletin, while optimistic, showed the first small hint of what was to come: "The President's condition is very much the same as this morning. His only complaint is of fatigue. He continues to take in a sufficient amount of food. Pulse, 126; temperature 100.2 degrees."[194]

Dr. Park told reporters that they had doubled the amount of beef juice the President was taking, thinking it important to continue to build his strength in order to enable him to heal. However, Dr. Mynter told them that the solid food that had been given the President that morning had not particularly agreed with him. After the afternoon bulletin was released, Secretary Cortelyou went to the press tent and was closely questioned to the meaning of that statement. He explained that it might be only natural that the President feel that way after his six day ordeal. The doctors that came and went did not appear particularly disturbed to observers.[195]

"The solid food given to the patient has not distressed him," explained Dr. Wasdin. "He digested it in a satisfactory manner. The subject was not discussed at our consultation.... He is naturally tired from lying in bed so long and from lack of nourishment for several days subsequent to the shooting."[196]

[192] *New York Times*, 13 September 1901, pg. 2, col. 2.
[193] "The Official Report on the Case of President McKinley" (*Buffalo Medical Journal 41-57*) 282.
[194] *New York Times*, 13 September 1901, pg. 1, col. 5.
[195] *New York Times*, 13 September 1901, pg. 2, col. 1.
[196] *New York Times*, 13 September 1901, pg. 2, col. 1.

Still, to be sure the patient received the best possible care, the President's doctors called in a stomach specialist for consultation, Dr. Charles Stockton. Stockton was an eminent general practitioner, the other doctors being surgeons. Stockton ordered a dose of calomel in addition to the castor oil that had already been administered. He also ordered the feeding to be stopped. When by the evening hours the President had still not passed the food, he was given an additional dehydrating cathartic enema. The President grew faint as a result, and Stockton was forced to administer heart stimulants.[197]

At 4:45, Dr Rixey made the following entry into his journal: "Mind wandering and restless."[198]

Senator Mark Hanna had previously scheduled an appearance before the Grand Army of the Republic, which was encamped near Cleveland. He had recently been elected a member and did not want to miss the opportunity. Before he left for the engagement, he asked the doctors for the most current condition of the President, so that he could pass it on to the troops at his speech. He was told that the President had passed the most critical point and that he would assuredly live. In Cleveland, right before his speech, Hanna received a telegram from Secretary Cortelyou, confirming the President's good condition. Hanna triumphantly announced it to the crowd amid wild cheers.[199]

But by 8:30 p.m. the tone of the doctor's bulletin markedly changed: "The President's condition this evening is not quite so good. His food has not agreed with him and has been stopped. Excretion has not yet been properly established. The kidneys are acting well. His pulse is not satisfactory, but has improved in the past two hours. The wound is doing well. He is resting quietly. Temperature, 100.2; pulse, 128."[200]

When Cortelyou handed out the bulletin, he admitted to the reporters that the President was not doing so well. "But," he was quick to add; "We all expect that the President will be better in the morning."[201]

---

[197] Selig Adler, "The Operation on President McKinley, *Scientific American* (March, 1963) 127.

[198] *Buffalo Courier*, 27 October 1901, pg. 1, col. 6.

[199] Herbert Croly, *Marcus Alonzo Hanna* (New York: The MacMillan Co., 1923) 358-359.

[200] Nelson W. Wilson, M.D. "Details of the McKinley Case" (*Buffalo Medical Journal, 41-57*) 223.

[201] *Washington Post*, 14 September 1901, pg. 2, col. 7.

During the day, the President had asked about his assailant.

"They did not hurt him did they?" he asked.

At first the doctors did not know what he was talking about. As they realized, the President said, "He is unharmed?"

"Yes." The President's face brightened. [202]

The President's doctors gathered an hour earlier than usual for their evening consultation. Afterward, the doctors retired for the evening, only to be called back to the Milburn House later that night.

At 9:35 p.m., Secretaries Hitchcock and Wilson arrived at the Milburn house in search of good news. Dr. Mann told them that the food that had been given the President was lying in his delicate stomach and was causing some trouble. They felt that by morning, he should be better.[203]

At almost this exact moment, Dr. Rixey was entering into his log the condition of the President, writing, "Whole body moist and cold. Pulse weak and thready. Slept quietly for 20 minutes."[204]

By midnight, the release simply said: "All unfavorable symptoms in the President's condition have improved since the last bulletin."[205] Cortelyou, with Milburn by his side, told newsmen that the President has responded to medical treatment, was better and was resting nicely.[206]

During the night the President had two bowel movements, and the doctors hoped this would help his wild heart beat. The President's pulse decreased from 128 to 120, but his temperature stayed at 100.2.[207]

"It has been said that the President was in a stupor at this time," commented one of his nurses. "That is not true. The patient was as bright and cheery as could possibly be expected, and occasionally conversed in a low tone. He was somewhat tired, however, and seldom moved in bed. As morning approached he became worse. The bulletins given out from time to time during the morning were absolutely correct. It was a gradual decline."[208]

[202] *Buffalo Express,* 13 September 1901.

[203] A. Wesley Johns, *The Man Who Shot McKinley* (New York: A. S. Barnes and Co., Inc., 1970) 155.

[204] *Buffalo Courier,* 27 October 1901, pg. 1, col. 6.

[205] Nelson W. Wilson, M.D. "Details of the McKinley Case" (*Buffalo Medical Journal, 41-57*) 223.

[206] A. Wesley Johns, *The Man Who Shot McKinley* (New York: A. S. Barnes and Co., Inc., 1970) 156.

[207] A. Wesley Johns, *The Man Who Shot McKinley* (New York: A. S. Barnes and Co., Inc., 1970) 156.

[208] G. Townsend, *Memorial Life of William McKinley* (Washington: Memorial Publishing Co., 1901) 268.

But the reporters outside suspected something was not quite right, even when Dr. Mynter told them that the President's condition was not alarming. The doctor's left by the back door of the house, avoiding the reporters for the time being. One person close to the case, but who refused to be identified, told the *New York Times*, "I do feel some concern about the President's case, but I think this will be dispelled by tomorrow morning, as a result of the treatment that is being administered to him."[209]

Secretary of State John Hay, a veteran of two presidential assassinations, had an uneasy feeling about the President's recovery. Later, in a letter to Henry Adams, he wrote, "Root and I left Buffalo on Wednesday [September 11] convinced that all was right. I had arranged with Cortelyou that he was to send a wire the next day telling me if the Doctors would answer for the President's life. He sent it, and I wrote a circular to all our Embassies saying that recovery was assured. I thought it might stop the rain of inquiries from all over the world. After I had written it, the black cloud of foreboding which is always just over my head, settled down and enveloped me, and I dared not send it. I spoke to Adee and he confirmed my fears. He distrusted the eighth day. So I waited— and the next day he was dying."[210]

Friday, September 13

As Thursday turned into Friday the thirteenth, the relief that the physicians had hoped for seemed briefly to come. The President had two bowel movements in quick succession, which eased the depression somewhat among his physicians. This gave them great encouragement and they changed the bulletin they had been working on to a more upbeat message.

Shortly after 2 a.m. on Friday, the President's condition suddenly became grave and he experienced what was described as a "sinking spell." A general alarm was sent out to the President's doctors and nurses, saying he was in extremely critical condition.

George Cortelyou sent an urgent telegram to Col. Montgomery at the White House saying, "The President is critically ill. Notify the Cabinet. The President's condition has grown worse during the night and he is extremely weak."[211]

---

[209] *New York Times*, 13 September 1901, pg. 1, col. 6.
[210] William R. Thayer, *The Life and Letters of John Hay, Vol. II* (Boston: Houghton Miffen Co., 1915) 267.
[211] *Washington Post*, 13 September 1901, pg. 1, col. 3.

As the President's secretary met with an anxious bunch of reporters, he read their faces and answered their questions before they were asked by telling them, "The President is much worse. He is weaker and the situation is extremely grave."[212]

Dr. Park reached the house after being summoned at 2:50 a.m., with Secretaries Wilson and Hitchcock soon following. Abner McKinley, the President's brother, was called to the house at 2:40 and arrived pale and anguished about eight minutes later by carriage, immediately rushing into the house.[213]

The downturn in President McKinley's condition came quickly, and the optimism of the previous days disappeared just as quickly. After the bowel movements, the President had rallied slightly but very briefly, giving rise to hopes that were soon cruelly dashed. The President's pulse fluttered, his heart weakened, and the doctors and nurses felt the end was near. By 3:00 a.m., all the doctors were at the President's bed side and they administered digitalis and strychnine and as a last resort injected a saline solution intravenously. The doctors who had left were summoned back to the house. Through the thunder and lightening of the evening, they conferred. Messages were sent recalling close friends, relatives and government officials to the Milburn house.[214]

At about 2:50 a.m., the following bulletin was issued: "The President's condition is very serious and gives rise to the greatest apprehension. His bowels have moved well, but his heart does not respond properly to stimulation. He is conscious. The skin is warm, and the pulse small, regular, easily compressible, 126; respiration, 30; temperature 100."[215]

George Cortelyou tried to reach Senator Hanna at home on the long distance telephone but was not successful. He then called Colonel Myron T. Herrick who was with Webb C. Hayes. They both tried to reach the Senator by phone but could not. Finally a neighbor was reached who went to the house and aroused the Senator.[216]

---

[212] *Washington Post*, 14 September 1901, pg. 1, col. 7.

[213] *New York Times*, 13 September 1901, pg. 1, col. 5.

[214] A. Wesley Johns, *The Man Who Shot McKinley* (New York: A. S. Barnes and Co., Inc., 1970) 157.

[215] Nelson W. Wilson, M.D. "Details of the McKinley Case" (*Buffalo Medical Journal, 41-57*) 223.

[216] Murat Halstead, *The Illustrious Life of William McKinley* (Privately Published, 1901) 56.

Senator Hanna received the alarming news at about 3 a.m., and within two hours, at 5:24, was on his way back to Buffalo with friends and family aboard a special train on the Lake Shore Road. The train reached speeds of eighty miles per hour, and made the scheduled four-hour trip in three hours and eleven minutes.[217] He arrived to find the President's condition critical.

Mrs. McKinley, being frail, was not told of the President's weakening state, and was permitted to sleep, unaware that the end was near.

The President struggled through the night. At four o'clock the saline solution seemed to have some effect, and at 4:45, Cortelyou sent word to the White House: "The President has rallied and is resting more comfortably."[218]

At 6 a.m., Secretary Hitchcock emerged from the house and told the waiting newsmen, "The President is rallying slowly, and we still think he has more than an even chance of recovery."[219] Dr. Rixey told the newsmen, "The President has rallied somewhat, but then, you know, the President is usually better in the morning."[220]

By daylight, the newspapers of Buffalo were on the street announcing to residents that the President was dying. As a result, a crowd began to form near Ferry and Delaware Streets. They stood behind ropes, some distance from the intersection, worriedly awaiting the morning bulletin.

Dr. Wasdin arrived at 8:15, telling reporters he had no new information as to the President's condition. Minutes later, Abner McKinley came out of the house and told his driver that he would not be going to his hotel for breakfast.

A new detail of soldiers from Fort Porter arrived shortly thereafter and took over sentry duties. Dr. Mann arrived at 8:25, refusing comment to reporters. Dr. Park was the last of the President's physicians to arrive at 8:45 a.m. The doctors immediately went into consultation.

An old woman approached one of the guards and insisted on seeing Mrs. McKinley, saying that she had something very important to tell her. She was kindly led away by a Secret Service agent, who listened to her long story of how the President could be healed by herbs and prayers.[221]

"It was reported down town that the President was dead," said George P. Sawyer, a friend of Mr. Milburn's, as he left the house about 9

---

[217] *New York Times*, 14 September 1901, pg. 2, col. 2.

[218] *Washington Post*, 13 September 1901, pg. 1, col. 3.

[219] *New York Times*, 14 September 1901, pg. 1, col. 5.

[220] *New York Times*, 14 September 1901, pg. 1, col. 6.

[221] *New York Times*, 14 September 1901, pg. 1, col. 6.

a.m. "The flag on the big liberty pole on the terrace at Exchange and May streets was half masted. I am glad to be able to say that the President is better than he was three hours ago. The surgeons are dressing his wound"[222]

At the President's bedside, the doctors thought he was asleep. Dr. Mynter gave him an injection of strychnine.

"What is that, doctor?" the President asked as he awoke.

"A heart stimulant," replied Mynter.

"Is the necessary great?" asked the President.

"Yes, Your Excellency," said the doctor. "You are a brave and very sick man."

"I realize it," replied the President.

The doctors' consultation lasted until 9:40 a.m. The doctors were reporting that his condition had "somewhat improved. There is a better response to stimulation. He is conscious and free of pain."[223]

The doctors all came out together and stopped on the lawn to tell the President's brother their opinion first. As Dr. Mann and Dr. Mynter came away together, Mann said, "We are very anxious, very anxious," as he entered a waiting carriage. He was asked he was giving up hope.

"By no means," he responded. "He is better than he was in the early hours of the morning."[224]

Dr. Mynter offered less hope, saying, "I am not absolutely without hope. The President has a fighting chance but I would be more hopeful if the day was passed and he had gained a little strength. The trouble lies with his heart. We are stimulating it and our treatment has been fairly successful."[225]

"Ordinarily the President was a man of remarkably clean and tidy personal habits, and never was known to pass from one day to another without a shave," explained one of his nurses. "His beard grew very fast, and naturally, after lying in bed almost a week without shaving, his face was very rough. He made many comments on it the day that he began to grow worse, and he asked me when I thought it would be permissible to have a barber shave him. He even joked a bit about it when the doctors came."[226]

---

[222] *Washington Post*, 14 September 1901, pg. 1, col. 4.

[223] Nelson W. Wilson, M.D. "Details of the McKinley Case" (*Buffalo Medical Journal, 41-57*) 224.

[224] *New York Times*, 14 September 1901, pg. 1, col. 6.

[225] *New York Times*, 14 September 1901, pg. 1, col. 6.

[226] G. Townsend, *Memorial Life of William McKinley* (Washington: Memorial Publishing Co., 1901) 267.

About ten o'clock, the President's friends and relatives who had been summoned began to arrive, among them Senator Hanna. They crowded into the downstairs of the Milburn house. Waiting for news were Secretaries Hitchcock and Wilson, former Secretary of State Day, Senator Fairbanks, Abner McKinley, Mr. and Mrs. Hermann Baer, the President's sisters Helen McKinley and Mrs. J. T. Duncan, Mrs. Lafayette Williams, John Milburn, Postmaster General Bissell, John N. Scatcherd of Buffalo, and Representative Alexander of Buffalo.[227]

"Friday morning Mrs. McKinley made her usual visit to the sick room," said one of the President's nurses. "The President knew he had grown worse, and here again his first thoughts were of his helpmate. It would worry her.

"He summoned one of the doctors, Dr. Wasdin, I believe, and asked that the truth of his condition be kept from her. This was a difficult proposition, however, as Mrs. McKinley had watched his condition closely, and quickly detected the smallest and most insignificant change. Then we offered to co-operate in keeping the news from her. He gathered all of his strength together, and made a Herculean effort to allay any suspicions she might have. He succeeded admirably, and she left the room after ten minutes with her husband in the belief that he was at least holding his own.

"When she left he lapsed into the state which characterized the very early morning. He was not in a stupor, however, and recognized everybody... Late in the afternoon, it became apparent that the President was not to last for long, his life was slowly ebbing away."[228]

Secretary Hitchcock said, "I refuse to surrender. I will not give up hope while life remains. I shall hope on and pray on to the end."[229]

The President was conscious throughout much of the morning. At one point the nurses started to adjust pillows to keep the light out of the President's eyes, and he told them, "No, I want to see the trees. They are so beautiful."[230] He also commented that the weather was brighter.

"Previous to the relapse suffered by the President he had become somewhat whimsical, and had several times asked that he be moved to a fresh bed, thus accounting for the presence of two beds in the room," explained one of his nurses. "A large easy chair occupied the northeast corner of the room, and when Mrs. McKinley visited her husband, the chair was drawn along side the bed for her comfort.

---

[227] *New York Times*, 14 September 1901, pg. 1, col. 6.
[228] G. Townsend, *Memorial Life of William McKinley* (Washington: Memorial Publishing Co., 1901) 268-269.
[229] *New York Times*, 14 September 1901, pg. 2, col. 3.
[230] *New York Times*, 14 September 1901, pg. 2, col. 3.

"The President lay with the foot of the bed westward, thereby preventing the sun from shinning in his face," she continued. "On the west wall there hung a large picture of Washington, a magnificent creation by Graves, and this particularly pleased the stricken President. Often during his confinement I heard him comment on the picture, characterizing Washington as a noble statesman, who was created to meet an emergency."

"The day which brought the fatal relapse brought surprise to us all. In the morning we had lifted him from one bed to another at his request. In his new bed he seemed to rest very easy. He turned without causing himself pain or suffering. 'See how I am progressing, doctor?' he said when Dr. Wasdin came in that morning, and he turned from one side to another without apparent effort. The doctor smiled and assured him that he was progressing well, but advised him to remain as quiet as possible."[231]

Representative Alexander, at 10:45 a.m., painted the most hopeful picture of the morning.

"It is not true that the physicians are without hope or that those gathered in the house are despondent," he said. "The lowering of the heart action is a natural result of the giving of a cathartic and was expected. It was found that the solid food given yesterday had not passed through the stomach, and it was found that a cathartic would have to be given. Then came the reaction. The physicians gave a saline solution, but in very small quantity, and this forenoon used some digitalis but also in small quantities. They did not want to use any more artificial means than absolutely necessary. The results so far are good, and the President is now sleeping, watched by Drs. Rixey, Park and Stockton. Everybody about the house is hopeful. The two men who know him best, Secretary Cortelyou and Senator Hanna are cheerful and as confident as the setback will allow. They both know his strong will and they think that will help."[232]

Rev. Dr. Corwin Wilson, of Canton's First Methodist Episcopal Church, called at the house. Upon leaving he said, "Yes, there is hope for the President. His brother tells me he is making the supreme fight for his life. I feel most deeply for the President, for in Canton, in by-gone days I was his pastor, and truly know his noble character."[233]

---

[231] G. Townsend, *Memorial Life of William McKinley* (Washington: Memorial Publishing Co., 1901) 266-267.
[232] *New York Times*, 14 September 1901, pg. 2, col. 3.
[233] *New York Times*, 14 September 1901, pg. 2, col. 3.

Dr. Mann, when pressed, refused to make any official announcement as to the President's condition.

"A patient may continue in the condition the President is now in for some time and then pick up or not, just as the case may develop," he explained. "The President is in a very serious condition, it is true, but it is absurd to say he is dying, as stated by some persons this morning. I cannot make any further statement about the case just now."[234]

Dr. Stockton simply said, "The President is holding his own. That is all I care to say publicly."[235]

A call went out for Dr. Janeway of New York and W. W. Johnston, both prominent heart specialists.

Senator Mark Hanna left the Milburn residence at 12:25, saying, "Well, there isn't any good news. I can only say that the President has a fighting chance. I am always hopeful. My faith is strong. I saw a rainbow in the sky as I came up here this morning. I hope it is prophetic."[236]

Around one o'clock, word was unofficially sent to the press tent that if the President made it through the night, his physicians had hopes for his recovery. The release was issued at 1:05 by Cortelyou, and was unsigned by the physicians, but it seemed to confirm that the President was indeed holding his own.

An official bulletin was issued at 2:30, saying that the President "has more than held his own since morning and his condition justifies the expectation of further improvement. He is better than yesterday at this time." At four, the bulletin said he had only slightly improved since the last bulletin.[237]

But the patient had suddenly taken a down swing and it was obviously very serious. McKinley's heart was now weak. Attempting to maintain optimism, doctors hoped that the President could overcome the "complication" of a weakened heart. Shortly after 2:30, Cortelyou had the words "he is better than yesterday at this time" stricken from the afternoon bulletin.[238] It was too late, however, as the passage still made its way into print.

---

[234] *New York Times*, 14 September 1901, pg. 2, col. 3.

[235] *New York Times*, 14 September 1901, pg. 2, col. 3.

[236] *New York Times*, 14 September 1901, pg. 2, col. 3.

[237] Nelson W. Wilson, M.D. "Details of the McKinley Case" (*Buffalo Medical Journal, 41-57*) 224.

[238] A. Wesley Johns, *The Man Who Shot McKinley* (New York: A. S. Barnes and Co., Inc., 1970) 160.

By 4 o'clock, the President's pulsations were alarming. He was again given saline solutions. He slipped into semi-consciousness and his lips were watered with no reaction.

"At this time he was in a stupor," confirmed his nurse. "I went to his bedside and touched his lips with water, but there was no response either by sign or action. He appeared to be conscious yet unconscious. Everyone considered the case hopeless, and knew that it was a question of vitality; that he must soon die."[239]

Still, shortly before five o'clock in the evening, Senator Hanna came out in a hopeful mood.

"There is a slight improvement," he said. "I feel and those in the house feel, that the improvement may continue. I am feeling better than I did this morning."[240]

The 5:35 bulletin had been the worst yet: "The President's physicians report that his condition is grave at this hour. He is suffering from extreme prostration. Oxygen is being given. He responds to stimulation, but poorly."[241]

At 6:21 George Cortelyou stepped to the door, saying simply, "The President is still alive."[242]

Late in the afternoon of Friday the thirteenth, President McKinley rallied and regained his mental faculties. He told doctors, "It is useless gentlemen, I think we ought to have a prayer."

Ansley Wilcox had already begun the task of trying to track down the Vice President, who had left to go camping and mountain climbing in the Adirondacks. Roosevelt, out of reach of telephones and telegraph, could not be reached.

"I telephoned and telegraphed to Vice President Roosevelt's secretary, Mr. Loeb, at Albany at 5 o'clock this morning," he told the reporters at the Milburn house. "He communicated at once with the railroad people and got a special train."[243]

By six o'clock, all at the President's bedside knew that now it was just a matter of time. Those closest to the President were given the opportunity to say their good-byes. Those members of the Cabinet who were in attendance and were huddled, teary eyed, in a downstairs room,

---

[239] G. Townsend, *Memorial Life of William McKinley* (Washington: Memorial Publishing Co., 1901) 269.

[240] *New York Times*, 14 September 1901, pg. 2, col. 3.

[241] Nelson W. Wilson, M.D. "Details of the McKinley Case" (*Buffalo Medical Journal, 41-57*) 224.

[242] *New York Times*, 14 September 1901, pg. 2, col. 3.

[243] *New York Times*, 14 September 1901, pg. 2, col. 3.

made the sad ascent up the stairs to see the President for what they knew was to be the last time. Secretary Root, Secretary Hitchcock, and Attorney General Knox each paid their final visit. Secretary Wilson did not go up to the death chamber but preferred to remain downstairs and not see the President in his final agony. As the Cabinet members left after very brief stays, they were choked in their grief.[244]

Dr. McBurney arrived in a speeding automobile, but one look at the reporters told him that it was too late.

The 6:30 p.m. bulletin announced, "The President's physicians report that his condition is most serious in spite of vigorous stimulation. The depression continues and is most profound. Unless it can be relieved the end is only a question of time. Cortelyou."[245]

There had been some discussion as to whether or not to release information about the true condition of the President to the nation. It was a haggard faced George Cortelyou who told the others, "Gentlemen, we have kept faith with the people hitherto. We must continue to do so."[246]

This was the last official bulletin, although at regular intervals verbal word was sent to the press tent as to the President's condition.

Secret Service Agent George Foster sent a telegram to Secret Service Chief Wilkie in Washington, saying in part, "President asking for Mrs. McKinley and friends. All hope seems to have gone." Later he cabled, "Mr. Cortelyou says President very bad could not be worse."[247]

Mr. Milburn broke the news to Mrs. McKinley that her husband was dying. She began to show symptoms of collapse. A friend, Herbert P. Bissell rushed to assist her as Mr. Milburn was literally supporting her. Dr. Wasdin was sent for and he gave her a restorative. She regained her normal composure and said, "I will be strong for his sake." She was urged to take a rest, but she refused, saying that she would remain in case the President awakened. She wished to have a last word of comfort with him.[248]

At about 7:45 p.m., oxygen was administered and the President, who had been unconscious, awakened and barely whispered for his wife,

---

[244] *New York Times*, 14 September 1901, pg. 1, col. 2.

[245] Nelson W. Wilson, M.D. "Details of the McKinley Case" (*Buffalo Medical Journal, 41-57*) 224.

[246] Murat Halstead, *The Illustrious Life of William McKinley* (Privately Published, 1901) 50.

[247] George Foster, *Telegram to John E. Wilkie*, 13 September 1901, Buffalo, N.Y.

[248] G. Townsend, *Memorial Life of William McKinley* (Washington: Memorial Publishing Co., 1901) 265.

telling Dr. Rixey that he knew the end was near. But by the time Mrs. McKinley could be brought to the room by Mrs. McWilliams, the President was once again unconscious. About fifteen minutes later, Mr. McKinley awoke and again asked for his wife.[249]

Mrs. McKinley came back to the room and tearlessly took the both Presidents' hands in hers, kissed him and wiped his brow, and as she leaned over the bed, they talked in whispers. The physicians and all but one nurse left them alone for ten minutes.

"I want to go too," she was heard to say. "I want to go too."

"We are all going, we are all going," was his reply.

"Good-bye to all, good bye all," the President was reported as saying by Dr. Mann, who recorded the words at his bedside. "God's will be done, not ours."[250] Another version had the President saying, "It is God's way. His will be done."[251]

One account said Mrs. McKinley, at one point, looked at Dr. Rixey and said, "I know that you will save him. I cannot let him go. The country cannot spare him."[252]

"The easy chair was drawn close to the bedside, and she was seated there," remembered the President's nurse. "The President's face lighted up. He recognized her, and it seemed as if the nurses and doctors would burst into tears. She took his hand, the hand which in one short week had become emaciated and thin, and held it."[253]

McKinley lay in his deathbed, his arm around his wife, smiling at her. As she leaned closer to him, he began to whisper the words of his favorite hymn, *Nearer My God to Thee, Nearer to Thee*. These were his last words to her. In their final moments together, others began entering the room. She put her arms around his neck for a final moment and was then led out and escorted back to her own room.

"Mrs. McKinley remained with him for a half hour and was led, weeping, from the room," said the nurse. "The President had lapsed into the sleep which knows no awakening. He was wholly unconscious."[254]

---

[249] Murat Halstead, *The Illustrious Life of William McKinley* (Privately Published, 1901) 53.

[250] Franklin Matthews, "The President's Last Days," *Harper's Weekly*, 21 September 1901, pg. 943.

[251] G. Townsend, *Memorial Life of William McKinley* (Washington: Memorial Publishing Co., 1901) 251.

[252] Murat Halstead, *The Illustrious Life of William McKinley* (Privately Published, 1901) 395.

[253] G. Townsend, *Memorial Life of William McKinley* (Washington: Memorial Publishing Co., 1901) 270.

[254] G. Townsend, *Memorial Life of William McKinley* (Washington: Memorial Publishing Co., 1901) 270.

Back in her room, Dr. Rixey gave Mrs. McKinley a stimulant. She continued to give way to her emotions, convulsing into bitter sobs, while Dr. Rixey and Miss Barber did their best to console her.

Outside, Senator Hanna's secretary Elmer Dover told the waiting newsmen that the President had asked for his wife. He told them that he did not think the President could live and that he groaned feebly and continually.[255]

After Mrs. McKinley left, the President expressed the wish to die, and oxygen was no longer given him. He began to sink slowly and his pulse was so weak it could not be felt in his extremities, which were growing cold.[256]

Charles Dawes, who had hurried back from Washington, arrived at about that time; about 9 p.m. McKinley looked at him. Slowly, life was beginning to slip away. The President tossed his head and muttered, his breathing became heavy and labored.

"He was surrounded by the family group," Dawes wrote in his journal upon returning from the President's funeral. "Mrs. McKinley was sitting by his side with her face near his. He had one arm around her and was smiling at her. He had ceased speaking some time before this but he seemed conscious and he looked up at me in the kindly way that was so natural to him."

"Silently we stood by his bedside," continued Dawes. "Abner took my hand in his. His sister, his nephew and nieces and others were there. Cortelyou stood at the foot of the bed. Mrs. McKinley made no outcry— her grief was past words. She was led away to see him no more alive. Before she went to rest she was told the President would not waken in this world."[257]

Another of the President's friends from years gone by, State Senator Martin Dodge from Cleveland, arrived but was not permitted to enter the President's sick room. Dodge lingered in the hall, trying to catch a last glimpse of his friend's face.

Dodge left the house, made his way over to the barriers where anxious crowds awaited.

"Gentlemen, the Nation's chief is dying," he told them. "There is absolutely no hope, no chance."[258]

---

[255] A. Wesley Johns, *The Man Who Shot McKinley* (New York: A. S. Barnes and Co., Inc., 1970) 160.

[256] Murat Halstead, *The Illustrious Life of William McKinley* (Privately Published) 48.

[257] Charles W. Dawes, *A Journal of the McKinley Years* (Chicago: R. R. Donnelley & Sons Co., 1950) 280-81.

[258] *New York Times*, 14 September 1901, pg. 1, col. 3.

"As the hour of 9 o'clock approached his condition became rapidly worse," described his nurse, "and I have since learned that even in the house the report was circulated that the President was dying."[259]

"The President is unconscious most of the time," said James B. Chard to reporters, perhaps a bit more objectively. "He is being kept alive by oxygen. His case is absolutely hopeless."[260]

At about 9:30 p.m., Secretary Cortelyou sent Harry Hamlin with a message to the waiting press, "Secretary Cortelyou cannot come out just now, but he says you boys—may as well know—that the President is dying."[261]

At about that same time, George E. Matthews emerged from the house saying, "All we learned is that the President is very feeble. But hope is not all gone."[262]

Crowds pressed toward the barriers, waiting for the word that would end their agony.

Dr. Rixey took Mrs. McKinley's place at the President's bedside, holding his hand after the President had reached for it. Senator Hanna had been asking to see the President and sobbed to his unconscious friend, "William, William don't you know me?" He nearly collapsed at the site of the President in his weakened condition and probably would have fallen down had it not been for Secretary Wilson and Colonel Herrick.[263] It was the only time that Hanna had been permitted to see his friend since the shooting, and upon leaving he broke down and cried like a baby. Days before, McKinley had been asking about the Senator, and Hanna was deeply touch when told of it.[264]

An emotionally spent Ida McKinley slept. Dr. Rixey, not wishing to awaken her said, "The worst has yet to come and there is no necessity for disturbing her."[265]

The Cabinet members periodically came and went. Secretary Gage walked outside and was asked about the President. "The night has not yet come," was his only reply.[266]

---

[259] G. Townsend, *Memorial Life of William McKinley* (Washington: Memorial Publishing Co., 1901) 269.

[260] *Buffalo Evening News*, 14 September 1901, pg. 5, col. 3.

[261] *Buffalo Evening News*, 14 September 1901, pg. 5, col. 3.

[262] *Buffalo Evening News*, 13 September 1901, pg. 1, col. 5.

[263] Murat Halstead, *The Illustrious Life of William McKinley* (Privately Published) 59.

[264] Herbert Croly, *Marcus Alonzo Hanna* (New York: The MacMillan Co., 1923) 359.

[265] Murat Halstead, *The Illustrious Life of William McKinley* (Privately Published, 1901) 50.

[266] G. Townsend, *Memorial Life of William McKinley* (Washington: Memorial Publishing Co., 1901) 251.

Dr. Janeway arrived, examined the patient and said what all knew, that the end was very near. Two more hours had passed while the President struggled to maintain life. At 11 o'clock, Dr. Mann predicted that Mr. McKinley would live another hour. Dr. Mynter thought he might last until 2 a.m.[267]

Outside a hushed crowd watched and waited. The Milburn house was the center of their attention. Each time small groups came out of the door to get a breath of fresh air, they were watched intently by the crowd, hoping for some hint of what was happening inside. The entire ground floor was aglow with lights, and inside the forms of friends, relatives and officials could be seen moving about. In the upper chambers the lights were low, and around the north side of the house, where the President's room was located, the lights would occasionally burn brightly, and then return to their dim glow.[268]

"At 11:15 o'clock Mrs. McKinley came again and this time remained with her dying husband for an hour," explained the nurse. "She said nothing and the President lay like one who had passed the river of death."[269]

The telegraphers and reporters were hearing the news from inside and were frantically sending news to all corners of the continent. Scores of bulletins were thrust upon weary operators. "Rush this to Roosevelt," was what Secret Service Agent Foster told one messenger, as he gave him a bulletin.[270]

About midnight, Secretaries Root and Wilson came out and strolled up and down the sidewalk in conversation. Root said, "The end has not yet come."[271]

Navy Secretary Long arrived at the Milburn residence at 12:08, in time to see the President alive, but unconscious. At 12:28, Buffalo Coroner Wilson arrived and caused a stir. He had come to the house on the orders of District Attorney Thomas Penney. Wilson had seen a report from a reputable local source that the President had died at 11:06. Dr. Mann, who told him his services were not yet needed, met Wilson at the door. Not wishing to show gruesome anticipation, Wilson left.[272]

---

[267] *New York Times*, 14 September 1901, pg. 1, col. 3.

[268] *New York Times*, 14 September 1901, pg. 1, col. 3.

[269] G. Townsend, *Memorial Life of William McKinley* (Washington: Memorial Publishing Co., 1901) 270.

[270] Murat Halstead, *The Illustrious Life of William McKinley* (Privately Published, 1901) 50.

[271] *New York Times*, 14 September 1901, pg. 1, col. 3.

[272] *New York Times*, 14 September 1901, pg. 1, col. 3.

Dispatches began to go out that the President had indeed died, probably spurred by the arrival of the coroner. But an official statement corrected them, saying that the President still lived.

President William McKinley's passing was almost imperceptible as he sunk into sleep and his pulse gradually became fainter. Relatives and friends stood by the bed watching.

"We are in the dark," noted Dr. Mann at the President's bedside. "The President's pulse had been rapid from the start. It had never behaved right. It had steadily and progressively grown weaker.

"For the last twenty-four hours he had been having sinking spells off and on, each one worse and each one harder to bring him back from.

"The President did not believe until late to-day that would die. He told me this morning that he had not lost heart. We were laughing and joking while I was dressing the wound. He said to me: 'I feel I will get well.'

"This evening he spoke to Dr. Rixey about dying," Dr. Mann continued. "He said he felt it was almost over."[273]

"As I watched him in the early evening the President did not seem like a dying man to me," wrote Charles Dawes. "He moved his limbs freely and did not seem to breathe with difficulty. He seemed to want to hold Dr. Rixey's hand and would reach out to him like a child in the dark. Once he said 'Oh dear' as if in distress.

"The President was breathing mechanically and audibly," Dawes continued. "Finally he ceased to breathe and it seemed he was gone. Then he drew another breath after a time. Then all was still."[274]

When his heavy breathing stopped, Dr. Rixey placed his stethoscope on the President's chest.

"The President is dead," he announced in a low voice. Another account quoted Rixey as saying, "It is over, the President is no more."[275]

Secretary Cortelyou was the first to arouse himself after the pronouncement of death. He left the room, slowly made his way down the stairs and into the large drawing room where members of the Cabinet and other officials waited. Looking up, they sensed what the loyal private secretary of the President was about to say.

---

[273] Murat Halstead, *The Illustrious Life of William McKinley* (Privately Published, 1901) 56.
[274] Charles W. Dawes, *A Journal of the McKinley Years* (Chicago: R. R. Donnelley & Sons Co., 1950) 281.
[275] Murat Halstead, *The Illustrious Life of William McKinley* (Privately Published) 55.

"Gentlemen, the President has passed away," Cortelyou told them. He then stepped outside and calmly moved down the walk to where the newsmen were waiting, telling them, "The President died at 2:15 o'clock."

It was September 14.

The lights in the upstairs room were turned down and the dead President was left alone with a white-clad, spectral guard.[276]

Another account reported that it was Webb Hayes who broke the news to the members of the Cabinet by saying, "It is all over."[277] But it seems more likely that it was George Cortelyou who had the regrettable honor.

"Mr. Cortelyou has borne up wonderfully under the fearful strain imposed upon him," commented an observer, Frank Baird, a friend of the McKinleys. "He seems to have the most marvelous powers of endurance. I am sure he has not slept more than four hours since the President was shot."[278]

"The undertaker came and laid the body on the bed which it had lain for a week," described the nurse. "The hands were folded across the breast, a sheet was drawn over the face. Private Hodgins of the Hospital Corps was detailed to guard the body, and throughout the remainder of the night he stood at attention at the foot of the bed. At 5:30 o'clock he was relieved by Private Voltmeyer, of the same branch of service."[279]

At the White House, the flag was lowered to half-staff.

Dr. Harvey B. Gaylord and Dr. Herman G, Matzinger in the presence of District Attorney Penney and other attending physicians of the President performed the autopsy on the President. In spite of a nearly three hour search, the fatal second bullet was not located. Finally, the McKinley family, in order to stop undue mutilation of the President's body, asked that the search be stopped.[280]

From the official autopsy report:

"The bullet which struck over the breastbone did not pass through the skin, and did little harm.

---

[276] Nelson W. Wilson, M.D. "Details of the McKinley Case" (*Buffalo Medical Journal, 41-57*) 220.

[277] G. Townsend, *Memorial Life of William McKinley* (Washington: Memorial Publishing Co., 1901) 254.

[278] *Buffalo Evening News*, 14 September 1901, pg. 1, col. 2.

[279] G. Townsend, *Memorial Life of William McKinley* (Washington: Memorial Publishing Co., 1901) 271.

[280] A. Wesley Johns, *The Man Who Shot McKinley* (New York: A. S. Barnes and Co., Inc., 1970) 165.

"The other bullet passed through both walls of the stomach near its lower border. Both holes were found to be perfectly closed by the stitches, but the tissues around each hole had become gangrenous. After passing through the stomach the bullet passed into the back walls of the abdomen, hitting and tearing the upper end of the kidney. This portion of the bullet track was also gangrenous, the gangrene involving the pancreas. The bullet was not found.

"There was no sign of peritonitis or disease of other organs. The heart walls were very thin, and there was no evidence of any attempt to repair on the part of nature, and death resulted from the gangrene, which affected the stomach around the bullet wounds as well as the tissues around the further course of the bullet. Death was unavoidable by any surgical or medical treatment, and was the direct result of the bullet wound."[281]

Signing the autopsy, along with those who performed it, were Drs. Mann, Park, Mynter, Rixey and Wasdin.

By Sunday, newspapers were reporting the cause of President McKinley's death as gangrene poisoning, but reports and rumors began to circulate soon after that the doctors had mishandled the case. In fact, no sooner than the autopsy was completed on the President, questions began to be asked, many of them caused by the autopsy itself. Adding to the discussion, Coroner James T. Wilson oversimplified the autopsy findings by making a notation on a police blotter that the cause of the President's death was gangrene found in both walls of the stomach and pancreas which had developed after the shooting.[282]

There was the question of gangrene being found behind the walls of the stomach in the bullet tract. But there was no free pus in the peritoneum, which explained the surgeons' failure to note postoperative complications. The upper portion of the kidney and the adjacent adrenal gland had sustained some minor bullet damage, but neither was considered important. The major postmortem finding was the damage to the pancreas and the complications that followed.[283]

But in fact, the autopsy did nothing to show incompetence on the part of the President's physicians. There was no way they could have known what was going on inside the President's body, especially when the

---

[281] *Literary Digest*, 21 September 1901, pg. 331.
[282] Selig Adler, "The Operation on President McKinley," *Scientific American* (March 1963) 128.
[283] Selig Adler, "The Operation on President McKinley," *Scientific American* (March 1963) 128.

medical knowledge of the time is considered. Their most glaring mistake was the premature reassuring of the public of the President's recovery. In reality, there was little they could have done to save the President under the circumstances. Laboratory analysis of body chemistry, antibiotics, intravenous feeding, blood transfusions and medical therapy for acute damage to the pancreas would all come only in the future.[284] President McKinley, as much as anything, was a victim of his time.

Among the criticisms that were pointed at the doctors in Buffalo; failure to identify the gangrene, limited knowledge of the possible complications, and wholesale ignorance of the nature of the lesions. Most of these charges were found to be invalid by most of the reputable medical journals of the day, but still, in a time of rabid newspaper competition, the charges found an eager audience in some newspapers.

There were rumors that the doctors were fighting among themselves over treatment and diagnosis during the President's fight for life. These rumors appeared often enough that the doctors involved felt it necessary to issue a statement to clear some of them up. Ansley Wilcox urged them to seek legal counsel to "save the profession and the city" from discredit.[285] After a consultation at Wilcox's home, on September 17, the doctors issued the following statement:

"The undersigned, surgeons and physicians who were in attendance on the late President McKinley, have had their attention called to the certain sensational statements published in the daily papers and particularly in one New York paper, indicating dissension and mutual recrimination among them.

"We desire to say to the press and the public, once and for all, that every such publication and all alleged interviews with any of us containing criticism of one another or of any of our associates, are false and are nothing but scandal mongering.

"We say again that there was never disagreement among the professional attendants as to any of the symptoms or as to the treatment of the case, or as to the bulletins which were issued. A very unusual harmony of opinion and of action prevailed all through the case.

"The unfortunate result could not have been foreseen before the unfavorable symptoms declared themselves late on the sixth day and could not have been prevented by any human agency.

---

[284] Selig Adler, "The Operation on President McKinley," *Scientific American* (March 1963) 128.

[285] Selig Adler, "The Operation on President McKinley," *Scientific American* (March 1963) 129.

"Pending the completion and publication of the official report of the post mortem examiners and of the attending staff we shall refuse to make any further statements for publication, and alleged interviews with any of us may be known to be fictitious."

Drs. Mann, Mynter, Park, Wasdin and Stockton signed the press release.[286]

Dr. Matthew D. Mann addressed the Academy of Medicine in Rochester on October 15, and defensively tried to explain what he thought was the cause of the President's death.

"Gentlemen, I do not know what killed the President, but I think that the cause of death was the fact that the walls of the right ventricle of the heart were very thin and atrophied," he explained. He also pointed out the lack of proper equipment during the operation, but said that he did not feel that it would have made the difference in the case.

Dr. Mann also said that the doctors should not have been surprised when the President suddenly deteriorated because he had not been responding properly to the treatment. He said that the President's blood count failed to show an increase in white corpuscles, which should have occurred if the President's body was responding and fighting off infection. He also curiously stated that the reason the search for the bullet was ended during the operation was because the President's family positively forbade further search. This is not consistent with any other account by the other physicians. They had stated that the search had been ended because the President was weakening and there was worry that if he was subjected to an extensive search he may have died on the operating table. More likely, Mann was referring to the autopsy, during which the McKinley family had stopped the search for the bullet.

But Mann told the doctors that he thought the cause of the President's death was due to the laceration of the kidney by the bullet, combined with atrophy of the heart. This, in spite of the fact that the official autopsy had determined gangrene poisoning as the cause.[287]

A few days later, on October 26, Dr. Presley M. Rixey issued his report, stating that gangrene poisoning of the stomach walls and pancreas had been the true cause of death. Dr. Rixey's report included almost

---

[286]*Buffalo Express,* 18 September 1901.
[287] *New York Times,* 16 October 1901, pg. 1, col. 2.

minute-by-minute descriptions of medication given to the President, including each morsel of food. It is the most detailed report concerning the treatment of the President.[288]

In its coverage of the report, the *Buffalo Courier* reported that Rixey's report proved that the President's true condition "belied the bulletins." It stated in headlines, "President's Mind Was Wandering When Bulletins Assuring His Convalescence Were Issued and He Was Said to Have Passed Comfortable Night, When He Was Restless and in Pain." Another headline read, "American Public Constantly Kept in Ignorance of Details That Would Have Been Alarming to the People Had They Known the Truth of Matters at All Times, as Doctors Knew Them." Always quick to sensationalize the news, the *Buffalo Courier* did not paint an accurate picture of Dr. Rixey's thoughts or words.[289]

But as would become apparent years later, there was indeed tension and disagreement among the President's doctors, regardless of what their press release stated.

Dr. Roswell Park had reservations about more than one of the attending physicians, and said so in an article he wrote in 1911. About Dr. Edgar Wallace Lee, he was most critical.

"Regarding this Dr. Lee," he wrote, "he happened to be on the grounds as a visitor; he had been medical director of one of the western expositions, and was on his way to New York where he proposed to, and later did locate. He manifested a tremendous amount of nerve in almost forcing his way into the operating room, talking with the President, and virtually offering to do the operation himself, it even appearing as though he tried to bring this about. He left for New York the same evening, and, in spite of our injunction to reticence and secrecy, he did a lot of talking the following day in New York. In reality he was more hindrance than help although it was a somewhat difficult matter to eliminate him."[290]

Dr. Park was not very charitable towards a doctor who offered his services in a time of crisis. He was not charitable toward the man who performed the operation either. In fact, he could be considered self-serving and arrogant.

"I do not believe that Dr. Mann had ever done a gunshot case before," he recalled. "Dr. Mynter had, however, of course, seen and handled them, but neither of them insisted upon a clean excision of the bullet track and tissues immediately surrounding it through the whole

---

[288] *New York Times,* 27 October 1901, pg. 5, col. 1.

[289] *Buffalo Courier,* 27 October 1901, pg. 1, col. 5.

[290] *Buffalo Evening News,* 15 September 1945, Magazine Section, pg. 1, col. 7.

thickness of the abdominal covering, i.e., some three inches and this contused and minutely ragged tubular was closed with the rest of the incision which all seemed to me unfortunate."[291]

If that was how Dr. Park felt during the operation, he certainly said nothing. Dr. Park even suggested that a primary reason for rushing the President's operation was to keep himself from performing it. He wrote of those who "have not hesitated to express their unreserved opinions to the effect that it was simply a matter of jealousy rather than of urgent haste because of the President's symptoms" that caused the rush to operate. "...there was no reason to fear immediate collapse nor to suspect serious internal hemorrhage. It was known that I was hurrying to the scene as rapidly as possible and would soon be there, but perhaps with these few words enough has been said on this score."[292]

Conversely, Dr. S. B. Harper who reexamined the McKinley case for the Mayo Clinic in 1944, praised Dr. Mann's decision to operate immediately, and went as far as to say that it would be considered entirely correct by 1944 standards at that in 1901 it had been remarkable.[293]

The *New York Medical Journal* stated, "It would have verged on madness to prolong the search for the bullet after it had been ascertained that it had not inflicted any very grave injury beyond that of the stomach..."[294]

Dr. George F. Shrady wrote an opinion of the case in *The Medical Record* within weeks of the shooting.

He agreed with the speed the operation commenced, saying, "The operation of suturing the stomach wounds was timely, proper, and, so far as it went, brilliant." But Dr. Shrady's overall opinion of the President's doctors and their decisions was less favorable.

"Time was precious, and prolonged search for the ball was impossible, consequently the condition and course of the wound beyond the stomach could not be positively ascertained at the time," he wrote. "The surgeons satisfied themselves, therefore, that it was safe to leave this terminal wound to itself and close up the abdomen. They used their best judgment under trying conditions; but unfortunately that judgment was in error.

---

[291] *Buffalo Evening News*, 15 September 1945, Magazine Section, pg. 1, col. 8.

[292] *Buffalo Evening News*, 15 September 1945, Magazine Section, pg. 1, col. 8.

[293] A. Wesley Johns, *The Man Who Shot McKinley* (New York: A. S. Barnes and Co., Inc., 1970) 263.

[294] *Literary Digest*, 5 October 1901, pg. 401.

"Then came the bulletins and interviews so eagerly read by an anxious nation," he continued, complaining more about the reports the doctors issued than their actual treatment of the President. "It was stated at first that the stomach wounds were the only causes for anxiety, that the ball having lodged in the muscles of the back would have safely encysted, and that septic peritonitis from possible leakage of the stomach contents was the only thing to be feared. When the latter danger was over, there came the surprising intelligence that the patient would certainly recover. This in the face of a continued high temperature and rapid pulse! Then it was announced that all the wounds had healed perfectly, and the only real danger was centered in a weak heart. Hardly had this bulletin been issued when it was announced that the external wound was found to be infected, necessitating the removal of some stitches. Still it was said that the distinguished patient was doing excellently well—in fact, even better than before. Next was the report of an attack of indigestion, claimed to be due to food given too soon, and last of all, without warning came the appalling accounts of his rapid collapse and surprisingly quick death.

"Worst of all, however, were the actual facts of the autopsy that seemed to prove to the public that the doctors had been wrong in their conception of the case from the beginning to the end. Sadly enough, not one of the principal lesions gave any evidence of its existence during life. The good condition of the wound behind the stomach, of which all the surgeons were so pronouncedly confident, was an illusion and a snare. Instead of the terminal track of the bullet being healed and the ball encysted, it was found at the autopsy to be gangrenous throughout. Thus a most startling error of diagnosis was flauntingly accentuated by an indignant and astonished press."[295]

Dr. Louis Sayre, a New York expert on gunshot wounds at the time, thought it was inexcusable for the doctors not to have known gangrene was developing.

"It is not generally an appreciated fact even in surgery that the treatment of a gunshot wound is not the same as that caused by a cut or stab," he explained. "The two wounds are totally different and require different treatment, and the first mistake made in treating the wound of the President was to sew up the bullet hole...here is a patient who has been shot through the stomach. The organ is simply laid bare and the holes in it are sewed. Nothing is done to remove the dead flesh. It is left there to clear itself in the only way that nature has provided it to clear

---

[295] *Literary Digest*, 5 October 1901, pg. 401.

itself, namely: It begins to sluff and develops into gangrene because that is the only thing that could develop under the circumstances."

In fact, it should be remembered that the President's doctors did have the white cells counted and found them to be nearly normal.

"The bruised and dead tissue about the wound should have been removed with the knife," Sayre concluded. "When the edges of the wound presented clean and healthy parts that could unite, they should have been sewed together. And more, the superficial wound in the stomach that was caused by the surgeon's knife should have been kept open and the healing of the wound in the stomach should have been watched day by day. But this dead tissue adjacent to the edge of the bullet hole was not considered and nothing but gangrene could have set in."

When asked if the surgeons could have known about the gangrene before the autopsy, Dr. Sayre replied, "Most decidedly, by the use of the microscope. An undue increase in the white cells in the patient's blood should have told the story and given ample warning. There was no medical excuse why the doctors should have been fooled by the apparently healthy condition of their patient."[296]

But Dr. Robert H. M. Dawbarn thought that the doctors should not be blamed.

"It is extremely unlikely that he (Czolgosz) was thoughtful enough of his victim's welfare to clean the weapon," he commented. "The bullet fired from such close quarters must have carried in a considerable amount of filth from the previous discharges, and though doubtless Dr. Mann did all that any surgeon could do in the way of mechanically cleaning the wound, the unfound bullet and its whole track must have been poisoned."[297]

As far as the high temperature and rapid pulse, the *New York Medical Journal* stated, "the record of the pulse and respiration seemed ominous, for the high rate might have been due to any number of conditions not in themselves of grave import. The hopeful view was taken, and quite naturally, that it could be so explained."[298]

The irrepressible Dr. Roswell Park also had reservations about the lack of drainage of the wound.

"While therefore," he wrote, "probably no one would, at least have drained posteriorly it certainly would have been wiser had an anterior drain been made. Whether this would have saved the patient or not I

---

[296] *New York Times*, 17 September 1901, pg. 2, col. 2.

[297] *New York Times*, 17 September 1901, pg. 2, col. 2.

[298] *Literary Digest*, 5 October 1901, pg. 401.

cannot say, but I have always regretted that it was not put into practice."[299]

Dr. Park compared the case to a woman he had treated with a similar injury weeks after the President's death.

"I found perforation of the stomach and injury to the pancreas; at all events I closed the stomach perforation and made posterior and well as anterior drainage; this case recovered without an untoward symptom."[300]

"My reason for not draining was that there was nothing to drain," explained Dr. Mann. "There had been no bleeding nor oozing; there was nothing to make any discharge or secretion; the parts were presumably free from infection, and were carefully washed with salt solution. As there was no peritonitis and the abdomen was found post mortem to be sterile, we may safely conclude that no drainage could have been provided which would have accomplished anything. My experience teaches me never to drain unless there is a good indication for it, as a drain may do harm as well as good."[301]

Again, however, other doctors refuted the importance of not draining the wound. Dr. Harper agreed with Dr. Mann, who had stated that there was nothing to drain, no undue bleeding, and that by doing so it could do more harm than good.

Finally, Dr. Park complained about the doctors not taking more control of the poor facilities question.

"...while the operating room was practically sufficient for all ordinary purposes, it must be acknowledged that both light and equipment were not all that could be desired.

"Had I been present at the time the President arrived at the hospital all this would have been changed or else I should have insisted upon his being taken to the General Hospital where the admirable facilities would have permitted easier work."[302]

In response to Park's criticism of her father, Dr. Mynter's daughter, Mrs. Agnes Robertson, wrote an article that appeared in the *Buffalo Evening News*. She pointed out that Dr. Park was not even there for most of the operation.

"This disposes of his statements that Dr. Mann and my father did sloppy work, that other doctors were urging him to take the operation away from them, and that he urged the wound be left open and drainage tubes put in."

[299] *Buffalo Evening News*, 15 September 1945, Magazine Section, pg. 5, col. 4.
[300] *Buffalo Evening News*, 15 September 1945, Magazine Section, pg. 5, col. 4.
[301] "The Official Report on the Case of President McKinley" (*Buffalo Medical Journal 41-57*) 276.
[302] *Buffalo Evening News*, 15 September 1945, Magazine Section, pg. 1, col. 8.

She also stated that the rush to operate was vital, saying the President would have died within half an hour had the operation not happened right away. She claimed that Dr. Simpson confirmed it and that when her father had arrived; the two young interns were frantic, thinking that the President was near death.[303]

Certainly there was a tension between at least some of the doctors who attended President McKinley. How much of it was due to professional jealousy is difficult to determine. Dr. Park had the luxury of hindsight, which is well known to be 20-20.

After the President died, *The World*, a New York paper, said in an editorial, "It is noteworthy that in the operation when the abdomen was opened no discovery was made of the serious injuries to the pancreas and kidney. But we must endeavor to judge this from the standpoint of the surgeons at the moment, for they presumably reasoned that they had upon their hands a desperate case; that there was probably little hope; that they would do what was absolutely necessary so far as they could see it, and would not add to the danger by endeavoring to do too much."[304]

Dr. Wasdin was quoted as saying, "These different areas [of gangrene all along the path of the bullet] were due to the same influence, acting about the same time. All these conditions lead me to believe that there has been an influence exerted by the passing bullet through the tissues entirely dissimilar to that influence exerted by an ordinary missile."

This statement was taken to mean that the bullet had been poisoned, but that rumor was later settled by lab tests.[305] Dr. Herbert M. Hill, the Buffalo City Chemist, at the direction of Buffalo District Attorney Thomas Penney, conducted the tests. Penney also directed Dr. Herman G. Matzinger to perform a bacteriological test and on September 22, a statement was issued saying no evidence of poison was found.[306]

The Medical News stated simply, "The President died because he could not carry on the processes of repair, and because the effort to do so was more than the vitality of the issues could support...It is clear that no human skill could have saved the President's life and that everything that modern scientific medicine could possibly suggest was done for him."[307]

---

[303] *Buffalo Evening News*, 14 November 1945, pg. 38, col. 5.

[304] *Literary Digest*, 21 September 1901, pg.331.

[305] *Literary Digest*, 21 September 1901, pg.331.

[306] *New York Times,* 23 September 1901, pg. 1, col. 7.

[307] *Literary Digest*, 5 October 1901, pg. 401.

"Never, I am sure, under like circumstances, was there a more harmonious or better-agreed band of consultants," Dr. Mann remarked. "That our endeavors failed was, I believe, no fault of ours; but it must be an ever-living and keen regret to each one of us, that we were not allowed the privilege of saving so noble a man, so attractive a patient, and so useful a life."[308]

---

[308] "The Official Report on the Case of President McKinley" (*Buffalo Medical Journal 41-57*) 276.

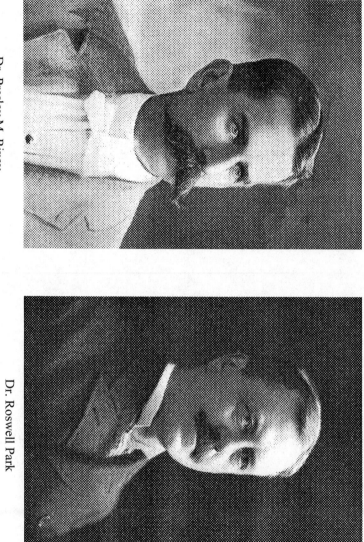

Dr. Presley M. Rixey

Dr. Roswell Park

Dr. Matthew Mann

Dr. Charles McBurney

Dr. Herman Mynter

**The Milburn house under guard as the wounded
President fights for his life.**

Press Tents Across the Street from Milburn House

Reporters at Rope Across from Milburn House

Back of Milburn House (X marks spot where McKinley's room was)

Cortelyou Gives Press Bulletin to Reporters

Vice President Roosevelt talks with Senator Mark Hanna
near the Milburn House.

The Milburn House under guard.

Organizing guards at the Milburn house.

Doctor Eugene Wasdin (center) and Dr. Herman Mynter (left) in a lighter moment when it was thought that the president would recover.

Senator Hanna & Secretary Hitchcock show the optimism of the moment before the President's fatal downturn.

Dr. Charles McBurney outside the Milburn house

The x-ray machine sent by Thomas Edison that was never used to locate the bullet lodged in the President

Senator Mark Hanna talking with reporters in front of the Milburn house.

The Glenny House, next door to the Milburn house on Delaware Avenue. In this house, the cabinet and other dignitaries met during the President's convalescence.

The Buffalo Club, about two miles from the Milburn house on Delaware Avenue. The Cabinet also met here during the week long ordeal.
The building still stands.

5. The Scapegoats

Immediately after the presidential shooting, because of Czolgosz's words, anarchists all over the country came under attack. Meetings were broken up and innocent people were arrested, often for doing no more than speaking their piece or giving an opinion. Being what authorities deemed to be an anarchist was reason enough to be taken into custody. The Constitution of the United States was put on hold.

Anarchists did not believe in government, law or rulers, whether they are kings or presidents. Anarchists had admittedly killed rulers of other countries, but the murder of McKinley brought them center stage in American thought.

Harper's Weekly questioned the basis of anarchy; "Anarchists are the common enemies of humanity. Their theory is that laws must be overturned, and that government must cease to exist..."

"The anarchist thinks that he wants liberty; but he really wants what the tyrant wants—license for his own passions and desires, a community where he and his kind may live as they please, unhampered by any government, or by their fellows, even to the offence of those fellows whom they would constrain to adopt and follow their notions, and to obey their decrees."

"But anarchy is insanity," *Harper's Weekly* concluded. "The belief that liberty is possible without law is a delusion, and anarchists will continue to be found here as elsewhere, as long as law reigns, and is therefore an offence to their disordered minds."[1]

Others, such as Buffalo Police Inspector Michael Donovan had an easier answer.

"Why in Buffalo every night we officers see knots of anarchists standing on street corners uttering sedition with every breath, but what can we do?" he declared. "My idea is whenever such gatherings are found the police should go after the whole bunch and break their heads."[2]

Anarchists had been viewed as a threat in the United States, particularly since May 4, 1886, when a bomb was thrown into Chicago's Haymarket Square. Anarchists had been holding a rally when Chicago Police Captain William Ward led a group of "blue coats" to disperse the crowd. Shortly after he told the leader to disperse, a terrific explosion

---

[1] *Harper's Weekly*, 14 September 1901, pg. 900.
[2] *Buffalo Evening News*, 8 September 1901, pg. 4, col. 1.

occurred. The bombing killed eight police officers, one immediately. Another sixty-nine was injured. Small arms fire commenced with the anarchists being spread in every direction.[3] Eight Chicago anarchists were eventually arrested and convicted, even though the actual bomb thrower was never identified. This incident did more to connect anarchism with murder and violence in the minds of Americans than any other single event.[4]

This impression was enhanced when on July 23, 1892 a Russian born anarchist named Alexander Berkman stabbed and shot Henry Clay Frick in an attempt to call attention to the plight of the working man, the unfair treatment by capitalists, and in retaliation for his acts during the Homestead strike. Frick had called in two hundred Pinkerton detectives to disperse a crowd and break a strike at the Homestead plant of the Carnegie Steel Company near Pittsburgh. The workers would not disperse and Frick, as manager of the plant and under the instructions of Andrew Carnegie, refused to negotiate. On July 6, the Pinkertons clashed with the steelworkers in the mill yards. A dozen or so men were killed on both sides, but the sixteen workers instantly became martyrs. Carnegie remained firm however, saying he would crush the strike, even if it took the rest of his life.[5]

Ultimately, the workers gave up the strike and it was considered a major loss to American labor. Berkman's attempted assassination of Frick in his Pittsburgh office served mainly to bring more attention to the violence of anarchists.[6]

Too many Americans, as the new century dawned, it appeared that the anarchists would stop at nothing to achieve their aims. As a result of the Haymarket affair and the attack on Frick by Berkman, most Americans thought that anarchism itself was responsible for the death of McKinley, and that Czolgosz was merely the instrument. The public not only wanted to execute the assassin, but also to get those who they supposed conspired with him and to take action against resident anarchists in general. The thinking was that all of the anarchists were accessories to the crime.

---

[3] Alexander K. McClure, *The Authentic Life of William McKinley* (W. E. Skull, 1901) 446.

[4] Sidney Fine, "Anarchism and the Assassination of President McKinley," *American Historical Review* (July 1955) 779.

[5] Joseph G. Rayback, *A History of American Labor* (New York: The MacMillan Co., 1959) 195-196.

[6] James W. Clarke, *American Assassins; The Darker Side of Politics* (Princeton, NJ: Princeton University Press, 1982) 45-46.

Saturday's newspapers, after Czolgosz's statements to police, were reporting that an anarchist, who had boasted of doing his duty, had assaulted the President. This excited the emotions of the country, which resulted in calls for reprisals against anarchists everywhere. Even though, from the start, Czolgosz insisted he had acted alone with no encouragement from anyone, many found it impossible to believe that he had committed the crime alone. It was reported that the police would detain Emma Goldman and Julius Schwab as soon as they were located, and other accomplices were being sought out.

A massive hunt for Czolgosz's accomplices was conducted in Cleveland, Detroit, Chicago and other cities. Literally hundreds of anarchist supporters and sympathizers were questioned, with many being arrested or detained. Many newspapers plainly stated that Czolgosz was a mere part of an anarchistic conspiracy as a matter of fact, regardless of the lack of evidence.

In Buffalo, five men were arrested and brought into headquarters for questioning after being found at Nowak's boarding house, the place Czolgosz had been staying. Police thought they belonged to an anarchistic society, but after extensive questioning, they could uncover no proof of a plot and were forced to release them.[7]

As early as the day after the assassination, Chicago police thought they were close to busting open "the nest of Anarchists which hatched the plot against the President."[8]

The day of the shooting, a telegram was sent to the Chicago police from the Buffalo police, saying, "We have in custody Leon Czolgosz, alias Fred Nieman, the President's assassin. Locate and arrest E. J. Isaak, who is editor of a socialistic paper and a follower of Emma Goldman, from whom Nieman is said to have taken instructions. It looks as if there might be a plot, and that these people may be implicated."[9]

By 11 p.m., the editor of the leading English language communist-anarchist newspaper in the United States, *The Free Society,* Abram Isaak, along with five other men, all closely associated with one of the country's leading anarchists, Emma Goldman, were arrested and taken by paddy wagon to the Central Station. Isaak was kept in Police Captain Colleran's office, while the others were taken to cells.[10] By the next day, three more associates were arrested, and police seized a quantity of

---

[7] *Buffalo Courier*, 8 September 1901, pg. 1, col. 6.

[8] *New York Times*, 7 September 1901, pg. 5, col. 6.

[9] Marshall Everett, *The Complete Life of William McKinley* (Privately Published, 1901) 84.

[10] *New York Times*, 7 September 1901, pg. 5, col. 6.

anarchist literature, including copies of "red" literature and photographs of Emma Goldman.[11]

Chicago Police Chief O'Neill questioned the detainees. First he spoke with Isaak, who relayed information about his association with Goldman and his meetings with Czolgosz.

"The last time I saw her was on the twelfth of July," Isaak told him. "On that day she left Chicago for Buffalo. I met her at the Lake Shore depot as she was leaving. When I reached the depot I found her talking to a strange man, who appeared about 25 years old, was well-dressed and smooth shaven. Miss Goldman told me that the fellow had been following her around wanting to talk to her, but she had no time to devote to him. She asked me to find out what the fellow wanted.

"The man made a bad impression on me from the first," Isaak explained, "and when he called me aside and asked me about the secret meeting of Chicago anarchists I was sure he was a spy. I despised the man as soon as I saw him and was positive he was a spy."

According to Isaak, Goldman left on the train and Czolgosz gave him his real name. Wanting to learn more about him, Isaak asked Czolgosz to accompany him home.

"On the way to my house he asked me again and again about the secret meetings of our societies, and the impression grew on me he was a spy," Isaak explained. "He asked me if we would give him money, and I told him no, but added that if he wanted to stay in Chicago I would help him get work.

"When we reached my house we sat on the porch for about ten minutes, and his talk during that time was radical. He said he had been a Socialist for many years, but was looking for something more active than socialism. I was sure then that the fellow was a spy, and I wanted to search and unmask him, so I arranged for him to come to my house on the following morning for breakfast."

Isaak then took him to Mrs. Esther Wolfson's rooming house at 425 Carroll Avenue and got him a room. But Czolgosz never appeared at Isaak's for breakfast the next day. Upon investigation, Mrs. Wolfson told Isaak that Czolgosz had slipped away without a word. This only seemed to confirm Isaak's suspicions.[12]

Isaak then wrote to his friend Emil Schilling, which was described in an earlier chapter.

---

[11] *New York Times*, 8 September 1901, pg. 4, col. 4.

[12] Marshall Everett, *The Complete Life of William McKinley* (Privately Published, 1901) 84-87.

After interviewing Isaak, O'Neill spoke with Hippolyte Havel, a close confidant of Emma Goldman's. An excitable 35-year-old Bohemian, Havel was a small man with disheveled jet-black hair.

Havel boldly said he was indeed an anarchist and that in Bohemia he had been an agitator. Havel had been arrested in 1884 and sentenced to two years in a Plzen prison for making incendiary speeches. He boldly admitted to O'Neill that he indeed knew both Goldman and Czolgosz, and that even if he had known that Czolgosz planned to shoot President McKinley, he would not have told police.[13]

While the members of the Free Society, which was reported as being a sub-group of the International Arbeiter Zeitung Association, refused to admit that they were proponents of violence, the Free Society platform seemed to indicate otherwise.

Supposedly in the possession of Chief William S. Bull, the platform gave detailed instructions on how assassinations, or "actions" as which they were referred, were to be carried out. The platform stated that it was obvious that the ruling class would not relinquish its power "without compulsion."

"It is therefore self-evident that the fight of the proletarian against the upper and middle classes must be of a violent character," it said. "Under all these circumstances there is only one remedy left—force."

The instructions for assassins at times seemed a blueprint for how Czolgosz had acted.

"As to the scene of action select personally that point of vantage which seems to absolutely assure success, even though some comrade must necessarily sacrifice himself," it instructed.

It even suggested how an assassin was to act in the event of capture.

"When all means of defense are exhausted then let the prisoner defend his deed from the viewpoint of true anarchy and convert the defendant's seat into a speaker's stand," it said. "Keep up hope as long as possible, but when you are irredeemably lost, use your respite for the propagation of your principles and meet your punishment, whether death or imprisonment, with the unfaltering calmness of a patriot."[14]

With these types of materials being distributed by anarchists, it is little wonder that police smelled a plot.

---

[13] Marshall Everett, *The Complete Life of William McKinley* (Privately Published, 1901) 88.

[14] *Buffalo Courier*, 12 September 1901, pg. 1-3.

While a nationwide search for Goldman herself continued, her associates were brought before Magistrate Prindville in Chicago's Harrison Street jail. Prindville denied release and set bail at $3,000 each. Their attorney, Leonard Saltiel, had requested the release. Those being held were Julia Mechtlanic, Maria Isaak, Maria Isaak, Jr., Michael Roz, Martin Rozinick, Morris Fox, Isaak and Abraham Isaak, Jr., Henry Travegelino, Hippolyte Havel and Alfred Schneider.[15]

Justice Chetlain, who listened to defense attorney's arguments for the release of the prisoners on the grounds of insufficient evidence on September 13, was inclined to believe that they could be held in spite of the confessed lack of evidence, as a precautionary measure.[16]

Captain Colleran, Chief of Chicago's Detective Bureau, described *The Free Society* as a "rabid Anarchist paper" and said that Czolgosz was "closely associated" with the publication. He further told newsmen that Isaak had been instrumental and a lead figure in anarchist meetings and the Czolgosz had apparently attended these meetings.[17]

"The arrests were in consequence of a telegram from Secret Service officials in Buffalo asking us to investigate and learn the whereabouts of the headquarters of a paper known as *Free Society*," Colleran explained. "We traced the owner of the house at 515 Carroll Avenue, and there found the persons arrested, apparently in the middle of an important meeting. All the prisoners admit they are Anarchists and do not hesitate to say that they have no regard for the laws as now enforced.

"Some of the men I have learned have several terms in prisons in their native countries for attempted crimes inspired by their Anarchist beliefs. The paper *Free Society*, published by Isaak, I have learned, was formerly issued on the Pacific Coast and it was only recently that Isaak opened an office here."[18]

The charges were filed: "Conspiracy to do an illegal act, on or about September 5, 1901. Specific act: Conspiracy to kill and assassinate President of United States William McKinley, conspired with Leon Czolgosz, alias Fred C. Neiman."[19]

Adding to the suspicions were two large dynamite bombs found buried nearby.[20] But no evidence was ever found to connect any of the prisoners to the bombs or to the presidential shooting and, eventually, all of the accused were released.

---

[15] A. Wesley Johns, *The Man Who Shot McKinley* (New York: A. S. Barnes and Co., Inc., 1970) 146.
[16] *New York Times*, 15 September 1901, pg. 3, col. 5.
[17] *New York Times*, 8 September 1901, pg. 5, col. 6.
[18] *New York Times*, 8 September 1901, pg. 4, col. 4.
[19] *New York Times*, 8 September 1901, pg. 4, col. 4.
[20] *New York Times*, 7 September 1901, pg. 5, col. 6.

Meanwhile, in Cleveland, Chief of Police George E. Corner was also very busy chasing down leads. But he did not believe from the start that a real conspiracy existed.

"It is my opinion that the shooting of the Chief Executive is not the result of a plot," he said as early as September 7. "I believe that Czolgosz went to Buffalo on a different errand, and while there decided to shoot the President. There was no plot hatched in this city to kill McKinley to my way of thinking. We are working hard on the case, and if he had any accomplices they will be brought to justice."[21]

In Pittsburgh, Harry Gordon, a friend of Emma Goldman's, was dragged from his home and was about to be lynched, with the rope literally around his neck. He was saved when some by-standers intervened, being sympathetic to the pleas of his wife and two children.[22]

It was estimated that there were about 1,000 Anarchists in the Cleveland area in 1901. Most of these were "wrought up" over the attempt on the President's life and loudly claimed that the act was 'unnecessary and uncalled for.'"[23]

On September 8, New York Police Commissioner Murphy stated that there would be no wholesale arrests of anarchists in his city. He claimed that there were only about 200 anarchists living in New York City and that they were harmless. He said they would be kept under close surveillance and that all laws would be enforced.

When questioned and told that other cities were arresting anarchists by the droves, Murphy said, "Conditions are different here from other large cities. The police in this city have always held the Anarchists in a determined way." [24]

Two days later, Murphy clarified his position.

"I don't propose, if I can help it, to have any Anarchist living in this city," he explained. "We will enforce the law drastically, and whatever means can be taken. When they hold open meetings we can stop them, of course, and we can also keep them under such close watch that they will soon tire of trying to do their work in this community."[25]

---

[21] *New York Times*, 8 September 1901, pg. 4, col. 2.

[22] Emma Goldman, *Living My Life* (New York: Alfred Knopf, Inc., 1931) 312.

[23] *New York Times*, 8 September 1901, pg. 4, col. 2.

[24] *New York Times*, 8 September 1901, pg. 4, col. 5.

[25] *New York Times*, 11 September 1901, pg. 2, col. 6.

The Commissioner, as a precaution, stationed a number of men in Wall Street to prevent any trouble he thought might occur in the crowd that he expected to congregate there. Many officers were in plain clothes, so as not to attract attention.[26]

In Rochester, New York Supreme Court Justice Davy, according to a report in the *New York Sun*, was initiating an investigation into an anarchist group numbering about one hundred persons. Any one found to be a member was to be indicted for conspiracy to overthrow the government.[27]

Police in Cincinnati searched for a band of anarchists that had supposedly hatched a plot in that city to kill McKinley. An E. Laux of 1430 Monroe Street was being sought for arrest, but Cincinnati police found that 1430 Monroe Street did not exist. According to sources, a Cincinnati man had traveled to Canton to kill the President, but could not accomplish his task. Emma Goldman had also supposedly visited the city incognito.[28]

A police officer in Newton, Massachusetts, Morris Kiley, was suspended from duty for declaring during a discussion with other police officers that the shooting of the President was a "good thing" and that "there are a lot of others out there who ought to get the same done." When Chief of Police Tarbox suspended him, Kiley admitted to making the statement but insisted that it was made with no malicious intent.[29]

In Paterson, New Jersey, a group of anarchists, "called Right of Existence Group," met to celebrate. This group was generally known as the largest organized anarchist organization in the country. From their number came Gaetano Bresci, the killer of King Humbert of Italy, who was chosen to commit the act as a strike against Italy.

The anarchists had intentionally chosen Paterson to be their headquarters in the United States; primarily because it was a small city where they could have their meetings without attracting much attention. They rightly assumed that authorities there would not be able to speak their language, which was principally Italian. They raised money and used it to fund a printing operation to publish anarchistic material. They

---

[26] *New York Times*, 8 September 1901, pg. 4, col. 5.

[27] *Literary Digest,* 5 October 1901, pg. 391.

[28] *Washington Post*, 9 September 1901, pg. 1, col. 5.

[29] *New York Times*, 8 September 1901, pg. 4, col. 3.

did not publicly distribute the material, but rather passed it along underground to their brethren in the anarchist movement.

The Paterson group actively recruited others from Europe to come join them in the United States. They were successful in helping Errico Malatesta escape from imprisonment on Lampodusa, a small island off the coast of Italy. Upon arrival in Paterson, he became the recognized leader of the Paterson group. At one meeting, Gaetano Bresci saved Malatesta's life by preventing an anarchist named Pazzaglia from firing another shot during an argument at a meeting where Malatesta spoke. Malatesta was wounded in the leg by a first shot, but afterward treated himself and recovered. It was Malatesta who ordered the murder of King Humbert from Europe, and it was Bresci who answered the call.

After the assassination of King Humbert, the Italian government requested that the American government turn over all those that had conspired with Bresci. Italy turned over evidence to the State Department, but the Federal government was unable to do anything but turn it over to the Governor of New Jersey and request a complete investigation. Insufficient evidence and the difficulty of finding a law in which to prosecute the charge of conspiracy against a foreign leader resulted in the escape of the accomplices of Bresci in Paterson. Italy was forced to stand by and watch the conspirators in the murder of her king go unpunished. It was generally believed in diplomatic circles that the perceived American inaction brought about the recall of Italian Ambassador Baron Fava. The killing of McKinley showed the Italian government that the Americans where helpless to anarchists, even where their own President was concerned.[30]

Emma Goldman had made frequent visits to Paterson. While no one admitted knowing of Czolgosz prior to the shooting, they toasted him, wishing him long life and power.

"We do not know him, but he is one of us," said one. "He did what it was his duty to do and we honor him while personally thinking his effort might better have been employed across the ocean upon some crowned head."[31]

While admitting to considering assassination plots on foreign leaders, members of the group denied that President McKinley had ever been the subject of such talk.

---

[30] G. Townsend, *Memorial Life of William McKinley* (Washington: Memorial Publishing Co., 1901) 452.

[31] *New York Times*, 7 September 1901, pg. 5, col. 5.

In denying knowing Czolgosz, one said, "He is probably some German lunatic and fool."[32] Many in the group feared that the city would rise up and expel them or put them in jail.

The *New York Times* reported this very thing, in commenting on the attitude of citizens toward the group: "The feeling of indignation is very strong. The Group of Existence has brought such abuse upon the city that the shooting of the President may lead to an upheaval that will drive the members of this gang from the city if they suffer no worse fate. The respectable citizens are tired of the subtleness of the authorities and will demand that this blot upon Paterson be wiped out. If the present authorities cannot do it, there will be a change. The general verdict seems to be that the Anarchists must go."[33]

On the evening of the shooting, a man tried to incite pedestrians on 125th street in New York City to follow him to Paterson and kill anarchists.

"If President McKinley dies there will be 10,000 Anarchists killed in Paterson to avenge his death," he reported as saying. "I am ready now to go and begin the slaughter. How many of you men will go with me?"

About a hundred men and boys followed the man down the street, presumably to catch the train to Paterson, but somewhere along the way, their nerve faded.[34]

Nearby, in Cliffside Park, Mrs. Bresci, the widow of assassin Angelo Bresci, was asked to move by the local mayor. At the time of the shooting she had expressed no support for the anarchists, but had since accepted their financial help. She ran a boarding house, but the presidential shooting had scared away all of her tenants.[35]

Other New York anarchists expressed that they also did not know of Czolgosz. One prominent anarchist, Johann Most, who had himself been arrested for producing a political essay on political violence and was out on bail, commented, "I don't know this man Leon Czolgosz, never heard of him before, and I don't believe that any of the Anarchists know him. He is likely a crank or perhaps downright crazy. If he is an Anarchist, he could not have come from Poland, for there are no Anarchists there. All the people there are Roman Catholics and go to church. Besides, Czolgosz is not a Polish name. The Anarchists had nothing to do with the matter, and know nothing of it.

---

[32] *New York Times*, 7 September 1901, pg. 5, col. 5.

[33] New York Times, 7 September 1901, pg. 5, col. 5.

[34] *New York Times*, 7 September 1901, pg. 5, col. 5.

[35] *New York Times,* 18 September 1901, pg. 4, col. 1.

"Every man who kills a President or a King is not an Anarchist," he continued. "Guiteau, who killed President Garfield, was not one."[36]

Yet Most did not do much to help his own cause in the world of public opinion. He was soon arrested for printing what was considered inflammatory statements in his paper, *Freiheit*, calling for the killing of "despots" and viciously attacking McKinley. The issue had already been on the street at the time of the shooting. In it, Most had reprinted material published in 1849 by the German revolutionary Karl Heinzen. In the article, Heinzen promoted tyrannicide as the chief means of historical progress. He did not believe that there was such a thing as a crime against despots, that they were outlaws, and that to spare them was the actual crime. His philosophy was to murder the murderers. After quoting him, Most had simply added that Heinzen's words were still true.[37]

When Most learned of McKinley's shooting, he tried to withdraw all the printed issues of the paper, but it was too late as a few copies had already been sold. He was arrested on September 12, and held for four days.[38]

After his arrest, while Most was still in jail, we wrote in *Freiheit*, "...since it has been said year after year that all citizens of this country are equal, there is no difference between a president and a street-cleaner, and no excuse for all this noise and nonsensical uproar..."

"It was said," he continued, "that there was a plot to assassinate the President. Notwithstanding all the excitement no one has yet discovered a plot, and it will be necessary to release all those who have been arrested, which will make the politicians, Government, and press ridiculous. Assassinations are not especially Anarchistic. We rejoice that Mr. Czolgosz is not a foreigner but a native."[39]

For the offense of publishing *Freiheit,* Most was charged with, in essence, inciting to disturb the peace. Most's attorney, socialist Morris Hillquit, argued that remarks Most had reprinted were talking about kings, not elected officials of a democracy. He asserted that Most's 'freedom of the press' rights were being violated. Justice Hinsdale nevertheless sentenced Most to one year imprisonment on Blackwell's Island on October 14. Hinsdale stated that it was unnecessary to prove a

---

[36] *New York Times*, 7 September 1901, pg. 5, col. 5.

[37] Sidney Fine, "Anarchism and the Assassination of President McKinley," *American Historical Review* (July 1955) 783.

[38] Sidney Fine, "Anarchism and the Assassination of President McKinley," *American Historical Review* (July 1955) 783.

[39] *Literary Digest*, 21 September 1901, pg. 336.

connection between the article and the assassination; that the offense was the same either way because of the published advocacy of crime. The decision was upheld upon appeal and sentence was pronounced on June 20, 1902. Most began to serve his sentence.[40]

Another leading New York Anarchist, Justus H. Schwab, had also defended his peers.

"Anarchists don't believe now in killing Kings or Presidents," he said. "They do not believe in the present order of things, but acts like that of Czolgosz do not do any good and would not change the order of things. Czolgosz was likely a fanatic."[41]

Johann Most had agreed, "It is too much the custom nowadays to immediately lay all these things to the doings of the Anarchists," he said. "But we are not in existence for any such purpose as this. The man who killed Garfield was a crank with a personal grudge. Bresci was a fanatic. This man is the same. I cannot say too strongly that we deplore this man's act. It is not calculated to evoke any more sympathy from the true Anarchists than from any other class.

"It is not right always to ascribe these things to the Anarchists," he continued. "It's getting to be here a good deal like China. There, if a man commits a crime, they hold his schoolteacher responsible. They say he ought to have taught his pupil better. And if the man's head goes off, well, the teacher's head is pretty apt to fall in the same basket. It's much the same over here nowadays with respect to the Anarchists."[42]

In Chicago, an anarchist paper titled *Lucifer* said, "We need not say that the shooting of President McKinley is wholly condemned by this office, as the suicidal act of a mad man...

"We believe that all acts of violence recoil on the party which institutes them. If a society of Anarchists had caused the assassination of Mr. McKinley, the act would do more harm to their cause than to the cause of governmentalism."[43]

Many people had doubts, however, about the sincerity of some of the Anarchist's statements, and thought them merely self-serving in light of the fact that they were finding themselves in imminent danger.

---

[40] Sidney Fine, "Anarchism and the Assassination of President McKinley," *American Historical Review* (July 1955) 784.

[41] *New York Times*, 7 September 1901, pg. 5, col. 5.

[42] *New York Times*, 8 September 1901 , pg. 4, col. 6.

[43] *Literary Digest*, 21 September 1901, pg. 336.

Politicians were quick to jump on the 'blame the anarchists' bandwagon. Henry C. Payne, a close friend of the President and a National Republican Committeeman from Wisconsin, said that he believed Czolgosz to be "only carrying out one detail of a general plan upon the part of the Anarchists to kill the rulers of the leading nations of the earth."[44]

Theodore Roosevelt wrote to Henry Cabot Lodge, urging the United States to wage war, not only against anarchists, but also against all active and passive sympathizers with anarchists.[45]

Justice Leonard A. Giegerich stated, "If, as is reported, the crime is due to the existence of an Anarchist conspiracy, the sooner Anarchy and its supporters in this country are stamped out the better for the civilized world..."[46]

Another Justice, John Henry McCarthy, agreed. "Laws should be enacted that would mete out special punishment for such acts as these. I believe that Congress should take some action against the Anarchists in this country. That they should be allowed to meet and thrive in this country, carrying out their dastardly deeds is an outrage to our civilization. The country has been entirely too apathetic with regard to the doings of Anarchists, until now it is brought directly home to them. Let the 'Reds' be swept out of the country."[47]

Neither of the Justices explained how this was to be done in spite of constitutional guarantees of freedom of speech and the right of assembly.

"Hanging? Why whether our President lives or dies, hanging is far too good for the man who tried to kill him," proclaimed Justice Schuchman. "Now that Anarchy has been brought so close to home to our people, maybe laws will be passed governing the doing of its agents. Right under our very noses the apostles of these people are working our schemes of murder, and we sit idly by and watch. It is high time that our lawmakers should do something toward putting an end to these Anarchists bloody work."[48]

Supreme Court Justice James A. Blanchard said, "It must have been the result of a conspiracy or the act of a lunatic. It appears to me that the crime was without justification or reason, and it was inflicted on one of the sweetest and noblest characters in American public or private life. A

---

[44] *New York Times*, 7 September 1901, pg. 5, col. 6.
[45] Sidney Fine, "Anarchism and the Assassination of President McKinley," *American Historical Review* (July 1955) 789-790.
[46] *New York Times*, 7 September 1901, pg. 5, col. 5.
[47] *New York Times*, 7 September 1901, pg. 5, col. 5.
[48] *New York Times*, 8 September 1901, pg. 4, col. 3.

sentence of ten years imprisonment for such an offense seems to be inadequate but the law does not look for vengeance, and no American citizen wants more than a justification or vindication of the law."[49]

The Assistant Secretary of the Treasury also thought Congress should enact something to get at the Anarchists, but he wanted to take a different route. He stated, "Undoubtedly something could be done, but I believe that the Secret Service should be greatly enlarged, and to it should be given supervision over other groups or bodies of men who plot against our form of government and against the officers of the government. The Secret Service force is so small that it is unable to do little more than keep down counterfeiting."[50]

New York Magistrate Flammer expressed a sentiment, which was ahead of its time, "There should be a strict law passed against carrying a firearm, as no one but those evil-minded do carry them."[51]

Senator Mark Hanna perhaps expressed the opinion of most people when he responded to a question about what to do about Anarchists.

"Something must be done," he said, "not only by the Federal Government, but by the States, but it is a hard question to figure out what to do."[52]

Senator Charles W. Fairbanks of Indiana, a close friend of President McKinley's, also wanted additional laws to crack down on anarchists, saying, "The Anarchist stands as the personification of the destroyer. His hand is raised against law and order. He strikes at the institutions, which are the foundation stones of our Government, rather than at the individual whom he directly attacks. So it certainly is consistent with our Constitution to protect ourselves against Anarchism by Federal action of a drastic character."[53]

"To my mind the new law covering treason should make it an offense punishable with death, to make a murderous assault upon the President or any member of his Cabinet," said Nebraska Senator Thurston.[54]

But even before the McKinley shooting, some legislators had already wanted restrictions placed on anarchist immigration, up to and including banning anarchists from entering the country. A measure advocated by U.S. Representative Stone would have excluded anarchists and provided

---

[49] *New York Times*, 8 September 1901, pg. 4, col. 3.

[50] *New York Times*, 8 September 1901, pg. 4, col. 6.

[51] *New York Times*, 8 September 1901, pg. 4, col. 3.

[52] *New York Times*, 10 September 1901, pg. 1, col. 3.

[53] *New York Times*, 9 September 1901, pg. 1, col. 5.

[54] *Buffalo Courier*, 12 September 1901, pg. 5, col. 1.

safeguards for identifying them. The measure ultimately did not pass because many thought that it would be a dangerous precedent to prosecute or punish a man for simply subscribing to a theory or opinion and never having committed any crime. Many also felt that the very word "anarchist" was too vague.

Even Commissioner of Immigration Powderly had asked Congress to provide him with the power to turn back at port known anarchists. And like many others, Powderly did not mind if the constitution was properly bent for this purpose.

"The man who shot President McKinley admits that he received his inspiration through the Anarchistic teachings of Emma Goldman," said Powderly, "who was permitted to enjoy the right of free speech in this country. The law should be so framed as to enable the authorities to place the strong hand of justice upon every anarchist who breeds such sentiments as Emma Goldman gave expression to and deport them at once.

"From the press dispatched this morning it will be seen that several Anarchist groups held meetings last night and rejoiced in the fiendish attempt on the life of the President," he added. "Every soul who assembled at every one of those meetings should be taken out and, if aliens, deported. If citizens, they should be promptly tried for their offense but, in any event, the authorities should prevent the assembly of such characters. They were not advocating reform nor the redress of grievances of any kind; they were applauding murder, and the man who applauds murder is himself a murderer at heart and should be punished. No maudlin sentiment should stand in the way of reaching these people." [55]

Both houses of Congress considered bills to deal with the anarchist problem.

In the Senate, the Hoar Bill called for the death penalty as well, with conspirators or instigators to serve a twenty-year sentence. Anyone who threatened or advised the killing, either in print or by the spoken word, would receive a ten-year prison term. The bill also provided that the Secretary of War was to dispatch officers and men from the regular army to guard the President. The Hoar bill narrowly passed on March 21, 1902 by a vote of 52-15.

The United States House of Representatives discussed the Ray Bill, which provided the death penalty to any person killing the President,

---

[55] *New York Times*, 8 September 1901, pg. 4, col. 6.

Vice President, anyone in line for presidential succession, or ambassadors, while performing their official duties. Unsuccessful attempts were to carry a mandatory ten-year sentence. It passed on June 9, 1902, by a vote of 179-38.[56]

After passing in the Senate, the Hoar Bill was sent to the House Judiciary Committee where it was found to be unacceptable. It was sent back to the Senate with only the number of the bill intact. The text was substituted with that of the Ray Bill, with an additional section calling for the assumption that any official attacked would be considered to be performing their official duties. Congressman George Washington Ray of New York explained that to do otherwise would be unconstitutional, arguing that crimes against high public officials must be in connection to their official duties, and not otherwise. He also objected to the government providing military guards for the president because it threatened the country's liberty.

The Senate refused to accept the House version of the bill and it was sent into committee conference. The compromise bill recommended the death penalty for anyone causing the death of the president, vice president, or any acting president, and a similar penalty for causing the death of a foreign ambassador or minister or persons in the line of presidential succession, providing they were killed because of their official duties. It also included provisions that those aiding, advising, or conspiring be deemed principle offenders.

The compromise was accepted by the House on February 20, 1903, but was stalled in the Senate. Senator George F. Hoar of Massachusetts asked the Senate to accept it without debate, but this was opposed. After hours of debate, no compromise was accepted.

Eventually a final bill passed on March 3, 1903, receiving the approval of President Roosevelt the next day. It took the form of anarchist-exclusion amendments to immigration legislation. It added "anarchists" or anyone who believed in or advocated the overthrow of the government to the list of excluded immigrants. In addition, those who did not believe in government, or belonged to organizations teaching such views, or to advocate the assassination of government officials were forbidden from becoming naturalized citizens.[57]

Various states also got into the legislative act. On April 3, 1902, New York made it a crime punishable by ten years in prison and/or a five

---

[56] Sidney Fine, "Anarchism and the Assassination of President McKinley," *American Historical Review* (July 1955) 790.

[57] Sidney Fine, "Anarchism and the Assassination of President McKinley," *American Historical Review* (July 1955) 791-793.

thousand dollar fine to advocate criminal anarchy, to be involved in groups advocating criminal anarchy, to justify assassination as a component of anarchy, or to assemble with two or more persons to advocate such doctrines. Twenty-seven days later, New Jersey passed a law that went a step further, including as an offense the encouragement of "hostility or opposition to any and all government." It also included provisions for the death penalty for those found guilty of assassination of government officials with intent "to show his or her hostility or opposition to any and all government." Wisconsin adopted a law that was practically word for word with the New York law on May 22, 1903.[58]

If the nation's politicians called for action against the anarchists, the country's newspapers were even more vocal, and constitutional guarantees were the farthest things from their minds.

The *Springfield Republican* wrote: "The plea or free speech, the pretext of political opinion, must no longer avail to protect what is simply a criminal organization. Its members should be dealt with as criminals, and should be put under the surveillance that attends criminals. Every one of them should be marked and followed by the oversight of the law, and be subject to arrest wherever found. There should be permitted no more publications of their evil teachings; there should be no more meetings allowed, no more street parades with 'Death to tyrants' and other angry legends on their banners; they should be driven to holes and corners. We have tried the plan of keeping everything in the open, and it has failed; now it is time to treat these conspirators with rigorous law. It might be well to consider the members of an anarchistic society should not be published on the proof of that fact with imprisonment for life."[59]

The *New York Herald* wanted "some cruel and unusual punishment" inflicted on Czolgosz. The *Tacoma Ledger* thought that anarchy should be a capital offense. "Admitted belief in Anarchy should mean loss of freedom to every person in this free country," said the *Milwaukee Sentinel.* Washington's *National Tribune* said, "This is one of those occasions when the aroused public vengeance should have full sway, unfettered by legal impediments, and any proclaimed Anarchist have no further grace than the time to take him to the nearest tree."

---

[58] Sidney Fine, "Anarchism and the Assassination of President McKinley," *American Historical Review* (July 1955) 793-794.

[59] *Literary Digest*, 14 September 1901, pg. 301-302.

The *Topeka Capital*, more reasonable, suggested, "Congress should declare the attempt, whether successful or not, to take the life of the President or Vice President to be high treason, punishable by death."[60]

"An avowed anarchist has no civil rights superior to those of the avowed thief," said the Seattle *Post-Intelligencer*. "The community can be rid of one as easily as the other. Every Anarchist nest in the United States can be broken up and its members dispersed, every public anarchist meeting or parade can be prevented, and the entire anarchistic propaganda checked, if not suspended, by local police regulations, and a few general state statutes, which will not conflict with the provisions of the Constitution."[61]

"Civilization has been tardy and weak in dealing with these demons," wrote the St. Louis *Globe-Democrat*. "They should be deprived of a citizenship they denounce and denied a place in the communities they seek to plunge into chaos."[62]

John R. Dos Passos, a prominent New York attorney who was regarded as an expert in constitutional law, urged that alien anarchists be banished. He thought that the government should "make it a misdemeanor for any person in public or private to profess anarchist principles as defined by law, or to counsel, advise, direct, command, or incite any one or more persons to become anarchists and commit the crimes of anarchy."[63]

Even in the face of unreasonable knee-jerk solutions to what the public perceived as the root cause of the shooting, some newspapers, to their credit, took a more reasoned approach to the problem.

"It must be remembered," wrote the *Philadelphia Press*, "that all [the restriction] now proposed in this country has existed for a decade in every continental country in Europe, without effect."[64]

William Jennings Bryan wrote is his *Commoner,* "We cannot give full protection to our officials merely by passing laws for punishment of those who assault them; neither can we give them adequate protection by closing our gates to those known to advocate anarchy. These remedies, good as far as they go, are incomplete. We can only bring absolute security to our public servants by making the Government so just and so beneficent that every citizen will be willing to give his life if need be to preserve it to posterity."[65]

---

[60] *Literary Digest*, 5 October 1901, pg. 391.

[61] *Literary Digest*, 5 October 1901, pg. 391.

[62] *Literary Digest*, 21 September 1901, pg. 335.

[63] *Literary Digest*, 5 October 1901, pg. 391.

[64] *Literary Digest*, 5 October 1901, pg. 391.

[65] *Literary Digest*, 5 October 1901, pg. 391.

"Rash or radical measures might do infinitely more harm than good," the *Chicago Tribune* agreed. "It would be unfortunate if too sweeping a law was enacted against immigrants."[66]

Certainly the freedom of speech, or the restriction of, was a key component to many of the proposed solutions.

"It may be sometimes difficult to draw the line where freedom of speech floods over and becomes license of speech, and regard must be had to time, place and circumstances," said the *Chicago Journal*. "What might be simple freedom of speech in one place would be gross license in another. 'I believe in free speech,' said the Duke of Wellington, 'but not on board a man-o-war.'

"The speech that makes such men as Czolgosz assassins, the cartoons that arouse hatred and malice of ignorant men against those in high authority- these must be stopped and ended forever. There is no longer room in free America for such freedom as this."[67]

"Free thought belongs properly to the intelligent and enlightened, the charitable and humane and right minded. The harm it is capable of when it is entrusted to the wicked, ignorant, and evil-disposed is a matter which deserves the attention of law-makers," said the *Topeka Capital*. "There is such a thing as throwing the gates open too wide or too soon. When the evil-minded or the ignorant and degenerate take advantage of privileges and immunities of law to destroy law, when anarchy runs amuck and treason is openly exploited, it is time to draw the lines."[68]

Perhaps the *Times-Democrat* of New Orleans said it best:

"The talk of imprisonment for life or a long period of years for a man's public avowal of anarchistic principles is absurd talk. If we sacrifice an American's inalienable right of freedom of speech- freedom perfect safe only when it incites to crime- we shall sacrifice one of the very dearest privileges, if not the dearest privilege, that a free American possesses; and that would mean purchasing immunity from anarchistic excesses at far too great a price."[69]

Anarchists concentrated on the free speech aspects, warning that efforts to suppress them could simply be a prelude to the suppression of

---

[66] *Literary Digest*, 5 October 1901, pg. 391.

[67] *Literary Digest*, 5 October 1901, pg. 392.

[68] *Literary Digest*, 5 October 1901, pg. 392.

[69] *Literary Digest*, 5 October 1901, pg. 392.

all unpopular views and all expressions of dissent. Citizens were urged not to take this dangerous route, and to check any encroachment on free speech.[70]

Due to the intense newspaper coverage, completely innocent people were put in harms way. For instance, on September 15, a group of about thirty armed men descended upon a small anarchist village, Guffey Hollow, Pennsylvania. They forced about twenty-five families to leave the area. Also that night, a mob attacked the offices of the New York Yiddish-language anarchist organ, *Freie Arbeiter Stimme*, and did considerable damage, forcing those in the office to run for their lives.[71]

The landlord of Czolgosz' family in Cleveland, accepting guilt by family association, ordered his tenants to move, and the *Cleveland Leader* demanded that the assassin's father, who had a city job digging water trenches, be fired from his job. Even as late as May, 1903, when President Theodore Roosevelt was visiting Los Angeles, the police arrested Leon Czolgosz's brother John, on the advice of the Secret Service, and kept him in custody until Roosevelt was gone.[72]

Since Leon Czolgosz had spoken with such admiration of Emma Goldman, and because of her fame and notoriety, she was immediately cast as the top suspect in the "conspiracy" to murder the President.

At the time of the assassination, Goldman was 32 years old, and was described as having coarse features, thick lips, a square jaw and prominent nose. She wore glasses because of nearsightedness, and her hair was light, almost red. Goldman had been born in Russia and had always considered herself a revolutionary.

"I am Russian through and through, although little of my life was spent there," she later said in an interview. "I was born in Russia but was brought up in Germany and graduated from a German school."

"When I was in Germany I did not think much about anarchy, but when I went back to St. Petersburg my whole attitude toward life changed, and I went into radicalism," she explained.

"I was an anarchist when I left Russia to come to America, but I had hardly formulated my belief," she said. "The final influence that crystallized my views was the hanging of the Chicago Anarchists in

---

[70] Sidney Fine, "Anarchism and the Assassination of President McKinley," *American Historical Review* (July 1955) 796.

[71] Sidney Fine, "Anarchism and the Assassination of President McKinley," *American Historical Review* (July 1955) 786.

[72] Sidney Fine, "Anarchism and the Assassination of President McKinley," *American Historical Review* (July 1955) 787.

1887. I followed that case carefully and it made me an active anarchist."[73]

Goldman's relatives in Rochester were put under surveillance. Her frequented places in Chicago, New York, and elsewhere were also checked. The police were unable to locate her.

"Her mother said she was in Rochester five weeks ago, and her sister said three weeks ago" said Secret Service Agent Samuel Ireland, who had left Buffalo and gone to Rochester in search of Goldman, "but both claim to have heard nothing from her since they last saw her."[74]

Goldman, who was staying at the time with a friend, Carl Nold, in St. Louis, described the moment she heard of the assassination attempt and what happened next in her autobiography:

"As I stood at a street-corner wearily waiting for a car, I heard a newsboy cry: 'Extra! Extra! President McKinley shot!' I bought a paper, but the car was so jammed that it was impossible to read. Around me people were talking about the shooting of the President.

"Carl had arrived at the house before me. He had already read the account. The President had been shot at the Exposition grounds in Buffalo by a young man by the name of Leon Czolgosz. 'I never heard the name,' Carl said; 'have you?' 'No, never,' I replied. 'It is fortunate that you are here and not in Buffalo,' he continued. 'As usual, the papers will connect you with this act.' 'Nonsense!' I said, 'the American press is fantastic enough, but it would hardly concoct such a crazy story.'"

The next day, Goldman went to a stationary store on business, selling one thousand dollars worth of goods to the owner. It was her largest sale ever and she was feeling good.

"While I was waiting for the man to fill out his order, I caught the headline of the newspaper lying on his desk: 'ASSASSIN OF PRESIDENT MCKINLEY AN ANARCHIST. CONFESSES TO HAVING BEEN INCITED BY EMMA GOLDMAN. WOMAN ANARCHIST WANTED.'"

"By great effort I strove to preserve my composure, completed the business, and walked out of the store. At the next corner I bought several papers and went to a restaurant to read them. They were filled with the details of the tragedy, reporting also the police raid of the Isaak house in Chicago and the arrest of everyone found there. The authorities were going to hold the prisoners until Emma Goldman was found, the papers stated. Already two hundred detectives had been sent out throughout the country to track down Emma Goldman.

---

[73] Marshall Everett, *The Complete Life of William McKinley* (Privately Published, 1901) 77-78.

[74] *New York Times*, 10 September 1901, pg. 2, col. 3.

"On the inside page of one of the papers was a picture of McKinley's slayer. 'Why, that's Nieman!' I gasped.

"When I was through with the papers, it became clear to me that I must immediately go to Chicago. The Isaak family, Hippolyte (Havel), our old comrade Jay Fox, a most active man in the labour movement, and a number of others were being held without bail until I should be found. It was plainly my duty to surrender myself. I knew there was neither reason nor the least proof to connect me with the shooting. I would go to Chicago."[75]

So Goldman said that she recognized Czolgosz from his photo in the newspaper. But upon being arrested and questioned, Goldman denied knowing Czolgosz, but admitted that he had approached her.

"I do not know Czolgosz," she said on September 9. "There is no plot implicating anybody so far as I know. I am sure the man who shot President McKinley acted without instigation. He was certainly not prompted by me, and I am sure none of the Isaaks or other Anarchists I know had anything to do with his foolish act. What he did was foolish. I am sorry it happened. Not that I am any more sorry for Mr. McKinley than for any other person who is shot, but because blood has been spilled. We do not believe in bloodshed."[76]

On the train from St. Louis to Chicago, she heard people outside her berth talking of stringing her up to a lamppost when she was found.

The Chicago police were already aware that Goldman might be coming to their city. After the arrest of her friends, they had captured a number of her letters that had given them the idea that she was in St. Louis. Through a telegram sent to a man who lived on Oakdale Avenue, the police surmised that Goldman would be coming to Chicago to the aid of her friends, and that she would be arriving on September 8. They watched the man's house, and a woman appeared and rang the doorbell, then checked around back. But no one was home and they followed her to the home of Mr. and Mrs. Charles G. Norris at 393 Sheffield Avenue. Immediately, Captain Herman Schuettler made his way to the house.[77]

When Emma Goldman arrived in Chicago, she had gone to the Norris home where she would stay. On her first day in Chicago, Mr. Norris accepted on behalf of Goldman, a five thousand-dollar fee for an

[75] Emma Goldman, *Living My Life* (New York: Alfred Knopf, Inc., 1931) 295-296.

[76] *Cincinnati Post*, 10 September 1901, pg. 1, col. 6.

[77] Marshall Everett, *The Complete Life of William McKinley* (Privately Published, 1901) 81.

exclusive interview with the *Chicago Tribune*. After the interview, Goldman had planned to turn herself in; the money was to be used in defense of herself and her friends.[78]

But before she could do anything, on September 10, after her hosts had left for the day, Goldman jumped into the shower. Hearing glass break, she slipped on a robe and got out to investigate and discovered a policeman on the window ledge. It was Detective Charles K. Hertz. Soon the place was full of the authorities. Goldman was at first able to convince them that she was a Swedish maid, alias Lena Larson, who could speak no English. But when they found a personalized pen of Goldman's, Captain Schuettler decided to leave a couple of men there in case Goldman returned. Realizing hope was gone; Goldman admitted her identity and was taken into custody.[79]

"If these officers had come twenty minutes later I would not have been here," she told Schuettler. "I would have been on my way to deliver myself to the police."[80]

"She said when she came to the house that she had come here to surrender herself to the Chicago police," explained Charles Norris when asked by police why he had not turned her in, "and I supposed she would do so when she got ready."[81]

After her arrest, Captain Schuettler asked Goldman why she had concealed her identity. She said that it was because she was not ready to show herself that her friends were still in jail and she wanted to do something for them first.[82]

Back in Buffalo, Leon Czolgosz was reportedly told of the arrest.

"She is a good woman," he supposedly said in tears. "A friend of the poor man and an enemy of the plutocrat and the monarch. I have heard her talk. I have believed in her teachings and I have done what I believed to be my duty. She has befriended me and it makes my heart ache, when I think that I am now in a position where I will be unable to help her."[83]

However, that same day, District Attorney Thomas Penney said that, to his knowledge, Czolgosz had not been told of the arrest.[84]

[78] Richard Drinnon, *Rebel in Paradise* (Chicago: University of Chicago Press, 1961) 69.

[79] A. Wesley Johns, *The Man Who Shot McKinley* (New York: A. S. Barnes and Co., Inc., 1970) 148.

[80] *Buffalo Courier*, 11 September 1901, pg. 3, col. 1.

[81] *Washington Post*, 11 September 1901, pg. 3, col. 3.

[82] *New York Times*, 11 September 1901, pg. 2, col. 4.

[83] *Buffalo Courier,* 11 September 1901.

[84] *Buffalo Evening News,* 11 September 1901.

Goldman was the prime suspect in the "conspiracy to kill the President." But Captain Schuettler admitted, "We have no evidence against her except that she is wanted by the Buffalo authorities."[85]

While in custody, Goldman at first did little to help herself. While she sat at the police station annex, Patrolman John Weber and Chief Matron Keegan reported Goldman saying upon hearing of the President's death, "Well, I do not care. There are thousands of men dying every day. No fuss is made about them. Why should any fuss be made about this man?"

"Haven't you any heart?" asked the matron. "Any sorrow for this man who was so widely beloved?"

"I tell you I don't care," came the reply.

"But as a woman you should at least show some feeling for the wife for whom he has always cared so tenderly."

"There are thousands of men dying every day," Goldman repeated. "I do feel sorry for Mrs. McKinley. But there are other wives who receive no comfort."[86]

At the police station Goldman was subjected to brutal interrogation, which she described in some detail:

"I had often heard of the third degree used by the police in various American cities to extort confessions, but I myself had never been subjected to it... On the day of my arrest, which was September 10, I was kept at police headquarters in a stifling room and grilled to exhaustion from 10.30 a.m. till 7 p.m. At least fifty detectives passed me, each shaking his fist in my face and threatening me with the direst things..."[87]

Goldman repeated her story to detectives, explaining where she had been and with whom. She claimed that the police did not believe her and continued bullying her and abusing her. Her head throbbed and she was so thirsty her lips were parched, but according to her, the police would not let her drink, even though a large pitcher of water was in plain view. Every time she tried to reach for it, the Detectives would tell her she could drink as soon as she told them what they wanted to know. This continued for hours, until finally she was taken to the Harrison Street Police Station, where she was locked in a cell with bars on every side.[88]

---

[85] *New York Times*, 11 September 1901, pg. 2, col. 4.

[86] Murat Halstead, *The Illustrious Life of William McKinley* (Privately Published) 36.

[87] Emma Goldman, *Living My Life* (New York: Alfred Knopf, Inc., 1931) 300-301.

[88] Emma Goldman, *Living My Life* (New York: Alfred Knopf, Inc., 1931) 300-301.

While being led to the carriage that was to take her to be locked up in the jail, for the first time, Goldman lost her composure, broke down and cried for a moment, but quickly recovered.[89]

"I woke up with a burning sensation. A plain-clothes man held a reflector in front of me, close to my eyes. I leaped up and pushed him away with all my strength, crying: 'You're burning my eyes!' 'We'll burn more before we get through with you!' he retorted. With short intermissions this was repeated during three nights ..."[90]

Goldman was held and not permitted to see any mail that was sent to her other than the ones expressing hate and threatening her. One threatened to cut out her tongue, soak her in oil and burn her alive. She did not think the authors of the letters were much better than the police officials holding her. Daily she was given many letters all of which had been opened and read by the guards, and all of which were non-supportive. At the same time, letters from friends were kept from her. She thought it was all designed to break her spirit.[91]

On September 11, the *New York Times* was reporting, "...up to this time the local authorities have no evidence to submit to the Grand Jury implicating anybody with Czolgosz except possibly Emma Goldman, who is under arrest in Chicago. In her case it is admitted that there is nothing resting against her except her known anarchistic ideas and the fact that Czolgosz has stated that he knows her and that her teachings had inspired him to attempt to take the life of the President."[92]

Goldman, referring to the fifth day after her arrest, "The same evening Chief of Police O'Neill of Chicago came to my cell. He informed me that he would like to have a quiet talk with me. 'I have no wish to bully or coerce you,' he said; 'perhaps I can help you.' 'It would indeed be a strange experience to have help from a chief of police,' I replied; 'but I am quite willing to answer your questions.' He asked me to give him a detailed account of my movements from May 5, when I had first met Czolgosz, until the day of my arrest in Chicago. I gave him the requested information, but without mentioning my visit to Sasha or the names of the comrades who had been my hosts...When I concluded—what I said being taken down in shorthand—Chief O'Neill remarked: 'Unless you're a very clever actress, you are certainly innocent. I think you are innocent, and I am going to do my part to help you out.' I was too amazed to thank him; I had never before heard such a tone from a

---

[89] *New York Times*, 11 September 1901, pg. 2, col. 4.

[90] Emma Goldman, *Living My Life* (New York: Alfred Knopf, Inc., 1931) 300-301.

[91] Emma Goldman, *Living My Life* (New York: Alfred Knopf, Inc., 1931) 300-301.

[92] *New York Times*, 11 September 1901, pg. 2, col. 5.

police officer. At the same time I was skeptical of the success of his efforts, even if he should try to do something for me."

After her talk with the Chief, Goldman noticed a decidedly different treatment. Her cell door was unlocked and left that way day and night. She was permitted to sit in the large room outside her cell, use a rocking chair and table, order food and newspapers, and to receive and send out mail.

"I began at once to lead the life of a society lady, receiving callers all day long, mostly newspaper people who came not so much for interviews as to talk, smoke, and relate funny stories. Others, again, came out of curiosity... Most attentive was Katherine Leckie, of the Hearst papers ... A strong and ardent feminist, she was at the same time devoted to the cause of labour. Katherine Leckie was the first to take my story of the third degree. She became so outraged at hearing it that she undertook to canvass the various women's organizations in order to induce them to take the matter up."[93]

Meanwhile, Buffalo District Attorney Thomas Penney was still trying to extradite Goldman to Buffalo. Chicago authorities refused and placed her under a twenty thousand-dollar bail. There was another fifteen thousand dollar bail for the Isaak group of defendants, and it was just too much money for Goldman's supporters to raise. [94]

In the effort to build a case against Goldman, authorities questioned her friends and relatives.

Hattie Lang, Emma's former landlord in Buffalo during a brief vacation there in July of 1901, was questioned. She admitted that while in Buffalo, Goldman had gone to the Exposition with Dr. Kaplin, who had invited her to Buffalo, and a friend of his, Dr. Saylin. They had simply toured the grounds as any tourist would, she said.[95]

In Rochester, her family was questioned intensely. Her teen-aged niece, Stella Cominsky, was interrogated for two days. Her nieces and nephews had to endure jeers at school about their aunt. Her father, Abraham Goldman, who owned a furniture store, lost many of his customers and was ostracized by his neighbors. He was also excommunicated from his synagogue. But police were still unable to uncover any evidence of her guilt.[96]

---

[93] Emma Goldman, *Living My Life* (New York: Alfred Knopf, Inc., 1931) 302.

[94] A. Wesley Johns, *The Man Who Shot McKinley* (New York: A. S. Barnes and Co., Inc., 1970) 252.

[95] Richard Drinnon, *Rebel in Paradise* (Chicago: University of Chicago Press, 1961) 71.

[96] Richard Drinnon, *Rebel in Paradise* (Chicago: University of Chicago Press, 1961) 71.

"Buffalo was pressing for my extradition, but Chicago asked for authentic data on the case," Goldman wrote. "I had already been given several hearings in court, and on each occasion the District Attorney from Buffalo had presented much circumstantial evidence to induce the State of Illinois to surrender me. But Illinois demanded direct proofs. There was a hitch somewhere that helped to cause more delays. I thought it likely that Chief of Police O'Neill was behind the matter."

Goldman received parcels containing fruit, candy, and liquor. Many of these gifts were from a "secret admirer" who supposedly owned a saloon around the corner from the station. She wondered about her admirer.

"One day she (the matron) brought me the message that he was going to send a grand supper for the coming Sunday. 'Who is the man and why should he admire me?' I inquired. 'Well, we're all Democrats, and McKinley is a Republican,' she replied. 'You don't mean you're glad McKinley was shot?' I exclaimed. 'Not glad exactly, but not sorry, neither,' she said; 'we have to pretend, you know, but we're none of us excited about it.' 'I didn't want McKinley killed,' I told her. 'We know that,' she smiled, 'but you're standing up for the boy.' I wondered how many more people in America were pretending the same kind of sympathy with the stricken President as my guardians in the station-house."[97]

Buffalo failed to produce any evidence to justify Emma Goldman's extradition. She was released under $20,000 bail, with the Isaak group being put under a $15,000 bail. She insisted on being released only after her friends and was thus transferred to the Cook County Jail.

"The night before my transfer was Sunday. My saloon-keeper admirer kept his word; he sent over a huge tray filled with numerous goodies: a big turkey, with all the trimmings, including wine and flowers. A note came with it informing that he was willing to put up five thousand dollars towards my bail. 'A strange saloon-keeper!' I remarked to the matron. 'Not at all,' she replied; 'he's the ward heeler and he hates the Republicans worse than the devil.' I invited her, my two policemen, and several other officers present to join me in the celebration. They assured me that nothing like it had ever before happened to them—a prisoner playing host to her keepers."[98]

The police were worried that angry mobs would try to get Goldman and indeed, reports to the affect had been published in the newspapers. But when she was led from the station, there were only a dozen or so

[97] Emma Goldman, *Living My Life* (New York: Alfred Knopf, Inc., 1931) 305.

[98] Emma Goldman, *Living My Life* (New York: Alfred Knopf, Inc., 1931) 306.

curious bystanders. Goldman thought the newspapers had intentionally tried to incite a riot.

"Ahead of me were two handcuffed prisoners roughly hustled about by the officers, she described. "When we reached the patrol wagon, surrounded by more police, their guns ready for action, I found myself close to the two men. Their features could not be distinguished: their heads were bound up in bandages, leaving only their eyes free. As they stepped up to the patrol wagon, a policeman hit one of them on the head with his club, at the same time pushing the other prisoner violently into the wagon. They fell over each other, one of them shrieking with pain. I got in next, then turned to the officer. 'You brute,' I said, 'how dare you beat that helpless fellow?' The next thing I knew, I was sent reeling to the floor. He had landed his fist on my jaw, knocking out a tooth and covering my face with blood. Then he pulled me up, shoved me into the seat, and yelled: 'Another word from you, you damned anarchist, and I'll break every bone in your body!'"[99]

When Goldman arrived at the jail, her waist and skirt were covered in blood. She said that no one showed the slightest interest or bothered to ask what had happened to her. They did not even allow her to clean up. She was held for two hours until finally a woman arrived who informed her that she would have to be searched. Goldman refused, telling the woman that she would have to kill her before she would allow it. The matron hurried out, and Goldman was again left alone to wait. Eventually another woman led her upstairs, where another matron was the first to ask what was the matter with her. She was then given a hot water bottle and it was suggested that she lie down and rest.

"The following afternoon Katherine Leckie visited me," Goldman wrote. "I was taken into a room provided with a double wire screen. It was semi-dark, but as soon as Katherine saw me, she cried: 'What on God's earth has happened to you? Your face is all twisted!' No mirror, not even of the smallest size, being allowed in the jail, I was not aware how I looked, though my eyes and lips felt queer to the touch. I told Katherine of my encounter with the policeman's fist. She left swearing vengeance and promising to return after seeing Chief O'Neill. Towards evening she came back to let me know that the Chief had assured her the officer would be punished if I would identify him among the guards of the transport. I refused. I had hardly looked at the man's face and I was not sure I could recognize him. Moreover, I told Katherine, much to her disappointment, that the dismissal of the officer would not restore my tooth; neither would it do away with police brutality...

---

[99] Emma Goldman, *Living My Life* (New York: Alfred Knopf, Inc., 1931) 307-308.

"Poor Katherine was not aware that I knew she could do nothing. She was not even in a position to speak through her own paper: her story about the third degree had been suppressed. She promptly replied by resigning; she would no longer be connected with such a cowardly paper, she had told the editor."[100]

Emma Goldman was again taken to court for a hearing and for the second time Buffalo authorities were unable to produce enough evidence to connect her directly with Czolgosz's act. After a two-hour verbal exchange between the Buffalo official and the Judge, Goldman was finally released. She complained that the press had loudly denounced her for her supposed involvement in the case, but that after she was released only a few lines were written to exonerate her.[101]

Max Hippolyte and other friends met Goldman when she was released and the group went to the Isaak's home. The charges against those arrested in Chicago had also been dismissed. Everyone was in high spirits and when Goldman expressed thanks for Chief O'Neill, her friends laughingly told her that the Chicago police chief had not cared anything about her, but had simply been trying to fuel a feud in the Chicago Police department in order to help himself politically. [102]

But at times, Emma Goldman's account of what transpired must be viewed as explicitly self-serving. As an example, in her autobiography, she tried to distance herself from being the cause of Czolgosz's act, even as there was ample evidence that Czolgosz himself had said she was an unwitting influence.

"I asked my friends their opinion as to how the idea of connecting my name with Czolgosz had originated. 'I refuse to believe that the boy made any kind of confession or involved me in any way,' I stated; 'I cannot think that he was capable of inventing something, which he must have known might mean my death. I'm convinced that no one with such a frank face could be so craven. It must have come from some other source.'

"It did!' Hippolyte declared emphatically. 'The whole dastardly story was started by a (Chicago) Daily News reporter who used to hang round here pretending to sympathize with our ideas. Late in the afternoon of September 6 he came to the house. He wanted to know all

---

[100] Emma Goldman, *Living My Life* (New York: Alfred Knopf, Inc., 1931) 307-308.

[101] Emma Goldman, *Living My Life* (New York: Alfred Knopf, Inc., 1931) 310-311.

[102] Emma Goldman, *Living My Life* (New York: Alfred Knopf, Inc., 1931) 310-311.

about a certain Czolgosz or Nieman. Had we associated with him? Was he an anarchist? And so forth. Well, you know what I think of reporters—I wouldn't give him any information. But unfortunately Isaak did.'

"'What was there to hide?' Isaak interrupted. 'Everybody about here knew that we had met the man through Emma, and that he used to visit us. Besides, how was I to know that the reporter was going to fabricate such a lying story?'"[103]

Another example of what would be called "spin" in another generation was her tale of Czolgosz's execution, which also appeared in *Living My Life*:

"It doesn't matter what Emma Goldman has said about me," she reported Czolgosz saying in the chair. "She had nothing to do with my act. I did it alone. I did it for the American people."

Certainly, no one heard Czolgosz say anything of the kind. He never mentioned Goldman at the execution. But Goldman did take an active interest in Czolgosz, in despair because of Czolgosz's fate and especially the torture of his body and spirit as execution approached. She feared that the warning that had appeared in *Free Society* had been a possible motive, by enticing Czolgosz to act to prove he was a true Anarchist and not a spy.[104]

"A trusted person was dispatched to Buffalo," Goldman later wrote, "but he soon returned without having been able to visit Czolgosz. He reported that no one was permitted to see him. A sympathetic guard had disclosed to our messenger that Leon had repeatedly been beaten into unconsciousness. His physical appearance was such that no outsider was admitted, and for the same reason he could not be taken to court. My friend further reported that, notwithstanding all the torture, Czolgosz had made no confession whatever and had involved no one in his act."[105]

Goldman was indeed very sympathetic to Czolgosz. In fact she was more so to him, than to his victim. Goldman asked at the time of McKinley's death if it was possible...that in the entire United States only the President had passed away. Her ill-timed point was that many others had died at the same time, perhaps in poverty and destitution, leaving helpless dependents behind. She said that she could not understand why more "fuss was made" over the "shooting of the President than of anyone else."[106]

[103] Emma Goldman, *Living My Life* (New York: Alfred Knopf, Inc., 1931) 310-311.
[104] A. Wesley Johns, *The Man Who Shot McKinley* (New York: A. S. Barnes and Co., Inc., 1970) 252-253.
[105] Emma Goldman, *Living My Life* (New York: Alfred Knopf, Inc., 1931) 315-316.
[106] *New York Times*, 11 September 1901, pg. 2, col. 4.

But when it came to the plight of Czolgosz, Goldman had a different opinion. She wrote an article for *Free Society*, which even its editor, Abram Isaak realized would be inflammatory. He tried to tone it down, only to have Goldman insist on printing it in its original form. She wrote in the article titled *Tragedy in Buffalo* that Leon Czolgosz and other men of his type were driven to some violence, even at the sacrifice of their own lives, because they could not sit by and watch the sufferings of others. She claimed that the blame for such acts must be on those who were responsible for the injustice and inhumanity, which dominate the world, meaning the world's leaders. She wrote that her heart went out to Czolgosz in deep sympathy, as it went out to all victims of oppression and misery, martyrs that die, and the forerunners of a better and nobler life.[107]

"The tragedy in Buffalo was nearing its end," wrote Goldman of the final days of Czolgosz's life. "Leon Czolgosz, still ill from the maltreatment he had endured, his face disfigured and head bandaged, was supported in court by two policemen. In its all-embracing justice and mercy the Buffalo court had assigned two lawyers to his defense. What if they did declare publicly that they were sorry to have to plead the case of such a depraved criminal as the assassin of 'our beloved' President!"[108]

Again, her sympathy to Czolgosz is apparent as she exaggerated Czolgosz's treatment by his jailors. She may well have thought he had been subject of such abuse, but again, she had demonstrated that she would not hesitate to "spin" the truth.

Goldman, later in a newspaper interview, talked about how a plot to assassinate might occur.

"He and perhaps one or two intimate friends or relatives make a plan," she explained. "They do not have orders. They do not consult other Anarchists. If a man came to me and told me he was planning an assassination I would think him an utter fool and refuse to pay any attention to him. The man who has such a plan, if he is earnest and honest, knows no secret is safe when told. He does the deed himself; runs the risk himself; pays the penalty himself. I honor him for the spirit that prompts him. It is no small thing for a man to be willing to lay down his life for the cause of humanity. The act is noble, but is mistaken.

---

[107] A. Wesley Johns, *The Man Who Shot McKinley* (New York: A. S. Barnes and Co., Inc., 1970) 254.

[108] Emma Goldman, *Living My Life* (New York: Alfred Knopf, Inc., 1931) 317.

"No, I have never advocated violence, but neither do I condemn the Anarchist who resorts to it. I look behind him for the conditions that made him possible, and my horror is swallowed up in my pity. Perhaps under the same conditions I would have done the same."[109]

Goldman went back to New York and stopped in Rochester for a month with her family, where she was generally snubbed, also being excommunicated from her synagogue.

In New York City, she could find no one who would rent her a room, and was forced to stay in the flat of a young prostitute she knew.

Emma Goldman was eventually deported from the United States on December 21, 1919, after serving a sentence of twenty-one months for a violation of the Espionage Act. Sailing with her aboard the Buford to Europe was Alexander Berkman and forty-nine other anarchists among a cargo off 249 being deported. [110]

Anarchists had been persecuted in the United States since prior to the McKinley assassination, but the shooting brought things to new heights. The fears after the Russian revolution of 1917 proved to be a catalyst for anti-anarchist actions, resulting in the 1917-1920 rounding up and deportation of about 3,000 known anarchists. These actions disrupted the anarchistic movement in the United States forever. After 1920, the country was more concerned with the threat of communism than the ideological doctrines of the anarchists.[111]

In Barcelona, thirty-six years after the assassination, Emma Goldman, who never gave up her sympathy for McKinley's assassin, remembered the anniversary of the execution of that "poor forsaken boy, Leon Czolgosz."[112]

Another "victim" of the McKinley Assassination was William Randolph Hearst, the tycoon owner of several newspapers, including the *New York Journal*, *Chicago American* and the *San Francisco Examiner*. Hearst had been one of McKinley's most venomous critics, and many thought he should shoulder much of the blame for the assassination.

Hearst had found reporting about the atrocities of the Cubans leading up to the Spanish American War was a huge draw to his paper's

---

[109] *Literary Digest*, 21 September 1901, pg. 336.

[110] Sidney Fine, "Anarchism and the Assassination of President McKinley," *American Historical Review* (July 1955) 799.

[111] Sidney Fine, "Anarchism and the Assassination of President McKinley," *American Historical Review* (July 1955) 799.

[112] Richard Drinnon, *Rebel in Paradise* (Chicago: University of Chicago Press, 1961) 71.

readership. Never mind if the stories were true. Most of the stories were plants from the Cuban revolutionary movement being run out of New York City, called the Cuban Junta.

Hearst continually encouraged the staff of the *New York World* to find more outrageous stories, and he felt himself unrestrained by the truth. His main goal was to outsell his boyhood idol, Joseph Pulitzer, and he would do that any way he could. Nursing a real dislike for the Spanish monarchy, he was also not opposed to spreading anti-Spanish propaganda, being sympathetic to the Cuban rebels.

Supposedly, Hearst had told Frederic Remington, his representative in Havana who wished to leave the city, "Please remain. You furnish the pictures and I'll furnish the war."

Hearst always denied the exchange, but whether or not it took place, William Randolph Hearst did not furnish the war. Forces much more powerful than yellow journalism furnished the war, when it came.[113]

Eventually, Hearst turned his venom on President McKinley for his reluctance to enter into the Cuban situation. His editorials and cartoons portrayed the President in an extremely bad light.

"What wonder that the weak Czolgosz answered such impulses as these," Secretary Elihu Root said in 1906 that it was little wonder that Czolgosz answered such impulses as the Hearst attacks on McKinley. Czolgosz, he said, never knew McKinley and had no had no wrongs of his own to avenge. He was simply answering to the lessons that it was a service to mankind to rid the earth of a monster, and that the foremost of the teachers of these lessons to him and his kind was none other than William Randolph Hearst and his yellow journals.[114]

Hearst used a sensational style of writing in his papers, a style that came to be known as "yellow journalism." Hearst wanted to shock his readers, and in light of the assassination, Hearst's previous attacks on McKinley were viewed by many as crossing the line.

Root continued his attack on Hearst in another speech in Utica, New York. Root claimed that Hearst had been sowing the seeds of dissension and hatred throughout the country. Hearst, he said, would play labor against capital, and capital against labor; poverty against wealth, and wealth against poverty. If Hearst had his way, said Root, he would destroy respect for the law and order and all confidence in the nation's

---

[113] G. J. A. O'Toole, *The Spanish War: An American Epic 1898* (New York: W. W. Norton & Co., 1984) 82.

[114] A. Wesley Johns, *The Man Who Shot McKinley* (New York: A. S. Barnes and Co., Inc., 1970) 139.

institutions. Root claimed Hearst was guided only by the selfish motives of a revolutionist.[115]

Dr. Allan McLane Hamilton, an alienist who had been at the trial of Czolgosz, agreed, though did not name Hearst or his papers by name.

"Undoubtedly the crime was precipitated by the outrageous attacks printed in one of the sensational and irresponsible journals of the time," he wrote. "This paper had for weeks been abusing McKinley, and accusing him of working in the interests of the trusts. In one issue it said: 'McKinley's fat white hand has tossed to the starving American peasant the answer out of the White House window,' 'A trust can do no wrong,' and again, 'Has his assassination changed world history?' We invite our readers to think over this question."[116]

As news of the assassination spread, there was a wave of hatred against Hearst and his papers, charging him with direct responsibility. In many places, Hearst was hung in effigy, sometimes next to figures representing Emma Goldman. Bonfires of Hearst papers lit the night. Hearst newspapers were boycotted by church and business organizations. Some businesses were even boycotted for just subscribing to Hearst papers.

Upon hearing news of the McKinley shooting during a meeting in the composing room of the *Chicago American*, Hearst turned to his Chicago publisher Charles Edward Russell and told him, that he thought things are going to be very bad.[117] His remark proved prophetic.

In anticipation of and in an attempt to head off trouble, Hearst fired off telegrams to his newspapers, the *New York Journal* and the *San Francisco Examiner* urging a softer line and a show of compassion and hope for the President's recovery.

William Randolph Hearst had been one of President McKinley's most vicious critics, and most people knew it. He disagreed heartily with McKinley's policies concerning powerful trusts; Hearst portrayed McKinley as being in their pockets and wanted more action taken against them. One of his editors had called McKinley "the most hated creature on the American continent." Trying to soften the blow, Hearst now said he hoped that the President would not leave his much beloved wife

---

[115] John Tebbel, *The Life and Good Times of William Randolph Hearst* (New York: E. P. Dutton & Co., Inc., 1952) 210.

[116] Hamilton, Allan McLane, *Recollections of an Alienist* (New York: George H. Doran Company, 1916) 361.

[117] John K. Winkler, *William Randolph Hearst* (New York: Hastings House Publishers, 1955) 123.

behind and that he may devote his remaining days to the program, which his last speech outlined.[118]

This statement, and its apparent hypocrisy, mainly served only to further infuriate Hearst's enemies. In fear for his life, Hearst began to keep a gun on his desk. Hearst's life was repeatedly threatened. Fearful of bombs, he refused to even open packages sent to him.[119]

Ironically, it had been Hearst's Albany correspondent, John Tremain, who was first to break the news of the presidential shooting by calling the *New York Journal* office. Copy boy Pete Campbell took the call and yelled to managing editor Foster Coates, "McKinley shot at Buffalo Exposition by a crank." After a fast and loose verification, which was a *New York Journal* trademark, Coates dictated the story.[120]

The bulletin had come in through John Tremain, an Albany correspondent for the Hearst papers. Tremain had earlier found the only telephone on the grounds while walking about with the presidential party. His bulletin arrived at 3:32 p.m. and the newspaper was on the street exactly twelve minutes later. In Buffalo, Tremain's telephone line went dead, which cause considerable confusion in the newspaper's office. No one could be reached to verify it for over an hour. Meanwhile, according to Campbell, every other newspaper had to quote the *New York Journal's* account.[121]

In another scoop, a man wandered into *New York Journal* office with a photograph he had taken at the Exposition, which, though blurry, showed the assassin at the scene. The editors feigned disinterest and paid the man five dollars for the picture, after which it was published.[122] Attempting to get yet another scoop, Hearst sent an agent to Chicago to talk with friends of Emma Goldman and made an offer of $20,000 for an exclusive interview. Goldman viewed the offer with suspicion, thinking Hearst was trying to divert attention from himself and his troubles. She was advised that her situation was bad enough without the help of Mr. Hearst.[123]

---

[118] A. Wesley Johns, *The Man Who Shot McKinley* (New York: A. S. Barnes and Co., Inc., 1970) 139.

[119] A. Wesley Johns, *The Man Who Shot McKinley* (New York: A. S. Barnes and Co., Inc., 1970) 152.

[120] John K. Winkler, *William Randolph Hearst* (New York: Hastings House Publishers, 1955) 123.

[121] John K. Winkler, *William Randolph Hearst* (New York: Hastings House Publishers, 1955) 124.

[122] W. A. Swanberg. Citizen Hearst (New York: Charles Scribner's Sons, 1961) 193.

[123] Emma Goldman, *Living My Life* (New York: Alfred Knopf, Inc., 1931) 303.

Among the most damning pieces to Hearst was unwittingly done by Ambrose Bierce, who after Kentucky Governor-elect William Goebel had been shot dead in an election quarrel months before McKinley's shooting, wrote the quatrain which became prophetic:

> "The Bullet that pierced Goebel's breast
> Can not be found in all the West
> Good reason: it is speeding here
> To stretch McKinley on the bier."[124]

"The lines took no attention, naturally, but twenty months afterward the President was shot," explained Bierce. "Everyone remembers what happened then to Mr. Hearst and his newspapers. His political enemies and business competitors were alert to their opportunity."

"As to Mr. Hearst," he added, "I dare say he first saw the lines when all this hullabaloo directed his attention to them."[125]

The Hearst newspapers, Bierce knew, had been very critical toward McKinley, and he also knew that he was unlucky in that it was his writing that had cost the Hearst paper tens of thousands of dollars, as well as political prestige. The matter was never mentioned between Bierce and Hearst, and Bierce thought it showed that William Randolph Hearst did indeed had a heart.[126]

But perhaps the most damaging of all was an editorial printed in the April 10, 1901 *New York Evening Journal*, which said in part, "If bad institutions and bad men can be got rid of only by killing, then the killing must be done."[127]

When the editorial came to Hearst's attention, he stopped the presses and had it removed from later editions, but the damage had already been done and his enemies filed it away. Later, after the assassination, Hearst enemies reprinted the editorial, probably written by the *Evening Journal's* Arthur Brisbane, as evidence of Hearst's irresponsibility.[128]

---

[124] John Tebbel, *The Life and Good Times of William Randolph Hearst* (New York: E. P. Dutton & Co., Inc., 1952) 199.

[125] John Tebbel, *The Life and Good Times of William Randolph Hearst* (New York: E. P. Dutton & Co., Inc., 1952) 199.

[126] W. A. Swanberg. Citizen Hearst (New York: Charles Scribner's Sons, 1961) 194.

[127] *New York Journal*, 10 April 1901.

[128] W. A. Swanberg. Citizen Hearst (New York: Charles Scribner's Sons, 1961) 191-192.

While the episode did cost Hearst money and political prestige, the *New York Journal* survived to continue to have the world's largest circulation. But competing newspapers, seeing their chance to damage their powerful rival, did all they could to add to Hearst's troubles, one printing in an editorial that was later recalled, that Czolgosz had actually been carrying a copy of the *New York Journal* at the time of the shooting.[129] This was of course, untrue. Czolgosz himself denied being a Hearst newspaper reader. Another story went around that Czolgosz had been offered ten thousand dollars for his family if he confessed to being inspired by the Hearst papers. Czolgosz denied even seeing a Hearst paper and repeated that it was Goldman's words which has spurred him to action.[130]

Among the attacks on the Hearst papers came an editorial in the *Chicago Journal*:

"What man now in office has not been assailed in terms too vile for repetition by the *New York Journal*, the *Chicago American*, and the *San Francisco Examiner*?

"These papers have vilified President McKinley in language so outrageous that billingsgate is respectful when compared to it.

"Day after day they have printed cartoons in which he is portrayed in the most despicable character and made food for the laughter of fools...

"It is strange, then, that in the public they have thus sought to educate and to sway, men are to be found who are capable of assassination—men who would consider it their duty to kill such a man as Hearst has taught them to believe McKinley is?"[131]

And the onslaught continued:

"Czolgosz was egged on to his crime not only by professed Anarchists," said the *Inter Ocean*, of Chicago, "but also by the newspapers that have continually depicted the President as a creature too contemptible to deserve the respect of a mongrel dog, is an unquestionable truth."

The *Brooklyn Eagle* thought that the cartoons of the yellow journals added to an atmosphere of popular passion against public officials and advocated a law to "make it an offense to hold the rulers of the country up to the scorn or hatred of the people."

---

[129] John Tebbel, *The Life and Good Times of William Randolph Hearst* (New York: E. P. Dutton & Co., Inc., 1952) 198.

[130] John K. Winkler, *William Randolph Hearst* (New York: Hastings House Publishers, 1955) 124.

[131] *Literary Digest*, 21 September 1901, pg. 364.

The *New York Press* said, "We have only to place Czolgosz in the back room of a Chicago beer saloon reading William R. Hearst's newspaper and we can place William R. Hearst at the bar of Erie County beside Leon Czolgosz, there to answer for the murder of William McKinley."

"We are well aware that no law can be framed to reach yellow journalism and the men who promote it," said the *Chicago Journal*, "but there is a higher law than the law of the land, that rests in the bosoms of all men of right feelings and just regard for the public welfare. That law can be invoked to condemn such men as William R. Hearst. That law can punish him with the scorn of honest men. It can place him in the pillory of public contempt. It can make him an object of obloquy to all mankind."[132]

The new President, Theodore Roosevelt, in his first message to Congress in 1901, even took a swipe. Czolgosz had, Roosevelt said, "inflamed by the teachings of professed anarchists, and probably also by reckless utterances of those who, on the stump and in the public press, appeal to the dark and evil spirits of malice and greed, envy and sullen hatred. The wind is sowed by the men who preach such doctrines, and they cannot escape their share of the responsibility for the whirlwind that is reaped."[133]

Years later, in 1906, Secretary Elihu Root put to rest any doubts that may have existed as to who Roosevelt had in mind with his statement.

"I say, by the President's authority, that in penning those words, with the horror of President McKinley's murder fresh before him, he had Mr. Hearst specifically in mind," said Root. "And I say, by his authority, that what he thought of Mr. Hearst then, he thinks of Mr. Hearst now."[134]

What worried Hearst more than the money he was losing, was how he should fight back. His response came in the form of an editorial.

"From coast to coast," Hearst wrote, "this newspaper has been attacked and is being attacked with savage ferocity by the incompetent, the failures of journalism, by the kept organs of plutocracy heading the mob. The Hearst papers are American papers for Americans. They are conservative papers, for the truest conservatism is that radicalism which would uproot revolution-breeding-abuses...All the enemies of the people, of the democratic people conscience and unconscious—all who reap where others have sown, all the rascals and their organs, and many fools

---

[132] *Literary Digest*, 21 September 1901, pg. 364.

[133] *New York Times,* 4 December 1901, pg. 1.

[134] *New York Times,* 2 November 1906.

caught by the malignant uproar, are yelling at the Journal. LET THEM YELL."[135]

But evidently, before any of his problems had transpired, and as witnessed by his reaction to the shooting, even Hearst had realized that he had gone too far in his criticism of President McKinley. Months earlier, Hearst had sent James Creelman to apologize to McKinley for excessive personal attacks in the heat of political battle. Ironically, at the time of his shooting, the President was on relatively good terms with Hearst.

Creelman claimed that Hearst had offered to exclude anything the President found personally offensive and also pledged his support in things in which the two men did not differ politically. The President, according to Creelman, seemed genuinely touched by Hearst's completely voluntary offer and sent Hearst a message of thanks. [136]

Much of what had appeared in his papers, Hearst had not had personal knowledge. Yet the charge of his complicity in the death of President McKinley was to haunt William Randolph Hearst for the rest of his life.

---

[135] John Tebbel, *The Life and Good Times of William Randolph Hearst* (New York: E. P. Dutton & Co., Inc., 1952) 200.

[136] John K. Winkler, *William Randolph Hearst* (New York: Hastings House Publishers, 1955) 125.

6. Trial and Execution

While the crowds and the nation waited for news of President's death, the rage against his assailant was rising. All over Buffalo there were crowds of people, wanting to be a part of history if only as spectators among themselves. But the crowds were largest near the police station and those in the throng threatened all sorts of violence. Authorities were ready with members of the police, militia and even federal troops being on guard. About ten thousand men began to rush the jail, shouting, "We'll break into the jail. We want Czolgosz."

The authorities acted promptly by charging the crowd and driving it two blocks from the jail. Reinforcements were immediately called upon, with the Seventy-fourth and Seventy-sixth regiments put on reserve in their armories.[1]

But on the night of September 13, as the President lay near death and the crowds waited in anticipation and anger outside the police station, Czolgosz was not even there. He had been secretly moved to the Erie County Penitentiary on Trenton Avenue, about a mile west of the city.

Shortly before noon on the thirteenth, Chief William S. Bull had ordered a carriage from C. W. Miller's livery stable on Huron Street for the transfer of the prisoner. It was brought right up to the front door of the headquarters.

Czolgosz was first brought from his dungeon cell to Chief Bull's office. Assistant Chief Cusack, with his revolver in his pocket, walked Czolgosz, without handcuffs in order not to attract attention, right out the front door and into the waiting carriage. Other plain-clothes officers were stationed outside near the entrance, talking in groups, in case of trouble. To the passersby who may have seen them get into the carriage, there was nothing at all to indicate it was the President's assailant; it simply looked like two men getting into a carriage.

Czolgosz was driven at a trot, without undue haste, to the penitentiary and given over to Sheriff Caldwell. He would remain in Caldwell's charge until he was indicted with the President's murder.[2]

Buffalo District Attorney Thomas Penney had been waiting to determine the charges and to arraign Czolgosz until the exact fate of the President was better determined. With the death of the President, justice moved swiftly.

---

[1] *New York Times*, 14 September 1901, pg. 1, col. 4.

[2] A. Wesley Johns, *The Man Who Shot McKinley* (New York: A. S. Barnes and Co., Inc., 1970) 191.

GRAND JURY INDICTMENT

Leon F. Czolgosz was indicted by the Erie County Grand Jury on September 16, 1901. The entire process took four hours and forty-three minutes and twenty-eight witnesses were called.

The morning session began at 10:15 a.m., and the first people to testify were the President's doctors; Mynter, Gaylord, Matzinger and Mann. During this portion of the testimony, the cause of the President's death was clearly established as a result of the gunshot wounds he sustained.

Next came the witnesses to the crime itself, and Secret Service Agent Albert Gallaher was the first to testify. He was followed by James L. Quackenbush, who testified longer than any of the other witnesses, from 11:15-12:15. Louis Babcock came next, followed by Major Alexander R. Robertson, commandant of the exposition police. Of the police, only Captain Damer and Officer's James and Westenfelder testified. Other officers stood ready to deliver testimony, but were not called. They included Officers Sullivan, Smith, Mahoney, Dougherty, Merkle, Warner, Taylor, and McCauley.

A recess was called at 12:38 p.m., and court was reconvened at 2 p.m. For twenty minutes, no witnesses were called, then for the next two hours, twenty witnesses were hurried through.

Five members of the 73rd Coast Artillery testified. Next was a visitor to the exposition, E. C. Knapp, followed by Mrs. Van Dozen Davis, a black porter in the Temple of Music. Another black porter, James Branch, followed her.

The omission of the testimony of James Parker was notable. He had been applauded and featured in the press, but his actions were now coming into question, and he did not testify.

According to a story that was being reported in the press told by men in Company C of the First Heavy Artillery, Parker had had nothing to do with the arrest.

"It was not the negro Parker but two privates of the Fourteenth United States Infantry that the credit of having seized and disarmed Czolgosz is due," said one of the men, "and in connection with this the part played by the Secret Service men is not altogether creditable.

"But while the hush was over the rest of the crowd two of the eleven men of the Fourteenth Infantry, O'Brien and Brooks, had fallen on the man who did the shooting, and bore him to the ground. O'Brien dragged the revolver from his hand, and with Brooks pulled him to his feet.

"Then the Secret Service men seemed to recover from their shock, and Detective Ireland jumped forward and struck Czolgosz in the face, and the other officers jumped on him and bore him back to the ground. When he was raised again he was bleeding from cuts and bruises, and shook his head to clear the blood from his eyes, much as a dog shakes himself to throw off water from his body.

"O'Brien and Brooks had been thrust aside by the onset of the Secret Service men, but O'Brien still held on to the revolver. Ireland demanded it from him but he was refused, O'Brien answering that he did not know the man who made the demand.

"Ireland then said he was a Secret Service officer, and again demanded the revolver. Again, it was refused..."

O'Brien refused until a Corporal told him to give up the weapon. It took about ten minutes for this to occur.[3]

In all probability, the soldier who gave the anonymous account to the newspaper was trying to steal the glory of James Parker for his own unit. All immediate accounts pointed to Parker being instrumental in the apprehension of Czolgosz, including the Secret Service's account, although Foster later denied Parker's involvement. But the doubt the stories created did prevent Parker from testifying.

"The evidence brought out in the trial of Czolgosz proved that the negro Parker, who is now lecturing about the country as 'the man who struck the gun from the assassin's hand,' had nothing to do with the capture of the President's murderer," said the *Buffalo Courier* later, in spite of much evidence to the contrary. A careful review of newspaper quotes and interviews makes it certain that Parker was involved in the fight, and it was never claimed that Parker had the gun in his possession. Some accounts say he knocked it away. But to say that Parker was not involved was to misrepresent the facts.

Captain James Vallely, Chief Bull and Assistant Chief Cusack were the next to testify, followed by eyewitnesses; Fred H. Leiter, timekeeper for the exposition; Charles L. Close, Temple of Music superintendent; exposition police officers James and Westenfelder, and Buffalo Police Detectives John Geary and Albert Solomon.

A man who waited outside the courtroom attracted attention of local news reporters. He refused to give them his name, but was called to testify. This man testified for seven minutes, after which the prosecution rested. It took the Grand Jury only five minutes to decide.

---

[3] *New York Times*, 10 September 1901, pg. 3, col. 2.

Judge Emery asked the foreman, "Have you any report to make?"

"Yes, your honor, we have a partial report," was the reply from foreman Theodore Krehbiel. He then presented a twenty-three-page report, which Emery looked at and nodded. He then excused the jury.

Adelbert Moot, President of the Erie County Bar Association, had written Judge Emery, "We deem it of the utmost importance that the counsel assigned will be men of such experience and of such a high sense of their professional obligations, that the highest traditions of the profession shall be upheld and that the trial shall be dignified, just and impartial...we respectfully suggest, that the Hon. Loran L. Lewis and Hon. Robert C. Titus, ex-Justices of the Supreme Court of the State of New York, be assigned as counsel and be requested to act."[4]

The commitment of the attorneys to defend the presidential assassin has been questioned since. They certainly gave Czolgosz only a half-hearted defense, seemingly apologizing for doing it at all. And make no mistake; they did not want the assignment.

Robert C. Titus was tracked down at the Ffister Hotel in Milwaukee and showed the dispatch naming him as a counsel for Czolgosz by reporters.

"I have had no notice of my appointment to act as counsel for Czolgosz and can hardly believe it is true," Titus responded. "I cannot understand why I have been, and have no hesitancy in saying that I will not defend that murderer, unless imperatively commanded to do so by the Court, when, or course, I will have no option.

"Czolgosz is, of course, entitled to counsel, but why I should have been selected for this unpleasant duty, I cannot understand."[5]

Titus expressed that he was very depressed by the announcement and he said that he thought Czolgosz should be defended by one of his own kind— an anarchist.[6]

---

[4] *Buffalo Evening News*, 17 September 1901, pg. 7, col. 3.

[5] *Buffalo Courier*, 17 September 1901, pg. 6, col. 2.

[6] A. Wesley Johns, *The Man Who Shot McKinley* (New York: A. S. Barnes and Co., Inc., 1970) 198.

ARRAIGNMENT

On September 16 at 2:00 p.m., Judge Loran L. Lewis, just arriving in town, visited his new client, Leon Czolgosz, for the first time in his cell in the Erie County Jail. But the assassin refused to talk to him, even to answer questions as to whether he wanted counsel.

"Czolgosz, I have been assigned by the court to defend you," Lewis told the prisoner. "Before undertaking the work, I thought I would call on you to learn if you had any preference in the matter. If you have an attorney of your own, whom would you like to have defend you? I will gladly retire in his favor. What do you have to say?"

Czolgosz simply stared at the floor, after he had curiously glanced at Justice Lewis.

"Do you care to say anything?" Lewis continued. "Have you any suggestions to offer?" [7]

Czolgosz was asked if he desired to meet the death penalty, but the question only elicited a blank stare. In spite of the lack of his client's cooperation, Lewis said that he would appear in his behalf at the arraignment, regardless whether or not he accepted the assignment to permanently defend Czolgosz.[8]

"No, I have reached no definite decision in the matter," he replied to a reporter's question in his office. "I will appear for him this afternoon, however, when he is arraigned in the County Court, and will enter a plea of not guilty for him. The case will then be transferred to the Supreme Court, and the trial will begin next Monday. In the meantime, I will confer with former Supreme Court Justice Titus who, as you know, was also designated by the Court to defend him. At the conference I will decide whether I will undertake to assist in his defense."[9]

On his way to his arraignment for the murder of the President of the United States, Leon Czolgosz was led through the "Tunnel of Sobs," a narrow underground passage leading from the jail, under Delaware Avenue, to Buffalo City Hall. The tunnel was about 300 feet long, six feet wide by nine feet tall, and was dark and damp. Mike Regan, with an escort of officers, escorted the prisoner to the court, who was led by Detective's Geary and Solomon and Assistant Superintendent Cusack. Czolgosz was handcuffed to Solomon. He passed the black mourning

---

[7] *Buffalo Evening News*, 17 September 1901, pg. 1, col. 8.

[8] *New York Times,* 18 September 1901, pg. 3, col. 1.

[9] *Buffalo Evening News*, 17 September 1901, pg. 1, col. 8.

and bunting that had decorated City Hall while the President was lying in state on Sunday. It did not appear to make the slightest impression on him. He was led into the second floor courtroom, just as the City Hall clock struck 3 p.m., with as many spectators as could fit into the packed room filing in behind him.[10]

A reporter who witnessed Czolgosz's arrival at City Hall said that the detectives did not use the elevators because they wanted to get the prisoner to the court as obscurely as possible. A spectator said Czolgosz was hatless with disheveled hair and somewhat slovenly in his gait.[11]

In this manner, Czolgosz was brought before Judge Edward K. Emery. The crowd in the courtroom surged around him, and Judge Emery instructed them to take their seats. Czolgosz looked around the courtroom, but according to a witness, his eyes were always downcast and not once did he look the prosecutor or the Judge in the face.[12]

Detective Solomon fumbled with the handcuffs for five full minutes, trying to get them unlocked. District Attorney Thomas Penney chided an attorney, who was trying to take a picture of Czolgosz.[13]

The gavel of Judge Emery silenced the courtroom murmur as the handcuffs were removed from the prisoner.

"The grand jury has found the following indictment against you," began District Attorney Penney. "I, as the prosecuting attorney will read it to you, and you may plead as you desire, or as your counsel directs."

Penney then read the charges and asked Czolgosz, "How do you plead, guilty or not guilty?"

Czolgosz stubbornly did not utter a word. His curly hair was disheveled and his clothes where crumpled. That, combined with his unshaven appearance, made him appear to be quite unkempt. Spectators commented that if Czolgosz had been shaved, which he had not been since the shooting, he would be a nice looking young man.[14]

During the proceedings, Czolgosz repeatedly licked his lips and occasionally glanced around the courtroom. Once his eyes met a reporter's and he looked away quickly. He seemed to try to maintain an attitude of indifference.[15]

---

[10] *New York Times*, 18 September 1901, pg. 3, col. 1.

[11] A. Wesley Johns, *The Man Who Shot McKinley* (New York: A. S. Barnes and Co., Inc., 1970) 195.

[12] *New York Times*, 17 September 1901, pg. 1, col. 3.

[13] A. Wesley Johns, *The Man Who Shot McKinley* (New York: A. S. Barnes and Co., Inc., 1970) 195.

[14] *New York Times*, 18 September 1901, pg. 3, col. 1.

[15] *New York Times*, 18 September 1901, pg. 3, col. 1.

Penney then asked him if he understood the charges, and Czolgosz looked at him as if he was about to speak. But he said nothing.

"Leon Czolgosz, you are charged with murder in the first degree, as described in the indictment read to you," said Judge Emery. "How do you plead? Are you guilty or not guilty?"[16]

Penney then asked Czolgosz if he had a lawyer, and still the prisoner did not reply.

"Speak up now—answer," snapped Penney. "Have you a lawyer?" Still no response.

"Have you got a lawyer? You have been indicted for murder in the first degree. Do you want a lawyer?"

Czolgosz looked at Penney, then at Cusack, then at the floor.

"You've answered before," commanded Cusack. "Answer now."

"If your Honor pleases, the defendant refuses to answer," said Penney, "and I would respectfully suggest to the court that counsel be assigned."[17]

"Czolgosz, do you want counsel?" asked Judge Emery. Still no response.

"Czolgosz, you have appeared for arraignment without counsel," the Judge continued. "The law makes it the duty of the court to assign counsel and the Bar Association has caused the names of gentlemen of high character to be submitted from which to select counsel for you. The court has considered the matter fully and has concluded to follow the suggestions of the Bar Association. The court, therefore, assigns Hon. Loran L. Lewis and Hon. Robert C. Titus as counsel."[18]

Justice Lewis rose and said, "If it please Your Honor, I have been assigned with a most respected colleague to defend this defendant and in defense of him and because the statutes of the state require it, I desire to enter a plea of not guilty."[19]

"I wish to say that I am accepting this assignment against my will and while it is more repugnant to me than my poor words can tell, I promise to present whatever defense the accused may have," Lewis continued. "In making the plea of not guilty, I wish to reserve the right to change that plea before the case is heard by the Supreme Court and I desire that such a notation be made by the clerks. It may be that after consultation with Judge Titus, my appointed colleague in this disagreeable case, that we may find it to the prisoner's advantage to enter a plea of guilty. The

[16] *Buffalo Courier,* 18 September 1901, pg. 6, col. 3.

[17] *Buffalo Evening News*, 17 September 1901, pg. 7, col. 2.

[18] *Buffalo Evening News*, 17 September 1901, pg. 7, col. 2.

[19] *Buffalo Courier,* 18 September 1901, pg. 6, col. 3.

Court may rest assured, however, that in appointing us the interests of the accused will be sought, and if he is not guilty as charged, every effort will be made to save him."[20]

District Attorney Penney gave notice that the trial would be held on the following Monday before the New York Supreme Court. Lewis said he did not see any reason that the assassin would not be ready.[21]

Lewis then added that the District Attorney had informed him that Czolgosz was being interviewed by some eminent physicians and alienists and stated that he may want to consult other alienists as well. He requested a court order permitting such consultation. Penney replied that he had already told Mr. Lewis that he would allow this. Judge Emery concurred, telling Lewis that the court would grant any desire he had in that regard.[22]

Czolgosz continued to look only at the floor and he was cuffed and hustled out through the crowd, which surged toward him. Four large policemen stopped the crowd's progress at the door.[23] Czolgosz was led back through the tunnel to the jail, where he was put in a third floor cell. Patrolman James Mahoney and two deputies were assigned guard detail. Czolgosz's court appearance had lasted no more than ten minutes.[24]

As the courtroom cleared, District Attorney Penney told reporters that Titus and Lewis would be given an opportunity to talk with Czolgosz and that he hoped to arraign him in the morning.[25]

After the courtroom appearance, one official who accompanied Czolgosz from the jail was asked why the prisoner had refused to speak, especially since he had been talking freely to the guards on the way to the courtroom.

"I thought that he would do lots of talking when we got him into court and was greatly surprised when he refused to answer a single question addressed to him by the District Attorney or the Judge," remarked the official. "He was in an especially talkative and defiant mood when we reached the jail, and certainly had enough to say there."

---

[20] *Buffalo Courier,* 18 September 1901, pg. 6, col. 4.

[21] *New York Times,* 18 September 1901, pg. 3, col. 1.

[22] A. Wesley Johns, *The Man Who Shot McKinley* (New York: A. S. Barnes and Co., Inc., 1970) 199.

[23] *New York Times,* 17 September 1901, pg. 1, col. 4.

[24] A. Wesley Johns, *The Man Who Shot McKinley* (New York: A. S. Barnes and Co., Inc., 1970) 196.

[25] *New York Times,* 17 September 1901, pg. 1, col. 4.

"On the way to the courtroom he evidently had his mind made up to say a great deal," he said, "probably to tell something from which important clues might be followed, but on seeing the Judge and jury and a somewhat crowded courtroom he changed his mind and said not a word. No, I don't think it was fear, for I don't consider that this is a part of this odd individual's makeup. Bullheadedness, I would term it.

"From my knowledge of the prisoner," he continued, "I don't think that he will have anything to do with lawyers, for I believe that he appreciates the enormity of the crime which he committed and I also believe that he is perfectly resigned to his fate."[26]

All during the period leading up to the trial, there was much speculation in the press and elsewhere as to Czolgosz's sanity. His behavior before the Grand Jury added to that speculation. Assistant Police Chief Cusack did not think Czolgosz was insane; thinking him much shrewder than some people gave him credit for being.[27]

District Attorney Penney and Assistant Chief Cusack commented on Czolgosz's silence before Judge Emery, saying it seemed to be a case of pure stubbornness. Penney explained that Czolgosz had had several stubborn fits during his confinement.[28]

But Assistant District Attorney Frederick Haller thought it was typical behavior of anarchists.

"That only shows that he is following out his anarchistic teaching," said Haller. "He has been taught to maintain silence until the death penalty is about to be imposed and then he will rant about anarchy."[29]

Czolgosz's behavior in jail was at times, less than sterling.

Once, when the Warden sent a priest to see Czolgosz, he threatened to smash the priest's head. The next day, Czolgosz apologized and on a couple of other occasions asked to see a priest. He became suspicious when they did not arrive quickly enough to suit him and then refused to see them.[30]

On September 19, Frank A. Olozanowski, the editor of The *Buffaloski*, a Polish newspaper, had an interview with Leon Czolgosz.

---

[26] *Buffalo Courier,* 17 September 1901, pg. 6, col. 4.

[27] A. Wesley Johns, *The Man Who Shot McKinley* (New York: A. S. Barnes and Co., Inc., 1970) 197.

[28] *Buffalo Evening News*, 17 September 1901, pg. 7, col. 2.

[29] *Buffalo Evening News*, 17 September 1901, pg. 7, col. 2.

[30] Dr. Walter Channing, *The Mental Status of Czolgosz* (Brookline, Mass: American Journal of Insanity, Vol. LIX, No. 2, 1902) 27.

"What's the use of talking about that," Czolgosz was quoted as saying. "I killed the President. I am an Anarchist, and simply did my duty. That's all I'll say."

"Czolgosz talked freely on every subject I suggested, except his crime," Olozanowski explained. "His conversation would have been entertaining, coming from a man other than the President's assassin. He talked on the Polish alliance and a variety of other subjects, but when I spoke of his crime he would not talk.

"Czolgosz spoke earnestly and determinedly," he continued. "I tried several ways but he would not add a word to his declaration. I don't believe that anyone has any more from him about the crime. Czolgosz is intelligent and I don't believe he will tell more."[31]

At the request of the defense, it was Dr. Carlos MacDonald, the eminent alienist from New York, who came to do a mental examination of Czolgosz on September 21. Judges Titus and Lewis were present during parts of the examination.

The meeting was held in District Attorney Penney's office and kept secret. At about 3:00 p.m., Titus and Lewis arrived; Czolgosz was brought in about 3:25 and waited alone with his counsel until MacDonald arrived about fifteen minutes later. MacDonald was then left alone with the prisoner.

MacDonald was with Czolgosz for exactly one-half hour. At 4:35, Czolgosz was taken back to the jail, handcuffed to Detective Solomon and guarded by Detective Geary, Jailor Mitchell and Patrolman Mahoney.[32]

"He is talking more freely but he is not a voluble chap," said Judge Lewis as he was leaving for home. "He said nothing upon we might work in basing a defense."[33]

Czolgosz had been shaved since his appearance before the Grand Jury and looked much better. He seemed also to be in much better spirits, dismissing his habit of always staring at the floor. He looked around and walked more spiritedly as he was led back to the jail.

"The prisoner talked but not freely," Judge Titus told reporters. "He talked considerably to District Attorney Penney and Dr. MacDonald but was not very communicative with Judge Lewis and myself. I would not care to say whether or not he said anything which would serve to help in forming a basis of defense."[34]

---

[31] *New York Times,* 20 September 1901, pg. 1, col. 3.

[32] *New York Times,* 22 September 1901, pg. 8, col. 1.

[33] *New York Times,* 22 September 1901, pg. 8, col. 1.

[34] *New York Times,* 22 September 1901, pg. 8, col. 1.

When asked whether or not MacDonald was going to testify at the trial, Judge Titus responded, "Well, we are not calling adverse witnesses just yet. We want to know just exactly what he thinks before we determine that question."[35]

This seemed to say that MacDonald had concluded that Czolgosz was indeed sane and that his testimony would damage the defense. Later that evening, Dr. MacDonald called the offices of the *New York Times* to make certain that everyone knew he was not there to "clear the assassin."[36]

The next day, Dr. MacDonald brought Dr. Arthur W. Hurd with him and again interviewed Czolgosz. The doctors held a conference with District Attorney Penney at 3:00 and were escorted to Czolgosz's cell at 3:15, where they remained until about 4:45, when they went back to City Hall and again spoke with Penney. Dr. James W. Putnam, a local alienist, joined the conference. The men, later joined by Assistant District Attorney Haller, talked until 6:30.

"I cannot say a word upon this subject until I have reported my definite conclusions to the counsel for the defense," MacDonald said as he left. "Judge Lewis is out of town over night, so that I shall do nothing until morning. I cannot tell whether or not I will be a witness." [37]

Another account had Dr. MacDonald saying, "I do not think I shall appear for the defense."[38]

THE TRIAL

The trial of Leon F. Czolgosz was held by the Buffalo's Part III of the Supreme Court of New York State and opened September 23, 1901, with Justice Truman C. White presiding. Over 53 newsmen and artists, as well as about 218 spectators packed the courtroom. After the room was filled, City Hall was cleared of everyone else. The path of the assassin from the jail to the courtroom was also cleared.[39]

The courtroom, located in the south side of the second floor of City Hall, just upstairs from the front entrance, and was lighted only by south end windows, near which were located the Justice's bench and witness stand. On the right were the jury's seats, with an unobstructed view of the room. There was no rail in front of the Jury, and their seats where

---

[35] *New York Times,* 22 September 1901, pg. 8, col. 1.

[36] *New York Times,* 22 September 1901, pg. 8, col. 1.

[37] *New York Times,* 23 September 1901, pg. 1, col. 7.

[38] *Buffalo Evening News,* 23 September 1901, pg. 8, col. 6.

[39] *New York Times,* 23 September 1901, pg. 1, col. 7.

placed upon a six inch platform. The Justice's bench and the bar occupied almost half of the space of the courtroom, with the rest accommodating seats for the general public, even though few common citizens occupied them during the first day of the trial.[40]

To accommodate the newspapermen, there were eleven tables of various sizes scattered around the front of Judge White's bench, some large enough for seven or eight people, others for just two.[41]

Long before the trial began, many curious people filled the streets around City Hall, hoping to be admitted. Police were everywhere and all entrances, except the one on Franklin Street, were closed and guarded. Blue uniformed officers were double lined near the entrance and mounted patrolmen paced all around the structure, with other enforcements waiting nearby should the crowd riot. No one was permitted to stand around on the sidewalk, so the crowd never became a problem. No one was permitted to enter the building without a pass signed by the Chief of Police, and even then, were checked by every officer on every landing and in every corridor. The elevator operators were instructed to not even stop on the second floor, which was the floor of courtroom.[42]

Guarding the courtroom itself were ten armed deputies, under the charge of Court Crier Frank Hess. They impressed upon all those in attendance the need for absolute quiet.[43]

Czolgosz and his counsel were placed directly in front of the Judge White. At the defense table were Titus, Lewis and attorney Carlton E, Ladd, Titus's law partner. At the prosecution's table sat Cusack, Haller, Drs. Mynter and Mann, and a group of alienists; Dr. Arthur W. Hurd, Dr. Allan McLane Hamilton, Dr. MacDonald, Dr. Floyd S. Crego, Dr. Joseph Fowler and Dr. James W. Putnam, any of whom may have been called to testify about the mental condition of Czolgosz.[44]

Judge White entered the courtroom just after ten o'clock, preceded by Hess and Deputy Sheriff A. W. Haskell. The attorneys soon followed.

Back in the jail, Czolgosz was stretched out on his cot, as his creaky cell door was opened. He sat up and looked at the officers at his door.

"Come with us, Czolgosz," said Superintendent Cusack.

---

[40] *New York Times,* 24 September 1901, pg. 2, col. 1.

[41] *Buffalo Evening News,* 23 September 1901, pg. 8, col. 5.

[42] *New York Times,* 24 September 1901, pg. 2, col. 1.

[43] *Buffalo Evening News,* 23 September 1901, pg. 1, col. 2.

[44] A. Wesley Johns, *The Man Who Shot McKinley* (New York: A. S. Barnes and Co., Inc., 1970) 203.

Czolgosz got up and showed no apprehension. His attitude seemed to be sullen indifference. He gazed at the floor.

"Hurry up, Czolgosz," urged Cusack. He moved toward the cell door and Detectives Solomon and Geary stepped inside and snapped handcuffs on him, and standing on either side, they walked into the corridor. Led by Cusack, the prisoner was taken in the "tunnel of sobs" to the courthouse. Lining the way were sturdy officers under the command of Police Inspector Donavan. Czolgosz was carefully moved into the basement of City Hall. Donavan formed some of the officers in front of the prisoner, others behind and with this blue coated escort, Leon Czolgosz was led up the stairs and into the courtroom.

During the trip, Czolgosz showed no emotion at all. He walked straight ahead and did not even react when spectators behind the officers on the second floor met him with a hiss.[45]

At 10:13, the words "here he comes" were heard in the corridor and Czolgosz was soon brought into the courtroom, handcuffed to Detectives Solomon and Geary.

"When they unshackled his hands he passed them over his thick damp locks," wrote one witness. "Then he crossed his legs, tapped a tattoo on the arm of his chair for a moment, and settled into the immovable attitude which has marked him throughout."[46]

The charge was read. For the first time in a courtroom, Czolgosz spoke during the exchange. When asked by Judge White if he understood the charge, Czolgosz shook his head. Penney then asked him how he would plead. "Guilty," was Czolgosz's low reply.

"He pleads guilty, but of course that plea cannot be accepted," commented Mr. Penney, referring to the fact that New York did not legally accept a guilty plea for murder.[47]

As the plea was quietly repeated around the courtroom for those who could not hear, it created a sensation. District Attorney Penney explained to Judge White that Judge Emery had assigned Titus and Lewis as Czolgosz's counsel and asked that the court confirm the assignment. Titus then addressed the court.

"I thought it best for my colleagues and myself that I should say something regarding our presence here as attorneys for the defendant," he began. "At the time my name was suggested I was out of the city and knew nothing of what was transpiring here with reference to the

---

[45] *Buffalo Evening News,* 23 September 1901, pg. 1, col. 4.

[46] G. Townsend, *Memorial Life of William McKinley* (Washington: Memorial Publishing Co., 1901) 461.

[47] *Buffalo Evening News,* 23 September 1901, pg. 1, col. 4.

selection of counsel for the defendant. I was out of the city at the time I was assigned, and when I returned and the circumstances of my selection were told to me I was extremely reluctant to accept. But the duty had been imposed, and I considered it my duty, in all the circumstances to defend this man.

"I ask that no evidence be presented here," he continued, "that the court will not permit the acceptance of any evidence unless it would be accepted at the trial of the most meager criminal in the land."

Justice White responded, "I am familiar with these circumstances and I wish to say that I will give you every assurance that the prisoner will have a fair and impartial trial, and that during the progress of the trial he will receive such treatment as the law demands in any criminal case."[48]

White then explained that the plea of 'guilty' would not escape the death penalty, according to New York law and that it could not be accepted. The course of the trial, the Judge explained, would be the same as if Czolgosz himself had pled 'not guilty.' He then settled speculation that it was not within his jurisdiction to appoint counsel for the defense, which had been appearing in some of the local Buffalo papers, confirming it was indeed his duty.[49]

The selection of jurors began. After selecting eight of the jurors, and approaching noon, court was recessed until 2 p.m. At 2:03 p.m., Judge White re-entered the room.

The selection of the jury took a total of two hours and twenty-nine minutes, with the last being selected at 2:43 p.m. The short time to select the jury was looked at as "an unprecedented record in any murder trial in the state," according to the *New York Times*. In addition, the *Times* stated that it was "noticeable that every man who acknowledged that he had not formed an opinion on the case was excused by the District Attorney. Men who had formed an opinion or stated that they were prejudiced but where willing to acknowledge that their opinion could be changed by evidence were accepted by both sides." In fact, reported the *Times*, "Counsel for both sides seemed to be in perfect harmony."[50]

The twelve selected jurors included: Frederick V. Lauer, 60, a plumber who lived at 1048 Michigan Avenue; Henry W. Wendt, a manufacturer from Buffalo; Silas Carver, 65, a farmer from Clarence; James S. Stygall, 45, a plumber who lived on Normal Avenue in Buffalo;

---

[48] *Buffalo Evening News,* 23 September 1901, pg. 1, col. 4.

[49] John D. Lawson, *American State Trials, Volume 14* (St. Louis: Thomas Law Book Co., 1923) 169-170.

[50] *New York Times,* 24 September 1901, pg. 1, col. 7.

William Loton, 65, a farmer from Eden; William E. Everett, 39, a blacksmith who lived at 176 15th Street in Buffalo; Ben C. Ralph, 40, an assistant cashier from 310 Woodward Avenue, Buffalo; Samuel P. Waldow, 59, a farmer from Alden; Andrew J. Smith, 60, an egg and butter dealer from 140 Leroy Avenue, Buffalo; Joachim H. Mertens, 42, a boot and shoe dealer who lived at 945 Exchange Street; and Robert L. Adams, a contractor from 200 Purdy Street, Buffalo.

While the jury was being selected, Czolgosz sat straight in his chair and stared ahead at the back of his counsel. His eyes blinked rapidly but he seemed to be oblivious to what was happening. He did not change his position and he made no effort to speak with neither his counsel, nor they with him.[51]

During the proceedings, Czolgosz was almost without movement. He was being watched carefully by the alienists in the courtroom, but gave them little to note. When he stood, he did so without fidgeting and held his brown slouch hat in his hands without twirling or moving it. About the only thing of note that he did during the day was frequently wet his lips with his tongue.[52]

Meanwhile, the reporters wrote furiously. There was almost no talking among anyone, as no one wanted to miss recording a single thing, no matter how insignificant. In the attic of the City Hall, telegraph machines clicked away, sending word of the trial to a waiting nation, with more than a score of expert operators at work.

During the recess called after the selection of the eighth juror, Solomon and Geary led Czolgosz back to his cell, where he ate his dinner heartily. Deputy Sheriffs Martin Long, A. W. Haskell and C.F. Brady were placed in charge of the jury and escorted them to the jail also, where Jailor George N. Mitchell served them an excellent dinner.[53]

As Czolgosz was led back into the courtroom shortly before 2:00, he was watched and commented upon.

"Isn't he a cowardly looking whelp?" asked one.

"Huh, he don't look as if he would kill a kitten," said another.

"What's the use of wasting time trying a pup like him," asked another, fortunately out of hearing range of the deputies. Otherwise, he may have been roughly escorted out.[54]

---

[51] *New York Times,* 24 September 1901, pg. 2, col. 2.

[52] *Buffalo Evening News,* 23 September 1901, pg. 1, col. 7.

[53] *Buffalo Evening News,* 23 September 1901, pg. 8, col. 4.

[54] *Buffalo Evening News,* 23 September 1901, pg. 8, col. 4.

After things got back underway, and the jury was selection was complete, Judge White turned to District Attorney Penney and asked, "Mr. District Attorney, I wish to learn, if I can, how long a time you anticipate it will require for you to present the evidence of your case?"

"I hope to complete it by to-morrow noon," replied Penney.

White then asked the defense, "And how long will it require for your defense?"

"That depends on the turn things take," answered Titus. "We are not prepared to say."

White then said, "Mr. District Attorney, the case is with you."[55]

Assistant District Attorney Frederick Haller opened the prosecution's case, and spoke for barely five minutes.

"May it please the court and gentlemen of the jury," he began, "this defendant is before you, charged with having committed the crime of murder in the first degree in the city of Buffalo on the sixth day of September of this year. It is alleged in the indictment that upon that day in this city he committed an assault upon William McKinley, and that with a revolver and firearm in his hands, then had and held, he fired upon William McKinley, inflicting upon him a mortal wound; that the said William McKinley languished from the sixth day of September of this year until the 14th day of September, upon which last-named day he died at the city of Buffalo, from the mortal wound so inflicted by this defendant.

"I shall but briefly indicate to you the trend of the evidence as it will be presented to you. The witnesses produced by the people will show to your minds, I believe, beyond any reasonable doubt, that this defendant for some days prior to the day on which he committed this crime, had premeditated and deliberated upon the commission of this crime; that he had been informed that the President of the United States would upon the 6th day of September, be at the Temple of Music in the exposition grounds, and that he would there receive the populace; that he would greet the people who came there to shake hands with him. The defendant, I say, had received information of that, and upon this day named, the sixth day of September, he went to the exposition grounds armed, prepared to commit this assault; that whilst there he learned that the President had entered the Temple of Music; that he entered the Temple of Music with the other people who entered at the time to shake hands with the President; he got into line with the people who were

---

[55] *New York Times,* 24 September 1901, pg. 2, col. 2.

passing before the President and awaited his opportunity and approached the President; that as he approached the President, he had this weapon concealed in his hand; that, as the President extended his hand to shake the hand of this defendant, the defendant fired the fatal shot; that he fired two shots; that one shot so fired by him inflicted this wound that I have referred to; that he was immediately apprehended at the time and disarmed, and has been in custody ever since; that the President was taken in charge—in care of—immediately by persons there with him, and was attended to in the city of Buffalo and afforded all the care that could be afforded him, and upon the 14th day of September thereafter he died from this mortal wound so inflicted by the defendant upon that day.

"These are, in brief, the main facts in this case. They will be presented to you by eye-witnesses, by people who were there at the time and saw the commission of this crime, by those who apprehended the defendant and who disarmed him at the time. You will be afforded an opportunity of judging as to the position that the President occupied and the people approaching him at this time, and the position occupied by the defendant. This opportunity will be afforded you by a diagram of the Temple of Music, the building in which this crime was committed.

"This is, in brief, gentlemen, the case of the People," Haller concluded, "and I have no doubt that when the evidence is presented to you, you will not find much difficulty arriving at a verdict in accordance with the evidence."[56]

The first witness for the prosecution was Samuel J. Fields, the Chief Engineer of the Pan-American Exposition and former city engineer, who with the help of a blackboard and a large poster of the ground plan of the Temple of Music, explained the layout to the jurors, including such details as the positioning of the furniture, plants, decorations and the entrances and exits.

The second witness was Harry A. Bliss, a photographer who had taken pictures of the interior of the Temple of Music the day after the shooting. He identified his five photographs which were passed around to the defense counsel and the jurors, then entered into evidence as exhibits A, B, C, D, and E.[57]

Witness number three was Dr. Harvey B. Gaylord, as the prosecution now focused on the results of Czolgosz's actions. Gaylord had done the autopsy and his testimony concentrated on showing that the care of the

---

[56] *Buffalo Express*, 24 September 1901.

[57] A. Wesley Johns, *The Man Who Shot McKinley* (New York: A. S. Barnes and Co., Inc., 1970) 210.

President had been the best and that his death had not been caused by any undue complications.

"The cause of death was a gunshot wound leading to changes in the important viscera," Dr. Gaylord explained. "The condition of the other organs which were not included in this area of the wound were those which a man of the President's age should have had. They were not especially robust organs, so to speak, but they were perfectly satisfactory and in sufficient condition to support life."[58]

Lewis, during his cross-examination, asked what organ the bullet injured, which caused the death of the President.

"I don't think that I could state specifically that the death of the President was due to injury in any organ made directly by the bullet," Gaylord responded. "The changes caused by the bullet, which resulted from the passage of the bullet through that space back of the stomach was what caused his death, and that was largely because of the fact that the pancreas was involved. It was caused by the absorption or breaking up of this material back of the peritoneal cavity."[59]

In his turn, Penney asked Gaylord to state the specific cause of death.

"He died as the result of absorption of the breaking-down material in this area back of the stomach," Gaylord explained. "The cause of the breaking down of the material was, in the first place, injury to the tissues and was probably further facilitated by the escape of the secretion of the pancreas into this cavity." "What was the cause of the injury to the tissues," asked Penney.

"That I should attribute to the bullet," Gaylord responded.[60]

Dr. Gaylord testified for a total of twenty-one minutes and left the stand at 3:28 p.m.

Dr. Herman Mynter was called next. He described the wounds, his part in the operation and help in the treatment of the President.

"The cause was blood poisoning from the absorption of poisonous matter caused by the gangrene," he responded to a query as the cause of death. "Primarily," he concluded, "it was the gunshot wound." [61]

During direct examination, Penney probed him as to why the doctors gave up on finding the second bullet. Dr. Mynter explained that further search would have been fatal.

---

[58] *Buffalo Express*, 24 September 1901.

[59] *Buffalo Express*, 24 September 1901.

[60] *Buffalo Express*, 24 September 1901.

[61] *New York Times*, 24 September 1901, pg. 2, col. 3-4.

"He was slightly under the influence of opium," Mynter said, describing how he found the President after being called to attend him. "I told the President that an operation was indicated at once to save his life and he acquiesced. I made preparations immediately, with the assistance of the other gentlemen present, for laperotomy (an operation of opening the abdominal cavity)."

"Dr. Mann turned around and asked the physicians whether they wanted him to operate," Mynter continued. "Dr. Van Peyma answered that they wanted Dr. Mann and me to do the operation. I acquiesced at once: told Dr. Mann I would take half the responsibility. He examined the President, told him the same, and we proceeded at once with the operation. The abdomen was opened in the line of the incision. As soon as it was opened, air escaped, showing that there was a perforation of one of the hollow viscus or organs. We, with some difficulty, pulled that out and found a bullet hole in the anterior end of the stomach, which was sewed together with two rows of silk sutures.

"On account of the stoutness of the President," Mynter continued, "it was difficult to get at the posterior wound in the stomach, which we judged to be present... Dr. Mann introduced his whole hand and tried to locate the forward course of the bullet. It showed itself to be impossible; the President's condition showed at that time shock, his pulse was getting higher, and it was time to close and to finish the operation. We, therefore, washed out the abdominal cavity with sterilized salt solution, cleaned everything, put the omentum back. Previously we had examined somewhat for injuries of the intestines, but found none. And at that time Dr. Park arrived from Niagara Falls...We all declared ourselves satisfied. We closed the wound with sutures and applied the bandages."

Judge Titus, during cross-examination, asked Mynter if it would have been advisable to continue to search and find the bullet.

"We couldn't have done that without taking out all the intestines," Mynter testified. "The President would have died on the table if we had gone further. We would have had to make a large incision, ten inches long, take all his intestines out. He was already under the influence of shock at the time. He would have died on the table if we had gone further."

"What was the object or what would have been the object in locating the bullet and removing it?" asked Titus.

"To get rid of it, so that it might not raise any disturbance afterward."

"If the bullet was left in the muscles, was it in a position where it would not create any disturbance?"

"It was it in a position where it would not create any disturbance."

"Was there any means by which this bullet could have been located at the time?" pressed Titus.

"Only the x-rays," Mynter replied.

"Were they used?"

"They were not used."

"Why not?"

"It was not considered necessary," Mynter explained. "And even if we had known where the bullet was not one of us would have thought at the time of trying to remove it."

Mynter went on to explain that even if the X-rays had disclosed exactly where the bullet was located, it could not have been removed without very much physical disturbance and that they may have had to use cocaine, and with a weak heart, it could have caused harm to the President.

"I do not suppose it would not have made the slightest difference either one way or another," Mynter explained as to finding the bullet. "The gangrene of the stomach would have occurred anyway."[62]

Titus then asked if there had been an open drain, if the passage of the bullet had been clearly diagnosed and determined, and if there would have been as much a chance of death had the wound been closed. Mynter testified that it would have made no difference; that gangrene of the stomach would have occurred anyway.[63]

When asked the cause of the gangrene, Dr. Mynter testified that it was not usual that gangrene appeared when a person received an internal injury.

"I attribute it, perhaps, partly to what Dr. Gaylord said, to leakage of the pancreatic fluid, although, to my idea, the pancreas was not wounded by the bullet, but it might have got into a state of injury by simply the wave of the bullet striking it—contre coup, as we call it—and in that way injury to the pancreas occurred. That is one idea. Another idea is that the bullet—or that the injury— was followed with bacterial growth. That we can not say yet, because the bacteriological examination is not finished. Another thing is that the proximity of the large solar plexus, the large ganglia near the heart, near the stomach wound, might have certain deleterious influence upon the nervous system, which already was weakened, and in that way favor gangrenous processes."[64]

---

[62] *Buffalo Express*, 24 September 1901.

[63] A. Wesley Johns, *The Man Who Shot McKinley* (New York: A. S. Barnes and Co., Inc., 1970) 213-214.

[64] *Buffalo Express*, 24 September 1901.

Titus then asked about the wound being reopened, and Mynter explained that they had only opened the outer wound but that it had not been opened enough to look into the stomach. Mynter was then asked why the bullet had not been located during the autopsy. He responded that the doctors tried for fours hours to locate it, but that the President's family had told them to stop, not wanting to cause undo damage to the corpse.[65]

Mynter's testimony concluded after twenty-one minutes, at 3:49 p.m.

The fifth witness was Dr. Matthew Mann, who confirmed what Dr. Mynter had said, as he described the operation.

"We opened the abdomen with a knife, making an incision some three inches in length, beginning just at the edge of the ribs and cutting down toward the naval, the incision being about three inches long at first. The opening was made down to the stomach. I introduced my finger and felt of the front wall of the stomach and found an opening in it. I then enlarged the opening in the abdominal wall somewhat and pulled the stomach up so that I could get at this opening; then, with a needle and thread, I sewed up the hole according to the usual methods. The parts were washed off and returned. I then cut away some of the fatty tissue, which is between the bowel and the stomach and got at the back wall of the stomach, and there we found another opening, a little larger than the one in front, the edges rather more frayed and bloody, and with great difficulty we got that up and closed that in the same way. The parts were then washed off with salt and water, warm, hot salt and water, and the parts returned. After this, the surgeons present expressing themselves as being satisfied that everything had been done, I introduced my hand into well down into the abdominal cavity to try and find the track of the bullet. This was entirely impossible. There were no evidences of blood or abdominal contents, intestinal contents there on my hand as I withdrew it. I, therefore, thought there was no serious injury, no large vessels, blood vessels injured, and I desisted, especially as the manipulation with my hand in the abdomen was making the President very weak, had a very bad effect on his pulse, as it always does. To find the track of the bullet, we should have had to take the entire intestines out of the abdomen, which would have increased the shock very much; probably would have killed him on the table, and it is doubtful whether we could have found the track of the bullet even then. In fact, there is not any doubt, as the autopsy showed, that we could not. After this we

---

[65] A. Wesley Johns, *The Man Who Shot McKinley* (New York: A. S. Barnes and Co., Inc., 1970) 214.

closed the abdominal wound with stitches, in the usual way, put on a dressing, bandages, and the President was then removed to the ambulance and taken to Mr. Milburn's."[66]

As for the autopsy, Dr. Mann testified, "We found, in the first place, that the abdominal cavity, intestines were all in a perfectly healthy condition; no evidence of inflammation of the bowels. There was a point in the front wall of the stomach, which had been closed by the suture and around, that was a spot as large as a silver dollar, which was entirely— where the tissue was entirely dead, the walls of the stomach were entirely dead. Raising up the stomach, we found a similar condition on the back wall, around the other bullet hole. Below this there was a cavity which contained a lot of fluid and which showed the evidences of gangrene. In this cavity was a portion of the pancreas, as was also the fat, which surrounds the kidney, and the upper end of the kidney was very near this cavity, whether it was in it or not I could not say. The cause of death of the late President was this bullet wound."[67]

As Mann was concluding his description of the autopsy, Judge White interrupted at 4:00 to say, "We will suspend here."

Penney then received permission from the Judge to ask one final question; the cause of the President's death. Mann stated that the cause of death was undoubtedly the bullet wound in the stomach.[68]

Further testimony by Dr. Mann waited until the following day, as Judge White recessed the court. The first day of the trial of Leon Czolgosz was over.

Trial: Day Two

Day two was September 24 and Czolgosz was led into the courtroom at 9:37 a.m. The day began shortly thereafter, as Samuel Fields was asked a few questions about the map depicting the Temple of Music and the murder scene. Loran L. Lewis then recalled and began to cross-examine Dr. Mann.

"Now, you spoke of the depleted condition of the President's body," asked Justice Lewis, as the testimony of Dr. Mann continued. "Do you mean that there were indications that the body was in that condition before he was assaulted?"

---

[66] *Buffalo Express*, 24 September 1901.
[67] *Buffalo Express*, 24 September 1901.
[68] A. Wesley Johns, *The Man Who Shot McKinley* (New York: A. S. Barnes and Co., Inc., 1970) 215.

"The President probably was not in a very good physical condition, he was somewhat weakened by hard work, want of exercise and conditions of that kind," replied Dr. Mann. "Undoubtedly that had something to do with the result."

"You agree with the other physicians that the kidney was not actually mutilated or struck by the bullet?"

"As well as could be determined, the bullet did not enter it. I could not say positively how it was injured, but it was injured in some way."

"A concussion?"

"Very possibly. Once the organ is injured then the pancreatic juice, the secretion of the gland would pass through, one part being healthy and the other diseased, the diseased part would allow the secretion to pass through and attack other parts of the body."

During his re-direct examination, District Attorney Penney turned to the witness.

"From your knowledge of the autopsy and the history of the case, was there anything that would have saved the life of the President known to medical surgery?" he asked.

"There was not," was Mann's firm reply.[69]

Louis L. Babcock, a member of the Committee of Ceremonies for the Exposition and Grand Marshal, was the next to testify. Babcock described the shooting to a riveted courtroom:

"I was standing in front of the east bay tree," said Babcock. "That was the nearest one to the point of entrance. I should say two or three seconds before the shooting I had left the point directly opposite the President. I was walking toward the east entrance of the Temple, and had taken five or six steps when the shooting occurred...I was possibly twelve feel toward the easy from the President."

"Were the people approaching the President already arranged in single file?" asked Penney.

"Yes."

"Go on and tell us what you saw from that point."

"I heard two shots which came very close together, and I immediately turned around toward the left, and saw the President standing," Babcock replied. "He was perfectly still, and he was deadly pale. Right in the range of my vision was a group closing in upon and bearing down to the floor, the defendant here."

---

[69] *Buffalo Courier*, 25 September 1901, pg. 7, col. 4.

After describing whom he recognized in the group, Babcock continued.

"These artillerists concentrated on the prisoner from all sides, and almost quicker than I can describe, bore him to the ground," Babcock said. "They were holding him on the floor by his coat, his arms and his legs. I could see eight or ten men on him almost immediately. I saw one man, whose name I didn't know, grab a revolver as he was going down and appear to take it away from him. Just as soon as the prisoner was on the ground, I ran toward the east and made a motion to the guard, like that (moving his arm), and shouted 'everybody out.' The guards immediately cleared the Temple of Music, toward the east. The man who had been borne to the floor was taken away. As soon as I came back from the east entrance to the Temple, I saw him surrounded by artillerymen and secret service men, among whom were Foster and Ireland, one or two Exposition guards and, I think, some Buffalo detectives, who were in attendance. There seemed to be a controversy as to who was entitled to the prisoner. That was soon settled and the prisoner was taken by three or four officers, in citizens' clothes, toward Mr. Henshaw's office. The man taken in there was the same man I had seen borne down by the soldiers."[70]

Babcock explained that he remained there until the District Attorney arrived. The defense had no questions.

The next prosecution witness to testify was Edward Rice, who was the chairman of the committee on ceremonies at the Exposition, and who was also near the President at the time of the shooting.

Rice testified, "I stood at the point indicated to get the signal from Secretary Cortelyou as to when he thought the ceremonies should close. The line had been passing more than ten minutes. I took my watch out in my hand indicating to Secretary Cortelyou that the time we had agreed upon was about up. And as I remember he took his watch in his hand indicating that he understood. Almost immediately after this and looking across at the Secretary I noticed the President's hand extended toward the next person in line. I noticed a line of white pushed towards the President. I was still looking toward the Secretary watching for the signal when I noticed the President's hand extended to shake with the next in line. I immediately noticed the line of white followed by two quick reports."

---

[70] *Buffalo Courier*, 25 September 1901, pg. 7, col. 4.

"By line of white, you mean some white object?" questioned Penney.

"Yes, something white," Rice continued. "It came within my vision as I was looking toward the President, almost immediately afterward. It looked to me black and white. It seemed to me as if someone had concealed a revolver in a newspaper. Then the whole thing went down to the floor."

"What went down?"

"This black and white object, and the individual holding it" Rice explained. "The people about fell in a mass. I immediately ran toward the east door, and had the space cleared. I moved toward the east where the people were coming in, and said, 'Close the door and clear the hall.' Then I ran to the south side and asked if an ambulance had been called. I found that it had. Then I went to the point I had started from, and I noticed that the President had been removed to the chair in the aisle"[71]

But the star witness for the prosecution was James L. Quackenbush, the Exposition committee on ceremonies member who saw the shooting and heard Czolgosz's confession at the police station the night of the shooting.

"I heard two shots fired very closely together," described Quackenbush in his testimony about the shooting. "I immediately looked toward the President and saw him straighten up. I saw standing directly before him and facing him, the defendant. Immediately after the artillerymen, who had been stationed on the left of the President, lunged forward toward the defendant. About the same time Mr. Gallagher, the Secret Service man, who had been stationed at the right of the President, a little toward his rear, plunged forward in an easterly direction and practically at the same time these same men caught defendant. I saw for an instant just a glimpse of something white as Gallagher lunged toward him. The artillerymen stationed directly opposite the President, and Foster and Ireland of the Secret Service, at the same time lunged toward these three, who were struggling and swaying. The defendant went to the floor and on top of him went a number of the artillerymen. At the time the shot was fired the President was standing at the point indicated by a round circle on the map. Directly in front of him and facing him were standing Foster and Ireland; and immediately back of them and extending in a line along the aisle, and facing the President were these artillerymen and their corporal. To the left of the President stood Mr. Milburn and on his left two artillerymen, Privates O'Brien and Mack

---

[71] *Buffalo Courier*, 25 September 1901, pg. 7, col. 4-5.

(Neff). Right behind the President was Buffalo Police Detective John Geary of the Buffalo headquarters. Immediately on his right stood Secretary Cortelyou, and a little back of him or near him, stood Secret Service Agent Gallagher and Solomon of the Buffalo headquarters. To their right were two other artillerymen, ranging just a few feet from each other. It seemed to me as if this entire mass went down in a heap on the defendant. They moved in a direction toward him in his struggle, so that they stood for a time at the point marked with a circle below the point where the President stood... I saw the defendant in the grasp of several of these men. He was then struck a blow by Foster that sent him to the floor again... He was then taken to the room of Mr. Henshaw."[72]

Describing the confession, Quackenbush said, "He described in detail in conversation extending over about two hours, his movements during the day of the shooting and for some time previous. He himself put the handkerchief on and showed how he concealed his revolver and how he fired it. He said that he had gone to Niagara Falls on the morning of the day of the shooting, but that he was unable to carry out his purpose there, not being able to get near to the President; that he took a street car from Niagara Falls to Buffalo, transferred to a car going to the Exposition grounds and went to the Temple of Music for the purpose of shooting the President. He said that he waited outside in line; that he had placed his revolver in his right hand, covered it with his handkerchief, placed his covered hand in his right hand pocket, and stood that way while in the crowd outside of the entrance to the Temple of Music, and as he entered the Temple of Music, but that when he came to the point where the people were singled into a file he took his right hand from his pocket and held the hand covered with the handkerchief across his stomach until he reached the President, when he fired."[73]

Penney asked him if Czolgosz had mentioned places he had been and subjects, which had been discussed. Quackenbush told him that he had mentioned Cleveland and Chicago.

"He said that he had been influenced by the teachings of Emma Goldman and another woman living near Cleveland, whose name I do not recall at this moment," said Quackenbush.[74]

Titus began to cross-examine and was interested to know whether Czolgosz gave the confession voluntarily.

Quackenbush told Titus that Czolgosz had answered the questions calmly.

[72] *Buffalo Courier*, 25 September 1901, pg. 7, col. 3.

[73] *Buffalo Courier*, 25 September 1901, pg. 7, col. 3.

[74] *Buffalo Courier*, 25 September 1901, pg. 7, col. 3.

"He talked just as I am now," said Quackenbush. "After the first half hour he talked with greater freedom." Quackenbush said that he had not been forced to confess.

Quackenbush related how Czolgosz made his famous statement that had been printed in the press.

"I asked him to make a statement for publication as to his reasons for shooting the President," he said. "He started to write it, but his hand shook some and he said that he would dictate to the reporter (pointing to Mr. Story) who stood on my left. He did dictate the statement."

"Are you using his exact language now?" asked Titus.

"I don't know whether he used the word dictate, he did use the word reporter. He said: 'Let the reporter write it down.'"

"Was it a voluntary statement?" asked Titus.

"I asked him to make a voluntary statement," replied Quackenbush. "I said that we could not hold the newspapers all night for his statement. He thought that I was a newspaperman when he offered to dictate the statement."

Quackenbush was permitted to refresh his memory by checking his notes. He then read for the hushed courtroom Czolgosz's statement, "'I killed President McKinley because I done my duty. I didn't believe one man should have so much service and another man should have none.' This statement he signed."[75]

The questioning then turned to Czolgosz's political beliefs. Quackenbush said that Czolgosz did not say he was an anarchist exactly.

'What he did say was that he did not believe in any government rulers. He thought that all rulers were tyrants and should be removed and that he had done his duty in removing the President."

"Did he say nothing about anarchy?" asked Titus.

"The District Attorney on several occasions used the word anarchy and talked with him about Anarchists of note, asking him whether he knew them. Whether he himself used that precise term I can't say," Quackenbush replied.

"Did he say it was his duty owing to any allegiance to some society, to slay the heads of the Government?"

"He did not put it under the grounds of allegiance," answered Quackenbush, "but on the ground of his belief. He claimed it was the result of his own individual theories."[76]

Quackenbush had testified for a full forty minutes.

---

[75] *Buffalo Courier,* 25 September 1901, pg. 7-8, col. 7-1.

[76] *Buffalo Courier,* 25 September 1901, pg. 8, col. 2.

Secret Service Agent Albert L. Gallaher was the next to testify. He described the moment of the shooting.

"I heard two shots, fired in rapid succession," he testified. "I looked around and saw smoke rising and something white in the hands of a man on whom a crowd was jumping."

"Where was that man?"

"Right in front of the President," Gallaher replied. "I immediately sprang forward, but struck the floor before I reached the crowd. I heard a voice calling, 'Get the gun, Al. Get the gun!' The gun was in the right hand of the defendant, sprawling in the crowd on the floor. I made a grab for the gun, but failed to get it, someone in that instant knocking it out of my possession. I secured the handkerchief, which I now produce."

"Is this the handkerchief which was around the gun in the hands of this defendant when he fired the fatal shot?" asked Penney.

"It was," answered Gallaher.

Gallaher pulled the handkerchief out of his pocket book and handed it to Penney. The handkerchief was viewed with interest in the courtroom, being mud stained, partially burnt, with a bullet hole in the center. He told the court that it was in the same condition it had been in when he obtained it, except that he had put identifying marks on it, and that it had been in his possession since he picked it up in the Temple of Music."[77]

Next came Secret Service Agent George F. Foster.

"The crowds were all lined up, and I made it my business to size up everyone as they came along," Foster testified. "This defendant came along and as he approached the President I looked him square in the face; and he looked at me in passing. I thought him a mechanic out to see the Exposition, anxious to shake hands with the President. I had noticed Secretary Cortelyou just a few minutes before with his watch in his hand; I took it as a sign that the ceremony was to be shut off quickly. I turned to look toward Secretary Cortelyou and saw the fellow put his hand that way (clapping his hands together). Immediately two shots were fired. Then I grabbed him on one side while someone made a dash from the other side. We pulled him backward and fell together on the floor. I started to strike him as I was going down, but I did not harm him very heavily. He got a twist as he fell and made a motion while lying back as if trying to get another shot at the President. Then I called to Gallaher,

---

[77] *Buffalo Courier,* 25 September 1901, pg. 8, col. 2-3.

'Al, get the gun!' He put his hand down and got the handkerchief and someone else got the gun. Then I gave the order to let him up. When he got up, I searched him and as I started to put my hand in his pocket I saw him look sideways over his shoulder as if to see what effect his shots had had upon the President. That made me so mad that I hit him on the jaw. I rode on the wagon to the Emergency Hospital with the President and was there while he was undressed. I found one of the bullets in is vest."

Foster handed the bullet to Penney, and then continued, "This is the bullet which was found there. The President called my attention to it while we were in the wagon. He said, 'I believe this is a bullet, Foster.' I reached for it and said, 'Yes, that's a bullet, Mr. President.' The bullet was marked for identification."[78]

During his cross-examination, Judge Titus asked Foster about the man with the black mustache, that police had at first thought might be an accomplice. Foster explained how he had noticed the man, had put his hand on his shoulder and moved him along because he was suspicious looking.

Later in his testimony, Foster referred to James Parker, stating that it seemed to him that he was in front of and not behind Czolgosz. He claimed that he had not seen Parker during the capturing of Czolgosz, saying that he only saw the artillerymen[79]

The three artillerymen, Francis P. O'Brien, Louis Neff and Corporal Louis Bertschey were called to the stand next.

"I kept looking down at the President and could hear him pass a remark to each one that passed," explained O'Brien. "About two seconds after I got the people into line I heard a sharp report. Then I heard another bang and seeing an opening, I jumped toward the defendant."

"Where was he?"

"In front of the President."

"What was he doing?" asked Penney.

"The shot had just been fired and I saw smoke coming from the revolver in his hand. I jumped at him and knocked him over. I don't know who it was I knocked him against. I made a grab for his arm and the revolver. I wanted to turn it over to the captain of my command."[80]

---

[78] *Buffalo Courier,* 25 September 1901, pg. 8, col. 3.

[79] A. Wesley Johns, *The Man Who Shot McKinley* (New York: A. S. Barnes and Co., Inc., 1970) 223.

[80] *Buffalo Courier,* 25 September 1901, pg. 8, col. 3.

"I was on the President's left," testified Louis Neff. "I heard two shots, one after the other. I joined in the rush toward the defendant and caught hold of the pistol point, when I saw that one of our men had a firm grasp on the weapon over the chamber of the revolver. I let go and bore down upon the defendant. I fell on my knees. Corporal O'Brien got the revolver and I left them to take care of the prisoner. I could not recognize the defendant in the crowd."[81]

Louis Bertschey also testified to hearing two shots in rapid succession, after about five minutes from the time the reception had begun. He said he turned to see the smoking revolver in Czolgosz' hand. He said he rushed over, grabbed the assailant by the shoulders and pulled him backward. As he was doing this, he testified, O'Brien wrenched the gun from his hand. Bertschey said he put his knee on Czolgosz' throat and his hand inside his coat. He said he yelled for the crowd to get back, that Czolgosz was his prisoner. Then a man he did not know grabbed and forced him off the pile. At that point, Bertschey looked at the President and saw him still standing, but looking very pale, looking at the struggling mass on the floor. He also saw Private Frank O'Brien with the gun and saw that two men who he thought were probably Secret Service men, were demanding the pistol from him. Bertschey went over to O'Brien and advised him not to turn over the pistol to them, but instead to turn it over to him. Bertschey testified that he then sent for Wisser, who arrived about fifteen minutes later, and that he gave the gun to him. Before turning it over, Bertschey alertly scratched his initials on the gun. Penney then showed Bertschey the revolver and he identified his initials, saying it was the same revolver O'Brien had given to him.[82]

Exposition Superintendent of Music Harry F. Henshaw was next. He described the shooting also.

"I was standing watching the people as they came up to the President," Henshaw testified. "I could see them very clearly, also the President. I noticed the prisoner in line as he approached. He carried his right hand in this position (pressing his closed hand to his breast). I noticed something around his hand. As he drew near the President he extended his left hand. I saw the President extend his right to shake hands, and like a flash I saw this man dash the President's right hand aside with his left and press forward. At the same instant two shots rang out in quick succession. I did not see the flash, but I saw a handkerchief

---

[81] *Buffalo Courier,* 25 September 1901, pg. 8, col. 4.
[82] *Buffalo Courier,* 25 September 1901, pg. 8, col. 4.

or bandage and smoke. I jumped over the aisle and noticed two artillerymen had grabbed the man and were bearing him down. A dozen or more gathered around and struggled to get at the defendant. When I got to the bunch I could not see anything of the defendant. Turning around, I saw Mr. Milburn and some other gentleman escorting the President to a seat."

Upon cross-examination, Henshaw explained that Czolgosz, upon his approach to the President, did not arouse suspicion.

"When you saw this man approaching with his hand up to his breast or abdomen, you thought that hand was sore or bandaged?" asked Judge Lewis.

"Yes, sir," Came Henshaw's reply.

"You did not see anything of a pistol?"

"No, sir."

"It did not excite your suspicion?"

"No."

"Did you see others approaching with hands bandaged?"

"No, but I saw people with handkerchiefs in their hands and capes in their arms."[83]

John Branch, a black porter who worked in the Temple, was called and testified that he had heard the President say, "Be easy on him, boys," as body guards were beating Czolgosz. This merely confirmed what had been reported in the press.[84]

At 2:12 p.m., Captain James F. Vallely, Captain of the Exposition Police, testified about Czolgosz in his cell back at police headquarters, talking about a conversation he had had with Czolgosz regarding smoking, and supplied some background that Czolgosz had told him about himself. He said he asked Czolgosz why he had shot the President, and that Czolgosz had told him he had done his duty. He testified that when he had asked Czolgosz if he was an anarchist, Czolgosz replied that he was. He said that Detective Solomon and the Assistant Commandant of the Exposition, Major Robertson, also heard the statement.[85]

---

[83] *Buffalo Courier,* 25 September 1901, pg. 8, col. 4.

[84] A. Wesley Johns, *The Man Who Shot McKinley* (New York: A. S. Barnes and Co., Inc., 1970) 224.

[85] John D. Lawson, *American State Trials, Volume 14* (St. Louis: Thomas Law Book Co., 1923) 191-192.

Buffalo Police Chief William S. Bull was the last prosecution witness and he primarily corroborated the earlier testimony of Quackenbush and others. He also told of the visit of Albert Nowak of Cleveland to see Czolgosz in jail, and their exchange.

He explained that he was with Czolgosz at the time of his questioning and that no threats were made to him or offers of immunity of any kind.[86]

"He said that he had been at the Pan-American grounds on several occasions prior to the President's visit to Buffalo," Bull testified, "and that he had been at the Exposition grounds on the day that President McKinley had delivered his speech," Bull said, talking about Czolgosz's confession. "Czolgosz told me that he had it is contemplation for some time. He said that he planned the shooting and knew what he was going to do and he finally made up his mind to kill the President, and went to the Exposition grounds for that purpose. He said that he thought it was right and was his duty to kill the President. I asked him if he was an Anarchist, and he said he was, and that he believed he was doing right in killing the President."[87]

Chief Bull was asked if Czolgosz had wanted to see an attorney, friends or family. Bull said Czolgosz told him that he did not wish to see a lawyer, that he had no friends and that he did not wish to see his father or mother.[88]

With that, the prosecution rested. It was 2:37 p.m.

Defense Counsel Lewis then asked Czolgosz if he wished to take the stand. Czolgosz simply closed his eyes and turned away. Then Lewis addressed Judge White.

"The defendant has no witnesses and as a consequence the testimony is closed," Lewis said. "We are somewhat embarrassed at the People's testimony closing at this point. We have not had much opportunity for consultation and I will ask your Honor to permit both of us to make some remarks to the jury."[89]

Judge White allowed them to proceed.

---

[86] John D. Lawson, *American State Trials, Volume 14* (St. Louis: Thomas Law Book Co., 1923) 192.

[87] *Buffalo Courier,* 25 September 1901, pg. 8, col. 4.

[88] A. Wesley Johns, *The Man Who Shot McKinley* (New York: A. S. Barnes and Co., Inc., 1970) 225.

[89] *Buffalo Courier,* 25 September 1901, pg. 9, col. 1.

"A great calamity has befallen our nation," Lewis said after a brief introduction. "The President of the country has been stricken down and died in our city. It is shown beyond any peradventure of doubt that that it was at the defendant's hands he was stricken down, and the only question that can be discussed or considered in this case is the question whether that act was that of a sane person. If it was, then the defendant is guilty of murder and must suffer the penalty. If the act was one of an insane man then he is not guilty of murder and should be acquitted on that charge and would then be confined in a lunatic asylum."[90]

Incredibly, rather than using the time to convince the jury of Czolgosz's insanity, Lewis then launched into a defense of himself and Titus for even daring to represent the President's killer.

"Much discussion and much talk has been carried on in our midst," Lewis said, "and has been called to my attention, as to the propriety of any defense being imposed in this case. Many letters have been received by me since I have been assigned, with my associates, to defend this man. You gentlemen know, perhaps, how Judge Titus and myself came into this case. The position was not sought by us, and we appear here in the performance of duty, which we have endeavored to discharge, notwithstanding it was exceedingly unpleasant one. His Honor, Justice White, as Justice of the Supreme Court, sits here because the law makes it is his duty to sit here and preside over this trial. Our very efficient and able District Attorney is prosecuting this action because the law makes it his duty to prosecute this action. You gentlemen are sitting as jurors because you were summoned to appear here, and under our system of jurisprudence it is your duty to sit here and hear the testimony in this case and perform the unpleasant duty of determining whether this man is to be executed or set at liberty"

"In a case of murder a man must have a trial," Lewis continued. "You gentlemen sat here and listened to the defendant's plea of guilty when he was arraigned by the District Attorney. But the law of our state will not permit a man to plead guilty of such a crime as this."[91]

He then tried to sway the jury against a lynch mob mentality, which was certainly prevalent throughout the country and in particular, Buffalo. He recounted a story, which had William Seward, Lincoln's former Secretary of State, saving from lynching, then defending in court, a black man accused of killing nearly an entire white family on the shore of nearby Owasco Lake.

---

[90] *Buffalo Courier,* 25 September 1901, pg. 9, col. 1.
[91] *Buffalo Courier,* 25 September 1901, pg. 9, col. 1.

His point was that Seward did not care anything for the defendant, but "he taught the people the significance of the law and the importance of maintaining the law and the desirability of there being nothing done by mob violence."[92]

Lewis said that the assassination of the President had touched every heart in the Buffalo community and in the world, and that the jury was now called upon to decide if Czolgosz was indeed responsible for his act. [93]

In trying to convince the jury of Czolgosz's apparent insanity, Lewis said "Every human being has a strong desire to live, and death is a spectre that we all dislike to meet, and here this defendant, without having any animosity against our President, without any motive, so far as we can see or learn, without personal motive, entered this building, and in the presence of hundreds of people, committed an act, knowing it would cause his death. Could a sane man perform such an act?"[94]

Lewis concluded with a tribute to the President, his client's victim, and sat down. The courtroom was silent. Titus got up and made a short statement, saying that Lewis had said it well, and that he would only be repeating. He deferred to Justice White, saying the remarks of his distinguished associate had so fully covered the ground, and so clearly set forth the views, which he intended to present to the jury that it was unnecessary for him to reiterate what had already been said upon this subject.[95]

So much for the defensive effort. It seems Czolgosz's attorneys wanted to hurry up and finish the fair trial so that the prisoner could be sentenced and executed.

District Attorney Penney then rose to give his summation:

"May it please your honor," he began, " and gentlemen of the jury: it is hardly possible for any man to stand before his fellow men and talk without the deepest emotion concerning the awful tragedy which came upon the entire world as described and demonstrated by the remarkable exhibition of feeling just presented to you by the distinguished jurist, forced by his duty as a citizen and a lawyer to carry out the absolute mandates of our law. He says to you that there is no question that has been proved beyond the peradventure of any doubt that this man was the instrument that caused the death of our beloved President, of our beloved statesman, and leaves you with the statement, 'That if this man is

---

[92] *Buffalo Courier*, 25 September 1901, pg. 9, col. 2.
[93] *Buffalo Courier*, 25 September 1901, pg. 9, col. 2.
[94] *Buffalo Courier*, 25 September 1901, pg. 9, col. 3.
[95] *Buffalo Courier*, 25 September 1901, pg. 9, col. 3.

mentally responsible he is fully and absolutely guilty of murder in the first degree."[96]

Penney then reviewed the evidence against Czolgosz. He pointed out that the prosecution had shown that Czolgosz had "attended meetings where he imbibed the theories and ideas which culminated in this awful crime, and which resulted in that fatal shot on that Friday afternoon."

Penney repeated that Lewis himself had said that Czolgosz was guilty if sane.

"Our law presumes every man to be innocent until he is proven guilty," the District Attorney continued. "Our law also presumes that every man is sane until he is proven insane."[97]

"Gentlemen, the question seems simple," Penney concluded. "Here are all the elements which go to make up the crime of murder in the first degree, and there is no testimony relieving him of responsibility of his criminal act."

In closing Penney said, "You know your duty. You have sworn to give this man a fair trial upon the facts and upon the evidence. The facts presented on the part of the People present every element of the crime charged and that is all there is to the case. The duty of counsel on both sides is now ended, and it will shortly be your duty to take up the case. I have the greatest confidence in each one of you and I have no doubt the same thought, the same idea and the same object is in all your minds."[98]

When Penney was finished, Justice White charged the jury, and spoke for twenty-one minutes.

White explained the term "reasonable doubt" saying that after sifting through all the evidence and testimony if there exists in a juror's mind a doubt as to the criminal responsibility of Czolgosz, the juror would be bound to acquit him.[99]

In reference to anarchism, Justice White explained that a man that is ready to go out on the street and commit a crime because some other man has committed a crime is as guilty in his heart as the man who has actually committed the act.

"Let me say in closing," White concluded, "that if on the sixth day of September, 1901, the defendant did wrongfully, without justification make an assault upon or shoot one President William McKinley at the place and in the manner and by the means alleged in the indictment, if

---

[96] *Buffalo Courier,* 25 September 1901, pg. 9, col. 3.

[97] *Buffalo Courier,* 25 September 1901, pg. 9, col. 3.

[98] *Buffalo Courier,* 25 September 1901, pg. 9, col. 3.

[99] A. Wesley Johns, *The Man Who Shot McKinley* (New York: A. S. Barnes and Co., Inc., 1970) 230.

such assault were committed from deliberate and premeditated design to effect the death of said William McKinley, or another person, and if he died, the defendant is guilty of murder in the first degree."[100]

The Justice went on to explain murder in the second degree, which would not include premeditation or deliberation.

There was then an exchange between District Attorney Penney and Justice White in regard to the responsibility of the defense to prove that Czolgosz was indeed insane. Penney wanted White to charge the juries that the law, as he had said, did indeed presume every individual sane until proven otherwise. White agreed and instructed the jury so. He also agreed with Penney that the burden of proving insanity was upon he who alleged it. But Titus objected and Penney conceded that the last part be stricken out. Titus then convinced the judge to instruct the jury that if they had a reasonable doubt that Czolgosz had acted under some defect of reason that he did not know what he was doing, that they necessarily acquit him. White agreed and so charged the jury. That being finished, White retired the jurors for their deliberations.[101] The jurors were then led to a second floor jury room and the door closed behind them at 3:50 p.m.

The jury did not take long, being gone a total of thirty-three minutes. Leon Czolgosz sat with head down in the courtroom while twelve men decided his fate. While a few of the jurors were hesitant about reaching a quick verdict, the fate of Leon Czolgosz or his guilt was never in doubt for a moment.

Speaking of the jury, the *Buffalo Courier* reported, "They overcame the opinion of the two or three who thought it wise to wait an hour before bringing in the verdict. The few who favored delay had no doubt of the assassin's guilt. They desired to avoid any appearance of unseemly haste or lack of proper deliberation and consultation. So deep was the disgust of some of the jurors that they were loath to linger even in discussion of the wretch's case."[102]

At 4:20 p.m., Justice White re-entered the courtroom, with the jury filing back in at 4:24.

Clerk Martin Fisher called the names of the jurors and asked, "Gentlemen of the jury, have you agreed upon a verdict?"

---

[100] *Buffalo Courier,* 25 September 1901, pg. 9, col. 4

[101] A. Wesley Johns, *The Man Who Shot McKinley* (New York: A. S. Barnes and Co., Inc., 1970) 232-233.

[102] *Buffalo Courier,* 25 September 1901, pg. 1, col. 1.

"We have," responded Forman Henry W. Wendt, who had been chosen as foreman by his fellow jurors without opposition.

"What do you find?"

"We find the prisoner guilty of murder in the first degree as charged in the indictment," said Wendt.

Fisher responded, "Gentlemen, listen to the verdict as the court has recorded it. You say you find the defendant guilty of murder in the first degree as charged in the indictment. So say you all?"

"We do," the jurors said in unison.[103]

"As the jury uttered the words which opened his grave," dramatically reported the *Buffalo Courier,* "his mental control, beneath the strain, gave way; his death-defying bravado disappeared; his rigidity of defiance was effaced and he appeared what expert criminologists have always believed him to be—an ordinary mortal whose courage had been screwed to the sticking point by insidious teachings and careful instruction in methods of assassination."[104]

However, later on the same page, the *Courier* seemed to contradict itself by stating that Czolgosz, "never by so much as a movement of the eye did he indicate the shock with which the words must have come home to him."[105]

"He was beginning to realize the hopelessness of it all," said the *Buffalo Evening News.* "He was assimilating appreciation of the awful consequences of his act. He was sinking beneath the crushing weight of the law, which he had sought to destroy. His fine bravado was disappearing. His melodramatic contempt for government and its institutions was oozing away. He was no longer a martyr even in his own eyes. He had fallen from the eminence on which he placed himself into a mire of cringing fear. He was groveling about in pitiful cowardice."

"His thoughts betrayed themselves in his appearance," the report continued. "As the afternoon wore away, his dejection increased. The color fled gradually from his face. His head sank slowly, slowly until it rested on his breast. His arms hung listlessly at his sides. His lips became parched and his breathing irregular. Once or twice one of the detectives offered him water. On each occasion the assassin gulped it down greedily. While the jury was out the murderer seemed on the verge of collapse."[106]

---

[103] *Buffalo Courier,* 25 September 1901, pg. 9, col. 5.

[104] *Buffalo Courier,* 25 September 1901, pg. 1, col. 1.

[105] *Buffalo Courier,* 25 September 1901, pg. 1, col. 1.

[106] *Buffalo Evening News,* 25 September 1901, pg. 8, col. 1.

"It was a dramatic moment when the foreman of the jury announced the verdict, but it was followed by no scene," reported the *Buffalo Courier* reporter. "Czolgosz sat immovable and apparently unheeding. There was not one expression from the crowd that packed the courtroom to its capacity. The court, the attorneys and the spectators expected the verdict. The prisoner was without hope. It surprised nobody."[107]

The *Buffalo Evening News* said that he "gave no indication that he heard what was said, save that the greenish pallor of his face became more livid, that his head sunk lower and lower, that he seemed to shrink smaller and smaller. He made no attempt to speak. When the shackles were snapped about his wrists he braced himself, rose to his feet and walked from the courtroom with wavering steps, with a detective on either side. When he reached his cell at the jail he threw himself heavily on his cot."[108]

Justice White adjourned the court and the sentencing was scheduled for 2 p.m., Thursday, September 26.

As they filed from the courtroom, reporters met the jurors. The verdict had taken four ballots, primarily to keep up appearances. The brevity of the trial was reported to be the cheapest murder trial in the history of Erie County.[109] The total cost of the trial of Leon Czolgosz was later determined to be only $1,799.50.[110]

"I could have voted for a verdict without leaving my seat," said Frederick Lauer, the first juror chosen. Others agreed.[111] Another juror said that it was only a few minutes either way and that Czolgosz would be dead for a long time.[112]

For the most part, the verdict was viewed with over-whelming satisfaction. So was the way the trial had been held.

"It was conducted in a proper and dignified manner," said Judge Edward Hatch of the Appellate Division of the New York Supreme Court. "It was a calm, proper and legal trial and the dignity of the Court was maintained to the minutest detail. The trial was all that it should have been, all that it possibly could have been where legal rights and decorum were to be maintained."[113]

---

[107] *Buffalo Courier*, 25 September 1901, pg. 1, col. 1.

[108] *Buffalo Evening News*, 25 September 1901, pg. 8, col. 1.

[109] *Buffalo Evening News*, 25 September 1901, pg. 8, col. 1.

[110] *Buffalo Commercial*, 11 November 1901.

[111] *Buffalo Courier*, 25 September 1901, pg. 9, col. 5.

[112] A. Wesley Johns, *The Man Who Shot McKinley* (New York: A. S. Barnes and Co., Inc., 1970) 234.

[113] *Buffalo Evening News*, 25 September 1901, pg. 8, col. 4.

"The case was conducted absolutely in the usual way," commented Judge White. "Every legal form was strictly observed, and any desire to expedite matters was not allowed to interfere with any rights which the accused had."[114]

"It's over now," said Police Superintendent Bull. "There are few people who are better pleased than I am. I am exceedingly glad that the police of Buffalo were not called upon to handle an attempt to harm the prisoner. They would have been compelled to protect him and there would have been some nasty things done."[115]

Czolgosz was taken back to his cell, and Jailor Mitchell told a reporter the next morning, "The man's manner is absolutely unchanged. He has not weakened one bit and he has made no remarks about the trial, the verdict or what is in store for him. He is as stoical as ever.

"As soon as he was brought back from court yesterday his supper was awaiting him and he ate it about 5:30 o'clock. I have been told he looked exhausted in court but he gave no evidences of it when he was brought back here. As soon as ate his supper, he slept like a log until midnight when his guard was changed. Then he turned over in his sleep but went to sleep again almost at once. He was awake at 6 o'clock this morning and had his breakfast at 7:30 o'clock. He ate heartily as he did last night."[116]

"There is not the slightest doubt but what Czolgosz intended to make a speech today, and he will do so when called upon as to what he has to say why he should not be sentenced next Thursday," said Detective Solomon, the officer who had been with the prisoner more than any other. "I expect a dramatic effort on his part. He is very weak at present. I noticed it several times today. The excitement and strain are beginning to tell upon him and I expect to see him break down completely in the last days before going to the chair. Thirty days to count off one by one awaiting death are apt to affect him greatly."

"I said to him after the jury went out today: 'Now is your time if you are going to make a speech.' He shook his head and said weakly: 'No, this is not the time, the Judge is not here.' He seemed to be short of breath after that, but did not seem to be affected by the verdict."[117]

---

[114] *Buffalo Courier,* 25 September 1901, pg. 8, col. 1.

[115] *Buffalo Courier,* 25 September 1901, pg. 8, col. 1-2.

[116] *Buffalo Evening News,* 25 September 1901, pg. 8, col. 6.

[117] *Buffalo Courier,* 25 September 1901, pg. 8, col. 2.

While Leon Czolgosz was meeting his fate in the courtroom, his father Paul, brother Waldek and Sister Victoria had arrived in Buffalo. After having been accompanied to Buffalo by Constable Jacob Mintz of Chicago, because it was feared they would be molested on the train, they sat in the District Attorney's office as the jury reached its verdict. Afterward, they were taken to police headquarters, where they were fed and then questioned for more than two hours by Bull, Cusack and Haller. They were permitted to spend the night at headquarters.

Waldek told the police that he thought Leon was a tool of other men and that he had been well supplied with money during his stay in West Seneca.

"My brother was a steady, hard-working young man for years," Waldek told police. "When he worked in the wire mill near Cleveland, he saved his money and studied, but he did not study the right things. He never drank, smoked little, and had no bad habits. If he had not become interested in anarchy, he would have amounted to something in time. But the papers and speeches, which he read about the rich and favored classes and inequalities in society made him dissatisfied, and he became lazy and shiftless. While he was in West Seneca, I sent him a money order for $10. He never said anything to any of the family about assassination."[118]

"I feel more than any of the others, the disgrace Leon has brought upon our family," Waldek told a reporter the next morning. "Leon was my chum in the old days and I liked him. I'm sorry, sorry all the way through that he should have gone and committed such a terrible crime."

Waldek denied having any knowledge of Leon being married in West Virginia or knowing he had ever worked there. Reports were coming from the region that Leon had been married near Charleston in January of 1900.

"If Leon was ever married, I do not know about it," was Waldek's reply. "Neither does my father nor my mother. I never knew he worked in West Virginia. He worked in Pennsylvania for a time, but never farther south."

Waldek was asked how their neighbors in Cleveland were treating the family.

"We have no trouble," he said. "The neighbors say that we can't help what Leon did and they let us alone. The newspapers in Cleveland printed a lot of stuff that wasn't true about the grocers not being willing to sell us food. That was all a lie. No one ever refused to sell us

---

[118] *Buffalo Commercial,* 25 September 1901.

anything when we had the money. No, we haven't had no trouble from the crowds. There are lots of people that come to look at the house, but that's all." [119]

At eleven o'clock the next morning, the family was permitted to see Leon in the Erie County Jail, in the presence of Haller and Cusack. The visit lasted 35 minutes, after which, they were escorted to the station for their trip home on the 12:00 train.

Czolgosz was taken out of the dungeon to a cell room to meet his family. It was an emotional meeting, especially when he kissed his young sister Victoria.[120]

"Leon, Leon, what have you done? What have you done?" she sobbed as she buried her face in his shoulder.[121] "Why did you do it Leon? Oh, God. Why did you do it?" she cried softly.[122]

Czolgosz did not cry, but his lip quivered. Then, he gently pushed his sister aside saying, "There is father. I must speak to him."

He approached his father, shook hands, and said something to him in Polish, but his father did not answer, seemingly devoid of emotion. Waldek then approached him.

"I am sorry you came to this, Leon," he said. Leon did not answer, but again his lip quivered. He quickly mastered his emotions.[123]

While Paul and Waldek had no sympathy for Leon due to his crime, they were still very emotional knowing he would soon meet his death. Seventeen-year-old Victoria cried during the entire visit, and by the end was convulsed in sobs, heartbroken. Czolgosz seemed grateful for the opportunity to see members of his family. Leon repeated to them that he had done the crime alone and that there was no one else involved. Waldek tried to get more out of him, but couldn't.

Then, all too quickly, it was time to leave. The father and brother shook Leon's hand, Victoria tearfully kissed him goodbye.

As she left on her father's arm, Victoria looked at Detective Cusack and with tear filled eyes said, "Be good to him, won't you? Don't hurt him, don't be cruel."[124]

Detective Albert Solomon escorted them to the station and was under orders not to allow reporters to talk to them. No one interviewed them, and alone with their sadness, they left Buffalo.[125]

---

[119] *Buffalo Express,* 26 September 1901.

[120] *Buffalo Commercial,* 25 September 1901.

[121] *Buffalo Commercial,* 25 September 1901.

[122] *Buffalo Courier,* 26 September 1901.

[123] *Buffalo Express,* 26 September 1901.

[124] *Buffalo Courier,* 26 September 1901.

[125] *Buffalo Commercial,* 25 September 1901.

Leon was taken back to his cell where he slept uneasily. The officials who had been with him during the interview with his family, noticed he was dejected. They expected him to now make a speech at his sentencing.[126]

"The little Czolgosz girl is far above the general run of her class," said Assistant Superintendent Cusack of the pretty, young sister of the assassin. "She is intelligent and is completely broken in spirit by the disgrace that has been thrust upon her and her family."

He was asked if Czolgosz had weakened.

"Yes, he did," Cusack replied. "He tried to be brazen, but he couldn't. The sight of that sister weakened him and he lost his entire defiant attitude. He was on the verge of breaking down completely but he managed to control himself until after they left. When he stepped back into his cell, he turned his back to the front of it, and I shouldn't be surprised if the tears he had been holding back came then."[127]

At 1:15 on September 26, the doors to the courtroom were opened and in rushed those lucky enough to have passes for the sentencing. For the next thirty minutes, there was excitement as people jostled for seats. The reporters had assigned seats and more than once people tried to take them, many claiming to be reporters only to be embarrassed when none of the other newsmen identified them as authentic. More than one hundred policemen had difficulty controlling the crush from outside. Finally, after ten minutes, Court Crier Hess ordered the doors locked, and busied himself getting those in the room seated.

Czolgosz was brought into the room at exactly 1:55. He looked "sallow and weak and beady drops of perspiration stood out on his forehead."[128]

Detectives John Geary and Albert Solomon removed the handcuffs and Czolgosz looked at the courtroom through half closed eyelids. He seemed to care nothing about the hundreds of eyes fixed upon him.

Justice White opened the proceedings of sentencing at 2:02 p.m., turning to the District Attorney and saying, "Mr. Penney, the court is at your service."

"I move sentence in the case of the people against Leon F. Czolgosz, please," came the reply.

---

[126] *Buffalo Commercial,* 25 September 1901.

[127] *Buffalo Express,* 26 September 1901.

[128] *Buffalo Evening News,* 26 September 1901, pg. 1, col. 8.

Clerk Martin Fisher called Czolgosz to the stand. He was asked to stand and place his hand on the Bible, which he did, and nodded his head in agreement with the words to the oath. However, he refused to say, "I do."

District Attorney Penney began by first asking, "What is your name?"

"Leon Czolgosz," came the quiet response, barely audible to the Judge or those in the courtroom.

"How old are you?"

"Twenty-eight," he responded after some hesitation.

"Where were you born?"

"Detroit."

"Do you know the street and number that you were born on?"

"Lawrence Street."

"Where did you last reside?"

"In Buffalo," whispered Czolgosz. He seemed not to make any effort at all to speak up and fidgeted while the questions were being asked.

"Where did you live in Buffalo?"

"On Broadway."

"Where on Broadway?" asked Penney. Czolgosz gave no response. "At Nowak's?"

"Yes," said Czolgosz, after some hesitation.

"What is your occupation? Do you understand the question?"

Czolgosz shook his head. It seemed as though he was hard of hearing and not understanding of all that was asked of him. Penney repeated the question distinctly and in a loud voice. Czolgosz responded as if dazed.

"Yes, sir; I was a laborer."

"What schools have you attended?"

"Small, common."

"Been to the church school too?" asked Penney.

"Yes."

"Catholic Church?"

"Yes."

"What church were you educated in? Did you used to go to the Catholic Church?"

"Yes."

"Are you married or single?"

"Single," came the ready response.

"Are your parents living or dead?"

"No, sir." was the answer.

"You don't understand me quite," said Penney. "Is your father living?"

"Yes, sir."

"Is your mother living?"

"No sir." Penney glanced at the jury.

"Mr. Czolgosz, have you been temperate or intemperate in the use of intoxicating liquors?" No reply.

"You don't understand the question?"

"No, sir. I don't."

Penney took a few steps toward Czolgosz and glared at him. "Do you drink much?"

"No, sir."

"Ever been drunk?" Again there was no response. "Come on, man! Do you drink much?"

"Mr. Penney, please pass on to something else," interrupted Judge White.

Penney turned and gave a slight bow to the judge acknowledging his request. "Mr. Czolgosz, were you ever before convicted of a crime?"

"No, sir."

Clerk Martin Fisher then interjected, "Have you any legal cause to show now why the sentence of the court should not now be pronounced against you?"

"I cannot hear that," replied the prisoner.

The Clerk repeated the question, and Czolgosz replied, "I'd rather have this gentleman here speak," looking toward the District Attorney. "I can hear him better."[129] Jutice White then told all in the courtroom to be quiet or they would be removed.

Penney then asked, "Czolgosz, the court wants to know if you have any reason to give as to why sentence should not be pronounced against you. Have you anything to say to the judge? Say yes or no."

Czolgosz did not reply, and Judge White addressed him, saying, "In that behalf, what you have a right to say relates explicitly to the subject in hand here at this time, and which the law provides, why now sentence should not be pronounced against you , and is defined by the statute.

"The first is that you may claim to be insane. The next is that you have good cause to offer either in arrest of the judgment about to be pronounced against you or for a new trial. Those are the grounds specified by the statute in which you have a right to speak at this time, and you are at perfect liberty to do so if you wish."

---

[129] *New York Times,* 26 September 1901, pg. 5, col. 1.

Czolgosz appeared dazed. "I have nothing to say about that."

The judge then said to Penney, "Are you ready?" Penney nodded that he was.

"Have you anything to say?" Judge White asked Czolgosz.

"Yes," replied the prisoner.

After some discussion between the Judge and the defense attorney, Czolgosz was then permitted to make a brief statement to the court.

"There was no one else but me," Czolgosz said in a low voice, barely above a whisper. "No one else told me to do it, and no one paid me to do it."

Mr. Titus repeated the words so that others in the courtroom could hear.

Then Czolgosz continued.

"I was not told anything about the crime and I never thought anything about murder until a couple of days before I committed the crime," he said.

Titus again repeated it to the courtroom.[130]

"Anything further, Czolgosz?" asked Justice White.

"No, sir," he replied.

Many were surprised that Czolgosz did not take the opportunity to make an anarchistic speech, as had been outlined in the *Free Society* platform.

Justice White then turned and looked directly into the assassin's eyes. "In taking the life of our beloved President, you committed a crime which shocked and outraged the moral sense of the civilized world. You have confessed that guilt, and after learning all that at this time can be learned from the facts and circumstances of the case, twelve good jurors have pronounced you guilty, and have found you guilty of murder in the first degree.

"You have said, according to the testimony of credible witnesses and yourself, that no other person aided or abetted you in the commission of this terrible act. God grant it may be so! The penalty for the crime for which you stand convicted is fixed by the statute, and it now becomes my duty to pronounce this judgment against you.

"The sentence of the court is that in the week beginning October 28, 1901, at the place, manner and means prescribed by law, you suffer the punishment of death. Remove the prisoner." [131]

The crowd filed out of the room and court adjourned at 2:26.

---

[130] *New York Times,* 26 September 1901, pg. 5, col. 1.

[131] *New York Times,* 26 September 1901, pg. 5, col. 1-2.

Czolgosz stood erect as the sentence was pronounced to him. He did not tremble. Detective Geary eased him back into his seat and slipped the hand cuffs on him.

Titus, who was his sole representation that day, approached him. "Czolgosz, Goodbye."

"Goodbye," replied Czolgosz as he half-heartedly shook his hand.

Back at the jail, Czolgosz said farewell to the detectives that had been his daily escort, Solomon and Geary. He then went into his cell, took off his coat, sat down and put his head in his hands.[132]

The death warrant, signed by Judge White and sent to the Warden of Auburn Prison, instructed that during the prescribed week, Czolgosz was to be executed; "to pass through the body of the said Leon F. Czolgosz a current of electricity of sufficient intensity to cause death, and that the application of the said current of electricity be continued until he, the said Leon F. Czolgosz, be dead."[133]

"I feel the disgrace of Leon keenly," said his father upon hearing the news. "He has cancelled all claim for sympathy by reason of his monstrous crime. He is an outcast from his family. We do not want or expect to see him again. He must meet his fate alone. His crime has brought us all disgrace."[134]

TRANSFER TO AUBURN PRISON

On September 26, Czolgosz was transferred to Auburn Prison to await execution. Handcuffed to Jailor George N. Mitchell, he was spirited out the back entrance of the Erie County Jail by Sheriff Caldwell and sixteen of his men. The move had been kept secret so as not to draw a crowd and to prevent possible harm to the prisoner. Czolgosz was hustled into a special railroad car that had been backed up to the entrance only moments before. The officers that made up the escort, by Caldwell's instruction, had arrived at the jail individually throughout the day so as not to attract the attention of the waiting reporters and curious observers. The car sped quickly to the train station, but so too did the word of the assassin's movement spread. By the time they arrived at the

---

[132] A. Wesley Johns, *The Man Who Shot McKinley* (New York: A. S. Barnes and Co., Inc., 1970) 243.

[133] *New York Times,* 26 September 1901, pg. 5, col. 1.

[134] *Buffalo Express,* 15 September 1901.

station, many of the railroad workers had taken a place on the platform to take a look at the prisoner. The train, which was scheduled to leave at 9:30, finally pulled out with its infamous prisoner at 10:06.[135]

Along the route, Czolgosz smoked on a cigar and a reporter asked him if the shooting was a mistake. He responded that it was and Jailer Mitchell, to whom Czolgosz remained handcuffed, asked him if he was sorry. Czolgosz said that he was.[136]

According to Auburn Police Chief MacMaster, Czolgosz had eaten a huge dinner in Buffalo before leaving and ate and smoked almost continuously during the train ride. He was even told by the Buffalo officers that he was a gormandizer, but he kept eating anyway.[137]

In Rochester, the car carrying Czolgosz was coupled to a train running to Auburn. The waiting crowd of mostly workmen had hoped that Czolgosz would be walked through the station to another car, but they were disappointed. A reporter noticed Czolgosz smoking a cigar and saw Jailor Mitchell sitting next to him, and Deputy Sheriff Hugh Sloan sitting opposite and facing them. The other guards where in front and behind the prisoner.[138]

In route to Auburn, Czolgosz talked as freely as he had since the days immediately following his arrest.

He became friendly and talkative with a *Buffalo Courier* reporter and when pressed about his movements between August 29th and 31st, he replied, "Where was I? Why, I went to Cleveland."

He talked with a smile and seemed quite relaxed.

Explaining his jaunt to Cleveland, he said, "I was a member of the Sila Society in Cleveland and attended meetings in the Superior Street Hall, where all addresses were made on the subject of anarchy. I have studied anarchy for many years."

He firmly denied knowing any of the suspects in the murder of the President except for Emma Goldman, Abraham Isaak and Marie Isaak. He refused to answer whether he had been in West Seneca or in Chicago on August 12. He also denied following McKinley to Niagara Falls on the day of the shooting.[139]

---

[135] *New York Times,* 26 September 1901, pg. 5, col. 2.

[136] A. Wesley Johns, *The Man Who Shot McKinley* (New York: A. S. Barnes and Co., Inc., 1970) 244.

[137] L. Vernon Briggs, *The Manner of Man That Kills* (Boston: R. G. Badger, Gorham Press, 1921) 255.

[138] *New York Times,* 26 September 1901, pg. 5, col. 2.

[139] *Buffalo Courier,* 26 September 1901, pg. 1, col. 5.

"I am sorry I killed the President," he said. "I was alone in what I did, I did it myself. There was one mistake about the trial. I did not go to Niagara Falls to kill the President. I only thought of killing him for about one day before I did it. My mind was stirred up and I don't know what was in it or what influenced me."[140]

"My trial was fair," he said. "The Judge could not help doing what he did. The jury couldn't either. The law was fair to me and it was right. It seems too late now, but I am sorry for Mrs. McKinley. I hope she does not die."[141]

"I wish the people to know I am sorry for what I did," he reportedly said. "It was a mistake and it was wrong."[142]

"I am especially sorry for Mrs. McKinley," he said.

He also told Jailer Mitchell to send a message to his father; "Tell him I am sorry I left such a bad name for him."[143]

He also said that he did not know anything of a man in St. Louis who was under arrest for allegedly tying the handkerchief. He declared that only he himself had gone behind the Temple of Music and arranged the handkerchief to conceal the gun, then had taken his place in line.[144]

Another account quoted Czolgosz's conversation as follows:

"I am sorry I done it. I would not do it again and I would not have done it if I had known what I was doing."

"It is awful to feel you killed somebody," he continued. "I wish I had not done it. I would like to live, but I can't now. I made my mistake. I was all stirred up and felt I had to kill him. I never thought of doing it until a couple days before. I did not tie the handkerchief to my hand. I only dropped it over the gun. I did not think it looked like a sore hand, but did not suppose I would be stopped, because the gun did not show. I did not try to kill him at Niagara Falls. I did not tell nobody and nobody set me on. I did it all myself."

He lapsed into quiet but began to answer questions.

"Did you know Count Malatesta or Madame Brusigloli or Bresci or any other foreign anarchists?"

"No, I heard of them, but I never met them," came Czolgosz's response. "I knew a lot of them in Cleveland but nowhere else. I did not know anyone from Paterson."

---

[140] *Buffalo Evening News*, 27 September 1901, pg. 7, col. 3.
[141] *Buffalo Evening News*, 27 September 1901, pg. 7, col. 3.
[142] *Buffalo Evening News*, 27 September 1901, pg. 7, col. 2.
[143] *Buffalo Evening News*, 27 September 1901, pg. 7, col. 2.
[144] *Buffalo Evening News*, 27 September 1901, pg. 7, col. 2.

"I knew Emma Goldman and some others in Chicago. I heard Emma Goldman speak in Cleveland. None of those people ever told me to kill anybody. Nobody told me that. I done it all myself."

"What do you think of your trial?" he was asked.

"It was all surprising to me," he said. "It was more than I expected. I thought I would be sentenced right off. What I heard there was more than I had heard before. I hated to hear about the wound and all that. I felt glad I killed him and then I felt sorry he did not live after I shot him."

"Had you thought of Mrs. McKinley?"

"I would be sorry if she died," he said after some hesitation.

"Would you like to have a priest before you die, or a minister?"

"Maybe a priest," Czolgosz replied after some thought.[145]

From still another account by the *Buffalo Express* reporter seated next to Czolgosz during this conversation:

"It is an awful thing to feel you killed someone. You do not feel the same after you kill them. It is hard and much different. You are not the same person after you do the crime. I wish I was my same old person again. You never can be the same. I wish I was the same for the little time left."

When the train arrived at Canadaigua at 1:21 a.m. there was heard the shouts of a crowd. A deputy sheriff riding on the train asked the crowd, "What's this all about?"

"Czolgosz," the crowd yelled in response.

"Czolgosz, why, he won't leave Buffalo until Saturday," answered the quick thinking deputy.

Auburn Prison was built in 1817 and at the time was the oldest prison in New York. It was located in the heart of the city, just across the street from the railroad depot. The gate of the prison was located on the principle street. It looked like an iron barred break in the high gray stone walls.

Waiting at Auburn was a crowd of not more than 100, (300 by other accounts) hoping to get a glimpse of the prisoner. Four guards had been sent by Auburn Police Chief MacMaster to prevent such a thing.

Earlier in the evening, when another train had arrived at Auburn, it was thought that it would be Czolgosz's transport. Nearly 1,500 angry

---

[145] Murat Halstead, *The Illustrious Life of William McKinley* (Privately Published, 1901) 462.

citizens waited and were disappointed to find the assassin was not aboard.

"If we had gone on that train," said Sheriff Caldwell upon his return to Buffalo, "We never would have landed the prisoner inside the jail. It was the worst crowd I ever faced as it was."[146]

At 3:11 a.m., the door of Car 1509 was opened and out popped Czolgosz with his bodyguards. The crowd surged forward surrounding the entourage and tried to reach the prisoner, still handcuffed to Mitchell. The grouped moved across State Street from the station to the prison gates. One punch landed on Mitchell, who instructed Czolgosz to stay close to him. Sheriff Caldwell told the officers not to use their guns, but their clubs to keep the mob back.

Just as they reached the gate of the prison, Czolgosz was struck a hard blow on the neck and another man grabbed him by the shoulder. The police got between Czolgosz and the crowd, with one officer pulling his revolver, which had the effect of cowing the crowd.[147]

Not more than a minute passed between the arrival of the train and Czolgosz entering the prison gates, and the distance from the railroad car to the gate was less than fifty yards.

Czolgosz was overcome with emotion and fear as the crowd shouted and tried to get him. He stumbled to his knees. The guards had to literally carry him in the gate. At the entrance, prison guard John Martin, a giant of a man, grabbed Czolgosz and pulled him inside the main hall, away from the throng. Czolgosz, only semi-conscious was dragged upstairs, where there was a large photo of President McKinley, framed in black crepe, next to photo of James Garfield. Czolgosz shuddered. The prisoner's shackles were removed and still unable to walk, he was dragged down the hall by Martin on his stomach and knees.[148]

Czolgosz was screaming hysterically and the guards called the prison physician, Dr. John Gerin. When he arrived, he found Czolgosz lying on the floor, screaming, "save me, save me," kicking his legs and waving his arms. His shrieks aroused other prisoners, who could hear him as his cries traveled through the corridors.

Chief MacMaster confirmed that Czolgosz had "shook or shivered, and trembled and went all to pieces."[149]

---

[146] *Buffalo Evening News,* 27 September 1901, pg. 1, col. 2.

[147] *Buffalo Evening News,* 27 September 1901, pg. 1, col. 1.

[148] *Buffalo Evening News,* 27 September 1901, pg. 1, col. 1.

[149] L. Vernon Briggs, *The Manner of Man That Kills* (Boston: R. G. Badger, Gorham Press, 1921) 257.

Czolgosz perspired, cried and drooled and one reporter who saw the scene thought he looked like a mad dog. The prisoner was taken to Deputy Warden Allan J. Tupper's office where Guard Martin had to carry him through the door. There he was stripped and put into a prison uniform.

At 3:26, Dr. Gerin came in to see the prisoner, and injected him with a hypodermic needle. Within seconds, the prisoner slumped to the floor. "Half fright—half fake," was Gerin's explanation.

Guards picked Czolgosz up and took him through the south wing to the condemned cells on 'Murderers Row,' and placed him in the last of the five cells. He was placed beside Clarence Egnor, who had killed a jail keeper named Benedict at the prison the previous winter. The other prisoners on death row included Fred Krist, who had shot Kittie Tobin of Waverly, New York in a jealous rage the previous December; John Truck, who had murdered a farmer named Miller in Virgil the year before and George A. Smith who had killed his wife two years before.[150]

Once Czolgosz was in his cell, Gerin made a more thorough examination of the prisoner. When he came out, he was quoted as saying, "It was just pure fright. He is a miserable coward and collapsed when he saw the crowd and the prison. Now that he is safe in his cell I guess he will brace up. He has partially recovered from his fright."[151]

In his cell, Warden J. Warren Mead, with John Nelson Ross, who worked taking measurements of Auburn prisoners among other duties, taking notes, interviewed Czolgosz. Mead stated that it was the only time that Czolgosz ever talked to them about anything substantive other than to say he was an anarchist. Mead had already made up his mind not to allow any outsiders access to Czolgosz, and refused to release the statements. They were kept at Mr. Ross's house, with no other copies being made.[152]

The notes of the only conversation Leon Czolgosz had at Auburn Prison were later shown to Dr. L. Vernon Briggs. They read:

"He was born in Alpena, Michigan, in 1873, where he resided until he was five years of age, when he removed to Detroit, where he resided for eleven years, when he went to Netrolia, Pennsylvania, near Pittsburgh, where he worked in a diamond factory (he afterwards said glass factory) for one year and nine months, when he went to

---

[150] *Buffalo Evening News,* 27 September 1901, pg. 1, col. 1.

[151] Murat Halstead, *The Illustrious Life of William McKinley* (Privately Published) 450.

[152] L. Vernon Briggs, *The Manner of Man That Kills* (Boston: R. G. Badger, Gorham Press, 1921) 257.

Warrensville, Ohio, where he invested his earnings with his family in a farm and worked on it for a time. It was afterwards sold, and he resided in Cleveland until July 1st, 1901, when he left there. He also spoke of being in Cleveland first and then going to Warrensville and returning to Cleveland. Of his family he said his own mother's name was "— Nebock," his stepmother's name Catrina— ."

There followed a listing of his family.[153]

When Czolgosz talked to the Warden, he asked him when his journey would continue. Mead told him that his journey had ended and Czolgosz said, "I thought I was going to Sing Sing—is it not Sing Sing where they do all the electrocuting?" When Mead told him he would be electrocuted at Auburn, Czolgosz seemed surprised. "In Ohio they only electrocute in one place, Columbus," he said.[154]

Guards Joseph Herman and Christopher Haas were given the duty of watching Czolgosz that first night, being relieved by Frank Murphy the next morning.

At 3:50 Dr. Gerin looked in on him, and Czolgosz was asleep. He was awakened at 8:00 a.m., and served breakfast.

The next evening, Warden Mead told reporters of Czolgosz's first day at the prison.

"Czolgosz has eaten his meals regularly and has had no conversation with any of the other condemned men," he said. "He answered questions in regard to his meals, such as inquiry if he would have salt, etc., which were put to him by the officers, but aside from that he has said nothing. Part of the time yesterday he lay in his bed and the rest of the time he spent walking up and down his cell."[155]

One report said that Czolgosz began to request books from the prison library and passed his days, in part, reading. But other reports claim that Czolgosz refused to admit that he could read or write, and in all the reports of Czolgosz inside the prison, no others mention him reading.

His fellow prisoners did not like him and Clarence Egnor, who was in the cell next to him, even obtained a photograph of McKinley, which he decorated in black crepe, hoping for Czolgosz to see it on the way to the electric chair.[156]

---

[153] L. Vernon Briggs, *The Manner of Man That Kills* (Boston: R. G. Badger, Gorham Press, 1921) 262..

[154] L. Vernon Briggs, *The Manner of Man That Kills* (Boston: R. G. Badger, Gorham Press, 1921) 257-258.

[155] *Buffalo Evening News,* 28 September 1901, pg. 1, col. 5.

[156] *Buffalo Evening News,* 4 October 1901, pg. 1, col. 7-8.

Leon's brother-in-law, Frank Bandowski, was causing some trouble and concerns while in Auburn. At least that was how the prison officials saw it. One said that he saw Bandowski talking to reporters and making up stories, as the reporters eagerly jotted down everything he said. Prison priest Father Hickey told of how Leon had asked for a priest shortly after his arrival at Auburn Prison, but that after a visit from Bandowski, Czolgosz suddenly refused to see him, even going as far as telling Warden Mead that if a priest came to visit him he would "smash his head." Later Czolgosz apologized for saying it, but when Hickey arrived, he refused to talk to him.

Another time Leon asked Dr. Gerin to send him a priest immediately. When one arrived after some delay, Czolgosz refused to see him. Gerin was under the impression that had the priest arrived promptly, Leon would have seen him. Warden Mead was quite put out by the incident and told Leon that prison officials were not in the habit of running errands for prisoners.[157]

In early October, Prison Superintendent Cornelius Collins interviewed Czolgosz in a secluded part of the prison. After trying for a while to get the prisoner to talk, Czolgosz finally began to speak somewhat freely.

"Now Czolgosz, I want you to talk to me," urged Collins. "I'm the only one that can do you any good, and if you tell me all I may help you to get out of here."

"I don't want to get out of here," Czolgosz replied. "They'd kill me outside," meaning the crowds.

"You mean the people who told you to kill the President?" asked Collins.

"No, nobody told me to kill the President. I mean the people."

"Who gave you the money to get to Buffalo?" Collins persisted.

"No one. A man in Chicago wanted to see me and I went there from Cleveland," was Czolgosz's reply.

"Who was this man?"

"I don't remember his name."

"Do you remember where he lived?"

"No. I don't know the names of the streets there."

"How did you get from Chicago to Buffalo? Did this man pay your fare?" asked Collins.

"No, sir. I had some money I earned at painting and carpenter work."

---

[157] L. Vernon Briggs, *The Manner of Man That Kills* (Boston: R. G. Badger, Gorham Press, 1921) 263.

"Didn't this man at Chicago and some others tell you to kill the President?"

"No, they didn't. I thought it out myself."

"Did you first follow the President to San Francisco to kill him?"

"That's a lie."

Throughout the interview, as he always did, Czolgosz denied any involvement in the crime by anyone other than himself. But Czolgosz was not truthful all the time. Later, when Collins asked him again about the money he had made in Chicago, Czolgosz responded, "What money?"

"Why, the money you told me about here earlier in the evening," responded Collins.

"Did I tell you that?" said Czolgosz. "I have forgotten if I did. I did not get any money. If I said so it was not true."

When asked about his father, Czolgosz said, "He is no good. He married a woman who made me cook my own food in the house after I had bought it."[158]

While most accounts have Czolgosz keeping his cool throughout his prison stay, the sensationalistic *Buffalo Courier* told of a different side of the assassin. Czolgosz, it reported, was taken to shaking in fear at unusual noises, shrinking back into the farthest corner of his cot. He supposedly was very dejected and sat for hours without saying anything. And he was in fear of the other prisoners and of the mob he had encountered upon his arrival at Auburn.

Once, when workmen where busy in the death chamber, the noises made Czolgosz sob and moan like a frightened animal. "What's the matter with you?" asked his guard. After a minute in which he was unable to reply, Czolgosz said, "I thought they were coming! I thought they were coming!"[159]

EXECUTION

The time leading up to the execution of Leon Czolgosz passed without incident. Members of the press were routinely denied interviews and were not permitted to witness the execution. In fact, as early as September 21, Auburn had received over one hundred requests to witness the execution by telegraph, telephone and by mail.[160] By the day

---

[158] *New York Times,* 30 October 1901, pg. 5, col. 4-5.

[159] *Buffalo Courier,* 29 October 1901, pg. 2, col. 2.

[160] *New York Times,* 21 October 1901, pg. 2, col. 2.

of the execution, there were over twelve hundred such requests, even though New York State law allowed only twenty-six witnesses. Warden Mead told reporters of numerous requests for Czolgosz's autograph coming into the prison and requests from medical men for portions of his brain after execution.[161] Czolgosz was receiving thousands of letters and also many parcels including fruit baskets and Bibles. None of the letters or the fruit made their way to the prisoner. He knew not even of their existence.[162]

One museum keeper offered $5,000 for either the body or the garments of the murderer. A kinetoscope owner offered $2,000 to be permitted to take a moving picture of Czolgosz entering the death chamber. These requests too were denied.[163]

Sheriff Caldwell went to Auburn from Buffalo on unrelated business and reported about the security at the prison.

"They are guarding the assassin closely," he said. "He is kept in solitary confinement and not even the death watch speak to him. Even the Warden of the prison hasn't seen him yet...a vigilant watch is kept on the other condemned men as it is known they would kill Czolgosz if they got a chance."[164]

Obviously, Caldwell was incorrect about Czolgosz's not having seen Warden Mead and that no one would talk to him. The only one refusing to talk was Czolgosz himself.

During his stay at Auburn, all of the prison officers agreed that Czolgosz was very secretive and they were unable to coax him into answering questions or to draw him into conversation about substantial things. When he did talk it was only about what he wanted and only then after slow deliberation.[165]

Reports said that Czolgosz wanted to commit suicide, but Warden Mead denied it and said that the prisoner was eating his meals and did not seem depressed. Superintendent Collins said that Czolgosz had told him that he knew he had to die. Collins said Czolgosz expressed no fear of the execution, but said that he did not care to go outside the prison, for he thought the people would kill him.[166]

---

[161] *Buffalo Evening News,* 28 September 1901, pg. 1, col. 6.

[162] *Buffalo Evening News,* 15 October 1901, pg. 5, col. 1.

[163] *New York Times,* 29 October 1901, pg. 1, col. 5.

[164] *Buffalo Evening News,* 8 October 1901, pg. 1, col. 5.

[165] Dr. Walter Channing, *The Mental Status of Czolgosz* (Brookline, Mass: American Journal of Insanity, Vol. LIX, No. 2, 1902) 28.

[166] *Buffalo Evening News,* 15 October 1901, pg. 5, col. 1.

Once when Warden Mead asked Czolgosz a question about his family, Leon stood at his cell door for almost half an hour before answering. On another occasion when the prison officials put Czolgosz with other prisoners to see if he would talk, he spoke only of snow and other unimportant matters. Usually, he would not speak at all.[167]

Another time, Czolgosz suddenly said to one of his guards, "How does it feel?"

"How does what feel?" came the reply.

"That—in there," he said, jerking his thumb toward the wall behind which rested the chair.

"Oh, you'll know," answered the guard. "It's soon over." Czolgosz started to say something else, but dropped his cigar to the floor, then went back into a corner of his cell and began to shake in fear, according to the guard.[168]

Warden Mead thought Czolgosz "way above the ordinary criminal" in intelligence, although at the prison they were never able to get him to even write his name, with Leon claiming he could not write. A guard was called in to take a letter to his brother Waldek in Warrensville, Ohio, and as Leon dictated, he became much affected. He stopped the letter.[169]

His fellow prisoners heckled him when possible.

"You'll go through there and you'll never come back," Fred Krist told him. "If you listen, you'll hear us cheer as you go."[170]

"Tell Leon that I hope that he may rest in peace; that he will become reconciled with God, and will meet his end bravely," was the message Paul Czolgosz wanted to send his son. "Tell him that as much as I and all our family regret his most unhappy plight that we can do nothing to interfere; that he is alone responsible for his unfortunate position and that he must meet his punishment as a consequence."[171]

---

[167] L. Vernon Briggs, *The Manner of Man That Kills* (Boston: R. G. Badger, Gorham Press, 1921) 258.

[168] *Buffalo Courier,* 29 October 1901, pg. 1, col. 7.

[169] L. Vernon Briggs, *The Manner of Man That Kills* (Boston: R. G. Badger, Gorham Press, 1921) 259.

[170] *Buffalo Express,* 30 September 1901.

[171] *Buffalo Courier,* 28 September 1901.

Warden Warren J. Mead spent part of October 21 meeting with Superintendent of Prisons Cornelius V. Collins making final preparations for the execution of Leon Czolgosz, including who would be invited to attend the execution from the over 1,200 requests. They tried to include Buffalo representatives, official government representatives and members of the press. Their work also included selecting the jurors who would sign the death warrant.[172]

The next day, Czolgosz asked to see a priest, and was visited by Rev. T. Szandinski, a Polish priest of the Roman Catholic Church, to which he spoke in Polish.

Czolgosz told Szandinski that he had given up the Catholic Church early in life and lost faith in its teachings. Szandinski urged him to renounce Anarchy and return to his faith in the church. Czolgosz said he was unable to do that and Szandinski told him that unless he could, the church would not console him.

The priest urged him to re-consider and to call for him if he changed his mind, but Czolgosz said he would probably not renounce the doctrines of anarchy. Szandinski left.[173]

Leon Czolgosz also spoke, according to press reports, with Rev. Father Hyacinth Fudzinski, a Polish priest from Buffalo, who was accompanied by the prison priest, Father Hickey. It is quite possible Fudzinski is the same priest mentioned in the account above, and it is possible that the *New York Times* misidentified him or got the information second hand. At any rate, no one knows what Czolgosz and Father Fudzinski discussed.[174] The Father did not answer questions of the reporters as he left the prison and did not reply to a letter of inquiry as to the conversation a year later.[175]

It was reported that Czolgosz refused to ask divine forgiveness and the priests told him they would answer his call at any hour. When asked if Czolgosz had denounced Christianity, Father Fudzinski replied, "He is a Christian. He was born a Christian and although he may have renounced Christianity, he is a Christian, I think. That is all I will say."[176]

---

[172] *Buffalo Evening News,* 22 October 1901, pg. 8, col. 1.

[173] *New York Times,* 23 October 1901, pg. 1, col. 6.

[174] L. Vernon Briggs, *The Manner of Man That Kills* (Boston: R. G. Badger, Gorham Press, 1921) 260-261.

[175] L. Vernon Briggs, *The Manner of Man That Kills* (Boston: R. G. Badger, Gorham Press, 1921) 265.

[176] *Buffalo Evening News,* 25 October 1901, pg. 1, col. 5.

Another report said that the Father, while reluctant to talk, stated that there had been a great change comes over the prisoner during their talk, a change for the better.[177]

It is interesting to note that Father Fudzinski had not known Czolgosz during his stay in Buffalo, even though the assassin was staying at a house in his parish, John Nowak's place on Broadway. [178]

On October 26, Warden Mead visited Czolgosz in his cell and informed him when the execution would take place and other details concerning it. Mead said that Czolgosz sat in his darkened cell and with head down, stared at the floor. His guards said they could not see any sign of emotion in him.

"Czolgosz has shown no more disposition to talk lately than when he came here on September 27th," said Warden Mead, who was suffering from a cold. "When he was informed of the hour fixed for his death he said nothing."

Fathers Hickey and Fudzinski again visited Czolgosz that afternoon. They sent in word via the Warden that they wished to see Leon, to help him prepare for his fate. He refused. Superintendent Collins then allowed them to go into his cell, and Czolgosz reluctantly allowed them to talk for three-quarters of an hour. But Leon would not hear them. They went away, without receiving any cooperation from him.[179]

"It seems hopeless," declared Father Fudzinski. "I have tried in vain to bring Czolgosz to God. When I left I told him I would be ready to go to his side at any time during the day or night. But I do not think he will call me. He is the most heartless man I have ever saw. He has not the grace to love God. I think he is so without conscience that he will actually sleep tonight. I think Czolgosz would have confessed if it were not for the presence of his brother."[180]

At 8:00 p.m., the night before the execution, Waldek Czolgosz, in town with his brother-in-law Frank Bandowski, visited his brother.

"Tell us, Leon, who got you into this scrape?" he asked, still trying to get Leon to name accomplices.

"No one," was his reply.

"That is not how you were brought up and you ought to tell us everything now," urged Waldek.

---

[177] *Buffalo Courier,* 26 October 1901, pg. 7, col. 2.

[178] *Buffalo Courier,* 26 October 1901, pg. 7, col. 2.

[179] *New York Times,* 29 October 1901, pg. 2, col. 3.

[180] *Buffalo Courier,* 29 October 1901, pg. 1, col. 6.

"I haven't got anything to tell," was Leon's surly reply.

"Do you want to see the priests again?" Waldek asked.

"No, damned them," Leon answered. "I don't want them and don't have them praying over me when I'm dead. I don't want any of their damned religion."[181]

Waldek asked Leon why he had done it.

"I did it—," he said, then stopped as if thinking or going to sleep and the suddenly finished, "because I done my duty."[182]

Then the men talked casually with Leon answering in monosyllables. Superintendent Collins was surprised when Bandowski requested that he and Waldek witness the execution.

"Yes, Superintendent, let them see me killed," was Leon Czolgosz's response.

But Collins told them in no uncertain terms that would not be permitted and ordered them to say good-bye. Leon walked to the back of his cell and sat down on his bunk. He did not answer the last farewell.[183]

Upon leaving the prison, Bandowski told reporters, "If anyone says that Leon has made a confession to a priest, don't believe it. He will refuse to have anything to do with clergymen."[184]

Waldek talked with a *Buffalo Courier* reporter, Thomas W. Streep, later that night.

"I talked with my brother for about twenty minutes this afternoon and again this evening," he said. "When I left tonight I said I would return to him about 3 o'clock in the morning and stay with him until the time of the execution. I asked Leon what he wanted done with his body and he said he didn't care what became of him. When I entered the prison the guards stood close beside me. They made me speak to Leon in English. I shook hands with my brother through the bars and then sat down close to the cell. We didn't talk very fast or say much to each other. I don't think Leon will weaken. He never shows any sign of crying. I asked him is he was sorry and he didn't answer. I asked him if he wanted to see a priest and he said, 'No. I never asked for any and I think they are humbugs.' I asked Leon if he wanted to see father and he said he did, if he was in town, but he didn't want him sent for."[185]

---

[181] *New York Times,* 29 October 1901, pg. 2, col. 3.

[182] *New York Times,* 29 October 1901, pg. 2, col. 3.

[183] *New York Times,* 29 October 1901, pg. 2, col. 4.

[184] *Buffalo Courier,* 28 October 1901, pg. 1, col. 3.

[185] *Buffalo Courier,* 29 October 1901, pg. 1, col. 5.

Bandowski said that Leon told him that he would talk to his father or his other brothers if they called.

"I am in doubt yet as to what I will do with my brother's body," Waldek told a reporter. "I have been talking with an undertaker about the expense of burial and I am inclined to think I will let the state take care of Leon."[186]

While Waldek was making that statement, Paul Czolgosz was described as "extremely anxious" in getting his son's body back to Cleveland for burial. He also reportedly wanted to see his son and there was talk of him coming to Auburn. But he never did.[187]

"I do not think my husband will go to Auburn," said Mrs. Czolgosz to a reporter while her husband was at work. "I am almost certain he will not. It costs too much. We cannot afford it. We have talked the matter over and over again and we cannot decide upon the best course to pursue in the matter of burial. We have almost decided that we will have the remains cremated. They may be sold, however."[188]

On October 28th, Warden Mead had released information to the press regarding the prisoner.

"Czolgosz has eaten his meals regularly and has had no conversation with any of the other condemned men," he said. "He answered questions in regard to his meals, which were put to him by the officers, but aside from that, he has said nothing. Part of the time yesterday he lay in his bed, and the rest of the time he spent walking up and down his cell."[189]

During the afternoon, Czolgosz was said to have had a 'nervous attack.' At about six o'clock, Dr. Gerin visited the prisoner who was perspiring heavily and had dilated pupils. After the examination, Czolgosz turned quickly and retreated to a corner of the room, refusing to talk to them.

Warden Mead had done his best to not enhance any notoriety achieved by the assassin of the President, and for this reason, even if Czolgosz said anything during his stay, it is doubtful if the press would have been told about it. Routinely, requests for interviews were denied and Czolgosz was kept in seclusion. There was no relaxation of those rules as the time grew short. In fact, during the last thirty hours before

---

[186] *Buffalo Courier,* 28 October 1901, pg. 1, col. 3.

[187] *Buffalo Courier,* 28 October 1901, pg. 1, col. 3.

[188] *Buffalo Courier,* 28 October 1901, pg. 1, col. 2.

[189] *New York Times,* 29 October 1901, pg. 12, col. 3.

the execution, no news was to be given out to newsmen of Czolgosz's condition or actions, in an attempt to squash any news stories about him. Mead made plans to, immediately following the execution, burn all the letters Czolgosz had received at the prison as well as all of his personal effects. He was determined not to relinquish Czolgosz's body or any part of it to anyone for any reason, including to Czolgosz's parents. His fear was that at some point, anything relating to Czolgosz would be put on display, thus adding to his notoriety. New York Governor Benjamin B. Odell sent word that the execution was to be conducted with as little display or notoriety as possible. As the execution drew closer, Mead had gotten over a bout of near pneumonia and was behaving rather irritably and discourteous to the reporters who tried to get information from him.[190]

Dr. MacDonald, who would perform the autopsy, requested to keep portions of Czolgosz's brain for further study. The Warden told him that he could examine it at the prison, but that in no event would it leave the prison. Dr. MacDonald understood and agreed.[191]

On Monday, October 29, Warden Mead arose feeling much better, after being quite ill. It had been doubtful whether he would be well enough to even attend the execution. He made the final preparations with his staff for the execution. He conferred with electrician E. F. Davis and the keepers and the guards who would assist in the proceedings. Extra guards were to be placed at the prison gates and a guard would spend the final hours inside Czolgosz's cell to prevent any suicide attempt. The Warden also instructed that any further conversations with the prisoner be conducted in English, except confessions to a priest.[192]

During that morning, Waldek walked around in front of the prison, stopping to peer in the gate, but never attempting to enter. Bandowski requested to see the prisoner, but was denied by Czolgosz himself, according to the warden.[193]

Warden Mead and Superintendent Collins, it was reported, had gone to bed at 10:00 p.m., the night before. Before the Superintendent retired, the deathwatch reported to him that Czolgosz was sleeping soundly. Two guards watched the corridor; a third spent the night in Czolgosz's cell.[194]

---

[190] *Buffalo Courier,* 29 October 1901, pg. 1, col. 3.

[191] *New York Times,* 28 October 1901, pg. 1, col. 7.

[192] *Buffalo Evening News,* 28 October 1901, pg. 1, col. 1.

[193] *Buffalo Evening News,* 28 October 1901, pg. 1, col. 1.

[194] *New York Times,* 29 October 1901, pg. 2, col. 3.

In the early morning hours of October 29, a crowd of perhaps one hundred gathered around the gate of Auburn Prison. The town of Auburn was quiet. Inside the penitentiary, the prisoners were quiet.

Leon Czolgosz was reported to have slept well during the last night of his life.

"He fell asleep after one o'clock, and I had to arouse him half past five to read the death warrant to him," explained Warden Mead.[195]

When he had been awakened, Czolgosz was so sound asleep that he had to be shaken by the guard. He made no reply to Warden Mead's "good morning." He sat listening as the Warden pulled a small paper from his pocket and slowly read the death warrant. Staring at the floor, Czolgosz barely raised his eyes. He asked to see Waldek again, but his request was denied.

"I would like to talk to the Superintendent," Czolgosz told Mead as he stepped out of his cell.

"He will be down presently," said the Warden.[196]

Czolgosz rolled back onto his cot and tried to go back to sleep, but fifteen minutes later a guard appeared with a pair of dark trousers with the left leg slit to allow for an electrode. He also brought with him a dark gray shirt. Czolgosz put them on, as well as the new shoes that were given him, and lay back on the cot.

When he arrived at 5:30, Czolgosz told Superintendent Collins that he wanted to make a speech in public at his execution.

"I want to make it when there are a lot of people present," Czolgosz told him. "I want them to hear me."

When he was told, this would not be permitted, he responded, "Then I won't talk at all."[197]

"Czolgosz said he wanted to make his statement in public, before all the people when he was going to the chair," Collins said. "He was told that this would be impossible and he then resumed his sullen almost ugly mood, and refused to talk anymore."[198]

And Leon Czolgosz still refused to see a priest.

"The prisoner has not asked for me," said prison priest Father J. J. Hickey, "and it is not our custom to the condemned cells without a request. Of course I would consider it my duty to see Czolgosz if he had not already seen a priest."[199]

---

[195] Murat Halstead, *The Illustrious Life of William McKinley* (Privately Published) 466.

[196] *New York Times,* 30 October 1901, pg. 5, col. 2.

[197] *New York Times,* 30 October 1901, pg. 5, col. 2.

[198] Dr. Walter Channing, *The Mental Status of Czolgosz* (Brookline, Mass: American Journal of Insanity, Vol. LIX, No. 2, 1902) 28.

[199] *Buffalo Courier,* 28 October 1901, pg. 1, col. 3.

The Rev. Cordello Herrick, the prison chaplain, also waited for a call from the prisoner. But it was a call that Leon Czolgosz never made.

A few minutes before seven, the witnesses who had assembled throughout the preceding hour, were told to file into the execution chamber. They took their seats near the electric chair. Behind the large iron door, the Warden's assistants prepared Czolgosz for death.

In the chamber, electrician Davis tested the chair, having hooked up lights that got bright with the current, a display not lost on the witnesses.

After they were seated, Warden Mead addressed the witnesses.

"You are here to witness the legal death of Leon F. Czolgosz," he said. "I desire that you keep your seats and preserve absolute silence in the death chamber, no matter what may transpire. There are plenty of guards and prison officials to preserve order and attend to the proper details."[200]

Doctors Gerin and MacDonald took their places to the left of the chair. Warden Mead stood directly in front. Electrician Davis went into the small room where the switchboard was located. Upon receiving a signal, he turned on the current, flooding the room with light. An assistant put two electrodes lined with sponge in two pails of water, in order to assure that the current would not burn the victim's flesh.[201]

At 7:10, Warden Mead gave the signal to bring the prisoner in. Chief Keeper Tupper swung open the door and Leon Czolgosz was led into the room, which was only a few steps from his cell. He had guards on each side, with two walking behind, and Tupper walking in front. As he stepped over the threshold Czolgosz stumbled. He stumbled again on the little rubber-covered platform on which the chair rested, each time being supported by the guards.[202]

Warden Mead claimed that the guards "had virtually to carry him to the chair, he so nearly collapsed.[203]

The electric chair was plain looking and seemingly built for strength. It had wide leather straps and heavy buckles. From the ceiling came a coil of wire no wider than a common pencil to which the electrode for the headpiece would attach. Electric lamps were along the wall behind the chair and about the ceiling. The chair was large enough to hold a

[200] *New York Times,* 30 October 1901, pg. 5, col. 2.

[201] *New York Times,* 30 October 1901, pg. 5, col. 2.

[202] *New York Times,* 30 October 1901, pg. 5, col. 2.

[203] L. Vernon Briggs, *The Manner of Man That Kills* (Boston: R. G. Badger, Gorham Press, 1921) 263.

man much heavier than Czolgosz, so a broad plank was placed on its edge across the seat and against the back of the chair, that there might not be any movement of the prisoner's body to break the circuit. The chair was situated near the north wall of the death chamber, facing south. Czolgosz would be the sixteenth person to die in this particular chair, with another scheduled to die the following Monday for killing his sweetheart.[204]

Czolgosz was pale and his lip quivered perceptively as he was place into the chair. His eyes seemed to be searching for the people to address.

Just before the electrocution was to begin, a leather-backed sponge soaked with salt water was tightly buckled below the knees, and on the head was placed a helmet, the top of which was filled with a wet sponge. The top of Czolgosz's head was not shaved so that perfect electrical contact could be made. At times, this is needed, but in the case of Czolgosz, it was not.[205]

"Just as he reached the platform he started to make, the warden thought, a speech, but was hurried to the chair, the straps placed on his head, face and chin, while he was yet talking, the last sentence being rather mumbled than spoken." [206]

As he was strapped into the chair, John Ross recorded Czolgosz's last words in shorthand as follows:

"I shot the President because I thought it would help the working people and for the sake of the common people. I am not sorry for my crime. That is all I have to say."[207]

As the broad leather straps with a slit for the mouth and nose were being adjusted on his chin, some witnesses thought they heard him say, "I am awfully sorry because I did not see my father."[208]

"He said nothing until he was seated in the chair," remembered Dr. Grosvenor R. Trowbridge, a witness from Buffalo. "Then, while they were strapping him in and applying the electrodes, he leaned forward with his hands on the arms of the chair, and facing the witnesses in front

---

[204] Murat Halstead, *The Illustrious Life of William McKinley* (Privately Published) 465-466.

[205] Murat Halstead, *The Illustrious Life of William McKinley* (Privately Published) 467.

[206] Dr. Walter Channing, *The Mental Status of Czolgosz* (Brookline, Mass: American Journal of Insanity, Vol. LIX, No. 2, 1902) 28.

[207] Dr. Walter Channing, *The Mental Status of Czolgosz* (Brookline, Mass: American Journal of Insanity, Vol. LIX, No. 2, 1902) 27.

[208] Dr. Walter Channing, *The Mental Status of Czolgosz* (Brookline, Mass: American Journal of Insanity, Vol. LIX, No. 2, 1902) 28.

of him, made his last speech. It was very short. I listened intently and I am sure of every word he said and the order in which he placed his words. These are all the words he spoke and just as he spoke them:

'I killed the President for the good of the laboring people, the good people. I am not sorry for my crime but I am sorry I can't see my father."[209]

Witness accounts of the electrocution vary. Some said Czolgosz screamed and swore, while others said he was calm until Warden Mead gave the signal to switch on the 1800 volts. Most published reports said that Czolgosz was calm at the execution. But Dr. Gerin, Warden Mead and John Ross all agreed that Leon "went all to pieces at the hour of execution, and that his face was the picture of abject terror." Dr. Gerin said that Czolgosz was "filled with fear and showed it."[210]

At 7:12:30, Electrician Davis turned on the current.

"The rush of the immense current threw the body so hard against the straps that they creaked perceptively," reported the *New York Times*. "The hands clinched suddenly, and the whole attitude was one of extreme tension. For forty-five seconds the full current was kept on, and then slowly, the electrician threw the switch back, reducing the current volt by volt until it was cut off entirely."

The time of death was recorded as 7:12 a.m. Dr. MacDonald checked his pulse, and suggested another surge of electricity. Two minutes later, Warden Mead pronounced him dead. From the time Czolgosz left his cell until he was dead, only four minutes had elapsed.

Before the current was stopped, Superintendent Collins was the first of the witnesses to leave the room. He did not wait for the pronouncement of death, as he was feeling ill and did not wish to see the execution through.[211]

When all was over, the witnesses filed from the room, many of them visibly shaken, and the body of Leon Czolgosz which had been full of vigor just five minutes before, was taken placed upon the autopsy table. The prison soon went back to its daily routine.[212]

[209] *Buffalo Express,* 30 October 1901.

[210] L. Vernon Briggs, *The Manner of Man That Kills* (Boston: R. G. Badger, Gorham Press, 1921) 263.

[211] *Buffalo Evening News,* 29 October 1901, pg. 1, col. 3.

[212] *Buffalo Evening News,* 29 October 1901, pg. 1, col. 3.

In Cleveland a small group of men gathered around the local Associated Press wire machine. The group included Paul Czolgosz, two of Leon's brothers and half a dozen of his former neighbors. When told that Leon had said he had wished he could have seen his father, Paul Czolgosz replied that he would have gone, but he was under the impression that he was not wanted. The assassin's father also said that he would not have been a witness to the execution. Some thought there was the slight tear in the father's eye, but other than that, the group held up well. After hearing the news, Paul Czolgosz went to work in the city park and the Czolgosz brothers headed off for their jobs as well.[213]

Leon Czolgosz was buried in a black stained pine coffin, in the prison cemetery at Auburn Prison. His brother Waldek had arranged it, and as a part of the agreement, the entire body would be buried there. He had originally wanted to take the body back to Cleveland, but Warden Mead, suspicious that the Czolgosz's would sell the body, convinced Waldek that if he tried that, he would be mobbed. Waldek later wondered if the body had indeed been buried. The Chief of Police in Cleveland, worried about crowds should the body be returned to Cleveland, urged Warden Mead to keep the body there.

"I did not see it and I don't believe what I do not see," Waldek said later.

Waldek had been put off numerous times by prison officials at Auburn in his efforts to view his brother's body. He had been told he could see it immediately after the execution, then after the doctors were finished with it, then just before burial. Finally, when he arrived at the prison about 2 p.m., they told him it was too late and that Leon had already been buried. Waldek felt he had been tricked into signing the agreement.[214]

The agreement read:

"Auburn, New York, October 28, 1901—J. Warren Mead, agent and warden of Auburn Prison—I hereby authorize you as warden of Auburn Prison to dispose of the body of my brother, Leon F. Czolgosz, by burying it in the cemetery attached to the prison as provided for by the law of the State of New York.

"This request is made upon the express understanding that no part of the remains will be given to any person or society, but that the entire body will be buried in accordance with the law in the cemetery attached

[213] *Buffalo Evening News,* 29 October 1901, pg. 7, col. 1.
[214] L. Vernon Briggs, *The Manner of Man That Kills* (Boston: R. G. Badger, Gorham Press, 1921) 310.

to the prison. Waldek Czolgosz, Witnesses John A. Sleicher, George E. Graham."[215]

All of the assassin's clothing and belongings were burned. As a last act of disgrace, sulfuric acid was dropped onto the body after it had been lowered into the grave. Doctors said the corpse would disintegrate within twelve hours.[216]

But there were those who wondered whether the execution and disposal of Czolgosz might have been too hasty.

"Czolgosz should have been kept alive under durance and scientific psychological surveillance," wrote Dr. Charles Hughes, "as the botanist would keep a newly-found exotic, until more might have been learned of his strange mental make-up, in order that our political future might profit by a better understanding of those anomalous integers and epochs of our anomalous present and recent past, when our Presidents have been slain by citizens."[217]

"Just consider that within about six weeks of the death of his distinguished victim Czolgosz has been executed for his crime," said Superintendent Collins proudly. "He was regularly tried, convicted, sentenced and executed and despite the fact that the law compelled us to give him four weeks to prepare for death the time was wonderfully short for our system of punishing criminals."[218]

Leon Czolgosz was the 50th person to die in the electric chair in the state of New York.

---

[215] *New York Times,* 29 October 1901, pg. 1, col. 5.

[216] A. Wesley Johns, *The Man Who Shot McKinley* (New York: A. S. Barnes and Co., Inc., 1970) 248.

[217] L. Vernon Briggs, *The Manner of Man That Kills* (Boston: R. G. Badger, Gorham Press, 1921) 339.

[218] *New York Times,* 29 October 1901, pg. 1, col. 5.

I killed President McKinley because I
done my duty. I didn't believe one
man should have so much service and another man
should have none.

[signed]
Leon F. Czolgosz

Auburn September 6th 1901.

Leon Czolgosz's signed confession

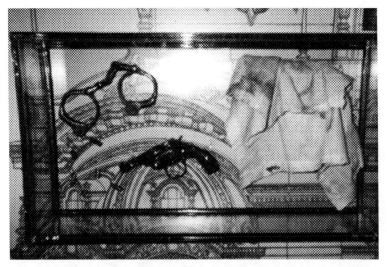

The gun, handkerchief, and cuffs on display during the 100th
Anniversary of the Pan American Exposition at the
Buffalo, NY Historical Society

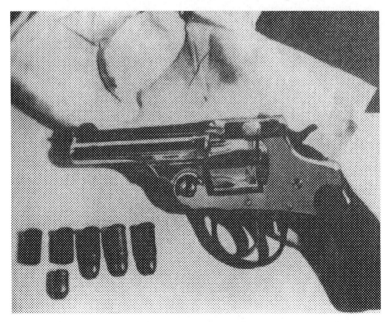

Original Buffalo, NY Police Photo of the Murder Weapon
and Handkerchief

The interior of the Temple of Music

The spot where the President was shot.

Buffalo City Hall

Erie County Jail

**Auburn Prison, where Czolgsz was held and executed.
Czolgosz's cell is marked with an 'x'.**

The execution room at Auburn Prison.

The Supreme Court courtroom where Leon Czolgosz was tried for
the murder of the President of the United States.

Warren Mead

Francis P. O'Brien

Thomas Penney

James B. Parker

Secret Service Agents Samuel Ireland (left) and George Foster.

James B. Parker

Emma Goldman

Judge Thomas C. White

Loran L. Lewis

Thomas Penney

Robert C. Titus

An artist's illustration of Leon Czolgosz in prison

Illustration showing Czolgosz being led to the death chamber.

7. The New President

At six o'clock in the morning of September 13, before the President experienced his fatal downturn, Vice President Theodore Roosevelt started out from the Tahawus Club in North Creek, New York, on a hunting trip through the woodlands of the Adirondack Mountains. Soon the news of President McKinley's condition reached the area, but the Vice President could not immediately be located. He was finally found about five o'clock in the evening atop Mount Marcy, where he received the dispatches to return at once to Buffalo. But what the Vice President read did not tell the true nature of the gravity of Mr. McKinley's plight. Another dispatch was sent to Roosevelt, describing better the President's condition and informing him that the President would not live. These reached the Vice President about 1:15 a.m. on Saturday, as President McKinley lay in his final moments of life.

Roosevelt immediately started out for the village of North Creek. The Adirondack Stage Company had established a relay of horses to enable the Vice President to cover the rugged ground as quickly as possible. The Vice President was located about thirty-five miles from North Creek and was driven at break-neck speed over those miles in the North Woods.[1] Orin Kellogg drove Roosevelt through the mountains to Aden Lair, where the Vice President jumped into another buckboard driven by Mike Cronin. Nicknamed the "Sphinx of the Mountains," Cronin was a burly man in his thirties who acted as the landlord of Aden Lair Lodge. When Kellogg pulled in, Cronin had been waiting for Roosevelt and he was ready.

"My! I made the last sixteen miles in one hour and forty three minutes," wrote Cronin, who drove the last leg of the Vice President's journey. "It was the darkest night I ever saw. I could not even see my horses, except the spots where the flickering lantern lights fell on them. This time beat the best record ever made before by a quarter of an hour, and that record I had made myself, with a two-seater, in daylight."[2]

In his pocket, Cronin carried a dispatch telling the news of President McKinley's death. He decided that if he gave the news to Roosevelt it would merely increase the Vice President's impatience and agitation. He decided to keep the news to himself until they arrived at North Creek.

---

[1] *New York Times*, 14 September 1901, pg. 1, col. 7.
[2] G. Townsend, *Memorial Life of William McKinley* (Washington: Memorial Publishing Co., 1901) 469.

"Did the President talk much? Very little about the situation," explained Cronin. "Most of the time he seemed to be deep in thought and very sad. About all the words he spoke were 'Keep up the pace.' He held his watch in his hand all the while, and kept continually asking how far we had come or how far we still had to go."[3]

"I tell you, Mr. Roosevelt is a nervy man," Cronin continued. "I shall never drive over that dark road again without seeming to hear him say, 'Push along! Hurry up! Go faster!'"[4]

A special fast train from the Delaware and Hudson Railroad, locomotive number 362, met the Vice President at North Creek, taking him from there to Saratoga and on to Albany. Company Superintendent C. D. Hammond took personal charge of the train. Roosevelt occupied coach number 200.

When Cronin and Roosevelt arrived at North Creek Station, the Vice President jumped out of the buckboard and one bound had him on the platform. His private secretary, William Loeb, met him and in hushed tones broke the news of McKinley's death. Roosevelt's face grew from anxious to sad as he listened. He then shook hands with Station Agent Campbell and rushed to his private car. The Vice President, Loeb and the conductor were the only ones on board.

The special train arrived in Albany at 8:04 a.m., and another special train took him on to Buffalo. The train sped past Syracuse at 10:00, past Rochester and a crowd of 50,000 that had turned out to meet him at 12:08, and arrived in Buffalo at 1:38 in the afternoon. [5]

The crowds in Buffalo awaited the arrival of Theodore Roosevelt, with many thousand waiting at the Exchange Street Station. In order to avoid the crowd, the train went on to the Terrace Station. Roosevelt leaped from the train, accompanied by twelve mounted patrolmen and several detectives, and dashed to a closed carriage driven by a coachman dressed in blue and white livery. He was met by Ansley Wilcox and General Roe and was immediately spirited to the home of Wilcox. As he left the station, three men leaped to his side. They were secret service agents.[6]

[3] G. Townsend, *Memorial Life of William McKinley* (Washington: Memorial Publishing Co., 1901) 469-470.

[4] G. Townsend, *Memorial Life of William McKinley* (Washington: Memorial Publishing Co., 1901) 470.

[5] G. Townsend, *Memorial Life of William McKinley* (Washington: Memorial Publishing Co., 1901) 471.

[6] G. Townsend, *Memorial Life of William McKinley* (Washington: Memorial Publishing Co., 1901) 472.

In route, a crowd of about 5,000 waited near the intersection of Allen and North Streets. At the Wilcox house, Roosevelt ate a light lunch and was brought up to date on the situation. The President was told that preparations had been made for him to take the oath of office and that it should be done immediately. Roosevelt agreed, but said that he first wanted to go to the Milburn house to pay his respects to President McKinley. He realized that he did not have a top hat, and John N. Scatcherd, who happened to wear the same size as Roosevelt, sent to his house for one. The President wore it throughout the day.[7]

Roosevelt was somewhat worried about the impression that would be left with the American people about his being on a hunting trip for pleasure at the time of the President's death. Accordingly, he had Secretary Loeb issue the following statement:

"The Vice President wishes it understood that when he left the Tahawus Club house yesterday morning, (September 13th) to go on his hunting trip into the mountains, he had just received a dispatch from Buffalo stating that President McKinley was in splendid condition and was not in the slightest danger."[8]

President Roosevelt came out of the Wilcox house about 2:30 p.m. for his trip to the Milburn house, and he saw the many soldiers and police that were acting as his guard. Among them were the Fourth Signal corps and two platoons of mounted police.

When Roosevelt saw this he called over Lieutenant Colonel Chapin and told him, "Colonel, tell your men that I don't want any escort. I only need two men—two policemen will do. I desire the military escort to remain here."[9]

Accompanied by Secretaries William Loeb and George L. Williams, the President was driven in a closed carriage guarded by three mounted policemen on either side. As the carriage pulled out, Roosevelt heard the hoof beats behind him and looked out of the carriage, thinking that the military was disobeying his orders.

"Hold on," the President told the coachman. Then he told the police officer in charge, "Sergeant, I do not want any escort to the Milburn house. Tell your men to stay here."[10] He then proceeded on with only an inconspicuous secret service detail riding in a carriage behind.

---

[7] G. Townsend, *Memorial Life of William McKinley* (Washington: Memorial Publishing Co., 1901) 472.

[8] G. Townsend, *Memorial Life of William McKinley* (Washington: Memorial Publishing Co., 1901) 467.

[9] G. Townsend, *Memorial Life of William McKinley* (Washington: Memorial Publishing Co., 1901) 473.

[10] G. Townsend, *Memorial Life of William McKinley* (Washington: Memorial Publishing Co., 1901) 47.

The spectators along the route knew the carriage contained Roosevelt and scattered applause could not be held back, however serious and solemn the occasion warranted. Upon arrival, Roosevelt crossed the Milburn lawn with head bowed and his hand to his face so the dozen or so photographers could not get a good picture, until he reached Secretary Cortelyou, who had come out to greet him. After inquiring of the condition of Mrs. McKinley, Roosevelt was lead to the upstairs room where Mr. McKinley rested.

Roosevelt stood silently with head bowed looking at the face of the fallen Chief Executive. After several minutes, he walked from the room with tears in his eyes, "and his strong frame shaking with convulsive sobs."[11]

It took the President some time to recompose himself, after which he met briefly with the cabinet members assembled in the Milburn house. After the meeting, Roosevelt quietly said to Secretary Root, "Let us take a little walk. It will do us both good."

As they walked onto the porch, Mr. Wilcox asked if he should go.

"No," replied the President. "I am going to take a short walk up the street with Secretary Root and will return again." He again shunned police protection, saying, "I do not want to set a precedent of going about guarded."[12]

Root and the new President attracted little attention as they walked until they neared the police lines on Delaware Avenue and Roosevelt shook hands with Root to say goodbye. Someone in the crowd recognized the President and Roosevelt was soon surrounded. The police drove the crowd back as Roosevelt realized that he could not help but attract attention. He went back to the Milburn house alone. He was then driven back to the Wilcox mansion, arriving shortly after 3 p.m.

Meanwhile, Secret Service Agent Foster was sending a telegram to his superior, John E. Wilkie in Washington.

"Mr. Cortelyou expects you to have a strong guard with the New President," Foster wrote. "He asked me impress this on you. No definite time set for leaving here."[13]

All of the Cabinet members were there, except Secretaries Hay and Gage, who were still in Washington. Also present were a number of other men and women. About a dozen cameramen stood about, but the

---

[11] *New York Times*, 15 September 1901, pg. 1, col. 7.

[12] G. Townsend, *Memorial Life of William McKinley* (Washington: Memorial Publishing Co., 1901) 474.

[13] George Foster. *Telegram to John E. Wilkie*. 14 September 1901, Buffalo, N. Y.

Vice President asked them to refrain from taking photographs and they complied with his wishes.

The library of the Wilcox home had been chosen for the place of swearing-in ceremony. It was a small, 18 by 25 feet room with a low ceiling. The room contained a bay window with green drapery and potted plants were artfully arranged. The general color of the room was green, but the walls were made up of well-filled bookcases. The only furniture in the room, other than the bookcases, was a library table and a few chairs.

Roosevelt was directed to the bay window alcove where he met and shook hands with Judge John R. Hazel, who would administer the oath. He was dressed in a long frock coat; waste coat buttoned high and not revealing much of the black silk tie. His pants were gray and a thin golden watch chain dangled across his waste coat. Secretaries Long, Hitchcock, Wilson, Root, Knox and Smith were assembled to his right. On his left were Ansley Wilcox, William Loeb, George Urban, Dr. Mann and Dr. Stockton. Also in the room were Secretary Cortelyou, John Milburn, Clerk George R. Keating of the U.S. District Court, Judge A. R. Haight, Senator Depew, John N. Scatcherd, George L. Williams, and about a score of reporters. In the doorway stood the wives; Mrs. Wilcox, Mrs. Milburn, Mrs. Mann, Mrs. Carleton Sprague and Mrs. Charles Carey. In all, there were forty-three people to witness the swearing-in of the new President.

Secretary Root approached Roosevelt and Judge Hazel and said, "Mr. Vice President, I have been requested by all the members of the Cabinet of the late President McKinley who are present in the City of Buffalo..."

As he referred to Mr. McKinley, an audible sigh was heard among those in attendance, forcing Root to stop briefly to clear his throat.

He continued, "Who are in the City of Buffalo and by all the members of the Cabinet who are not here, to request that, for reasons of weight affecting the administration of the Government, you should proceed without delay to take the Constitutional oath as President of the United States."

Roosevelt replied, "Mr. Secretary, I am one mind with the members of the Cabinet. I will show the people at once, in accordance with the request of the members of the Cabinet that the administration of the Government will not falter, in spite of the terrible National blow from which we are suffering.

"I wish to say that it will be my aim to continue, absolutely unbroken, the policy of President McKinley for the peace, the prosperity, and the honor of our beloved country," he added. While he said this, his voice never rose above a normal conversational tone.[14]

After a brief moment, Roosevelt turned and slightly bowed to Judge Hazel, giving him the signal that he was ready for the ceremony to begin.

With his right hand high in the air, Roosevelt repeated the oath after Judge Hazel in a voice so low that those farthest from him in the room could barely hear. His high-pitched voice showed nervousness but his words were stronger as he proceeded. By the time he reached his final touch, "And so I swear," his words were strong and forceful.[15] The oath was completed at exactly 3:30 p.m., only eight minutes after he had entered the Wilcox house.[16]

His hand dropped to his side, and President Roosevelt seemed almost to be praying for almost two minutes. Judge Hazel broke the silence, asking the President to sign the official document. Roosevelt turned to a small table off to the side and affixed his signature as "Theodore Roosevelt."

"I should like to see the members of the Cabinet a few moments after the others retire," commented the President.[17]

For a moment, no one moved, not wanting to be the first to break the silence after the oath. Finally, Secretary Root stepped forward and extended his hand.

"God bless you and keep you, Mr. President, and may you have every success," he said.

"I thank you from the bottom of my heart for your well wishes," replied the President.[18]

At that, the others present began to descend upon the President with similar greetings and good wishes. Within about four minutes, the President had spoken to each of the forty-three persons in attendance.

When John Milburn's son approached, the President recalled that a few days earlier he had promised the young man that he would accompany him on a fishing trip at some future date.

"I am afraid that we will have to postpone that fishing trip for some time," Roosevelt told him.[19]

---

[14]*New York Times*, 15 September 1901, pg. 2, col. 1.

[15] Nathan Miller, *Theodore Roosevelt: A Life* (New York: William Morrow & Co., 1992) 352.

[16]*New York Times*, 15 September 1901, pg. 2, col. 1.

[17] G. Townsend, *Memorial Life of William McKinley* (Washington: Memorial Publishing Co., 1901) 473.

[18]*New York Times*, 15 September 1901, pg. 2, col. 1.

[19]*New York Times*, 15 September 1901, pg. 2, col. 1.

Seeing another man with whom he was acquainted, Roosevelt said, "Ah, here is mine ancient enemy, but we are all of one mind and one heart in such a sad crisis as this."[20] To another, he lamented, "And to think that it was so short a time ago that you and I were trying to straighten out the police force of New York City."[21]

President Roosevelt then called Secretary Cortelyou aside and asked him to continue serving him as he had President McKinley. Cortelyou readily agreed.

Some of the people around him then suggested a group photograph be taken to mark the event. The new President agreed and several shots were taken.

President Roosevelt then attended a fifteen minute informal Cabinet meeting, at which no official business was discussed, other than to decide that no official Cabinet decisions need be made until after President McKinley's funeral.

Mark Hanna was the first visitor to the house after the ceremony. Roosevelt greeted him warmly.

"How do you do, Senator, I am glad to see you," he said.

"Mr. President," said Senator Hanna as his voice quivered. "Mr. President, I wish you success and a prosperous administration; I trust that you will command me if I can be of service."

The two men then clasped hands for a full minute but neither could say another word.[22]

"In the evening Senator Hanna, by arrangement came to call," remembered Roosevelt later. "The dead man had been his closest friend as well as the political leader whom he idolized and whose right hand he himself was. He had been occupying a position of power and influence, because of his joint relationship to the President and the Senate, such as no other man in our history whom I can recall ever occupied.

"He had never been very close to me, although of course we had worked heartily together when I was a candidate for Vice President and he was managing the campaign. But we had never been closely associated, and I do not think that he had at the time felt particularly drawn to me.

---

[20]*New York Times*, 15 September 1901, pg. 2, col. 1.

[21]*New York Times*, 15 September 1901, pg. 2, col. 1.

[22] G. Townsend, *Memorial Life of William McKinley* (Washington: Memorial Publishing Co., 1901) 478.

"As soon as he called on me, without beating around the bush, he told me that he had come to say that he would do all in his power to make my administration a success, and that, subject, of course, to my acting as my past career and my words that afternoon gave him the right to expect, he would in all ways endeavor to strengthen and uphold my hands."[23]

At his first official Cabinet meeting in Washington on September 17, Roosevelt asked each member of the McKinley team to stay on throughout his administration. He repeated his intention to continue with the McKinley policies, stating that the President's speech in Buffalo of September 5 would be considered the basis for that policy.[24]

As people greeted the new President, they generally wished him success. One reporter commented that he never once heard anyone congratulate the new President. There were no congratulations over President McKinley's death.[25]

Theodore Roosevelt passed a quiet evening in the Wilcox house his first night as President, dining late. New York Governor Benjamin B. Odell, Congressman Lucius Littauer of New York, and William Warden of Buffalo all called during the evening.

Roosevelt's first official act as President was to issue the following proclamation:

"A terrible bereavement has befallen our people. The President of the United States has been struck down; a crime committed not only against the Chief Magistrate, but against every law-abiding and liberty-loving citizen.

"President McKinley crowned a life of largest love for his fellowmen, of most earnest endeavor for their welfare, by a death of Christian fortitude; and both the way in which he lived his life and the way in which, in the supreme hour of trial, he met his death, will remain forever a precious heritage of our people.

"It is meet that we, as a nation, express our abiding love and reverence for his life, our deep sorrow for his untimely death.

"Now, therefore, I, Theodore Roosevelt, President of the United States of America, do appoint Thursday next, September 19, the day in which the body of the dead President will be laid in its last earthly resting place, as a day of mourning and prayer throughout the United States. I

---

[23] Herbert Croly, *Marcus Alonzo Hanna* (New York: The MacMillan Co., 1923) 360-361.
[24] *New York Times,* 18 September 1901, pg. 1, col. 3.
[25] G. Townsend, *Memorial Life of William McKinley* (Washington: Memorial Publishing Co., 1901) 478.

earnestly recommend all the people to assemble in their respective places of divine worship, there to bow down in submission to the will of Almighty God, and to pay out of full hearts their homage of love and reverence to the great and good President, whose death has smitten the nation with bitter grief.

"In witness whereof I have hereunto set my hand and caused the seal of the United States to be affixed.

"Done at the city of Washington, the 14th day of September, A.D., one thousand nine hundred and one, and of the Independence of the United States the one hundred and twenty-sixth.
"THEODORE ROOSEVELT"[26]

At forty-two, Theodore Roosevelt was the youngest man ever to serve as President up to that time and was the fifth to succeed to the Presidency due to the death of a sitting President. His strength of personality, bravery and vigor were known throughout the country.

"In a large and true sense Theodore Roosevelt is typical of the country over which he presides," wrote Avery D. Andrews, Roosevelt's Chief of Staff from his gubernatorial days, in *The Independent.* "Young, strong progressive and ambitious, yet steadied by a wide experience in public life and a conservatism which has grown as responsibilities have increased, he looks forward with confidence to the future, fully believing in all that is best in the American character to aid and support him in his work. He knows the weak as well as the strong epochs in our national career, and will profit to the utmost thereby. He represents no faction, and is bound by no ties or promises, except only his oath of office and his pledge to the whole people 'to continue, absolutely without variation, the policy of President McKinley for the peace, prosperity and honor of our beloved country.'"[27]

Avery also pointed out that among Roosevelt's strong points was his ability to accurately judge his associates.

"He knows the type of man he wants for each position at his disposal, and gets him if he possibly can. His record as Governor of the State of New York shows that, whatever his relations to a political party may be, he will never appoint a man whom he believes or suspects to be unfit for office. He fully appreciates that the Chief Executive of a great business or Government cannot do all the work, or even direct in person all of the

---

[26] G. Townsend, *Memorial Life of William McKinley* (Washington: Memorial Publishing Co., 1901) 480.

[27] Avery D. Andrews, "Theodore Roosevelt," *The Independent* (26 September 1901) 2274-2275.

work, for which he is ultimately responsible, and he therefore depends largely and properly upon his chosen advisors and assistants. He confides fully in those in whom he confides at all, and holds his appointees to a strict accountability for the tasks to which they have been assigned."[28]

When Theodore Roosevelt was born October 27, 1858 at 28 East Twentieth Street in New York, his mother Mittie looked at him and exclaimed, "He looks like a turtle." But "Teedie," as his father called him, was anything but turtle-like and he quickly began to wear out his mother and father with his mischief and energy.

His father, Theodore Roosevelt Sr. taught Teddy, as a young man, that each person had a duty to mankind. Theodore Sr. founded the Children's Aid Society and volunteered many hours at a lodging house for boys.

"I was brought up with the constant injunction to be active and industrious," said Roosevelt later. "My father, all my people, held that no one had a right to merely cumber the earth; that the most contemptible of created beings is the man who does nothing. I imbibed the idea that I must work hard, whether at making money or whatever. The whole family training taught me that I must be doing, must be working—and at decent work."[29]

During his youth, Roosevelt grew up in a house somewhat divided by the Civil War. His mother's family kept slaves, while his father disapproved. Theodore Sr. paid a substitute to fight in the war in his place, a common practice. He explained that he feared he would fight against Mittie's relatives.

Theodore Sr. did help the union cause by lobbying congressmen and even meeting with President Lincoln in support of a bill that encouraged soldiers to send part of their salaries to their families, many of whom had become destitute during the war.

In New York City, when he was only seven, Teddy watched the funeral procession of Abraham Lincoln pass beneath his window. In fact, there is a photo that many think show young Teddy Roosevelt watching the spectacle.

Teddy was a sickly child and suffered from asthma.

---

[28] Avery D. Andrews, "Theodore Roosevelt," *The Independent* (26 September 1901) 2276.
[29] Alexander K. McClure, *The Authentic Life of William McKinley* (W. E. Skull, 1901) 467.

"One of my memories is of my father walking up and down the room with me in his arms at night when I was a very small person, and of sitting up in bed gasping," he wrote later.[30]

At an early age Teddy developed an interest in natural history that would remain with him his entire life. He began a collection of rocks, fur, birds' wings and snakeskins, which he arranged on a shelf with a sign that read "The Roosevelt Museum of Natural History."[31] His "museum" would eventually number over one thousand items and he dreamed of being a zoologist. Once, during a family trip to the Middle East, Teddy preserved over 200 specimens of area animals and birds. After all, his father had helped to establish the American Natural History Museum. Few could accuse young Theodore Roosevelt of not being enthusiastic. And he was just as enthusiastic in his academic studies.

In the fall of 1878, Theodore met Alice Hathaway Lee, a beautiful tall blonde. After their third date, he decided he would marry her. They spent considerable time together, but when they were reunited after a summer apart, Alice showed little interest. But she changed her mind and on December 26, 1879 they resumed their courtship. Theodore proposed and Alice accepted.

Theodore wrote in his diary, "How she, so pure and sweet and beautiful can think of marrying me I cannot understand, but I praise and thank God it is so."[32]

The couple was married on October 27, 1880, on Theodore's twenty-second birthday, becoming members of New York's high society, frequently visiting the homes of the Astors and Vanderbilts. His father, who had become a multi-millionaire, left Theodore one hundred twenty-five thousand dollars, which earned him about eight thousand dollars in interest per year.[33] The result was that Roosevelt did not have to devote all his energies to making money, and was freer to choose a career path.

Roosevelt would eventually bring to the White House a background of preparation and accomplishment that was, perhaps, unequaled by any of his predecessors. Roosevelt was a devout student and master of

---

[30] Nancy Whitelaw, *Theodore Roosevelt Takes Charge* (Morton Grove, IL: Albert Whitman & Co., 1992) 17.

[31] Nancy Whitelaw, *Theodore Roosevelt Takes Charge* (Morton Grove, IL: Albert Whitman & Co., 1992) 18.

[32] Nancy Whitelaw, *Theodore Roosevelt Takes Charge* (Morton Grove, IL: Albert Whitman & Co., 1992) 32.

[33] Nancy Whitelaw, *Theodore Roosevelt Takes Charge* (Morton Grove, IL: Albert Whitman & Co., 1992) 32.

American political history and graduated from Harvard University in 1880.

H. E. Armstrong, a correspondent for the *New York Sun* during the Cuban campaign, remembered Roosevelt from his Harvard days, seeing him in a boxing class where he was being soundly beaten by a bigger man. The man asked Roosevelt if they should stop.

"Roosevelt showed his teeth in a strenuous smile and shook his head with the motion of a terrier worrying a rat," Armstrong described, "and rushed at the big man as soon as he put up his hands. The result was never in doubt, but it made no difference to Roosevelt."[34]

"When I was in Harvard and sparred for the championship," Roosevelt later remembered, "I suffered a heavier punishment than any man there did, and I have been knocked out at polo twice. I thoroughly believe in boxing and football, and other rough and manly games."[35]

Roosevelt entered politics as a Republican, as his father had been a Republican. The Republican Party of the time was strongly for a united country. In New York, the Democrats of Tammany Hall, while dominating state politics, stole millions of dollars. This corruption infuriated Roosevelt, and he entered politics determined to do something about it.

"I have always believed that every man should join a political organization and should attend the primaries; that he should not be content to be merely governed, but should do his part of that work," remembered Roosevelt. "So after leaving college I went to the local political headquarters, attended all the meetings and took my part in whatever came up. There arose quite a revolt against the member of Assembly from the district, and I was nominated to succeed him, and was elected."[36]

He began to work with the Republican Club, a group of working men who had joined together to choose and work for candidates. Though at first scorned by some because of his wealth, he won their trust and was endorsed and elected to the New York Assembly in 1881, the same year James Garfield was assassinated.

He became somewhat famous as a reformer when he demanded an investigation of Republican State Supreme Court Justice T. R. Westbrook. Roosevelt thought the judge had used his position to

---

[34] H. E. Armstrong, "Theodore Roosevelt as a Volunteer Soldier, *The Independent* (26 September 1901) 2277.

[35] *New York Times*, 14 September 1901, pg. 2, col. 5.

[36] Alexander K. McClure, *The Authentic Life of William McKinley* (W. E. Skull, 1901) 467-468.

embezzle thousands of dollars for him and friends. His subsequent investigation proved the charges to be true.

While his attack of a fellow Republican angered those in his own party, Roosevelt forged a reputation as a straight shooter and idealist. Politicians from both parties thought he involved himself in issues that were none of his concern. But Roosevelt saw government service as an opportunity for more than just lining his own pockets.

During this time, he also published a book about the War of 1812, and donated some 600 wildlife specimens to the Smithsonian Institution. Theodore Roosevelt was always busy.

New York Governor Grover Cleveland asked Roosevelt to help end the spoils system in the state. Roosevelt introduced and got passed a bill that forced the state to hire ten percent of its workers from written tests and protected government workers from being fired for anything short of incompetence.

Roosevelt made a trip to the Badlands in 1883 to shoot a buffalo. His love of the outdoors motivated him to purchase a cattle ranch, the Maltese Cross, in what is now North Dakota. Later he purchased another with a thousand heads of cattle, the Elkhorn.

He returned to the New York Assembly in the fall of 1883 and resumed his work fighting government corruption in New York. On February 13, 1884 he received a telegram informing him of the birth of his daughter, Alice Lee, the night before. A few hours later he received a second telegram informing him that both his wife Alice and his mother, who lived together, were seriously ill. He immediately rushed to New York City, arriving after midnight to find his wife in a coma and dying of kidney failure. Two hours later he learned that his mother was dying as well, of typhoid fever. He went to her side and spent an hour with her before she died at three in the morning. He then rushed back to his wife's bedside. At two o'clock in the afternoon, Alice Roosevelt also died.

At twenty-five, Roosevelt was a widower. He wrote in his diary, "The light has gone out of my life."[37]

Roosevelt was stunned throughout the funeral. He accepted his sister's offer to look after the new baby and returned to Albany the day after the funeral saying, "There is nothing left for me except to try to so live as not to dishonor the memory of those I loved who have gone before me."[38]

---

[37] Nancy Whitelaw, *Theodore Roosevelt Takes Charge* (Morton Grove, IL: Albert Whitman & Co., 1992) 49.

[38] Nancy Whitelaw, *Theodore Roosevelt Takes Charge* (Morton Grove, IL: Albert Whitman & Co., 1992) 49.

Roosevelt served three terms in the New York Assembly, eventually as Minority Leader. He was the New York delegation chairman at the Chicago Republican convention in 1884, making a name for himself when he refused to follow the Republican leadership and support incumbent president Chester A. Arthur or Maine Senator James Blaine for president. Instead he stubbornly backed Senator George Edmunds of Vermont. Blaine eventually won the nomination with Roosevelt supporting him in the fall.

In June, Roosevelt refused a forth term as an assemblyman and instead took a trip to the Bad Lands. There he again enjoyed the rugged outdoor life of a ranchman, going on frequent hunting trips. During the next two years, he continued to write. He wrote two more books during this period, *Hunting Trips of a Ranchman* and the *Life of Thomas Hart Benton*. Roosevelt remained in the west for two years, rekindling his body and spirit. During that time he had been making frequent trips to New York, visiting his daughter Alice. He was also courting his childhood friend, Edith Carow. Roosevelt had proposed and Edith had accepted. Roosevelt was ready to return to the east for a family life and a public life.

Upon his return to New York, Roosevelt was urged by fellow Republicans to run for mayor of New York City. Roosevelt thought it hopeless, but he ran for the post in 1886, often campaigning eighteen hours a day, and was defeated by ex-Mayor Hewitt.

After the defeat he sailed to England with Edith Carow on December 2, 1886 where they married. After a honeymoon of fifteen weeks, they returned to a house Roosevelt had started for Alice at Oyster Bay, New York. They called the twenty-eight-room house Sagamore Hill.

Roosevelt had no job and, with Sagamore Hill expenses high, needed to support his family. After a freezing winter out west in which two thirds of his cattle were lost, Roosevelt sold his property in the Bad Lands for a loss of seventy thousand dollars. He then turned to writing for income. In three months in 1887, he researched and wrote a biography of American Revolutionary statesman Gouverneur Morris. In September of 1887, the Roosevelt's had their first child, Theodore Roosevelt, Jr.

Roosevelt made a five-week trip to the west and discovered that the animals were endangered because of the rapid expansion in the area, the unregulated trapping and hunting, and the severe weather of the previous winter. He, along with a few other men, formed the Boone and Crockett

Club. This was the very first conservationist club in America. Their goal was to keep large portions of the west free from development and to protect the forests from lumbering interests.

Roosevelt continued to earn a living writing, doing many articles and books. He worked seven years on a series, *Winning the West*, which covered the period from Daniel Boone to Davy Crockett. In his spare time, he campaigned for Benjamin Harrison for President.

As a result and because of his work against the spoils system in New York, in 1889, Roosevelt was appointed by newly elected President Benjamin Harrison as a member of the United States Civil Service Commission, on which he served with distinction until 1895. It was looked at as being a minor job of little importance. But Theodore Roosevelt thought no job unimportant.

Ironically, it had been the assassination of President Garfield by a disappointed job seeker that had precipitated a movement to eliminate patronage. The Pendleton act of 1883 established the Civil Service Commission with three commissioners who over-saw the hiring and firing of government workers. Since its inception the commission had been complacent. Theodore Roosevelt changed that. After quickly learning the rules of hiring and firing, he shot letters off to hundreds of officials telling them that the rules would be followed.

In 1890, Roosevelt went about the work of cleaning up patronage violations in the United States Post Office. After the election of Harrison, about thirty thousand Democratic postmasters had been fired, with Republicans installed in their places. He sent a report to Congress describing literally thousands of violations. Congressmen were forced to admit that Roosevelt was correct and he earned a reputation across the country as a fearless government reformer.

Meanwhile Roosevelt's family was growing. On October 10, 1889, Kermit, Roosevelt's second son, was born. In August of 1891, Ethel Roosevelt, his second daughter was born. That winter the brood moved from New York to Washington to live. Benjamin Harrison was running for reelection against Grover Cleveland, and Roosevelt figured that no matter who won, he and his family would be headed back to Sagamore Hill. But upon election, Grover Cleveland asked Roosevelt to stay in his position.

In 1894 Archibald was born, Roosevelt's fifth child. That same year, Roosevelt's brother Elliot, after a long battle with alcoholism, committed suicide. In October, Roosevelt reluctantly turned down his party's nomination for mayor of New York City because of his wife's wishes.

Theodore Roosevelt left his Civil Service job in Washington and went back to New York City, being appointed President of the Board of Police Commissioners in 1895 by New York City Mayor William Strong, serving in that capacity for two years. He inherited a police department that was filled with corruption, complete with internal and external bribery and extortion. Ever the reform specialist, Roosevelt would patrol the streets night after night making sure officers were patrolling their beats rather than off somewhere sleeping. He took along a reporter, Jacob Riis, and newspaper readers enjoyed the escapades. Riis's stories served to enhance Roosevelt's reputation. He even found evidence of wrongdoing by another Commissioner, Andrew Parker, who was reluctantly dismissed by the mayor for accepting a four hundred-dollar bribe from a job seeker.

Roosevelt, while retaining his job as police commissioner, campaigned vigorously for fellow Republican William McKinley for President.

Theodore Roosevelt was then called back to Washington in 1897, and was named Assistant Secretary of the Navy by President McKinley, a post he held during the preparations for the Spanish-American War.

McKinley had had reservations about naming Roosevelt to the post. He worried about him being a "jingo," as war advocates were then called. He thought he might be too aggressive for the position. Roosevelt was fully aware that war with Spain was a possibility and immediately began preparing for it.

In a speech to the Naval War College, Roosevelt's fiery words seemed to confirm fears about him. Roosevelt claimed in the speech that war would only vanish in some distant age and that, in his view diplomacy was a waste of time, there being no force behind it. He advocated a strong navy and that no national life was worth having unless that nation was willing to risk everything in war.[39]

Overlooking Roosevelt's fiery rhetoric, Senator Henry Cabot Lodge continued to push for the appointment, after having first approached McKinley about Roosevelt in Canton.

Secretary of the Navy John D. Long, when asked about the possible appointment, worried with good reason that within six months Roosevelt would be dominating the Navy Department.[40]

---

[39] G. J. A. O'Toole, *The Spanish War: An American Epic 1898* (New York: W. W. Norton & Co., 1984) 96.

[40] G. J. A. O'Toole, *The Spanish War: An American Epic 1898* (New York: W. W. Norton & Co., 1984) 85.

Roosevelt eventually received the nomination with the help of Senator Thomas C. Platt, who thought Roosevelt would cause him less trouble in Washington than in New York City.

Roosevelt brought with him the vigor he had displayed in other jobs. Secretary Long allowed his under-secretary the freedom to virtually run the Navy Department. Within two months Roosevelt was publicly calling for a strengthening of the navy using George Washington's axiom, that to prepare for war was to secure the peace.[41]

Navy Secretary Long took one of his frequent vacations away from Washington and Roosevelt revealingly confided to a friend that we was having great fun running the Navy.[42]

After Long had been gone about three weeks, Roosevelt wrote him, urging him to stay away for as long as he wished. There was no reason to return until October unless something unexpected occurred and all was running smoothly, Roosevelt wrote.[43]

In Long's absence, Roosevelt was thrilled to be asked to join President McKinley in a carriage ride. McKinley was worried about war with Spain over Cuba. Roosevelt told him that the Navy Department needed advance warning if any action was to occur. But if there was to be a war, Roosevelt assured the President, he would guarantee that the navy would be ready.

Roosevelt then told the President that if war indeed came that he did not intend to sit it out in Washington. McKinley asked what Mrs. Roosevelt thought about that, and Roosevelt told him that in this one instance, he did not intend to consult his wife, or even the President. McKinley laughed and told him he thought he could make sure he saw action if the war came.[44]

Two days later, Roosevelt was invited to dinner at the White House. The next week, President McKinley again asked Roosevelt to join him in a carriage ride.

Roosevelt had been studying contingency plans for war with Spain. During the ride, he talked naval strategy with the President, even bringing along a map of Cuba for illustrative purposes.

---

[41] Nancy Whitelaw, *Theodore Roosevelt Takes Charge* (Morton Grove, IL: Albert Whitman & Co., 1992) 82.

[42] G. J. A. O'Toole, *The Spanish War: An American Epic 1898* (New York: W. W. Norton & Co., 1984) 101.

[43] G. J. A. O'Toole, *The Spanish War: An American Epic 1898* (New York: W. W. Norton & Co., 1984) 101.

[44] G. J. A. O'Toole, *The Spanish War: An American Epic 1898* (New York: W. W. Norton & Co., 1984) 101.

Roosevelt showed McKinley the exact positioning of the American ships and told the President what he thought ought to be done if Spain seemed threatening, urging the taking of immediate and prompt action if McKinley wished to avoid some serious trouble, and to keep Japan from entering into the situation. Roosevelt wrote Cabot Lodge about the talk during the ride, saying that he doubted if the war would last six weeks. He also thought that the Asiatic Squadron should blockade, and if possible take, Manila.[45]

Roosevelt was also instrumental in getting Civil War Veteran George Dewey appointed as head of the Asiatic command. He intercepted a letter from Senator William E. Chandler of New Hampshire recommending Commodore John A. Howell for the post. Roosevelt did not approve, thinking Howell "irresolute" and "afraid of responsibility." Roosevelt immediately began pushing for Dewey, and with the help of Senator Redfield Proctor of Vermont, the President through Navy Secretary Long requested Dewey for the post. Long had been leaning toward Howell, but Roosevelt had circumvented the channels to get his man appointed, ruffling some feathers in the process.[46]

When reports came out of Cuba of Spanish mistreatment of Cubans and Americans, Roosevelt was characteristically quick to urge war. He wanted the United States to send the navy to the Philippine Islands to establish a naval base. Likewise, he supported the annexation of the Hawaiian Islands for the same purpose in the Pacific. Roosevelt was criticized by many as being too quick to go to war.

The yellow journals of the day sent stories from Cuba that were sensational and seldom true. Roosevelt and many Americans believed the reports. Roosevelt continued to pressure for the building of more battleships and the training of troops for possible confrontation.

In January of 1898, President McKinley sent the battleship *U. S. S. Maine* into Havana Harbor, where it exploded. Roosevelt thought the explosion was "an act of dirty treachery on the part of the Spaniards."

Left in charge of the Navy Department for an afternoon while Long was away, Roosevelt ordered Commander Dewey to prepare for war with Spain. Dewey was told to allow no Spanish ships to leave the Pacific and head for Cuba. He sent similar orders to other officers and ordered huge supplies of ammunition, and even requested Congress to

---

[45] G. J. A. O'Toole, *The Spanish War: An American Epic 1898* (New York: W. W. Norton & Co., 1984) 101.

[46] G. J. A. O'Toole, *The Spanish War: An American Epic 1898* (New York: W. W. Norton & Co., 1984) 102-3)

authorize the recruitment of more sailors. When Long returned he vowed never to leave Roosevelt in charge again, but changed no orders.[47]

The Senate investigated the explosion of the *Maine* and could not fix the blame. Later in 1976, it was found that a fire that ignited the Maine's ammunition had caused the explosion. President McKinley accepted the fact that the Spaniards may not have attacked the American ship. This infuriated Roosevelt.

"McKinley has no more backbone than a chocolate éclair!" Roosevelt exclaimed.[48]

In spite of no evidence of Spanish involvement in the sinking of the *Maine*, and despite Spanish assistance in fishing the survivors out of Havana Harbor, the yellow journals stirred up American sentiment to the point that President McKinley could no longer ignore it. At the end of April, McKinley requested that Congress declare war on Spain. Congress consented.

Immediately, Roosevelt resigned as Assistant Secretary of the Navy to go and fight in Cuba. Secretary Long disagreed with his decision. He thought that his resignation would not be of benefit to the Navy Department and that he was much more valuable there than in the field. Long thought that Roosevelt was acting a fool and that he had lost his mind. He knew his heart was right, but he felt he was misguided.[49]

Regardless, Secretary of War Russell Alger offered the command of a regiment of volunteers to Roosevelt, but Roosevelt, citing his inexperience, requested that his friend Leonard Wood be given the command. This was done; Wood was named colonel, with Roosevelt as a lieutenant colonel.

Roosevelt, of course, served in the war, becoming a household name for his escapades with the "Rough Riders." What vaulted Roosevelt to national prominence more than anything else, were his actions during the Spanish-American War.

On May 15, Roosevelt, decked out in a uniform he had designed himself, met his troop of volunteers in San Antonio, Texas for training. The press dubbed the regiment the "Rough Riders" because of informal attitude and lack of military experience. Roosevelt quickly whipped

---

[47] Nancy Whitelaw, *Theodore Roosevelt Takes Charge* (Morton Grove, IL: Albert Whitman & Co., 1992) 89.

[48] Nancy Whitelaw, *Theodore Roosevelt Takes Charge* (Morton Grove, IL: Albert Whitman & Co., 1992) 89.

[49] G. J. A. O'Toole, *The Spanish War: An American Epic 1898* (New York: W. W. Norton & Co., 1984) 195.

them into shape, thrilled to be a part of the exciting times. In early June, they left for Cuba.

Roosevelt and his men had barely landed in Cuba when they came under fire at Guasimas. During the battle a rumor spread that the commanding officer, Colonel Wood, had been killed. Lieutenant-Colonel Roosevelt said that he would assume command and order the entire regiment to advance, but first he wanted conformation that Wood had indeed been killed. He sent out a soldier to find out, and when he was receiving the report that it was true, an unharmed Wood came riding up, much to Roosevelt's relief. Wood then ordered Roosevelt to take his men and continue his advance, which he immediately did.

"At every halt we took advantage of the cover, sinking down behind any mound, bush or tree-trunk in the neighborhood," wrote Roosevelt. "The trees, of course, furnished no protection from the Mauser bullets. Once I was standing behind a large palm, with my head out to one side, very fortunately, for a bullet passed through the palm, filling my left eye and ear with the dust and splinters." [50]

In spite of heavy losses, Roosevelt charged his men up Kettle Hill. At the top, he began firing on the Spanish who held San Juan Hill. San Juan Hill was a strategic stronghold with a view of Santiago Harbor. Roosevelt ordered his men to charge the hill. Up the hill they rushed, through a stream and over a wire fence, dodging enemy bullets the entire way.

"When we came to make the final charge that took this possession, some of the officers wanted to fall back and leave it in possession of the Spaniards, but Colonel Roosevelt pulled his pistol and said: 'You can fall back if you want to, but my men will hold it till the last man dies,'" wrote Rough Rider Will T. Palmers in a letter home. "We held it and did not die, either...we fought ninety hours without sleep or rest." [51]

When it was over, Roosevelt held San Juan Hill with Santiago Harbor below. The army joined the navy and successfully blockaded the harbor. After a siege of three weeks, the Spanish in Santiago surrendered.

After the battle, a writer was trying to get the true story of what had happened, and Roosevelt was more than happy to give him the details, even referring him to others for confirmation. Roosevelt, with his high

---

[50] Alexander K. McClure, *The Authentic Life of William McKinley* (W. E. Skull, 1901) 477.

[51] Alexander K. McClure, *The Authentic Life of William McKinley* (W. E. Skull, 1901) 478.

profile government experience, was used to being interviewed, while Colonel Wood was not. Usually, it was Roosevelt who talked to the reporters and those back home read the stories.

"I have heard army officers say that Colonel Roosevelt, who commanded the Rough Riders at San Juan, claimed too much credit for himself on July 1, and did no more than his duty," wrote H. E. Armstrong. "He would be the last person to take issue with them on this latter point, for his conception of the performance of duty is that a man must always do his best. There is no doubt that he led the charge of the cavalry on Kettle Hill, and but for his resolution to move forward when other officers had halted their men and were waiting for orders the hill might have remained in the possession of the Spaniards for some time after Ford's infantry had taken San Juan hill, the key to the enemy's position."[52]

At one point during the charge, Roosevelt was seen arguing with another officer in command of a battalion at the front. One of the Rough Riders heard him say, "If you have no orders to advance, let me and my men through. I will take the responsibility."[53]

Roosevelt was prominent in the charge on San Juan Hill and General Sumner who had witnessed Roosevelt's 'headlong bravery," recommended him for the Congressional Medal of Honor.

"I would sooner have that medal to transmit to my children than any promotion in rank," Roosevelt declared.[54]

Early in the morning of July 2, Roosevelt had a bomb burst over his head, wounding the two officers who were with him. He immediately ordered everyone under cover, taking none himself. Later that evening, he stubbornly stood on a ridge while deadly fire burst all around him.

On August 12, Spain agreed to give up control of Cuba. Also transferred to United States control were Guam and Puerto Rico. Spain also agreed to allow the United States to occupy Manila in the Philippine Islands until a more permanent arrangement could be worked out. This was important to the future of the United States in its quest to become a world power, and these countries became the nation's first overseas territories.[55]

---

[52] H. E. Armstrong, "Theodore Roosevelt as a Volunteer Soldier," *The Independent* (26 Sept 1901) 2278.

[53] H. E. Armstrong, "Theodore Roosevelt as a Volunteer Soldier," *The Independent* (26 Sept 1901) 2279-2280.

[54] H. E. Armstrong, "Theodore Roosevelt as a Volunteer Soldier," *The Independent* (26 Sept 1901) 2281.

[55] Nancy Whitelaw, *Theodore Roosevelt Takes Charge* (Morton Grove, IL: Albert Whitman & Co., 1992) 94.

When the regiment returned to New York on August 15, a reporter asked Roosevelt if he would be the state's next governor. Roosevelt was surprised, but refused to talk about anything but the regiment. After a brief quarantine because of yellow fever contracted by many of the troops, Roosevelt left for Sagamore Hill. There he was met by a swarm of reporters and soon it was obvious that he would indeed become New York's next governor. The people wanted him and the politicians knew it. Roosevelt, during the campaign that followed made the most of his new found military fame, with six Rough Riders in full uniform accompanying him everywhere.

On November 8, 1898, he was elected governor by eighteen thousand votes.

The new governor immediately became embroiled in an internal party conflict. Senator Thomas Platt, called "Boss Platt" because of his ranking in the Republican Party, expected Roosevelt to reward Republicans with state jobs. Roosevelt, as always, thought they should awarded on merit. Platt wanted to reappoint Louis Payn, a man who Roosevelt knew had used his position to secure a half million-dollar loan. Roosevelt told Platt that he could choose from among three other men for the position and Platt refused. Roosevelt then told Platt that if he did not make a choice in three days, he would have no choice in the matter. Platt threatened never to support Roosevelt again if he did not choose Payn, and Roosevelt called his bluff. Platt finally accepted and made his choice.

Roosevelt would have ran for re-election to that post, but was convinced to accept the Vice Presidential nomination of his party as the running mate of William McKinley.

Actually New York politicians had had enough of Roosevelt, and many worked behind the scenes as much to get him out of New York as anything. His investigations, charges, and reforms had rocked too many boats. McKinley needed a Vice President, but wanted the convention to choose the candidate, and with Roosevelt's intense popularity it looked like they could get him out of New York politics once and for all. Actually the Vice Presidency represented a two thousand-dollar per year pay cut for Roosevelt, and Edith liked living in the Governor's Mansion. But of course, the Vice Presidency offered too great a challenge for Roosevelt not to accept.

There was an attempt involving Senator Marcus Hanna to try to keep Roosevelt off the Republican ticket. Pennsylvania political boss Matthew Quay and Roosevelt's old New York nemesis Tom Platt were trying to orchestrate a stampede to force Roosevelt onto the ticket. Hanna was infuriated and wanted it blocked, and said he would refuse to be the Republican Party Chairman if they succeeded. Charles Dawes phoned McKinley and Cortelyou, explaining the situation. McKinley issued an ultimatum to Hanna, dictating it to Dawes who delivered it to Hanna.[56]

"The President's close friend should not undertake to commit the administration to any candidate," McKinley instructed. "It has no candidate. The Convention must make the nomination. The Administration would not if it could. The President's close friend should be satisfied with his unanimous nomination and not interfere with the Vice Presidential nomination. The Administration wants the choice of the Convention and the President's friend must not dictate to the Convention."[57]

Hanna, who had already scheduled a conference to decide whether to make an effort to unite the convention behind another candidate, said he would follow the President's instruction.

To his credit, Roosevelt was a tireless campaigner for the Republican ticket and since McKinley made very few public statements, Roosevelt became the chief spokesman for the party.

On November 6, the Republicans won a sweeping victory. McKinley and Roosevelt were inaugurated on March 4, 1901. Roosevelt presided over the Senate for just five days when it recessed on March 9. The Senate would not meet again until December. Roosevelt planned to spend the time with his family, writing and studying law, intending to get a law degree after his term as Vice President was up. But after serving only six months, Theodore Roosevelt was President of the United States.

Roosevelt's popularity had put him on the Republican ticket and in a very real sense, he was the choice of the people for the presidency. Roosevelt had been the first choice of many in the country for the presidency, especially in the west. But with McKinley securely at the head of the ticket, the country demanded Roosevelt as Vice President.

However, others thought Roosevelt inexperienced, and reckless. Senator Mark Hanna called him "that damned cowboy." Many thought Roosevelt was too unpredictable and dangerous.

Roosevelt promised to move slowly and stick to President McKinley's policies. Characteristically, he was soon embroiled in yet another controversy, this time with American business interests when he invoked the Sherman Antitrust Act against a company owned by J. P.

---

[56] Charles W. Dawes, *A Journal of the McKinley Years* (Chicago: R. R. Donnelley & Sons Co., 1950) 232-233.

[57] Charles W. Dawes, *A Journal of the McKinley Years* (Chicago: R. R. Donnelley & Sons Co., 1950) 233.

Morgan. It created a storm from nervous businessmen on Wall Street who feared the legislation. Up until that time, the act had not been used to interfere seriously with large corporations. Businessmen warned that Roosevelt would paralyze the economy.

One newspaper rebutted sarcastically, "Wall Street is paralyzed at the thought that a President of the United States should sink so low as to try to enforce the law."[58]

For better or worse, the amiable and gentle William McKinley was gone. In his place was a young, energetic, dynamo who later bragged of carrying a big stick. And it was a stick that Theodore Roosevelt fully intended to use.

---

[58]Nancy Whitelaw, *Theodore Roosevelt Takes Charge* (Morton Grove, IL: Albert Whitman & Co., 1992) 115.

Vice President Roosevelt talks with reporters.

Vice President Roosevelt speaks with Senator Hanna near the Milburn house.

The Wilcox Mansion on Delaware Avenue where Theodore Roosevelt stayed and where he was sworn in as President of the United States

8. A Question of Sanity: Czolgosz Analyzed

From the start, about the only line of defense in the case was the sanity of Leon Czolgosz. He had obviously committed the act in front of hundreds of witnesses, and the prosecution did a good job of establishing that fact. All his defense could hope to do was to prove Czolgosz insane and allow him to spend his life in an insane asylum. But proving Czolgosz insane had its difficulties.

Doctors Floyd S. Crego, an alienist from Buffalo and Joseph Fowler, the prison physician, and James W. Putnam spent a half an hour with Czolgosz on the night of September 9, but would not make any comments to the press other than to say they were absolutely certain that he was sane.[1]

Three doctors had been called in by District Attorney Penney to examine Czolgosz. Drs. Fowler, Putnam and Crego all saw Czolgosz four times, each time having him under observation for two hours. They applied all the tests known to them. After the first examination, they thought Czolgosz was sane and all subsequent meetings simply seemed to confirm their first hypothesis.

In addition, the two experts called by defendant's attorneys, Drs. MacDonald and Hurd, examined Czolgosz three times, two hours at a time. Their conclusions were the same as the prosecution's team of doctors. In fact, there was only one conclusion reached by all six of the doctors that examined the prisoner. Leon Czolgosz was sane.[2]

Dr. Joseph Fowler later explained that he had been on the grounds and heard the shots, and had even beaten the President to the hospital. He had seen Czolgosz every day he was kept in Buffalo, with the exception of the five days he was secreted away in the jail, and he had looked forward to seeing the saga concluded at Czolgosz's execution. But Fowler was ultimately not permitted to attend the electrocution.[3]

Fowler talked of Czolgosz's extreme cleanliness and his repeatedly requests for a comb or brush to groom his disheveled hair. Fowler had promised to bring him these articles, but Czolgosz was spirited away

---

[1] *New York Times*, 10 September 1901, pg. 2, col. 3.

[2] A. Wesley Johns, *The Man Who Shot McKinley* (New York: A. S. Barnes and Co., Inc., 1970) 255.

[3] L. Vernon Briggs, *The Manner of Man That Kills* (Boston: R. G. Badger, Gorham Press, 1921) 272-273.

before Fowler saw him again. Czolgosz kept asking the guards where the brush and cigars Dr. Fowler had promised him were.

The prisoner, according to Fowler, continually wound a handkerchief around his had while talking to the physicians, and alluded to his crime and how his stepmother worried him. He was also very particular about the water and milk he drank, making certain they were "clear."[4]

The three doctors had a lengthy interview with Czolgosz on September 7, during which he talked freely about the commission of the crime. During the second interview the doctors covered much of the same ground looking for inconsistencies in Czolgosz's story. They found his statements to be totally consistent. During the interview, Czolgosz also discussed his association with anarchy and his political beliefs and activities. The doctors solicited information about Emma Goldman and his short day trip to Cleveland from Buffalo. It was during this examination that Czolgosz, continuing to complain about his clothes, was purchased a change. Over all, the alienist questions seemed to be more a police interrogation rather than a medical investigation. There were no questions about his family background and childhood. Unfortunately, the doctors spent more time trying to catch him in lies about the commission of the crime itself than in trying to get new information that could shed light on his motives.

The doctors did spend a lot of time on his anarchistic beliefs, but did little to go beyond Czolgosz's statements to the root causes of his actions; his motivations to become involved politically and to rebel against government in general in the form of first socialism, and then later anarchism. Unfortunate, because the second interview was to be the last time Czolgosz would talk in depth to anyone concerning substantive subjects.

On September 8, Czolgosz' attitude suddenly changed. He refused to answer most questions and even denied killing the President or meaning to kill him. Finally, upon being told that it was too late for him to deny things he had already said, he blurted, "I am glad I did it."[5]

"At all subsequent interviews he declined to discuss the crime in any of its details with us, but would talk about his general condition, his meals, his sleep and how much he walked in the corridor of the jail, or upon any other subject not relating to the crime," the doctors wrote in

---

[4] L. Vernon Briggs, *The Manner of Man That Kills* (Boston: R. G. Badger, Gorham Press, 1921) 273.

[5] L. Vernon Briggs, *The Manner of Man That Kills* (Boston: R. G. Badger, Gorham Press, 1921) 244.

their report. "From the daily reports filed with us, we note that be talked freely; that his appetite was good; that he enjoyed his walks which he took in the corridor of the jail. He told his guards that he would not talk with his lawyers because he did not believe in them and did not want them."[6]

Fowler, Putnam and Crego filed their report with District Attorney Thomas Penney on November 2, dated September 28, 1901 in which they explained their findings on Czolgosz's mental state:

"In conclusion, as a result of the frequent examinations of Czolgosz, of the reports of his watchers during his confinement in the jail, of his behavior in court during the trial and at the time he received his sentence, we conclude that he was sane at the time he planned the murder, when he shot the President and when on trial. We come to this conclusion from the history of his life as it came from him," concluded the report. "He had been sober, industrious and law-abiding until he was twenty-one years of age; he was, as others in his class, a believer in the government of this country and of the religion of his fathers. After he cast his first vote he made the acquaintance of anarchistic leaders who invited him to their meetings. He was a good listener, and in a short time he adopted their theories. He was consistent in his adherence to anarchy. He did not believe in government, therefore be refused to vote. He did not believe in marriage, because he did not believe in law. He killed the President because he was a ruler, and Czolgosz believed, as he was taught, that all rulers were tyrants; that to kill a ruler would benefit the people. He refused a lawyer because be did not believe in law, lawyers or courts.

"We come to the conclusion that in the holding of these views Czolgosz was sane, because these opinions were formed gradually under the influence of Anarchistic leaders and propagandists. In Czolgosz they found a willing and intelligent tool; one who had the courage of his convictions, regardless of personal consequences. We believe that his statement, 'I killed the President because I done my duty,' was not the expression of an insane delusion, for several reasons. The most careful questioning failed to discover any hallucinations of sight or hearing. He had received no special command; he did not believe he had been specially chosen to do the deed. He always spoke of his motive for the crime as duty; he always referred to the Anarchists' belief that the killing of rulers was a duty. He never claimed the idea of killing the President was original with him, but the method of accomplishing his purpose was

---

[6] L. Vernon Briggs, *The Manner of Man That Kills* (Boston: R. G. Badger, Gorham Press, 1921) 244-245.

his; and he did it alone. He is not a case of paranoia, because he has not systematized delusions reverting to self, and because he is in exceptionally good condition and has an unbroken record of good health. His capacity for labor had always been good and equal to that of his fellows. These facts all tend to prove that the man has an unimpaired mind. He has false beliefs, the result of false teaching and not the result of disease. He is not to be classed as a degenerate, because we do not find the stigmata of degeneration; his skull is symmetrical, his ears do not protrude, nor are they of abnormal size, and his palate not highly arched. Psychically he has not a history of cruelty, or of perverted tastes and habits. He is the product of Anarchy, sane and responsible."[7]

Two other alienists examined Czolgosz for the defense, Dr. Carlos F. MacDonald and Dr. Arthur W. Hurd, after MacDonald had been recruited by Adelbert Moot to examine Czolgosz for the defense. MacDonald agreed and brought Hurd into the picture to be associated with him in the case.

"Being unable to establish communication with Dr. Hurd before evening of that day, and in view of the short time intervening before the trial," wrote MacDonald, "I decided to make a preliminary examination of Czolgosz alone, and did so that afternoon, in the District Attorney's office, first disclosing to him my identity and the object of my interview and informing him of his legal right to decline to answer any question I might ask him.

"I examined him again on the following day—in the jail jointly with Dr. Hurd, and in the presence of one of his guards who was questioned at length, respecting his observations of him in the jail, as to his habits of eating, sleeping, talking, reading, etc. We subsequently interviewed the District Attorney and the Superintendent of Police, General Bull, who gave us all the facts and information in their possession respecting the case. The statement which Czolgosz made to the District Attorney shortly after his arrest throws much light on his mental condition on the day of the crime, but that official deemed it his duty to refuse to allow me to publish it. We also conferred at length with the people's experts— Dr. Fowler, Crego and Putnam—who stated to us separately and in detail their observations and examinations of him. We also observed him carefully in the court room throughout the trial."[8]

---

[7] L. Vernon Briggs, *The Manner of Man That Kills* (Boston: R. G. Badger, Gorham Press, 1921) 245-246.

[8] "Report of Dr. Carlos F. MacDonald and Dr. Arthur Hurd, Experts for the Prisoner" (1901). Reprinted in *American State Trials,* edited by James D. Lawson, vol.14, (St. Louis: Thomas Law Book Co., 1923) 200.

"After our examination of Czolgosz on Sunday, we reached the conclusion, independently of each other, that he was sane," wrote MacDonald later, "and we so informed his counsel on Monday morning before the trial began. It should be said that, owing to the limited time—two days—at our disposal prior to the trial, and the fact that his family relatives resided in a different State and were not accessible for interrogation, we were unable to obtain a history of his heredity beyond what he himself gave us."[9]

"My last examination of Czolgosz was made jointly with Dr. Gerin, physician of Auburn Prison, the evening before his execution," MacDonald continued. "This examination revealed nothing in either his mental or physical condition which tended to alter the opinion I gave his counsel at the time of his trial; namely, that he was sane—an opinion which was concurred in by all the official experts on either side: namely, Drs. Crego, Fowler and Putnam for the people and Dr. Hurd and myself for the defense, also by Dr. Gerin, the only other physician who examined him. Moreover, neither of the three careful personal examinations which I made of him—one alone, one with Dr. Hurd and one with Dr. Gerin—the measurements of his body by the Bertillon System, nor the post-mortem findings, disclosed the slightest evidence of mental disease, defect or degeneracy."[10]

MacDonald effectively argued that while Czolgosz was suffering from a delusion, it was not an "insane delusion or false belief due to disease of the brain. On the contrary, it was a political delusion...founded on ignorance, faulty education and warped—not diseased—reason and judgment—the false belief which dominates the politico-social sect to which he belonged and to which he was a zealot...The course and conduct of Czolgosz from beginning down to his death are entirely in keeping with this creed."[11]

"Careful inquiry failed to elicit any evidence of delusion, hallucination or illusion," wrote MacDonald. "When questioned as to the existence of enemies, persecutions or conspiracies against him, he replied in the negative. He evinced no appearance of morbid mental depression, morbid mental exaltation, or of mental weakness or loss of mind; nor did he display any indication of morbid suspicion, vanity or

---

[9] L. Vernon Briggs, *The Manner of Man That Kills* (Boston: R. G. Badger, Gorham Press, 1921) 247.

[10] L. Vernon Briggs, *The Manner of Man That Kills* (Boston: R. G. Badger, Gorham Press, 1921) 247.

[11] L. Vernon Briggs, *The Manner of Man That Kills* (Boston: R. G. Badger, Gorham Press, 1921) 247.

conceit, or claim that he was 'inspired' or bad 'a mission to perform,' or that he was subject to any uncontrollable impulse. In fact, as regards the existence of evidences of mental disease or defect, the result of the examinations was entirely negative. On the contrary, everything in his history as shown by his conduct and declarations, points to the existence in him of the social disease, Anarchy, of which he was the victim."[12]

"In view of the great importance of the case, it is regrettable that no experts were called to testify on the trial as to the prisoner's mental condition in order that it might appear on the record of the trial that his mental state was inquired into and determined by competent authority," explained MacDonald. "Had the experts on either side been given the opportunity of thus stating officially their unanimous conclusion, together with the grounds on which it was based and the methods by which it was reached, it would have left in the public mind no reasonable doubt as to its absolute correctness, and that it had been arrived at only by the rules of professional conduct governing the examination of such cases."[13]

"In conclusion," MacDonald wrote, "the writer having viewed the case in all its aspects with due regard to the bearing and significance of every fact and circumstance relative thereto that was accessible to him, records his opinion unqualifiedly that Leon F. Czolgosz on September 6, 1901, when he assassinated President McKinley, was in all respects a sane man—both legally and medically—and fully responsible for his act."[14]

The most notable alienists who thought Czolgosz was insane never interviewed him face to face. Dr. Walter Channing, Dr. L. Vernon Briggs and Dr. Allan McLane Hamilton all thought Czolgosz was insane.

Channing, who with Briggs did considerable research into Czolgosz's background, thought that he was suffering from the delusion that it was his duty to kill the President and said that from the facts he had seen, "insanity appeared the most reasonable and logical explanation of the crime."[15] It was Channing and Brigg's work which today gives the most detailed glimpse into Leon Czolgosz's personal life.

[12] "Report of Dr. Carlos F. MacDonald and Dr. Arthur Hurd, Experts for the Prisoner" (1901). Reprinted in *American State Trials,* edited by James D. Lawson, vol.14, (St. Louis: Thomas Law Book Co., 1923) 201.

[13] L. Vernon Briggs, *The Manner of Man That Kills* (Boston: R. G. Badger, Gorham Press, 1921) 249.

[14] "Report of Dr. Carlos F. MacDonald and Dr. Arthur Hurd, Experts for the Prisoner" (1901). Reprinted in *American State Trials,* edited by James D. Lawson, vol.14, (St. Louis: Thomas Law Book Co., 1923) 203.

[15] Dr. Walter Channing, *The Mental Status of Czolgosz* (Brookline, Mass: American Journal of Insanity, Vol. LIX, No. 2, 1902) 4.

Hamilton came to the same, possibly pre-determined conclusion. He wrote, "Had I been allowed, and had the trial not been hurried on with such indecent haste, I would have made the same examination subsequently undertaken by Dr. Walter Channing, the learned psychiatrist of Brookline, Massachusetts, who after the execution established without doubt the family's degeneracy and the prisoner's mental disease, but the newspapers were impatient and something had to be done, and at once, to appease the vengeful and restless public."

About Czolgosz's mental condition, Hamilton wrote, "The assassin was really a defective who had long been drifting to paranoia, and whose actual delusions of persecution and grandeur found soil in which to grow. As early as 1901 his family said he had 'gone to pieces;' he neglected his trade, and became a vagabond. He had delusions that he was being poisoned, for he bought and cooked his own food, and would not let even his mother prepare his meals. He talked a great deal about anarchy and murder, and eagerly read the accounts of the assassination of King Humbert; he likewise had religious and 'exhaulted' delusions. His ordinary conduct before the commission of the crime had been orderly and gentle; he was fond of children and simple things, and a week before his act had played with the little daughters of the people with whom he stayed."

Hamilton thought Czolgosz was weak of nature and susceptible to the teachings of the Anarchists, and "absorbed the doctrines of anarchism in the same manner that certain morbid adolescents undergo a religious change, which leads to a familiar kind of breaking down. Unlike the ordinary anarchist, who when he kills takes means to save his neck and escape, this boy carried his fanatical recklessness to the extreme danger point with complete indifference to his fate."[16]

Dr. Sanderson Christieson also felt Czolgosz was insane.

"At the age of 28 and after a life record of an exceptionally (abnormally) retiring and peaceful disposition, he suddenly appears as a great criminal," Christieson, wrote. "Had he been sane, this act would imply an infraction of the law of normal growth, which is logically conceivable.

"Such a monstrous conception and impulse as the wanton murder of the President of the United States, arising in the mind of so insignificant a citizen, without his being either insane or degenerate could be nothing short of a miracle, for the reason that we require like causes to explain

---

[16] Allan McLane Hamilton, *Recollections of an Alienist* (New York: George H. Doran Company, 1916) 365-366.

like results. To assume that he was sane, is to assume that he did a sane act, i. e., one based upon fads and for a rational purpose.

Insane Egotism, e. g., his reason for killing the President was 'I done my duty; I don't believe in one man having so much service and another having none.'"[17]

Christieson then listed the events of Czolgosz's life which seem to point to a developing mental condition, including his difficulty associating with other children when young, the way he avoided the opposite sex and had apparently had no close friends, the fact that he was always complaining of being sick and taking medicine even thought to others he did not appear distinctly ill, his habit of falling asleep at odd times, and his sudden departure from his work life, retiring to his fathers farm to spend his time in idleness.

"We thus see that his previous history reveals the development of a distinctly abnormal condition in his character and which could hardly be expected to continue much longer without a break or some peculiar overt manifestation, the precise form of which would depend upon the suggestions made to such a peculiar mind by passing events," he concludes. "And yet he has been declared an Anarchist, sane and responsible, by the state's medical advisers."[18]

The Post Mortem

The post-mortem examination of Leon Czolgosz was performed by Dr. Edward Anthony Spitzka only a few feet from the chair in which the assassin died, under the supervision of Dr. MacDonald. MacDonald had been asked by the New York State Superintendent of Prisons to oversee the examination with Prison Physician Dr. John Gerin. The examination began immediately following the execution at 7:50 a.m. and ended at 12:30 p.m. When the body temperature was taken at the outset it was 97 degrees. It cooled very slowly throughout the remainder of the procedure, with the brain seeming to retain the heat best. Rigor mortis set in about three hours after Czolgosz's death. A witness, Murat Halstead, described Czolgosz's corpse:

"The spectacle was interesting: the assassin had been dead but a few minutes, and was lying at full length on his back on the table provided

---

[17] L. Vernon Briggs, *The Manner of Man That Kills* (Boston: R. G. Badger, Gorham Press, 1921) 338.
[18] L. Vernon Briggs, *The Manner of Man That Kills* (Boston: R. G. Badger, Gorham Press, 1921) 338-339.

for the surgeon, his body white as marble, his face not at all distorted," Halstead wrote. "One might say he was as if sleeping, but that would not describe the expression of the features, though that was almost of perfect repose. The head rested on the back part of the table so as to elevate the chin and allow the forehead to slope downward. There was no sign of a great agony; the hair had not been removed for the electrode, but was full of water from the sponge, and in disorder. If there was any mark on the head made by the deadly shock it was not visible. There was a red blotch on the right leg below the knee... .The strong throat, with a distinct Adam's apple was prominent The lips were slightly parted with more than the curl they had in life. There was nothing in the appearance of the body of the emaciation from imprisonment so often referred to. Any physician would say the corpse was that of a well-nourished young man. The figure was of good proportions, his limbs especially so. The arms were not muscular Evidently he was not a man who had cultivated his muscles by exercise or expanded them by labor. The arms were of a young man of leisure—smooth, round and fair. His hands were not in any way notable. He had high insteps, *neat* ankles and long toes. The muscles of the legs were better developed than those of his arms, indicating he was swift of foot. He was not noticeably spare in body; his chest was round and symmetrical—not lean—but the ribs quite distinct. With his head thrown back, it seemed to have been well poised in life, more so than is shown in his pictures—all of which that are familiar having been taken in prison. Nothing in his face or his person gave indication of heavy feeding or drinking, or of evil indulgence. There were none of the inevitable traces of confirmed dissipation."[19]

The doctors took detailed measurements of Czolgosz's head and made complete plaster molds of the entire head. The cranium was next opened and the brain was removed.

"Supernumerary or abnormally developed bones were not discernable," wrote Spitzka.[20]

"The base of the skull was normal in every respect," Spitzka continued. "The pia-arachnoid was of normal thinness, and devoid of opacities or any other signs of disease—past or present. The only unusual appearance was an injection of bright red blood in the finer

---

[19] Edward A. Spitzka, "The Post-Mortem Examination of Leon F. Czolgosz, the Assassin of President McKinley," *American Journal of Insanity* 58 (January 1902) 397-398."

[20] Edward A. Spitzka, "The Post-Mortem Examination of Leon F. Czolgosz, the Assassin of President McKinley," *American Journal of Insanity* 58 (January 1902) 389.

vessels of the pia, due, if we may judge from previous reports of autopsies on electrocuted criminals—to the high electro-motive force exerted by the fatal current in this part of the body."[21]

About the brain itself, Spitzka wrote, "In general the brain presents no marked peculiarities of shape or size. It is firm to the touch and no portion of it despite most careful examination feels softened or indurated."[22]

The brain was then dissected and drained.

"Examination of the paracceles (lateral ventricles) in both hemicerebra revealed the veins of the striatum (striatal veins) injected with deep-violet colored blood. The cornua were of normal extent and conformation throughout. The endyma was smooth, the choroid plexus normal and contained little blood, the velum interposition ("velum" of Wilder) was normal."[23]

After further examination of the brain, Czolgosz's thorax and abdomen were examined. Only a small residue of food was found in the stomach, because despite reports in the newspapers that Czolgosz had eaten a hearty breakfast prior to execution, he had actually not eaten since the evening before. Czolgosz was found to be normal in all respects.

Spitzka had intended to do a more extended examination, but "the peculiar circumstances which arose in the matter of the disposal of the body, and the anxiety of the Prison Warden to put the body under earth, forced me to conclude my researches after having obtained the most essential data for purposes of record and future study."[24] The autopsy on Czolgosz was completed within four hours of his execution.

"The results of the necropsy can be summed up by saying that Czolgosz was in excellent health at the time of his death," concluded Spitzka. "The question as to whether his body invested a healthy mind opens up a wide topic for discussion which it is not entirely in the

[21] Edward A. Spitzka, "The Post-Mortem Examination of Leon F. Czolgosz, the Assassin of President McKinley," *American Journal of Insanity* 58 (January 1902) 390.

[22] Edward A. Spitzka, "The Post-Mortem Examination of Leon F. Czolgosz, the Assassin of President McKinley," *American Journal of Insanity* 58 (January 1902) 391.

[23] Edward A. Spitzka, "The Post-Mortem Examination of Leon F. Czolgosz, the Assassin of President McKinley," *American Journal of Insanity* 58 (January 1902) 391-392.

[24] Edward A. Spitzka, "The Post-Mortem Examination of Leon F. Czolgosz, the Assassin of President McKinley," *American Journal of Insanity* 58 (January 1902) 397.

writer's province to pursue. So far as our knowledge of the correlation of brain-structure and brain-function extends, nothing has been found in the brain of this assassin that would condone his crime for the reason of mental disease due to intrinsic cerebral defect or distortion."[25]

Spitzka also wrote, "Of course it is far more difficult, and it is impossible in some cases, to establish sanity upon the results of an examination of the brain, than it is to prove insanity. It is well known that some forms of psychoses have little ascertainable anatomical basis, and the assumption has been made that these psychoses depend rather upon circulatory and chemical disturbances."[26]

In summary, Spitzka editorialized, "Taking all in all, the verdict must be, 'socially diseased and perverted, but not mentally diseased.' The most horrible violations of human law can not always be condoned by the plea of insanity."[27]

So was Leon Czolgosz insane? While Czolgosz had some emotional issues, it is doubtful that he was insane in the true sense of the word. Those who believed him insane explained the insanity in more in ideological terms than in medical ones.

Most who promote the theory of insanity cite Dr. Walter Channing and Dr. L. Vernon Brigg's work in the investigation of Czolgosz's background as the reason. Repeatedly, Czolgosz's sleeping and eating habits are seen as important clues. Also emphasized are his behaviors in regard to other people and his political "delusions."

But when viewed in the context of Czolgosz's times, the political beliefs are not as far fetched as some would purport them to be. Leon Czolgosz worked in a labor system that was often times cruel to the workers. Long days and terrible, often dangerous, working conditions were the norm, and the rewards for the workers were little. Czolgosz spent much of his reading time with publications and books, which called attention to this situation, and his own personal experiences reinforced the views. When one takes into consideration the conditions of Czolgosz's life and the views of the anarchists he read, it can be easily

---

[25]Edward A. Spitzka, "The Post-Mortem Examination of Leon F. Czolgosz, the Assassin of President McKinley," *American Journal of Insanity* 58 (January 1902) 398.

[26] L. Vernon Briggs, *The Manner of Man That Kills* (Boston: R. G. Badger, Gorham Press, 1921) 334.

[27] Edward A. Spitzka, "The Post-Mortem Examination of Leon F. Czolgosz, the Assassin of President McKinley," *American Journal of Insanity* 58 (January 1902) 400.

understood how he could have acted out his political frustration in assassination.

Channing and others have argued that Czolgosz must have been insane because he saw McKinley as an enemy of the people and that this delusion was a part of his insanity. This is a convenient and simplistic explanation that ignores the very real economic conditions in which Czolgosz lived, and in which his desire to act was bred.

"We are left sitting in the dark, still wondering how such a deed could have been done by a man in his sound and sober senses in fair and free America and appalled at the possibility of a sane man murdering a President of the United States," wrote Henry Holt, a prominent publisher of the times and a founder of Holt, Rinehart and Winston. [28]

Abraham Isaak argued, "One of the reasons for Czolgosz's insanity is stated as follows:...'Moral chaos, e.g. He declared he did not believe in marriage nor in law, nor in government nor in God.'—This probably puts Wat Tyler in the direct way of being declared a lunatic. Certainly all Anarchists come under this head. 'Wat Tyler' bears a rather suggestive pseudonym to be engaged in the attempt to excommunicate Leon Czolgosz. I reject it utterly and entirely."[29]

Wat Tyler had written an article disclaiming Czolgosz as an anarchist, but Ross Winn in the same issue also wrote, "I do not think Czolgosz was insane. His act was not an insane act, neither was he a criminal. I cannot bring myself to approve of his act—I do not believe in violence except in defense of human life and liberty, and I do not think the death of McKinley has served that purpose. We who denounce vengeance and retaliation when done in the name of the law can not consistently approve of this spirit when resorted to by individuals in the name of Anarchy. But I do not see that anyone can call Czolgosz a criminal. If his deed was a crime, the cause of it was tenfold more a crime."[30]

The economic justification of the McKinley assassination was not something the vast majority of Americans were prepared to accept. While it was certainly a delusion to think that the killing of McKinley would lessen the economic strife of Czolgosz's class, it was a delusion of political belief and not of an insane mind.

---

[28] James W. Clarke, *American Assassins: The Darker Side of Politics* (Princeton: Princeton University Press, 1982) 62.

[29] L. Vernon Briggs, *The Manner of Man That Kills* (Boston: R. G. Badger, Gorham Press, 1921) 323.

[30] L. Vernon Briggs, *The Manner of Man That Kills* (Boston: R. G. Badger, Gorham Press, 1921) 322.

Czolgosz was impressionable and misguided, but not insane.; certainly no more insane than John Wilkes Booth. He acted from political motivation, no less real than that of Booth's.

But regardless of Czolgosz's sanity, finding a jury that would accept insanity as fact and allow the killer of the President to escape the ultimate penalty would have been nearly impossible in those times of retribution. In a very real sense, whether Czolgosz was insane would not have mattered in 1901. His fate was sealed when the President died.

Immediately following the speedy trial and execution of Leon Czolgosz, most people were very happy about the swiftness of American justice. In less than two months, the President's killer had been arrested, tried and executed. Praise for the legal system and those who took part in the trial was almost universal in the press.

"In the dignity, impartiality, and celerity with which the trial of Czolgosz was conducted," remarked the *New York Herald,* "the judiciary of this State has set an illustrious example for sister commonwealths and vindicated the majesty of the law as administered in this country."[31]

The *New York Journal* compared the Czolgosz trial to that of Charles Guiteau, the assassin of Garfield, noting it had taken two days shy of a year to execute him after the commission of the crime.

"Czolgosz will die within two months after McKinley was shot," the *Journal* wrote. "It is a notable advance in civilized procedure, especially when we remember the long disgrace of Guiteau's trial was perpetuated in the nation's capital."[32]

But there were others who questioned the competence and commitment of the Czolgosz's defense team. In fact, the *New York Times* reported following the first day of the trial, "'The mental condition of the assassin will absolutely be the only defense to be offered,' are the words of Mr. Titus and there is no little expectancy that they will publicly abandon the idea of an active defense to-morrow, and merely represent Czolgosz formally during the trial."[33]

"I really do not think in all my experience that I have ever seen such a travesty of justice, nor have I heard of such a tribunal except in the clever *Grand Guignol* little horror of *Les Trois Messieurs du Havre,*" wrote Dr. Allan McLane Hamilton, an alienist who claimed to have been brought in by the defense to examine Czolgosz, but who was never given the opportunity.

---

[31] *Literary Digest*, 5 October 1901, pg. 393.

[32] *Literary Digest*, 5 October 1901, pg. 393.

[33] *New York Times,* 24 September 1901, pg. 2, col. 1.

"On arriving, I found that the three people's experts, and the two physicians retained by the Erie County Bar association had made up their minds that the prisoner was *sane,*" he wrote. "It seems that they were a long time reaching a conclusion, and had made their report only an hour before they heard I was coming to Buffalo. A secret meeting, to which I was not invited, was held that night by the experts with the attorneys of *both* sides, and it was decided to go on with the trial....I was then told that no further examination was necessary, after I had been informed the night before that I was to see the prisoner at nine o'clock on Monday morning. I was, however permitted to attend the trial, which I did."

Dr. Hamilton recorded his impressions of the trial, "The two superannuated and apparently self satisfied ex-judges assigned for the defense apologized freely and humbly for *their appearance in behalf of this wretched man,* referred to 'the dastardly murder of our martyred President,' and really made nothing more than a formal perfunctory effort, if it could be called such. Long and fulsome perorations were indulged in by these remiss members of a great and distinguished profession, and others who praised the dead President, and flattered each other, the District Attorney, the Presiding Judge, the Medical Faculty of Buffalo, and every one they could think of."[34]

Dr. Carlos F. MacDonald, another alienist at the trial, agreed. Having been an observer of many murder trials, MacDonald was in a position to judge. He wrote, "Having in view the nature and importance of the case, the fact that no testimony was offered on the defendant's behalf and that practically no defense was made, beyond a perfunctory examination of jurors and a mild cross examination of some of the people's witnesses, which was limited to efforts to elicit information respecting the President's condition during his illness and of his body after death, and a summing up of one of the counsel—Judge Lewis—which consisted mainly of an apology for appearing as counsel for the defendant and a touching eulogy of his distinguished victim, renders the case, in this respect, a unique one in the annals of criminal jurisprudence."[35]

As to the preparation of the defense team, MacDonald observed, "beyond a fruitless effort of counsel to confer with the prisoner and the examination made of him at their request by Dr. Hurd, and the writer in

---

[34] Allan McLane Hamilton, *Recollections of an Alienist* (New York: George H. Doran Company, 1916) 363-364.

[35] Carlos F. MacDonald, "The Trial, Execution, Autopsy and Mental Status of Leon F. Czolgosz, Alias Fred Nieman, the Assassin of President McKinley," *American Journal of Insanity* 58 January 1902, 374.

reference to his mental condition...It also appears that no plea was entered by the attorneys for the defense, but Czolgosz speaking for the first time in court, entered a plea of guilty to the indictment which plea the court promptly rejected and directed that a plea of not guilty be entered...

"Each juror on qualifying said, in answer to the usual question, that he had formed an opinion as to the guilt of the prisoner, but that this opinion could be removed by reasonable evidence tending to show that the defendant was innocent. And yet, to one accustomed to being in court...it was difficult to avoid the impression that each of the jurors in the case held a mental reservation to convict the prisoner. Had Czolgosz been on trial for the murder of a common citizen, instead of the President, it is safe to say that not one of the jury as completed would have been accepted by the defense; and instead of getting a jury in approximately one hour and a half, that feature of the trial alone would probably have occupied several days."[36]

The *Baltimore Herald* remarked that Judge Lewis had displayed a "remarkable exhibition of bad taste," because his oration "was, in brief, an elaborate and needless defense of the counsel and a symposium on lynch law, instead of defense of the prisoner."

Certainly, the defense attorneys did nothing for Leon Czolgosz. However, in their defense, Czolgosz did nothing to help himself and refused to help them in any way. He would not talk to them and did not want them. He refused, except on rare occasions, to even answer questions in court. But his attorneys did not call even one witness in his defense. That was inexcusable, but admittedly, their hands were somewhat tied.

There were questions at the time, which have persisted that anarchists supplied Czolgosz money to finance his assassination scheme. He later produced a roll of bills, according to one witness, which would seem to indicate that he had a ready source of cash. And he seemed to always have money when he needed it, in spite of that fact that he was unemployed. His sister-in-law had given him seventy dollars when he left the farm. If he worked at odd jobs occasionally, this could have financed him.

---

[36] Carlos F. MacDonald, "The Trial, Execution, Autopsy and Mental Status of Leon F. Czolgosz, Alias Fred Nieman, the Assassin of President McKinley," *American Journal of Insanity* 58 January 1902, 373-374.

But what would the anarchists have gained by shooting McKinley?

The whole point of assassination, in the eyes or anarchists, was not only to bring about social change, but also to bring attention to their views. By denying complicity in the assassination, even anonymously, it would seem that anarchists would have been defeating their purpose had they organized and financed it by not claiming credit.

As always happens in investigations, there are questions about the details of the assassination that will never be answered. But the final conclusion seems clear—Leon Czolgosz was sane, and he acted pitifully alone.

9. The Funeral and Aftermath

After the death of the President, the morning of September 14, all was quiet in the Milburn house. At the rope barriers there was no great crowd. Word had been passed that there would be a public service at City Hall and that the President could be viewed at that location. Most people began to amass there, rather than on Delaware Street. Weary messenger boys peddled their bikes to their destinations. Inside the house, faithful Secretary George B. Cortelyou was sleeping. Since the shooting, he had slept but eight hours.

As September 14 dawned, with an eerie damp fog in place, quiet prevailed in the neighborhood surrounding where President McKinley lay in rest. The body remained in the upper room of the house and had been guarded throughout the night by a detail of non-commissioned officers from the Marine Hospital Corps. The men alternated so that two were with the deceased President at all times.[1]

A large American flag hung from the front of the house, and since there was no way to hang it at half-mast, it simply hung where it had since the start of the Exposition.

The police continued to hold the lines along Delaware Avenue and the streets that intersected it. Throughout the day, passersby stopped along the ropes to stand in silence and stare at the house. Men from the Grand Army in the crowd begged with police to allow them to opportunity to guard the President, who had fought with them during the Civil War. But police held their ground, and would not allow it.

Secretary Cortelyou was up early, solemnly attending to the funeral arrangements and other details. The Superintendent of Public Buildings and Grounds in Washington arrived to assist in the arrangements.

Down at the jail, Czolgosz seemed a forgotten man and barely a sole bothered to keep a vigil at that location. The Pan American Exposition closed its gates, even though the city was crowed with visitors. Flags, as they did everywhere else, began to fly at half-mast. Plans were being finalized for the President's funeral, with a brief service planned for the next day at the Milburn house. The Cabinet began to make arrangements to return to Washington, where the President was to lie in state in the Capital building on Wednesday. President Roosevelt, in his first official act the night before, had named Thursday, September 19, as an official day of mourning.

---

[1] *New York Times*, 15 September 1901, pg. 3, col. 5.

"I earnestly recommend all the people to assemble that day in their respective places of divine worship, there to bow down in submission to the will of almighty God and to pay out of full hearts their homage of love and reverence to the great and good President whose death has smitten the Nation with bitter grief," Roosevelt had said.[2]

Not until about ten o'clock did the Milburn house seem to stir. It was at that hour that Abner McKinley arrived, soon followed by other McKinley relatives and friends. Former Vice President Garret A. Hobart's wife and son paid their respects also.

Mrs. McKinley awoke early and stayed in her room with Miss Barber. Having been given sedatives the preceding evening by Dr. Rixey, the inhabitants of the house were relieved that she had not yet asked to see the President. They were very concerned about how she would take the news.

Throughout the morning, though no one would tell her the news, Mrs. McKinley wandered from room to room, intuitively sensing the worst had come, but fearing the finality of being informed of the sad news. Perhaps that is why she did not ask to see the President.

Finally, the time came when she must be told.

"The President is dying," she told the doctors. "You can't deceive me. I must see him."

Dr. Rixey was assigned the task of breaking the news to her and he went to her room where she waited with Miss Barber.

"I understand the President is sleeping, doctor," said Mrs. McKinley.

"He is sleeping," replied Dr. Rixey. "He is sleeping that sleep which knows no awakening."

There was no reply and no tears.[3]

The night before, a McKinley family friend, Frank B. Baird, had told newsmen that if the President indeed died, there might be a double funeral, referring to Mrs. McKinley's inability to handle the news.

Dr. Charles B. Locke, son of the former pastor of the McKinleys' church in Canton and currently working as pastor of the Delaware Avenue Methodist Episcopal Church in Buffalo was chosen to conduct the funeral services the next day. Upon leaving the Milburn house, he was asked about the condition of Mrs. McKinley, and seemed to confirm the fears.

---

[2] *New York Times*, 15 September 1901, pg. 1, col. 3.
[3] *New York Times*, 15 September 1901, pg. 1, col. 5.

"All great ideals have been consecrated in blood," he said. "Mrs. McKinley's nobleness and piety are her own. She is keeping up wonderfully well, although there may be a double tragedy."[4]

At 11:15, Abner McKinley's companion, Col. Brown, told of Mrs. McKinley's state, saying she "does not seem to fully realize the awful blow. She is in sort of a dazed condition, and acts mechanically. We expect her to collapse during the day, but we do not anticipate any fatal results."[5]

Shortly after, John Milburn added, "Although I have not seen her this morning, I understand that she is bearing the terrible misfortune better than was anticipated. Dr. Rixey, Miss Barber and Mrs. Lafayette McWilliams are with her almost constantly."[6]

Later, Milburn talked more about her condition.

"Mrs. McKinley, all things considered, is bearing up wonderfully well—the doctors say as well as can be expected," he told newsmen with a hint of irritation in his voice. "I think medicines and stimulants are being administered, but I do not know whether she is under the influence of opiates."

But only a moment later, Milburn admitted her true state, "Mrs. McKinley is deeply bereaved, utterly grief stricken, and very, very much broken down."[7]

Throughout the day, she remained in the dazed state, but did tell the President's advisors that she wished to go to Washington with the funeral train and remain in the White House while the body was lying in state. President Roosevelt immediately agreed.

James Wilson, Buffalo's coroner, arrived shortly after 10 a.m. to officially view the body. After the autopsy, he would issue the proper death certificate, without empanelling a Grand Jury, to allow for the removal of the President's body.

By 10:30 a.m., the Cabinet was assembled in a rear room of the house in conference. The surgeons who were to perform the autopsy also were arriving and meeting in the room where the President lay. Dr. McBurney refused to comment to reporters as to the treatment the President had received, saying that Dr. Mann should first be permitted to issue his report on the matter.

---

[4] *New York Times*, 15 September 1901, pg. 1, col. 4.
[5] *New York Times*, 15 September 1901, pg. 1, col. 4.
[6] *New York Times*, 15 September 1901, pg. 1, col. 4.
[7] *New York Times*, 15 September 1901, pg. 1, col. 5.

Almost immediately after the announcement of the death of the President, thousands of telegrams began to arrive, with many for Mrs. McKinley. Thinking it unwise to give them to her in her distressed state, these were laid aside. The Mexican Commissioners to the Pan American Exposition called at the Milburn house to express their sympathy, as well as representatives from other South American countries who were in Buffalo for the event.

The crowds that had been in the streets of the nation's capital had mostly retired for the evening, when the word reached Washington that President McKinley had died. Most of the Cabinet members and government officials had retired as well. Secretary of State John Hay had left word with the Navy Department as to what to do if official conformation of the President's death should come.

Hay instructed that upon receipt, cables were to be sent to every United States Ambassador abroad, telling of the news and instructing them to officially notify the government of the country in which they were charged. The messages included few details. Soon thereafter, the executive departments of the government as well as the navy yards and army posts were closed in official mourning. Military orders went out to fly all American flags at half-staff. Thirteen guns were to be fired in the morning, with one being fired throughout the day at intervals at one half hour. At sunset, forty-five guns would be fired.[8]

The White House sent official word to Secretary Hay and Secretary Gage, who were the only two Cabinet members in town. The White House announced that it would be closed until after the funeral and the flag was lowered to half-mast.

In New York City, people crowded around public bulletin boards, usually located near newspaper offices. As new dispatches arrived, they would be written on the boards, with people pushing forward in silence to see the words. Others gathered around telegraph tickers to read the latest news from Buffalo. Everywhere there was a ticker, in bars, in the offices of stockbrokers and in hotels, people grouped together in search of the latest news. Some people arranged with telegraph offices to receive the dispatches with all haste. Even in saloons, people spoke in hushed tones.

Theatres prepared to close in the event word came of the President's death. At the end of acts, patrons would try to get word of the President's condition. Even the actors, sensing that they may not have to

---

[8] *New York Times*, 14 September 1901, pg. 2, col. 2.

finish their performances, lost their spirit and interest. Like those who watched, their thoughts were on the news from Buffalo.

The bulletin that caused the most anguished reaction other than the President's death was the one that told of him asking for Mrs. McKinley. Women and men alike were moved to tears.

At the Waldorf-Astoria, crowds of businessmen, politicians, bankers, railroad men and brokers gathered to await the news. The corridors were crowded throughout the evening. Men and women sat wherever they could to await the bulletins. Nearly all the brokerage houses near the hotel stayed open all night, both to do business with London and to wait for news on their ticker machines.[9]

J. P. Morgan, after a day in his Wall Street office of watching the ticker, had taken his yacht to Great Neck that evening. Upon returning, he went to the Union League Club, where he learned the news of the President's condition and that he was not expected to live much longer. He was too shocked to comment to reporters. While at the club, he was told that the President had perhaps an hour to live. Morgan was driven back to the yacht club, and refusing to comment, went to bed on his yacht.[10]

There was much speculation about the effect the President's death might have on the stock market.

"I do not believe the financial prosperity of this country is dependent upon the life of any man," said A. A. Housman, a prominent New York broker. "The business buoyancy of the United States is founded upon the actual economic prosperity of the country at large and the death of the President would affect it."[11]

"The situation is too complicated to forecast just what will happen," said businessman James P. Keene. "Mr. McKinley has stood for a particular economic and foreign policy, and the country has been and is prosperous under that policy. I don't know what effect the unfortunate news of the day will have upon the street but I hope no serious breaks will occur."[12]

"There isn't going to be nearly so great a change in the market as many people are supposing," said E. L. Oppenheim, Vice President of the Chicago and Western Railroad. "Mr. Roosevelt is a safe man and there is no reason to fear anything that would happen under him as President. We have been trading for a week with the idea that the

[9] *New York Times*, 14 September 1901, pg. 3, col. 1-3.

[10] *New York Times*, 14 September 1901, pg. 3, col. 2.

[11] *New York Times*, 14 September 1901, pg. 3, col. 3.

[12] *New York Times*, 14 September 1901, pg. 3, col. 3.

President might grow worse and die at any time, but the market has suffered very little from it."[13]

Newspapers around the United States and the world were filled with expressions of sympathy from virtually every political leader of importance. Pages were full with reviews of the life of President McKinley and stories introducing the new President Roosevelt.

The eulogies and comments began to pour in from home and around the world.
"This is dreadful news and the more cruel because it strikes down the confident and comforting expectation which all our people were encouraged to entertain that their President would be saved from death," said former President Grover Cleveland from his home on Bayard Lane in Princeton, New Jersey, upon hearing the news of McKinley's death. "In the afflictive gloom surrounding this third Presidential murder within the memory of men not yet old, we can scarcely keep out of mind a feeling of stunning amazement that in free America, blessed with a Government consecrated to popular welfare and contentment, the danger of assassination should ever encompass the faithful discharge of highest official duty. It is hard at such a time as this to calmly and patiently await the unfolding of the purpose of God."[14]

In London, the morning papers were filled with sympathetic words for England's American cousins, as Union Jacks flew at half-staff and the stock and commercial exchanges were closed.
"The tragic end of his honorable career would ensure for William McKinley a permanent place in the memory of his countrymen, even if he had not won it already by good and faithful service to the State," wrote the *London Times*.[15]
"There was the same anxious look in the faces of Londoners yesterday as they wore when our late beloved Queen was fighting her battle with death," wrote the *London Daily Telegraph*, referring to Queen Victoria. "It was then that America stretched out its hand to us. Today, in her hour of bitter trial, we return the grasp."[16]

---

[13] *New York Times*, 14 September 1901, pg. 3, col. 3.
[14] *New York Times*, 14 September 1901, pg. 1, col. 7.
[15] *New York Times*, 14 September 1901, pg. 2, col. 4.
[16] *New York Times*, 14 September 1901, pg. 2, col. 4.

King Edward wrote, "Most truly do sympathize with you and the whole American Nation at the loss of your distinguished and ever-to-be-regretted President."[17]

Paris saw its buildings decorated with furled black crepe-draped American flags to honor the fallen President and its citizens could speak of little else.

The French paper, *Gaulois*, wrote, "The death of President McKinley will have a greater reverberation throughout Europe than had the disappearance of Garfield, Lincoln, or Carnot. He played a bigger part on the world's stage than any of his predecessors. Bolder than they, he threw down the gauntlet to one of the nations of the Old World and inaugurated at the expense of Spain a policy of expansion and conquest."[18]

In the *Figaro*, "We also salute President Roosevelt, whose chivalrous mind is known to all, and who undoubtedly will continue, especially in the relations with France, the traditions of his predecessor. There is not another man who better responds to the ideal of his countrymen."[19]

French Ambassador Porter had been very ill and the news of the change in the President's condition had so upset him the day before that his physicians ordered the news of the President's death kept from him. French President Emile Loubet drove to the embassy but was told by Porter's doctor that the Ambassador had not yet been told the news and that he was in poor health. President Loubet expressed his sympathy for the Ambassador and told the doctor to inform him of his personal visit and to convey his condolences over the loss of President McKinley. Porter was told of the President's death later in the day.

President Loubet then wrote to Mrs. McKinley, saying, "I learn with deep pain that his Excellency Mr. McKinley has succumbed to the deplorable attempt on his life. I sympathize with you with all my heart in the calamity which thus strikes at your dearest affections and which bereaves the great American Nation of a President so justly respected and loved."[20]

"The Anarchist Czolgosz flattered himself with a vain hope if he thought that by a revolver shot he could root up the famous gibbet, the golden cross on which Bryan wished to prevent humanity from being crucified," wrote the *Temps*, a French newspaper. "The Buffalo murder,

---

[17] *New York Times*, 15 September 1901, pg. 4, col. 1.

[18] *New York Times*, 15 September 1901, pg. 1, col. 3.

[19] *New York Times*, 15 September 1901, pg. 1, col. 3.

[20] *New York Times*, 15 September 1901, pg. 4, col. 5.

therefore, was perfectly useless, even from the viewpoint of the Anarchists themselves. Political murder is always formidable to dynasties, but quite inoffensive to republics."[21]

Germany's Emperor William sent condolences from Berlin, "I am deeply affected by the news of the untimely death of President McKinley. I hasten to express the deepest most heartfelt sympathy of the German people with the great American Nation. Germany mourns with America for her noble son, who lost his life while he was fulfilling his duty to his country and people."[22]

To Mrs. McKinley, the Kaiser wrote, "Her Majesty the Empress and myself beg you to accept the expression of our most sincere sorrow in the loss which you have suffered by the death of your beloved husband, felled by the ruthless hand of a murderer. May the Lord, who granted you so many years of happiness at the side of the deceased grant you strength to bear the heavy blow with which he has visited you."[23]

The funeral of William McKinley in reality began in the house were he died, on Sunday morning, September 15, and lasted for a week. The casket was carried down into the drawing room from the upstairs chamber in which he died and placed between two windows in the library, a silken folded American flag drawn about the bier. At 11:00, the upper lid was drawn back and those assembled gazed upon the President's face.

The dead President's head rested on a white satin pillow, with his left hand placed upon his breast. He had been dressed in black, with a black tie and white stand-up collar. In his lapel was a bronze Grand Army button. His face was drawn and sunken, indicating his suffering. His skin was somewhat yellow.[24]

Senator Hanna had picked out the casket. It was framed with red cedar, covered with black cloth, and inside a copper box with white satin lining. The handles were of ebony finish. The cover of the copper box had a full-length pane of plate glass, which made the box airtight. On the outer box of the casket read the inscription, "William McKinley, born January 29, 1843, died September 14, 1901."[25]

---

[21] *New York Times*, 15 September 1901, pg. 4, col. 5.

[22] *New York Times*, 15 September 1901, pg. 4, col. 5.

[23] *New York Times*, 15 September 1901, pg. 4, col. 5.

[24] G. Townsend, *Memorial Life of William McKinley* (Washington: Memorial Publishing Co., 1901) 299.

[25] G. Townsend, *Memorial Life of William McKinley* (Washington: Memorial Publishing Co., 1901) 318.

Mrs. McKinley was led in by Dr. Rixey and sat a while alone with him, fondling his face, seeming not to realize he was dead. After her visit, she was led back upstairs during the service.

Because of her weakened condition, Abner McKinley requested the service be simple and short. Barely 200 people were admitted to the service and few still found a place in the small room, most of them McKinley's family and closest friends. Shortly after ten o'clock they began to arrive. At first they came one and two at a time, or in small parties. As the time of the service drew nearer, many decided to wait on the lawn.[26]

At three minutes until eleven, President Roosevelt's carriage arrived, with the President getting out and shaking hands with a few members of the Cabinet before entering the house. He entered the room, came up and looked at his dead predecessor, and as he took his assigned seat near the head of the casket, tears could be seen in his eyes. [27]

Dr. Charles Edward Locke raised his right hand as a signal that the service was about to begin. At that moment an audible pitiful sob was heard from the top of the stairs by nearly everyone in the room. Recognized as being Mrs. McKinley, all were greatly affected. Abner hurried upstairs to console his sister-in-law and ask her to remain calm. Dr. Rixey also helped and Mrs. McKinley calmed as the service began.[28]

A quartet from the First Presbyterian Church sang a hymn, *Lead, Kindly Light*. Dr. Locke concluded the brief but touching services with the *Lord's Prayer* and many of the mourners joined him.[29]

After the service, Senator Hanna approached the casket. He was under control emotionally, but he stood gazing at his friend for a full minute with a look on his face that drew the sympathy of all those around him. As he turned around, those in the Cabinet saw tears trickling down his face. Secretary Long and Attorney General Knox helped him to his seat, where he bowed his head in grief.[30] After that, the casket was closed.

---

[26] G. Townsend, *Memorial Life of William McKinley* (Washington: Memorial Publishing Co., 1901) 302.

[27] G. Townsend, *Memorial Life of William McKinley* (Washington: Memorial Publishing Co., 1901) 302.

[28] *Buffalo Courier,* 16 September 1901, pg. 1, col. 1.

[29] G. Townsend, *Memorial Life of William McKinley* (Washington: Memorial Publishing Co., 1901) 307.

[30] Murat Halstead, *The Illustrious Life of William McKinley* (Privately Published, 1901) 229-230.

The nurses and attendants who had served the President during his final hours, assembled on the side porch of the house to watch as the body was taken away. Through their tear filled eyes and the ivy that grew on the house, they watched until the hearse was out of sight.[31]

The funeral cortege left the Milburn House at 11:45. In the first carriage, President Roosevelt was seated with Secretary Root, Attorney General Knox and Postmaster-General Smith. In the second carriage were Secretaries Long, Wilson, Hitchcock and Cortelyou. General Brooke sat alone in the third carriage and Dr. and Mrs. Locke occupied a fourth.

Then came the hearse, drawn by four black horses with pallbearers marching beside and soldiers and marines walking behind. There followed a detail from the Grand Army of the Republic, a company of marines from Camp Haywood, the Sixty-fifth Regiment Band, a company of the Fourteenth Regiment stationed at Fort Porter, and companies from the Sixty-fifth and Seventy-fourth regiments and finally sailors and marines from the steamship *Michigan*.[32]

An estimated fifty thousand people witnessed the movement to Buffalo City Hall. Along both sides of the street, in a scene that would be repeated many times in the coming days, men, women and children lined the two mile route.

City Hall was a granite building in the heart of Buffalo, which occupied an entire block, and was about two miles from the Milburn house. The outside had been decorated with black bunting, but much of it was gone due to the rainstorms of the night and morning. On the spacious main floor of City Hall, which was reached by climbing a few stone steps, the walls were decorated in black. Palms and palmettos were placed in the recesses on either side. In the center of the hall, beneath four lighted six-branch chandeliers, was a slightly inclined platform for the coffin. Directly above the spot where the casket would lie, there was a dome of black bunting and within that structure four American flags hung straight down above the coffin, forming a cross, which pointed in all directions of the compass.[33]

The funeral procession marched slowly and deliberately down Delaware Avenue as thousands looked on. Outside the hall thousands

---

[31] Alexander K. McClure, *The Authentic Life of William McKinley* (W. E. Skull, 1901) 341.

[32] Murat Halstead, *The Illustrious Life of William McKinley* (Privately Published, 1901) 235.

[33] G. Townsend, *Memorial Life of William McKinley* (Washington: Memorial Publishing Co., 1901) 299.

waited until about one o'clock when was heard the strains of Chopin's *Funeral March*. Soon the head of the procession swung onto Eagle Street, then into Franklin Street to the main entrance. The soldiers and marines wheeled into their places and formed lines along the curbs.[34]

At this moment, the rains came again, sweeping across the square in a gusty wind. The horses drawing President Roosevelt's carriage became frightened, but alert policemen grabbed their reigns. As the band played *Nearer My God to Thee*, the pallbearers took up their load in the rain.[35]

The coffin was placed beneath the arrangement, while President Roosevelt, members of his Cabinet and the others looked on. The upper half of the casket was opened, with the lower half draped in a flag upon which were masses of red and white roses.

When the casket was opened, funeral director Drullard noticed that the lapel pin of the Grand Army of the Republic, an organization for former comrades of the Civil War, was missing from the President's clothing.

"I thought I had everything," he sad in a low tone, "but it must have been forgotten."

One of the members of the GAR's honorary guard heard the words and quickly gave Drullard his own lapel pin, which was placed on the President's coat. [36]

As soon as the casket was in place and all was arranged, President Roosevelt led the Cabinet past, and then made their way our the western entrance, followed by about one hundred mourners who had waited at City Hall or who had accompanied the body from the Milburn house.[37] They left at 1:18, and afterwards, after a delay while the guard was placed, the display was opened to the public.

More than twice the number that could hope to view the body came from all over western New York to Buffalo. About 200,000 people patiently lined up, and stood through a pounding rain hoping to view the remains. For ten hours they filed by in City Hall, an estimated ten thousand per hour. Others estimated about 200 viewers per minute. One report said that not less than 100,000 viewed McKinley. Rain fell in torrents during much of the afternoon, but it could not deter the crowd

[34] G. Townsend, *Memorial Life of William McKinley* (Washington: Memorial Publishing Co., 1901) 313.

[35] G. Townsend, *Memorial Life of William McKinley* (Washington: Memorial Publishing Co., 1901) 313.

[36] *Buffalo Courier,* 16 September 1901, pg. 2, col. 2.

[37] G. Townsend, *Memorial Life of William McKinley* (Washington: Memorial Publishing Co., 1901) 315.

from its mission. The weather and weariness ended the lines at about 11 o'clock that night.[38]

The crowds entered the eastern entrance from Eagle and Church Streets. The police formed them into two lines, so that four people could view the casket at a time from either side. As the afternoon wore on, the police hurried people through so as to allow as many as possible to enter.

One of the first men to reach the coffin shook his fist and said to the dead President, "Curse the man that shot you!" He was escorted out while he shook his head and muttered threats again the anarchists.[39]

When Mrs. McKinley had originally given permission to have the body lie in state at City Hall, it had been done so with the request that it be returned by six o'clock. She could barely stand to have it out of her sight. But with the outpouring of citizens, she was persuaded to allow it to remain longer. Originally, the doors had been scheduled to close at 5:00. At that hour 35,000 people had been through the lines and 100,000 still waited. Special trains brought thousands of people from Lockport, Niagara Falls, Rochester and other towns in the western part of the state. It was estimated that less than half of those who viewed the body were from Buffalo.[40]

About four o'clock, a group of one hundred and fifty American Indians from the Exposition came through, two-by-two, to the see the Great Father, who so many of them had come to the Exposition to see. Dressed in many colored blankets with painted faces, they filed past, each placing a white aster on the coffin.

On one of the floral arrangements near the casket, there was the following inscription, "Farewell of Chief Geronimo, Blue Horse, Flat Iron and Red Shirt and the 700 braves of the Indian Congress. Like Lincoln and Garfield, President McKinley never abused authority except on the side of mercy. The martyred great White Chief will stand in memory next to the Savior of mankind; we loved him living; we love him still."[41]

James Parker, who had helped apprehend Czolgosz at the Temple of Music, was in line, unnoticed by most. He waited like everyone else and

---

[38] Murat Halstead, *The Illustrious Life of William McKinley* (Privately Published, 1901) 236.

[39] G. Townsend, *Memorial Life of William McKinley* (Washington: Memorial Publishing Co., 1901) 316.

[40] G. Townsend, *Memorial Life of William McKinley* (Washington: Memorial Publishing Co., 1901) 311-312.

[41] G. Townsend, *Memorial Life of William McKinley* (Washington: Memorial Publishing Co., 1901) 300-301.

silently made his way past the President. As he walked away he looked back for one final look at the man he almost saved.[42]

One man and his two little boys approached the coffin. The smaller boy said, "I was fer McKinley last time, an' I wore a McKinley cap all fall."

The large well-dressed man behind the boys in line put his hand on the boy's shoulder and responded, "I was for McKinley too."[43]

Another man in line became agitated when a young boy of about four whimpered in line in front of him.

"It's a wonder you couldn't leave the kid at home," he complained to the mother.

"I'm sorry he annoys you," she said apologetically. "I know he's too young to understand it, but he will remember it when he grows up and he will be proud to say he saw President McKinley. I couldn't bear to leave him at home."[44]

At 10:42 p.m., the thin line of mourners making there way to the doors was suddenly halted. The guards on the steps of the building announced that the doors would be closed.

"Too late," were the words that echoed along the line, as disappointed people began their march home through the rain.

After the doors of City Hall were closed, Edward L. A. Pausch of Hartford, Connecticut made a death mask of plaster of McKinley's face. He had done this for many other notable figures in recent years. His cast fixed the features of the dead President forever.[45]

The sun was bright, but a crisp wind blew as September 16 began in Buffalo. Mrs. McKinley was awakened at 7 a.m., and asked what she had been asking for nearly a day, "When will I see him?"

From the Milburn house, two truckloads of baggage were being removed, including the hospital bed that could possibly be used if Mrs. McKinley needed it. Soon after, at 7:35, Mrs. McKinley, supported on either side by Dr. Rixey and Abner McKinley, made her way to her carriage for the ride to the train station. She was erect and in surprisingly good control of her self. She was taken to the station and placed in her car, which had already been arranged that morning by her nieces. President Roosevelt arrived at the station shortly after Mrs. McKinley.[46]

---

[42] *Buffalo Courier,* 16 September 1901, pg. 2, col. 3.

[43] *Buffalo Courier,* 16 September 1901, pg. 2, col. 2.

[44] *Buffalo Courier,* 16 September 1901, pg. 2, col. 2-3.

[45] Marshall Everett, *The Complete Life of William McKinley* (Privately Published, 1901) 344.

[46] *New York Times,* 17 September 1901, pg. 2, col. 1.

Just after 7 o'clock, President Roosevelt had been awakened, quickly dressed, and had taken breakfast with the Wilcox family. At a few minutes past 8:00, he left in his carriage for the train station with Ansley Wilcox and his secretary, William Loeb. A few mounted police, detectives and Secret Service men followed closely.[47]

Soon, Delaware Avenue, which had seen so much excitement and action during the preceding few days, returned to its former state. The press tents and reporters, the high government officials and guests, the crowds and the police and military presence all became forevermore just a memory.

Meanwhile, preparations had been made for the removal of the President's body from Buffalo City Hall to the Exchange Street Station.

At about 7:00 the gates, which surrounded the building, swung open. Forty sailors from the *Michigan* moved into Franklin Street and drew into line across from the entrance to the building. Four minutes later, the four-horse drawn hearse arrived. A company of marines filed into place and the members of the Cabinet began to assemble.

At exactly 7:45, the appointed time, the escort was in place and Major Mann barked the orders "present arms." Soon after, the flag-draped coffin emerged from the building, carried by eight body bearers, four sailors and four soldiers. The Sixty-fifth Regimental Band played *Nearer my God to Thee* as the coffin was gently paced into the hearse and the door was closed.

The procession soon moved down Franklin Street while the band played *Chopin's Funeral March*. First marched the troops, followed by carriages containing dignitaries, then the hearse, followed by members of the Grand Army, with local Buffalo militia bringing up the rear.

The scheduled departure time from Buffalo was 8:30 a.m. The route from City Hall to the station was lined with people. Business was practically suspended in the mourning-draped city until the train had left. The brisk, cool winds off Lake Erie whipped the bunting of the buildings.

In route to the station, near Ellicott Street, President Roosevelt's carriage met the procession. The President ordered it stopped and waited for his predecessor to pass. [48]

When the procession arrived at the Exchange Street Station, as the band played solemnly, the body bearers, with the casket resting on their

---

[47] *New York Times,* 17 September 1901, pg. 2, col. 2.
[48] *New York Times,* 17 September 1901, pg. 2, col. 2.

shoulders, carefully loaded it into the observation car. President Roosevelt, who had waited and watched the ceremony, was one of the last to board. He raised his hat in salutation to the people of Buffalo, spoke quietly to a man he recognized from Chicago, and entered his car.[49]

A pilot locomotive would run ten minutes ahead of the funeral train, Pennsylvania Limited Locomotive No. 168, draped in mourning. The pilot car would alert crowds to the approach of the train as well as assuring that the track was clear.[50] A compartment car called Hungary would contain President Roosevelt and his party. The private car, the Olympia, would accommodate the First Lady, and her closet friends and family. The observation car Pacific carried the President and his honor guard, commanded by Captain Leonard of the Marine Corps. The guard consisted of ten sailors from the battleship, *Indiana*, Four men each from the Seacoast Artillery and Fourteenth Infantry and three United States Hospital Corps orderlies.[51] The only mourning decorations on the train were located on the locomotive itself and the car containing the casket, across which rested a shaft of wheat.

The President's body was on the train by 8:35, and the pilot train departed two minutes later. In about ten minutes, the funeral train followed.

Along the route from Buffalo, it is impossible to determine the number of people who turned to watch the funeral train pass. In the rural areas, lone farmers stood a vigil. In the cities, such as Harrisburg and Baltimore, tens of thousands turned out. In many of the smaller towns, schools and business was suspended. Many times a minister and his congregation were seen singing and kneeling in prayer as the train passed. People, wishing to have a souvenir of the event, placed coins on the track to be smashed by the funeral train. To the satisfaction of many who turned out, they discovered that they could actually see the President's casket through the large window in the observation car, partially covered by a large, silk American flag and attended by the military honor guard. All along the 450-mile trip, which traversed some of the most beautiful scenery in the country, the citizens turned out. The somber mood, whether it was a crowd of a hundred or a thousand, was always the same.

---

[49] *New York Times,* 17 September 1901, pg. 2, col. 2.

[50] *New York Times,* 17 September 1901, pg. 1, col. 7.

[51] *New York Times,* 17 September 1901, pg. 1, col. 7.

"The people loved him. They loved him more than I knew," Mrs. McKinley said to Abner as she watched from her birth as the train passed the mourning crowds.[52]

During the ride, Mrs. McKinley, who had been requesting to see her husband repeatedly for more than twenty-four hours, was finally granted her wish. Accompanied by Dr. Rixey, she stood by as the coffin was opened. When she saw the President's features, she sobbed, but there was no outburst of grief. She knelt beside the casket for a full hour, virtually alone, because no one made a sound to disturb her. Finally, Dr. Rixey asked her to return to her cabin, which she did without protest; after she was assured that she was not taking her last look at her husband.[53]

Somewhere along the route between Harrisburg and Baltimore, Mrs. McKinley was subject to frequent fits of hysteria and Dr. Rixey gave her some light doses of opiates to help quiet her nerves. When the train arrived in Baltimore, she was composed, but the sounds of the crowd started her weeping again.

"We must go home," she exclaimed. "Can't we go back to Canton? There is peace there. We love our home."[54]

President Roosevelt spoke in his car with Exposition President John Milburn, Mayor of Buffalo Conrad Diehl and other members of the Buffalo Reception Committee and thanked them on behalf of himself, the nation, and the McKinley family, for all they had done since the shooting. [55]

The day had been cloudy and dull. Due to arrive in Washington at 8:25 p.m., the funeral train pulled into the station a bit late at 8:38. The soldiers and sailors who had been awaiting the train's arrival made their way through a cleared pathway in the crowd to the door of the train, where an officer was admitted. The funeral director removed the many flowers that accompanied the casket, and prepared them for transport to the White House. The sailor with drawn cutlass and soldier with fixed bayonet who stood guard at the head of the casket gave way to the new honor guard.

Secretaries Hay and Gage quickly made their way to the mourners car and helped those they could descend. A veiled Mrs. McKinley was

[52] *Buffalo Courier*, 17 September 1901, pg. 1, col. 5.
[53] *New York Times*, 17 September 1901, pg. 1, col. 7.
[54] *Buffalo Courier*, 17 September 1901, pg. 1, col. 5.
[55] *New York Times*, 17 September 1901, pg. 2, col. 2.

aided by Abner McKinley and Dr. Rixey, and despite the worry and circumstances, was holding up remarkably well. She was hurried to a carriage and was soon headed back to the White House, without waiting for the procession. Immediately behind her, in more carriages, rode other family and friends.

President Roosevelt came off next, arm in arm with his brother-in-law, Navy Commander Cowles. With members of his Cabinet and high-ranking military officials trailing behind, Roosevelt walked erect to the carriageway next to the gates of the station, where he waited.

Meanwhile, the body bearers were removing the coffin. They removed a large window and the casket was brought through the open window of the observation car. Four artillerymen from Fort McHenry, Maryland, were on the right, with four sailors on the left. The body bearers slowly walked, with four officers marching ahead, through a line of bareheaded soldiers, and placed the casket into the hearse on Sixth Street. A bugle, sounding out 'taps' was the only sound that broke the silence. Just as the body was being placed into the hearse, a photographer flashed a picture from a window nearby. The resulting noise and flash startled many and drew some disdainful looks.[56]

The hearse was hand carved and was pulled by six coal black horses, each with its own African-American groom in black livery. It began its journey with the President, in his carriage, directly behind. Riding with President Roosevelt were Secretaries Gage, Hay, Root and Hitchcock, Attorney General Knox, Commander Cowles, and Postmaster Smith. Behind, in other carriages, rode Cortelyou, Secretaries Wilson and Long, and Senators Hanna and Fairbanks. The Citizen's Committee from Buffalo, military officers and friends followed.[57]

As the procession began its way from Sixth Street to Pennsylvania Avenue, the military was already in place. The thoroughfare was decorated in black, with signs of mourning evident from every building. Lining the street were tens of thousands of common citizens. Little was said, and many of the people had tears in their eyes as they watched the President travel to the White House for the last time.

A platoon of mounted police led the procession, followed by representatives of the Grand Army of the Republic. Then came members of the Union Veteran's Union, veterans of the Spanish-American War and troops from the Eleventh Calvary from Fort Myer, Virginia. The hearse followed, flanked on each side by the body bearers. A detachment of Signal Corpsmen marched directly behind the hearse, with

---

[56] *New York Times,* 17 September 1901, pg. 1, col. 6.

[57] *New York Times,* 17 September 1901, pg. 1, col. 6.

the dignitaries following. It was about 9:30 when the head of the column turned into the White House gates.[58]

The soldiers got into formation and presented arms. A lady standing across from the scene began singing the President's hymn. At first, she received questioning glances, but soon other had joined in.[59]

President Roosevelt and his entourage took up a prominent place and the body was slowly and somberly carried into the White House. It was placed in the East Room with its head to the east. Piled around it were about fifty floral arrangements, with others placed in the halls. Standing guard were two marines, a soldier and a sailor, one at each corner of the casket. Seated on each side were two members of the Grand Army and two members of the Loyal Legion. The guards were changed every two hours.

By midnight, the White House was quiet and dark; dark except for the room where the guards watched over their fallen chief.

At 9:00 the next morning, September 17, President McKinley was borne the mile from the White House to the Capital building with another impressive procession, made up of detachments of the army, District military, bodies of marines and sailors, and various civic organizations.

"At precisely 9 o'clock a silent command was given, and the body bearers silently and reverently raised to their stalwart shoulders the casket containing all that was mortal of the illustrious dead," wrote one eyewitness. "They walked with slow, cadence step, and, as they appeared at the main door of the White House, the Marine Band, stationed on the avenue opposite the mansion, struck up the hymn the dead President loved so well, *Nearer My God, to Thee.*

"As the hearse moved away, the mourners from the White House entered carriages and followed the body on its march to the Capital, where the funeral services were to be held. It was thought early in the morning that Mrs. McKinley might feel strong enough to attend the services there, but it was finally decided that it would be imprudent to tax her vitality more than was absolutely necessary, and so she concluded to remain in her room under the immediate care of Dr. Rixey, Mrs. Barber, her sister, and her niece, Miss Barber."[60]

---

[58] *New York Times,* 17 September 1901, pg. 1, col. 6.

[59] *New York Times,* 17 September 1901, pg. 1, col. 6.

[60] G. Townsend, *Memorial Life of William McKinley* (Washington: Memorial Publishing Co., 1901) 336.

Slowly the cortege wound out the White House gate and onto Pennsylvania Avenue. The entire parade occurred under a rain that was pounding at times, and some where reminded that it was the anniversary of Antietam, the bloodiest day of the Civil War and a battle in which President McKinley had valiantly participated. Included in the procession were President Roosevelt and the only living former president, Grover Cleveland. The bands that accompanied the procession were silent, until reaching the capital, when they began playing *Nearer My God to Thee*, now being called by many "the President's hymn." All the way, bells tolled, bringing a hush to the crowd.

"The universal sadness was too deep to be turned back by the force of the elements," wrote one contemporary account, "and the sorrowful multitudes which viewed the funeral pageant to-day were almost as great as those which, on a more joyous occasion, six months ago, saw President McKinley driven to the Capital for his second inauguration. The weather on the two occasions was similar, with a difference only in temperature, but the crowds which cheered and applauded on March 4 were silent and weeping to-day."[61]

"Solemnly the funeral party wound down past the Treasury Building and into the broad sweep of Pennsylvania Avenue amid a profound silence that was awful to those who only six months ago had witnessed the enthusiastic plaudits which greeted the dead man as he made the same march at assume for a second time the honors and burdens of the Presidential office," wrote one observer.[62]

At the Capital, the casket was taken up the steps by the honor guard, between rows of soldiers and sailors.

"As the eight sturdy body-bearers, four from the army and four from the navy, tenderly drew the flag-draped casket from the hearse, the band, sweetly wailed the pleading notes of *Nearer My God, to Thee*," wrote an observer. "Every head in the vast attendant throng was bared. Tear bedimmed eyes were raised to Heaven and a silent prayer went up from the thousands of hearts. With careful and solemn tread, the body-bearers began the ascent of the staircase with their precious burden, and tenderly bore it to the catafalque in the rotunda." [63]

---

[61] Murat Halstead, *The Illustrious Life of William McKinley* (Privately Published, 1901) 236.

[62] G. Townsend, *Memorial Life of William McKinley* (Washington: Memorial Publishing Co., 1901) 337.

[63] G. Townsend, *Memorial Life of William McKinley* (Washington: Memorial Publishing Co., 1901) 339.

Brief services were held in the Capital, packed with distinguished mourners, with Presidents Roosevelt and Cleveland occupying prominent places, side by side. There were about 800 seats, but even the immense rotunda was inadequate to hold all that wished to attend. The chairs where placed in circles around the casket, with a space of about six feet between the first row and the catafalque.

Among the first visitors came the choir for the ceremonies and they were seated on each side of the parlor organ that sat at the head of the catafalque.

A woman entered the rotunda, dressed in black, and it was soon learned that it was Mrs. Garret A. Hobart, wife of the late Vice President and a close personal friend of Ida McKinley. She was placed directly behind the family section.[64]

There were no decorations of mourning except for the black draped catafalque in the center. There were hundreds of floral arrangements, many of the most expensive kind, and they filled all the space behind the rails in front of the historical pictures on display. The body rested on the same bier that had held Lincoln and Garfield, and which would later hold Kennedy. At about 10:30 a.m., there was a more rushed arrival, with Senators and Congressmen taking their place for the services. To the left of the catafalque, some 75 reporters representing the country's newspapers were seated. The President's Cabinet came into the room and it was known that the funeral procession had arrived. President Roosevelt and former President Cleveland, looking slightly tanned and somewhat thinner than he had been during his tenure as President, soon followed them.

"Secretary Hay looks white and far from strong," wrote a witness, "but evidently steeling himself for a ceremony certain to bring his own recent bereavement—the loss of his son—painfully before him. His dark beard, with its powdering of white, his parted hair and glasses give him a stern autocratic look, far from his bearing of the moment. Abner McKinley, very pale, poor man! and leading his wife, heads the family party from the White House, where Mrs. McKinley remains for the afternoon—her last in the home of the Presidents. Senator Hanna, still pale and shaken, is with the family party."[65]

Soon, the body was brought in by privates of the army and navy and carefully placed upon the catafalque. Former President Cleveland was among the first to rise. Shortly thereafter, the family mourning party

---

[64] *New York Times,* 18 September 1901, pg. 1, col. 7.

[65] G. Townsend, *Memorial Life of William McKinley* (Washington: Memorial Publishing Co., 1901) 343.

came in and was seated. It was immediately noticed that Mrs. McKinley was not among them.

Mrs. McKinley, upon the advice of Dr. Rixey, did not attend the Capital services. Instead, because of her feeble condition, she rested and conserved her strength for the last rites to be held in Canton. Those who were there, were not told why she was not there, but they understood.

At 10:50, after a brief prelude on the organ, the choir sang *Lead Kindly Light*, followed by a prayer by Rev. H. R. Nayler, an elder of the Methodist Episcopal Church in Washington. The echoes of the rotunda made his words undistinguishable to most in attendance. The prayer ended with *The Lord's Prayer*.

Mrs. T. C. Noyes then sang *Some Time We Will Understand*, then E. G. Andrews from Ohio, the oldest Bishop of the Methodist Episcopal Church, gave the funeral address, as a gentle breeze stirred the delicate blooms that rested on the coffin. He spoke of how the President had developed and how many loved him.

After Bishop Andrews was finished, the choir sang *Nearer My God to Thee*, with many joining in singing the song. Rev. W. H. Chapman of the Metropolitan Church gave the benediction, and the ceremony was over.

At that point, as the dignitaries left, the chairs were noisily removed and all was made ready for the entrance of the large crowd that had patiently been waiting outside for the ceremonies to end. The undertaker removed the lid of the coffin, exposing the face of President McKinley to view.

At about 12:30 the crowd, which had been waiting since early morning, entered in two lines, viewing the body from each side. They entered from the east door and moved out the west door in a seemingly endless line. The crowd that had been waiting outside suddenly pushed through the doors when they were opened, brushing aside the military guards and police. Tens of thousands pushed their way toward the great staircase inside. The crowd pressed forward for some time and the cries of women and children in pain made it apparent that the situation was becoming dangerous. Women and children, many of them infants, were crushed in the push. Men held some children above the crowd. But little seemed to be able to be done as pale and flushed-faced people were crushed and pushed into the bottleneck. The police were forced to draw clubs and threatened the crowd to get back. In the rush, several people were crushed or trampled on, and some of the injured were taken into the room directly below the rotunda where the President's body lay. From there, seven of the more severely injured were taken on to the hospital.

Afterwards, when order had been restored, at the base of the staircase could be seen many tattered bits and pieces of wearing apparel. The police injured none of these people, but it was bad mark on the day's events.[66]

It has been estimated that 130 people were enabled to view the remains per minute. All the while the pressure from outside was tremendous, with people being pushed along. More than one person entered the rotunda in a fainting condition. Many women and children actually did faint. [67]

As the body of President McKinley was lying in state, representatives of all branches of service guarded it. On each side, through two sentinels, the crowd passed. This continued throughout the day.

At 6:25, the doors of the rotunda were closed and a near riot ensued. By that time, the crowd, which had become larger as the day went on, had been drenched by intermittent rain. Those closest to the door, after having waited since one o'clock in unbearable conditions, where the most angry. A rush at the door was nearly successful and was stopped only by the threat of violence by the police guarding the entrance. Finally, the crowd retreated to the lawn and was finally dispersed by a concerted police action.[68]

Soldiers began to amass outside the Capital building under dark, stormy skies. On the Library of Congress grounds, and elsewhere, thousands of people waited, unable to see because of the intense darkness, in hopes of catching a glimpse of the last act of the Washington drama. As the soldiers took their places to form the escort, their dark forms were all that could be seen, with an occasional glitter of a bayonet. The soldiers and the crowd waited, neither able to see the other well. At 7:00, a cannon thundered and the doors of the rotunda swung open. Taps was the only sound that could be heard as the President's body was taken down the Capital steps. The flag-draped casket moved downward toward the hearse in darkness, and witnesses strained to see. Then it appeared under the electric lights that had been put in place for a moment, then disappeared again into the shadows. Nothing more was seen until movement showed that the hearse had begun its journey.

---

[66] *New York Times,* 18 September 1901, pg. 2, col. 5.

[67] G. Townsend, *Memorial Life of William McKinley* (Washington: Memorial Publishing Co., 1901) 358.

[68] *New York Times,* 18 September 1901, pg. 2, col. 3.

In the dark, the President's body was escorted to the Pennsylvania station. Along the route, people stood in the rain and darkness, pushing up close to the military line on both sides of the avenue. At the station, there were more people, and those entitled to admission where unable to get inside the station due to the silent, well-behaved crowd.

The soldiers and sailors placed the casket into the observation car, which was located in the second section of the funeral train. It was placed on flag-draped standards and covered with floral arrangements. In all, over twenty cars made up the train. Another train left the next day to carry a large contingency of Senators, Congressmen, and other mourners to Canton.

It was just prior to 8:00 when Mrs. McKinley was driven from the White House to the station. Her carriage failed to find the correct gate of the station to enter and it was some time before the problem could be rectified, there being no one to direct the driver. Awaiting the First Lady was a wheel chair, in case she had difficulty walking. But Mrs. McKinley, escorted again by Dr. Rixey and Abner, firmly walked to her car.

President Roosevelt had arrived fifteen minutes early and gone to his car with Secretary Hay. Senator Hanna arrived shortly thereafter.[69]

The observation car, in which the casket was placed, was flooded with light. As the trained moved trough the countryside, those that waited easily saw it. Also seen standing guard was a soldier at its head and a sailor at its foot.

The funeral entourage was divided into three sections, with each train leaving at ten-minute intervals. The first section included eight cars, and carried forty newspapermen and a host of dignitaries. The second portion was the presidential train and was made up of virtually the same cars that had come from Buffalo. It included the observation car with President McKinley, President Roosevelt and his entourage, and Mrs. McKinley and her family and friends. The third section was devoted entirely to army and navy officers.[70]

The lead train pulled out at 8:20, slightly behind schedule due to the late arrival of Mrs. McKinley.

As the train sped on, from inside, it appeared to be traveling in a tunnel, the darkness was so complete. It arrived in Baltimore at 9:24 and thousands stood in the drizzle for a view. The story of the train was much the same as the other two trips, with mourners dotting its path. The train arrived in York at about 11:30, with nearly ten thousand people

[69] *New York Times,* 18 September 1901, pg. 1, col. 6.
[70] *New York Times,* 18 September 1901, pg. 1, col. 6.

waiting at the station. After midnight it passed through Harrisburg, with thousands discouraged not by the rain or the late hour. It stopped for a short time to change engines and crew before resuming its journey through the blackened night. It gave the citizens of Harrisburg a great opportunity to view the guarded casket.[71]

Canton, Ohio, perhaps more than anywhere else, was a city in deep mourning. The entire town was decked in black; with perhaps the only house not being so decorated being the McKinley home on North Market Street. Not only had this city lost a President, a friend and a neighbor, but it had also lost a huge source of pride. Many an important man had made the journey to Canton to participate in the fabled "Front Porch Campaign." Now, the McKinley Presidency was over and would very soon begin fading into memory. But not before Canton said farewell to its favorite son.

The funeral train arrived at 11:20 a.m. in Alliance. The final eighteen miles of the journey was marked with black bordered flags at half-mast, and it seemed that every man woman or child was at the station. Across Main Street, a large white banner proclaimed, "We Mourn Our Nation's Dead." Church bells droned on as the train passed.

Then came the final half-hour ride to Canton. With each passing mile, more and more evidence of deep personal affection was apparent. The faces of the people showed the sense that they had lost, not just a President, but a family member. Through Maximo the train moved, then Lewisville, a mere six miles from Canton. Soon, the shops and stores of the late President's much loved native city were coming into view.

The sun finally appeared just as the train pulled into the Canton station at exactly noon. All around the station were the friends and neighbors of the fallen President. Canton had suddenly become a city of 100,000 and all seemed to be in the streets.[72]

Meeting the train was a local committee led by Ohio Secretary of State William R. Day. For a full minute after its arrival, no one departed the train. Then, Abner McKinley appeared, his face drawn and tense, followed by Dr. Rixey and another frail and broken form.

Mrs. McKinley, beneath her black veil, held her handkerchief to her eyes and her slight figure shook convulsively as she was practically carried to her carriage at the east end of the station. She was quickly driven to her home, where only two weeks earlier, she had enjoyed the company of her husband.

---

[71] *New York Times,* 18 September 1901, pg. 2, col. 6.
[72] *New York Times,* 19 September 1901, pg. 1, col. 6.

The casket was removed from the observation car after a window had been removed. The flowers were carefully placed on the ground near the train.

President Roosevelt came out of his car, and took a position, along with his entourage, on the west side of the station. The casket was then removed, carried past the President and Ohio officials and placed in the hearse. The new President's carriage fell in behind the hearse.

The procession went to Tenth Street, turned onto Cherry Street, then onto Tuscarawas, all the way between masses of people lining the streets and beneath black curtains of mourning strung across the streets from the tops of buildings.

As the funeral procession reached the Town Square, the city militia ranks swung about to face the coming hearse. It pulled up to the curb and the body bearers again took up their burden. They carried the casket up the wide stone steps leading to the entrance to City Hall, while a band player *Nearer My God to Thee*, and disappeared into the building. The body was placed in the rotunda of the building shortly before one o'clock. Outside, President Roosevelt got out of his carriage, talked with Secretary Gage and others at the curb, then walked up the steps and into the building, followed by other government officials and military officers in splendid uniforms.

The silk banner was removed from the coffin, the flowers taken off, and it was opened. President Roosevelt approached and took a look, then moved on. The other men, Cabinet members and other officials, followed him one by one to pay their final respects.

As the President started to leave he was unsure of what exit to take and he was shown to the one on the east. He exited and went to his carriage, being driven to the home of Mrs. Elizabeth Harter, where he would be staying, with others in the Cabinet.

Members of President McKinley's old Commandery of Knights of Templars, Canton Commandery No. 38 had asked to be able to place an honor guard over the casket while it lay in state. Charles L. Oberly, a businessman from Canton was the first to stand guard. The guard was changed every thirty minutes. At the foot of the bier stood a member of the Ohio National Guard, on the right a Sergeant of the Infantry and on the left a sailor. [73]

Detachments of soldiers took their places by forming lines from the entrance to the bier. When all was ready for the public, Joseph Saxton, an aging uncle of Mrs. McKinley's, was helped in. He stood for a full

[73] *New York Times,* 19 September 1901, pg. 2, col. 1.

two minutes gazing at the President, then was helped out as his lips quivered.

Finally the doors opened, and the public was admitted. Two little girls were the first to enter, followed by a large man with a red mustache. When he looked at the President, the man gasped audibly and literally passed out. Many of the visitors were shocked at McKinley's appearance, his face looking much thinner than it had in life.

Four abreast, the people were hurried by the casket, without stopping to gaze. Many left in tears. Almost all had personal remembrances of the President.

"Fathers brought their children and held them over the bier for a fleeting glance at the upturned face," reported the *New York Times*. "A sleeping babe was roused by its mother for a sight its little mind could not comprehend. Toilers came from the factories, and dinner pails in hand, trooped by the bier of him whom they call their benefactor and their friend. Now and then knots of school children hurried past, awestruck at the gloom of this chamber of death."[74]

One old man on crutches talked his way into the chamber without having to stand in line. He was a comrade of the President's and had served with him during the war. He was permitted to place a small flag on the coffin, which he took with him as a remembrance.

Some little girls places flowers upon the casket and even though they had orders not to allow anyone to place anything on the casket, the guards allowed them to stay. They were still on the coffin when it was carried out the door to be taken to the McKinley cottage. [75]

A little girl leaned over and kissed the glass above the President's face. She then ran from the hall in tears. One of the guards thought she had dropped something and he found a small bouquet of common late blooming flowers on the ground among the expensive orchids. Attached was a note that read, "Dear Mr. McKinley: I wish I could send you some prettier flowers, but these are all I have. I am sorry you got shot. Katie Lee."

The guard thoughtfully placed the flowers in a prominent place among the orchids.

"I thought I saw the President smile," he said when he told a comrade of the event.[76]

[74] *New York Times,* 19 September 1901, pg. 2, col. 1.
[75] *New York Times,* 19 September 1901, pg. 2, col. 1.
[76] Marshall Everett, *The Complete Life of William McKinley* (Privately Published, 1901) 411.

The undertaker from Buffalo, who had made the trip to turn the duties over to the local funeral director, stopped by and made a point of dispelling rumors that the President had not been embalmed properly. He had received a telegram from his Buffalo assistant, saying that the casket had hurriedly been closed because of the poor condition of the embalming. He explained that because of the condition of the body after the autopsy, it had been impossible to perform the usual tasks associated with embalming.[77]

It was estimated that 100 people every minute passed in front of the catafalque. During the five hours it was open to the public, an estimated 30,000 people passed, a number nearly equal to the population of Canton. When the doors closed at 6 p.m., the line stretched for over a mile, with people from the side streets adding to its length almost by the minute.

It was here that the face of the President was seen for the last time. The coffin was not opened afterwards and the family was not given an opportunity to see his features again. The casket was sealed before it left the courthouse.[78]

Afterward, the casket was taken to the McKinley residence, where it was placed in the front parlor for the night. The Grand Army of the Republic acted as the only escort on this trip, and there was no following. Guards were placed around the house and a number of sentries were placed in the front yard of the residence.

As church bells tolled, the next morning there was a brief private service for the family in the house before departure for the church. Mrs. McKinley was in such a state of grief that she stayed in her room and listened from the door to the minister as the body was taken from the house. Dr. Rixey remained close to Mrs. McKinley, who did not attend any more services for her husband. She had held up well, but finally, her grief had overcome her. Those around her felt that her crying was doing her good, as it released the anguish of her heart.[79]

Dr. Rixey had performed his duties to the President and First Lady well. President Roosevelt noticed and knew of President McKinley's intentions to name Rixey as the new Surgeon General, upon the expiration of the current Surgeon General's term. Through George Cortelyou, the President sent word to Mrs. McKinley that he would

---

[77] *New York Times,* 19 September 1901, pg. 2, col. 2.

[78] Murat Halstead, *The Illustrious Life of William McKinley* (Privately Published, 1901) 249.

[79] *New York Times,* 20 September 1901, pg. 1, col. 5.

follow through with the late President's plans. In the meantime, plans were made for Dr. Rixey to be able to provide, if needed, continued care for Mrs. McKinley.[80]

On the way to the church, soldiers formed triple lines to keep the citizens out of the street. The people formed masses on lawns and anywhere else they could get a clear view of the procession, surging all the way up to the line of soldiers.

At one o'clock, the black chargers of the Cleveland Troop paraded down the street, their riders four abreast in brilliant uniforms. They carried flags wrapped in crepe and their sabers bore fluttering emblems of mourning. Their coming was the signal for President Roosevelt and his Cabinet to take their places, which they did to the left of the entrance to the house.

In double file, the body bearers entered the darkened parlor, raised the flag covered casket up onto their shoulders and took it out the door and again loaded it into the hearse. In majestic silence, the white roses could be seen above the heads of those in the crowd as it was loaded.

The procession to the church passed under giant black arches draped across the streets. Masses of onlookers crowded both sides of the route. They sat on rooftops and peered from nearly every window. The church bells tolled while the sound of the funeral cadence filtered through the crowds.

At about 1:50 the procession passed the Courthouse turned onto Tuscarawas Street. At the stone First Methodist Church, where the services were to be held, lines of soldiers stood with bayonets drawn, keeping clear a broad path for the casket and the mourners who followed. As the hearse arrived, President Roosevelt and his Cabinet got out of their carriages and lined the way as the body was carried into the church through the black draped entrance.

"The scene within the church when the casket was carried in on the brawny shoulders of the soldiers and sailors was profoundly impressive," reported the *New York Times*. "A black border, twenty feet high, relieved at intervals by narrow white bands falling to the floor, swept completely around the interior. Only the gold organ pipes, back of the pulpit rose above it. The vestibules on either side of the chancel, leading into the church, were black tunnels, stained glass windows on either side were framed in black and the balcony of the Sunday school to the rear, thrown open into the church by large sliding doors, was shrouded in the same somber colors."[81]

---

[80] *New York Times,* 20 September 1901, pg. 2, col. 3.
[81] *New York Times,* 20 September 1901, pg. 1, col. 6-7.

As all rose, the body bearers, to the sounds of Beethoven's Funeral *March* being played by the organ, gently lowered the coffin onto its supports. The generals and admirals of the army and navy, all in full uniform, represented the honor guard as they came in and occupied the first pew. The President and the Cabinet, all dressed in black with gloves, followed and sat in the second pew to the right of the center aisle. Roosevelt was so close to the coffin that he could nearly bend over and touch it. Immediately behind the President sat Cortelyou, Milburn, Scatcherd and others. The mourning relatives occupied the left of the center aisle.

The services consisted of a brief oration, prayers by three different ministers and a singing quartet. Dr. John A. Hull, the pastor of the Trinity Lutheran Church, read from the Bible, after which the quartet sang the hymn, *Lead, Kindly Light.* Dr. C. E. Manchester then delivered a twenty-four minute eulogy about the life of President McKinley and the lessons learned from it.

"Our President is dead," he said. "We can hardly believe it. We had hoped and prayed, and it seemed that our hopes were to be realized and our prayers answered, when the emotion of joy was changed to one of grave apprehension. Still we waited for we said: 'It may be that God will be gracious and merciful unto us.' It seemed to us that it must be His will to spare the life of one so well beloved and so much needed.

"Thus, alternating between hope and fear, the weary hours passed on. Then came the tidings of defeated science and of that failure of love and prayer to hold its object to the earth. We seemed to hear the faintly muttered words: 'Goodbye, all, goodbye. It is God's way. His will, not ours, be done.' and then 'Nearer My God to Thee.' So, nestling nearer to his God, he passed out into unconsciousness, skirted the dark shores of the sea of death for a time, then passed on to be at rest. His great heart had ceased to beat. Our hearts are heavy with sorrow."[82]

Dr. Manchester went on to describe the life of the fallen President and how Canton had always been his true home. When he had finished, Bishop I. W. Joyce followed with a brief prayer.

"And the people without, the people who had loved him, crowded close, some of them inside the church, more on the steps and far out into the street, listening with bared heads and bated breath to the beliefs on which had been built so fine a life and so noble a death," wrote Maud

---

[82] *New York Times,* 20 September 1901, pg. 2, col. 1.

McDonald. "Then once more the march of death was taken up to music, which now wailed of the woe of the people bereft, and again told in almost triumphant solemnity of a rest well earned."[83]

The service was concluded with the singing of the hymn, the President's hymn, as it was not being called, *Nearer my God to Thee*. Father Voltman of Chicago, chaplain of the 29th Infantry did the benediction and to the music of the organ the coffin was carried back outside to the hearse.

The procession to the cemetery was two miles long and the long line of carriages consisted of representatives from the Army and Navy, the full military strength of the state of Ohio, and hundreds of civic, fraternal and other organizations. Included were Senators and Congressmen from every section of the country, Supreme Court Justices, governors and mayors, and the dead President's fellow townsmen.

They left the church at about 3:00 for the one and a half mile trip to West Lawn Cemetery. For the final time, crowds lined the streets. From the church the procession moved down Tuscarawas Street to Lincoln Street, then to West Third Street and north one block to the gates of the cemetery. For hours before the event, the people had thronged the route, and again taken up every window. There was nearly an unbroken line of soldiers from the church to the cemetery. Here too, the houses were decorated in black. Along the way, people sobbed. At the cemetery gates, where the crowd was the heaviest, two women passed out.

Meanwhile, across the United States, services were being held. In Washington, New York, and every village and hamlet, the people gathered. In Oyster Bay, the home of the new President, business was suspended, as it was in most places. In unison, the nation offered its prayers.

At exactly 4:04, the procession passed into the gates of the cemetery. Bishop Joyce read the burial service of the Methodist Church and eight buglers played taps.

"And for the last time the boys in blue lifted the weight of a nation's woe to their stalwart shoulders and, the good Bishop leading them in, bore it from the light of day to the gray gloom of the tomb," wrote Maud McDonald. "With streaming eyes, they who had been the President's family, official and unofficial, watched it pass into the shadow. With heavy hearts they acquiesced in the posting of the guard, three men at the entrance to the tomb and one at the head, one at the foot of the bier, to

---

[83] G. Townsend, *Memorial Life of William McKinley* (Washington: Memorial Publishing Co., 1901) 387.

which seemed to shut them who loved and shared his life out from him as effectively as it did the veriest stranger.

"Then, since on the isolation of death even they must not intrude, they turned sadly away. Following them came Senators and Representatives, the great majority of the people's representatives at Washington, each, as he passed the guarded doorway, reverently uncovering. After them walked the federal employees of four great cities. It must have been nearly 7 o'clock when the last of these filed past the door of the open tomb, when the last head was bared, and the last tear-rimmed eyes that sought over the vague shape of the bier in the shadow behind the impassive guard."[84]

In twenty minutes the ceremony was over and the distinguished men of the nation who had come so far with him were leaving for home. Within an hour and forty minutes, under orders, the cemetery was cleared and President McKinley rested alone under the watchful eye of the military guard.[85]

"Just inside the stately entrance stands the gray stone vault, where for a time the casket will repose," reported the *New York Times*. "Its dreary exterior was relieved to-day by great masses of flowers, banked all about and above until the gray walls were shut out from view. But in due time, the body will be taken from the vault and committed to the little plot of ground lying further on. This is the McKinley lot and here lies his father, whose name he bore, the mother he guarded so tenderly in his life, his brother James and his sister Anna, and his two children. And when that time comes a stately shaft of granite will arise above the grave, telling of the civic virtues, the pure life, and the martyred death of William McKinley."[86]

Back in Buffalo, the inside of the Temple of Music was a mere shell. It was already being visited by hundreds of people on September 8, who wished to see the spot where the President had been shot. Guards were placed in the building to prevent souvenir hunters from doing damage.

"If I ever get in there," said one man with a pocket knife on the day of the shooting, "I will cut out a piece of the floor just where the President stood."[87]

---

[84] G. Townsend, *Memorial Life of William McKinley* (Washington: Memorial Publishing Co., 1901) 389-390.

[85] *New York Times,* 20 September 1901, pg. 2, col. 3.

[86] *New York Times,* 20 September 1901, pg. 2, col. 4.

[87] *Buffalo Commercial*, 7 September 1901.

There was erected a railing around the spot, and on the floor a star marked the spot where the President stood. Around the room where scattered chairs and the only decorations where American flags. The Temple had been erected as a temporary building and was later torn down. A small stone to mark the spot of the Temple and of the presidential assassination can presently be found on Fordham Street, in the middle of a residential neighborhood, which were once the Pan-American grounds.

The Exposition Hospital also became a point of interest as people flocked to see it, particularly the cot used for the President and the operating room where the President was temporarily saved.

"I just want one good look at the room in which the dear President was first placed," said Elizabeth Mahley of Syracuse. "It will be so good to tell my friends at home that I really saw the cot, don't you know."

Another of the Exposition's temporary buildings, it was eventually torn down. The hospital had been located just inside the Amherst gate at the corner of Elmwood and Amherst.[88]

The Milburn house, built in 1861, which had for a week commanded the attention of a nation, was to eventually meet the same fate as the Temple of Music. John G. Milburn suggested that the city buy the home when he was about to leave the city, but the house was sold in 1904 to Philip Mark Shannon, who made it his home. Three years later, in 1907, a fire occurred in the house and destroyed the "McKinley apartment" in the rear of the home. A movement to have the city buy the house to preserve it failed, with the city refusing to purchase it for $30,000 in 1927. An appropriation of $200,000 was sought from Congress in 1930, but met with defeat as well. The home was remodeled and additions were added and it was eventually made into eight apartments. The house then became a home for Jesuit fathers of Canisius High School. Finally, on November 9, 1957, Rev. Gerald A. Quinn, president of the high school, announced that the house would be demolished to make room for "additional campus space." Rumor has it that the building was torn down quickly to keep preservationists from interfering. No building was ever erected in its place, and a high school parking lot now exists on the site of the Milburn home at 1168 Delaware Avenue, just north of West Ferry Street.

---

[88] *Buffalo Courier*, 10 September 1901.

The Wilcox mansion still stands today on Delaware Avenue, as a tribute to Theodore Roosevelt, and is a national historic site. About 25,000 people visit the site each year. The Buffalo Club also still stands about a block from the Wilcox mansion on Delaware.

Czolgosz' gun, handkerchief and cartridges were turned over to the Buffalo Erie County Historical Society on March 26, 1902. They can be viewed today at the Society, located in what was once the New York State Building of the Pan-American Exposition on Nottingham Court, within a few blocks of where the Temple of Music stood.

A guard was attacked at the McKinley tomb on September 29, 1901, with two men being involved in some unknown plot. The guard, Private DePrend, saw a suspicious man lurking in the shadows behind the tomb. He told the man to come forward and he refused. As he raised his gun to shoot, a second man jumped him from behind as he discharged his pistol. The blow sent DePrend rolling down a small hill. Before he could recover, or before other officers could come to his aid, the men had escaped. Police at the time thought the plan was to blow up the tomb with explosives. The men were never caught.[89]

It was only after President McKinley was killed that systematic and continuous protection of the President was instituted. Protection before McKinley was intermittent and spasmodic. During the Spanish-American War, McKinley had had four Secret Service agents assigned to him with round the clock protection. Upon the conclusion of the war, the protection was relaxed, with only Secret Service Agent Foster, at the President's request, usually accompanying him. The problem of protection had existed from the days of the early Presidents, but no action was taken until the third presidential assassination had occurred.

This third assassination of a President in a little more than a generation; it was only 36 years since Lincoln had been killed; shook the nation and aroused it to a greater awareness of the dangers to the Chief Executive. The first congressional session after the assassination gave more attention to legislation concerning attacks on the President than had any previous Congress, but still no measures for the protection of the President were passed. Nevertheless, the Secret Service assumed full-time responsibility for the safety of the President and this now became

---

[89] *Buffalo Evening News,* 30 September 1901, pg. 1, col. 1-2.

one of its major permanent functions. In 1907, the agents were, for the first time, officially funded for Presidential protection. Until that time, they had merely been paid out of funds appropriated to investigate counterfeiting. Treasury Secretary Lyman J. Gage assigned Secret Service agents to protect the President on a regular basis. Additional agents were provided when the President traveled or went on vacation.

Theodore Roosevelt, the first President to experience the extensive system of protection that has surrounded the President ever since, voiced an opinion of Presidential protection that was probably shared in part by most of his successors. In a letter to Senator Henry Cabot Lodge, from his summer home, he wrote:

"The Secret Service men are a very small but very necessary thorn in the flesh. Of course, they would not be the least use preventing any assault upon my life. I do not believe there is any danger of such an assault, and if there were, as Lincoln said, "though it would be safer for a President to live in a cage, it would interfere with his business." But it is only the Secret Service men who render life endurable, as you would realize if you saw the procession of carriages that pass through the place, the procession of people on foot who try to get into the place, not to speak of the multitude of cranks and others who are stopped in the village."[90]

The establishment and extension of the Secret Service authority for protection was a prolonged process. Although the Secret Service undertook to provide full-time protection for the President beginning in 1902, it received neither funds for the purpose nor sanction from the Congress until 1906 when the Sundry Civil Expenses Act for 1907 included funds for protection of the President by the Secret Service. Following the election of William Howard Taft in 1908, the Secret Service began providing protection for the President-elect. This practice received statutory authorization in 1913, and in the same year, Congress authorized permanent protection of the President. It remained necessary to renew the authority annually in the Appropriations Acts until 1951.[91]

Though it was talked about that time, the murder of a President did not become a federal crime until 1964, after the assassination of President Kennedy in Dallas.

It is interesting to note that three of Czolgosz's brothers served in the World War and one gave up his life for his country.

---

[90] Warren Report
[91] Warren Report

Joseph Czolgosz tried to join the United States Army but was not accepted because of his age, 49 years, so he joined the Canadian Expeditionary Force at Winnipeg on the 8th of May, 1918, under the name of Joe Peterson. He served in France and was discharged April 11, 1919; his War Service badge is No.15, 436.

Charles Czolgosz was anxious to join the Army at the beginning of the War, but his parents then being old persuaded him not to go until he was called. He was called in June, claimed no exemption and was placed in Class AI. He was sent to the University of Cincinnati Training School, transferred to Fort Sheridan, Illinois, and then with a detail of sixty boys was sent to Camp Mills to the Eighth Division for immediate service overseas. He was placed in Company D, Motor Supply Train, which was ready to sail when the Armistice was signed. He received an honorable discharge on the 7th of February, 1919.

Antoine Czolgosz, who was usually called "Tony," was Leon's youngest brother. He joined the Army at Los Angeles, California, and was transferred to Camp Lewis, Washington, where he was placed in Company K, 363d Infantry, 91st Division, American Expeditionary Force, and served with them in France. A shell killed him on the 4th day of the Argonne Drive.

THE AMERICAN RED CROSS
National Headquarters
Washington, D. C.

Jan. 31, 1919.

Private Tony Czolgosz,
Co. K, 363 Inf., Am. E. F.

Mr. Paul Czolgosz,
3557 East 59th St.,
Cleveland, Ohio.

My dear Mr. Czolgosz:
It is with deep regret that I am writing to confirm the death of your son, who died bravely fighting for his country and the glorious cause of freedom.

A grateful nation will never forget the debt it owes to all who have paid such a price for the cause, and as he lies in his soldier's grave he will be honored by the whole world, as one of the brave American soldiers who gave his life that the world might become a better and a safer place. I am enclosing a letter to you from the Chaplain of the 363rd Inf.

Please accept my very sincere sympathy for you in your great sorrow and believe me to be,

Faithfully yours,
(Signed) W. R. Castle, Jr.,
Director Bureau of Communication.

Leon's brother Waldek Czolgosz died in 1933 at the age of 67.

Leon's younger sister, Victoria, sued his other sister, Celia, in 1933 over a life insurance policy on Leon Czolgosz. Victoria had been to young to collect from the insurance at the time of the execution, and Celia promised to pay her some of the money for years, but had never done it. Victoria Gralewicz (later shortened to Graull for convenience) lived with her husband at 3624 East 64th Street in Cleveland and was considered a bit off by her brother Jacob, who thought her demands groundless. She had finally appealed to courts for her share of the insurance money because of "dire need." Victoria was awarded a default judgment for a share of the $483 that was paid in 1901 to Celia and Paul Czolgosz. The award was for $400, but it is unclear whether or not she was ever able to actually collect the money.

Paul Czolgosz, Leon's father, lived on into his nineties, cared for by his remaining children, and living with his daughter, Celia Bandowski at 5718 Fleet Avenue in Cleveland. He never learned English and drew a pension from the death of Tony during World War I.

Emma Goldman spent her last years in Canada, close enough to be visited by her friends in the United States. She suffered a stroke in February of 1940, which left her unable to speak. She died on May 14, 1940. A memorial service was held in New York City, attended by some of the most prominent reformers and radicals of the age, to pay tribute to Goldman's life work. Meanwhile, thousands of mourners flocked to see her flower laden casket as she was buried in Chicago. It took so long to raise money for her tombstone that her birthday and the date of her death are both recorded inaccurately. She is buried at Waldheim Cemetery in Chicago, only a few feet from the Haymarket monument.

A controversy arose when it came time for the President's physicians to be paid. Dr. Mann was widely criticized for maintaining that the government had retained the doctors rather than by the McKinley family. He also stated that the dignity of the medical profession demands that Congress pay their bill, and that the doctor's services should be handsomely rewarded.[92]

The government had doled out $27,500 for medical fees incurred during President Garfield's treatment, but the doctors were accused of trying to get big money from Congress rather than sending a bill to McKinley's estate. Eventually, the doctors were indeed handsomely paid, with Mann receiving $10,000 for his week of services. Mynter received $6,000, Park and McBurney $5,000 each, and Stockton $1,500. The President's nurses each received $100.

Dr. Roswell Park had his standing in the medical profession enhanced, because many believed that he could have indeed saved the President's life. He continued to be one of most famous doctors in the world. His name is now synonymous with cancer research. One evening, about 2:30 a.m., Park got out of bed to get a drink of water in the night and succumbed quickly to a heart attack. His son found him and called for help but it was too later. Dr. Park died at 3 a.m. on February 15, 1914.

Dr. Mann, the villain to many in the case, came out financially undamaged and maintained a successful practice, holding a professorship of obstetrics and gynecology at the University of Buffalo. He retired from teaching in 1910. On March 2, 1921, Dr. Mann went to a Lenten Noon Day at St. Paul's with his wife. After the service, Mrs. Mann went to the hospital to visit a friend, while the doctor went to his office for his customary nap. When he did not appear at the normal time, Mrs. Mann went to his office and found him; he had died peacefully in his sleep. He was 76.

Dr. Herman Mynter was known for his quick wit and sense of humor. Once, a lady called him on the telephone and apparently having the wrong number, asked if she was speaking to Miller the baker. "No, Madam, this is Mynter the butcher," the doctor quipped before hanging up the phone.[93]

---

[92] Selig Adler, "The Operation on President McKinley," *Scientific American* (March 1963) 130.
[93] *Buffalo Express*, 10 February 1903.

Mynter had heart disease and suffered for about a year, but practiced medicine until two weeks prior to his death. The doctor had been ill for about ten days and at first, it was not suspected that it was nearly so serious. But he gradually grew worse and died with his family around him at 10:30 p.m. on February 10, 1903. He was 58. Dr. Stockton was one of the attending physicians and was the last survivor of the President's principle doctors, dying in 1931.

Dr. McBurney was not harmed by his faulty prognosis, and practiced medicine until just prior to World War I. Dr. Parmenter died in June of 1932 in Geneva, New York. Dr. Eugene Wasdin died ten years after the assassination in a sanitarium near Philadelphia on November 11, 1911. He was only 53.

Louis L. Babcock lived to the ripe old age of 87, dying in his home on West Ferry Street on November 5, 1956. All his life, he kept scrapbooks and anything else he could find pertaining to the McKinley assassination. His collection is now housed at the Buffalo Erie County Historical Society.

Big Jim Parker became a celebrity of sorts in the days following the assassination, and before the President died, as the man who saved McKinley. Fair goers paid twenty-five dollars each for the buttons from the shirt he was wearing that day, another person offered to take his picture and sell photographs on the Midway. He was also offered a job as a Midway side show exhibit.[94]

The week of the shooting, Parker began to receive a hundred envelopes a day containing money. The people were trying to thank him. He was given many opportunities to cash on his newfound notoriety, but he refused.

"I happened to be in a position where I could aid in the capture of the man," he said. "I do not think that American people would like me to make capital out of the fortunate circumstance. I am no freak anyway. I do not want to be exhibited in all kinds of shows. I was glad that I was able to be of service to the country."[95]

After the assassination some questioned his role in the apprehension of Czolgosz. A report issued by the Treasury Department in 1910 denied that Parker had been involved in the apprehension of Czolgosz.

---

[94] *Buffalo Evening News*, 8 September 1901, pg. 4, col. 4.
[95] *Buffalo Evening News*, 14 September 1901, pg. 4, col. 7.

"Out of this incident grew the widely heralded statement, cunningly fostered by a notoriety-loving negro, that he was the 'hero' who had 'falled the President's assassin,'" read the report. "The negro's story was contradicted by every witness of the tragedy but from time to time the alleged incident is revived to discredit the officers of this Service who were present."[96]

Contrary to what the Treasury report claimed, virtually all of the eyewitnesses confirmed Parker's story the day of the shooting. Some, doubtless upon reflection, changed their stories later, to discredit Parker, possibly for racist reasons. And Parker's actions after the assassination did not seem to be those of one seeking notoriety. But there is no doubt as to the part James Parker played. Parker would be rightfully proud of his quick action for the remainder of his life.

Czolgosz attorney Robert C. Titus died in 1928, after a distinguished career in law. Loran L. Lewis died a few short years after the Czolgosz trial. Judge Edward K Emery, who presided over the arraignment of Czolgosz, died in 1919. Justice Truman C. White, the judge in the Czolgosz trial, resigned from the New York Supreme Court on December 31, 1910 because he had reached the mandatory retirement age. Two years later he developed bladder trouble and was ill for five weeks, until doctors decided an operation would be best. After the operation, White, like McKinley, seemed to be rallying, but then took a downturn and suddenly died on February 6, 1912.

John Nowak was a prominent Polish leader in Buffalo. He served a deputy sheriff from 1905-1913 and was active in the Polish National Alliance. He died in 1938 at the age of 71.

Detective Albert Solomon moved to Duluth, Minnesota, where he worked as a police chief in a steel mill for twenty years. He died three years after retiring, at age 75 in 1935.[97]

Secret Service Agent Albert Gallaher requested that he be permitted to witness the execution of Czolgosz. "I still have the marks of the kicking I received, to say nothing of the about the choking and I feel that the only satisfaction I can get out of it will be to see the 'curr' in the chair," Gallaher wrote in his request. He was to be dead within ten years of the assassination.

---

[96] Franklin MacVeigh, *Papers of Franklin MacVeigh*, Box 27, 1910 folder, Library of Congress, pg. 4.
[97] *Buffalo Evening News*, 8 November 1935.

William S. Bull resigned as Buffalo Police Superintendent in June of 1906, after serving longer than anyone else in that position. Following his retirement, he was named assistant adjutant general of the New York detachment of the Grand Old Army, a Civil War veterans association. He served in that capacity until he died at his home at 806 Elmwood with his family at his bedside in 1919.[98]

Thomas Penney, after serving only two years as Buffalo's District Attorney, resigned the position in 1902, retiring to private practice, becoming one of the finest trial lawyers in New York State and practicing in Buffalo for a total of 43 years; 32 years after the Czolgosz trial. On November 11, 1933, Penney spent the afternoon with friends at the Buffalo Club, then a happy evening at home. He retired for the evening, and suddenly died of a heart attack. Seemingly in good health, his death was a shock to those around him.[99] He was buried in Forest Lawn Cemetery in Buffalo.

On February 1, 1904, John Milburn left Buffalo and moved to New York City to practice law. His house had become the center of attention to tourists, with public tours complete with megaphones frequently going by the house. But John Milburn always handled the situation with a generous spirit, with grace and in stride. After he moved, in New York City, he served on the board of trustees of Columbia University and as President of the New York Bar Association. John Milburn died on August 11, 1930 in London, only 17 days after the death of his wife.

John Hay had lived through the deaths of three assassinated Presidents. He had been an assistant to Lincoln's private secretary and had worked as an editorial writer for the *New York Tribune*. Among his books, he wrote a ten volume series, *Abraham Lincoln: A History* (1886-1890). He continued to serve President Roosevelt as Secretary of State, until his death in 1905.

Charles G. Dawes went on to become Vice President of the United States (1925-1929) under Calvin Coolidge. He won a Nobel peace prize in 1925 for arranging a plan for German reparation after World War I. After his Vice Presidency, he was named Ambassador to Great Britain, a post he held from 1928 until 1932. Born in Marietta, Ohio, he died in 1951.

---

[98] *Buffalo Commercial*, 27 June 1907.
[99] *Buffalo Evening News*, 11 November 1933.

James Wilson served as Secretary of Agriculture from 1897-1913, serving in the Cabinets of McKinley, Roosevelt and Taft. He died August 26, 1920. He has a building of the Department of Agriculture named after him in Washington, D. C.

Elihu Root also went on to win a Nobel peace prize in 1912. Though he was an avid critic of the League of Nations, Root helped plan the Permanent Court of International Justice, or World Court, that the League sponsored. He continued to serve as Secretary of War under President Roosevelt, and was named Secretary of State by Roosevelt upon the death of John Hay, a post held until 1909, when the New York legislature elected him to the Unite States Senate, where he served until 1915. He failed in an attempt to secure the Republican nomination for President and died in 1937.

Philander Chase Knox became Secretary of State from 1909-1913 under William Howard Taft. He died in 1921.

Dr. Presley M. Rixey continued to serve as the President Roosevelt's official physician and even served after Roosevelt as the official White House physician. Rixey was decorated by Alphonso XIII, King of Spain for service performed for the officers and men of the Santa Maria following an explosion on that vessel. He died June 27, 1928 in Arlington, Virginia.

Surviving his good friend by only three years, Marcus Alonzo Hanna was a viable candidate for the Republican nomination for President against Theodore Roosevelt. However, he died suddenly in 1904. Abner McKinley, the President's brother, also died in 1904.

Capable George Bruce Cortelyou went on to a distinguished career in government service. He stayed on as personal secretary to President Roosevelt, until he was appointed as the first Secretary of Commerce and Labor in 1903, a job he held for two years, until 1905. He served as Postmaster General from 1905-1907, then as Treasury Secretary, 1907-1909. Cortelyou also was chairman of the National Republican Committee, 1904-1907. In 1909 he left government service to take a job as President of Consolidated Gas Company in New York, a position he held until 1935. He was the honorary President of the McKinley Memorial Association. He lived in Huntington, New York, on Long Island. He died October 23, 1940, at the ripe old age of 78.

On September 20, 1901, shortly after noon, Ida McKinley asked to be taken for the first time to the cemetery. She had missed the funeral the day before due to her distressed condition. Dr. Rixey readily agreed and took her there in a closed carriage. They were joined by Mrs. Barber. Upon their arrival, a throng of citizens who gathered around the carriage were quickly dispersed by the soldiers on guard. She was driven to the front of the vault where she received a salute.

She expressed gratitude when she saw all the flowers, but was somewhat apprehensive about someone doing damage to her husband's body. Dr. Rixey assured her that the guards would remain for ninety days, after which the President's body would be locked in the vault.

"I am happy over the effect of the drive on Mrs. McKinley," Rixey said. "She is much better today, I have finally achieved success in getting her to take an interest in affairs going on in Canton. She asked many questions while riding, and seemed in good spirits."[100]

The next day, she said she had slept better since any day since her husband had been shot. She went on her customary carriage ride with Dr. Rixey and Mrs. Barber. When she looked out her window to see guards in front of the house, she insisted they be removed as being unnecessary.

"I do not feel so confident as earlier this week," said Dr. Rixey upon their return. "Mrs. McKinley's grief is crushing her, though she is bearing up bravely and doing as well as could be expected under the circumstances. However, too much encouragement should not be taken at this early day."[101]

On September 26, George Cortelyou made a trip to Canton to facilitate in the business of the President's will. The President left his widow approximately $250,000 worth of assets, including $67,000 in insurance. He also left $1,000 per month to his sister, Helen. Whatever property remained after Mrs. McKinley's death, was to be dispersed equally among the President's surviving siblings.[102]

The following year, Mrs. McKinley suddenly remarked to friends, "This is the anniversary of the shooting of my husband at Buffalo." Her friends had not mentioned it to her, but Ida was fully aware.[103]

Ida McKinley lived on wishing to join her husband. Charles Dawes visited the President's widow in 1903.

---

[100] *New York Times,* 21 September 1901, pg. 3, col. 3.

[101] *New York Times,* 22 September 1901, pg. 1, col. 5.

[102] *Buffalo Courier,* 28 September 1901, pg. 1, col. 7.

[103] *Buffalo Times,* 8 September 1902.

" Mrs. McKinley greeted us in tears and was depressed in spirits which is always the case with her now," Dawes wrote. "Owing to rain, we could not go the cemetery as she desired. A friend (Miss Cross I think the name is) and a nurse are now with her at the house. Mrs. McKinley refers to her husband constantly. She will not or cannot keep her mind from him, and hopes that she will be soon be called to follow him.... The McKinley home in which, while the President lived, there was so much happiness is now the saddest into which I have ever entered. I talked of the President as best I could, for Mrs. McKinley is best satisfied when he is the subject of our conversation.... The day was a sad one at best."[104]

Mrs. McKinley lived out her remaining days in Canton, and died in 1907. She is buried next to her husband at the McKinley Memorial.

In an irony of history, following his terms as President, and while again running for the presidency as a third party candidate, Theodore Roosevelt was himself shot.

On October 14, 1912, Roosevelt was shot in the chest while entering an automobile during a campaign trip to Milwaukee in front of the Hotel Gilpatrick. His life was spared because the bullet struck him in pocket where he carried a fifty-page speech, which had been folded, and his glasses' case, slowing the bullet. The crowd apprehended his assailant, and like McKinley, Roosevelt instructed them not to hurt him.

Refusing to go to the hospital, Roosevelt went on with his speech in the Milwaukee Auditorium, though he had was bleeding enough that there was blood on his shirt and trousers and in his shoe.

"Please excuse me from making a long speech," he said to the crowd of nine thousand as he began his speech. "I'll do the best I can. You see, there is a bullet in my body."

After a heckler had doubted his being shot at all, Roosevelt pulled his bullet riddled speech from his pocket, held it over his head and exclaimed, It takes more than one bullet to kill a bull moose! I'm all right, no occasion for any sympathy whatever, but I want to take this occasion within five minutes after having been shot to say something to our people which I hope no one will question the profound sincerity of."[105] He then spoke for an hour and a half before going to the hospital.

---

[104] Charles W. Dawes, *A Journal of the McKinley Years* (Chicago: R. R. Donnelley & Sons Co., 1950) 349-350..

[105] James W. Clarke, *American Assassins: The Darker Side of Politics* (Princeton, NJ: Princeton University Press, 1982) 215.

Roosevelt had been assaulted by John Schrank, a thirty-six year old man who had been spurred to action because of, he said, visits to him by McKinley's ghost. Schrank was concerned about Roosevelt seeking a third term, something he felt was the first step toward dictatorship.

"I did not want to kill the candidate of the Progressive Party. I shot Roosevelt as a warning to other third termers."

The first visit Schrank said McKinley had paid him came the day after his death on September 15, 1901. He described the vision in a scrawled note, writing, "In a dream I saw President McKinley sit up in his coffin, pointing at a man in a monk's attire in whom I recognized as Theo. Roosevelt. The dead President said, 'This is my murderer, avenge my death.'"[106]

Then on September 14, 1912, almost eleven years to the minute of his first dream, Schrank said McKinley reappeared to him in another dream.

"While writing a poem, someone tapped me on the shoulder and said: 'Let not a murderer take the presidential chair. Avenge my death.'" he wrote. "I could see clearly Mr. McKinley's features."

"Before the Almighty God, I swear that the above written statement is nothing but the truth," he added.[107]

Schrank followed Roosevelt during a campaign swing through the south, until he finally had his opportunity in Milwaukee. He was found to be insane after the shooting and spent the remainder of his days in the prison hospital at Waupon, Wisconsin. He died on September 15, 1943, the anniversary of the two McKinley visions. He never received a card or a visitor in thirty years of confinement. Upon his death, his body was donated to Marquette University Medical School. [108]

Shortly after his inauguration, President Theodore Roosevelt initiated a memorial to be dedicated to William McKinley. Ironically, the site in Canton had been picked by President McKinley himself to build a memorial in tribute to Stark County soldiers. After the necessary funds were raised, construction on the memorial began in 1905, with President Roosevelt traveling to Canton on September 30, 1907 for the dedication ceremonies. An Act of Congress on March 4, 1911, set in motion a movement to mark the birthplace of William McKinley, and the National

[106] James W. Clarke, *American Assassins: The Darker Side of Politics* (Princeton, NJ: Princeton University Press, 1982) 218.

[107] James W. Clarke, *American Assassins: The Darker Side of Politics* (Princeton, NJ: Princeton University Press, 1982) 219.

[108] James W. Clarke, *American Assassins: The Darker Side of Politics* (Princeton, NJ: Princeton University Press, 1982) 221.

McKinley Birthplace Memorial Association was incorporated to complete the project in Niles, Ohio.

The city of Buffalo tried to get out from under the cloud that had been left in the wake of the McKinley assassination. The Pan American Exposition continued, but there was now an interest in the Temple of Music for a different reason.

"There must be no faltering in our efforts now, considering how much of the success of the Pan-American Exposition means in the development of closer and political relations between the peoples of the western hemisphere," said Exposition President John Milburn. "There are six weeks more of the life of the Exposition, and it is in the full bloom of its beauty and interest. Every feature of it has been developed to its highest point, and it is being operated on a more elaborate scale than ever. It is a complete mass of varied activities and entertainments, more than adequately carrying out its aims and purposes. It is a National enterprise, and should be supported as such, for the credit of our country as the leading Nation of this hemisphere. That support I feel certain it will have in fullest and overflowing measure."[109]

The Pan American Exposition did not die. It continued to draw large sized crowds. President's Day had been the biggest day of the fair, but the next day's shooting of the President was what was etched in the minds of the people.

The assassination of President McKinley has been said to have been a turning point for the City of Buffalo. Until that time, Buffalo had been an up and coming port city. Afterward, the city never quite fulfilled its promise. Whether the assassination itself was the cause could be argued. But from that point on, a city on the rise, became a city in decline.

---

[109] *New York Times,* 23 September 1901, pg. 2, col. 1.

Leaving the Milburn house.

Taking the casket into Buffalo City Hall.

Removing the casket from the hearse at Buffalo City Hall.

McKinley's casket taken into Buffalo City Hall.

McKinley funeral procession in Buffalo passing St. Paul's Cathedral en route to funeral train.

Lying in State in the Buffalo City Hall.

The line of mourners waiting to see the President in Buffalo City Hall.

The train tracks near East Palestine, Ohio

The casket on the way to the funeral train in Buffalo.

Independence Hall in Philadelphia decked out in mourning.

Lying in state in the White House.

Members of Congress in the McKinley funeral procession pass the Treasury Building from the White House to the Capital.

The President's casket is born up the steps of the Capital.

The casket being taken into the Rotunda of the Capital.

The east front of the Capital as the casket enters.

Another view of the umbrellas in the plaza near the Capital.

The Rotunda of the Capital ready for the President's funeral service.

Rev. Dr. Manchester

Bishop Andrews

Reverend Locke

Arrival of the funeral train in Canton, OH.

McKinley home under military guard in Canton, OH.

The funeral train at Canton, OH.

One of the specially constructed funeral arches in Canton, OH.

Taking the casket into the church in Canton, OH.

McKinley funeral procession moves through Canton, OH

Stark County Courthouse in Canton, OH.

Taking the casket from the church in Canton, OH.

Funeral in Canton, OH. President Roosevelt can be seen, second from left with the hat.

Canton City Hall at the time of the McKinley funeral.

McKinley's casket being placed into the vault at burial site in Canton, OH.

Photograph showing floral arrangements at burial site in Canton, OH.

The McKinley Monument in Canton, OH.

The Caskets inside the Monument.

The Marker that stands in place where the Temple of Music once stood.

Parking lot where the Milburn House once stood.

Bibliography

Books

Barry, Richard H. *The True Story of the Assassination of President McKinley at Buffalo.* Buffalo: Robert Allan Reid, 1901.

Briggs, L. Vernon. *The Manner of Man That Kills.* Boston: R. G. Badger, Gorman Press, 1921.

Carnes, Cecil. *Jimmy Hare: News Photographer.* New York: MacMillan Co., 1940.

Caroli, Betty Boyd. *First Ladies.* New York: Oxford University Press, 1987.

Clarke, James W. *American Assassins: The Darker Side of Politics.* Princeton, NJ: Princeton University Press, 1982.

Croly, Herbert. *Marcus Alonzo Hanna.* New York: The MacMillan Co., 1923.

Dawes, Charles G. *A Journal of the McKinley Years.* Chicago: Lakeside Press, R.R. Donnelly & Sons, 1950.

Donovan, Robert J. *The Assassins.* New York: Harper & Brothers, 1952.

Drinnon, Richard. *Rebel in Paradise, A Biography of Emma Goldman.* Chicago: University of Chicago Press, 1961.

Everett, Marshall. *The Complete Life of William McKinley and the Story of His Assassination.* Privately Published, 1901.

Fallows, Samuel. *Life of William McKinley: Our Martyred President.* Chicago: Regan Printing House, 1901.

Goldman, Emma. *Living My Life.* New York: Alfred A. Knopf, *1931.*

Halstead, Murat. *The Illustrious Life of William McKinley: Our Martyred President.* Privately Published, 1901.

Hamilton, Allan McLane. *Recollections of an Alienist.* New York: George H. Doran, 1916.

Johns, A. Wesley. *The Man Who Shot McKinley.* London: AS Barnes and Co., 1970.

Kent, Zachary. *William McKinley* Chicago: Children's Press, 1988.

Leech, Margaret. *In the Days of McKinley.* New York: Harper and Brothers, 1959.

McClure, Alexander K. & Morris, Charles. *The Authentic Life of William McKinley: Our Third Martyr President.* Washington, DC: Act of Congress, 1901.

McKinley, James. *Assassination in America.* New York: Harper & Row Publishers, 1975.

Miller, Nathan. *Theodore Roosevelt.* New York: William Morrow & Co., 1992.

O'Toole, G. J. A. *The Spanish War: An American Epic 1898.* New York: W. W. Norton & Co., 1984.

People V. Leon F. Czolgosz (1901). Courthouse Archives, Erie County, Buffalo, New York. Reprinted in American State Trials, edited by John D. Lawson, vol. 14, pp. 159-231. St. Louis: Thomas Law Book Co., 1923.

Rayback, Joseph G. *A History of American Labor.* New York: MacMillan Company, 1959.

Renehan, Edward J. Jr. *The Lion's Pride: Theodore Roosevelt and His Family in Peace and War.* New York: Oxford University Press, 1998.

Swanberg, W. A. *Citizen Hearst.* New York: Charles Scribner's Sons, 1961.

Tebbel, John. *The Life and Good Times of William Randolph Hearst.* New York: E. P. Dutton & Co., Inc., 1952.

Thayer, William Roscoe. *The Life and Letters of John Hay.* 2 vols. Boston: Houghton Miffen Company, 1915.

Townsend, Col. G. W. *Memorial Life of William McKinley.* Washington, DC: Memorial Publishing Company, 1901.

Whitelaw, Nancy. *Theodore Roosevelt Takes Charge.* Morton Grove, Illinois: Albert Whitman & Co., 1992.

Winkler, John K. *William Randolph Hearst.* New York: Hastings House Publishers, 1955.

Magazines & Journals

Adler, Selig. "Operation on President McKinley." Scientific American (March 1963), pp. 118-30.

Channing, Walter. "The Mental Status of Czolgosz, the Assassin of President McKinley." American Journal of Insanity 59 (October 1902) 233-278.

Fine, Sidney. "Anarchism and the Assassination of President McKinley." *American Historical Review 60* (July 1955) 777-799.

Matthews, F. "President's Last Days." Harper's Weekly 45 (September 21, 1901) 942-943.

Parmenter, John, M.D. "The surgery in President McKinley's Case." *Buffalo Medical Journal* 41-57:205-6.

Spitzka, Edward A. "The Post-Mortem Examination of Leon F. Czolgosz, The Assassin of President McKinley." *American Journal of Insanity* 58 (January 1902) 386-388.

Unsigned. "The Assault Upon President McKinley." *Literary Digest* 23 (14 September 1901) 301-303.

Unsigned, "The Official Report on the Case of President McKinley" *Buffalo Medical Journal* 41-57:271-93.

VanPeyma, P. W., M. D. "Last Hours of McKinley" *The Daily Bazaar* (28 November 1945.) 5.

Wilson, Nelson W., M.D. "Details of the McKinley Case" *Buffalo Medical Journal* 41-57:207-225

Documents

Foster, George. *Official Secret Service Report,* 6 September 1901.

Fowler, Joseph; Crego, Floyd S.; and Putnam, James W. "Official Report of the Experts for the People in the Case of the People v. Leon Czolgosz" (1901). Reprinted in *American State Trials,* edited by James D. Lawson, vol.14, pp. 195-199. St. Louis: Thomas Law Book Company, 1923.

Gallaher, Albert L. *Official Secret Service Report,* 6 September 1901.

Ireland, Samuel R. *Official Secret Service Report,* 6 September 1901.

"Report of Dr. Carlos F. MacDonald and Dr. Arthur Hurd, Experts for the Prisoner" (1901). Reprinted in *American State Trials,* edited by James D. Lawson, vol.14, pp. 195-199. St. Louis: Thomas Law Book Company, 1923.

MacVeigh, Franklin. *Papers of Franklin MacVeigh*. Library of Congress: Box 27, 1910.

Newspapers

Buffalo Commercial
Buffalo Courier
Buffalo Enquirer
Buffalo Express
Buffalo Evening News
Chicago Tribune
Cincinnati Enquirer
Cincinnati Post
Cleveland Plain Dealer
New York Times
St. Louis Post-Dispatch
Wall Street Journal
Washington Post

Photo Credits

Cover

An artist's rendition of the shooting. (Everett, Marshall. *The Complete Life of William McKinley and the Story of His Assassination.* Privately Published, 1901, pg.355.)

Frontispiece

President McKinley

Chapter 1

President McKinley. (McClure, Alexander K. & Morris, Charles. *The Authentic Life of William McKinley: Our Third Martyr President.* Washington, DC: Act of Congress, 1901. pg. 134)

President McKinley. (McClure, Alexander K. & Morris, Charles. *The Authentic Life of William McKinley: Our Third Martyr President.* Washington, DC: Act of Congress, 1901, pg. 273)

President William McKinley. (McClure, Alexander K. & Morris, Charles. *The Authentic Life of William McKinley: Our Third Martyr President.* Washington, DC: Act of Congress, 1901, pg. 97

Ida McKinley, the First Lady. (McClure, Alexander K. & Morris, Charles. *The Authentic Life of William McKinley: Our Third Martyr President.* Washington, DC: Act of Congress, 1901, pg. 98)

The McKinley Home in Canton. (McClure, Alexander K. & Morris, Charles. *The Authentic Life of William McKinley: Our Third Martyr President.* Washington, DC: Act of Congress, 1901, pg. 189)

Secretary of State Day signing the peace treaty with Spain while President McKinley and others look on. (McClure, Alexander K. & Morris, Charles. *The Authentic Life of William McKinley: Our Third Martyr President.* Washington, DC: Act of Congress, 1901.)

Theodore Roosevelt at his desk. (McClure, Alexander K. & Morris, Charles. *The Authentic Life of William McKinley: Our Third Martyr President.* Washington, DC: Act of Congress, 1901, pg. 108).

Charles Emery Smith. (*Harper's Weekly*, 1901)

Chapter 2

George B. Cortelyou, the President's personal secretary. (Halstead, Murat. *The Illustrious Life of William McKinley: Our Martyred President.* Privately Published, 1901.)

Marcus Hanna, Senator from Ohio and a close personal friend of the President. It was Hanna who engineered McKinley's presidential campaigns. (Halstead, Murat. *The Illustrious Life of William McKinley: Our Martyred President.* Privately Published, 1901.)

Lyman C. Gage. (Halstead, Murat. *The Illustrious Life of William McKinley: Our Martyred President.* Privately Published, 1901.)

Elihu Root. (Halstead, Murat. *The Illustrious Life of William McKinley: Our Martyred President.* Privately Published, 1901).

Grover Cleveland, the only living former President at the time of the shooting. (*Harper's Weekly*, 14 September 1901.)

Charles Dawes, McKinley's Comptroller of the Currency and friend. (*Harper's Weekly*, 28 September 1901.)

Judge Emery, who presided over the Czolgosz arraignment. (*Harper's Weekly*, 5 October 1901, pg. 1014.)

The President giving his September 5th speech at the Exposition. (*Harper's Weekly*, 14 September 1901, pg. 910).

McKinley in the reviewing stand at the stadium the day before the shooting. (*Harper's Weekly*, 14 September 1901, pg. 912).

The President and Mrs. McKinley leave the Milburn house for their trip to Niagara Falls the morning of the shooting. (McClure, Alexander K. & Morris, Charles. *The Authentic Life of William McKinley: Our Third Martyr President.* Washington, DC: Act of Congress, 1901, pg 317.)

President McKinley viewing Niagara Falls on September 6, 1901, the morning he was shot. Secret Service Agent Foster is second from right in the light colored jacket. (McClure, Alexander K. & Morris, Charles. *The Authentic Life of William McKinley: Our Third Martyr President.* Washington, DC: Act of Congress, 1901, pg. 272).

The last photograph of Mr. and Mrs. McKinley together, as they arrive back in Buffalo from Niagara Falls. Mrs. McKinley speaks to George Cortelyou as Secret Service agent George Foster follows. (*Leslie's Illustrated Weekly*, 14 September 1901).

The President on the way to Niagara Falls on the morning of the shooting. (*Leslie's Illustrated Weekly*, 14 September 1901).

The President on the way to the Temple of Music. The photo reveals his extraordinary good mood. (*Leslie's Illustrated Weekly*, 14 September 1901).

President McKinley reviews troops at the Exposition Stadium the day before he was shot. (*Leslie's Illustrated Weekly*, 14 September 1901).

The President reviews troops at the Exposition Stadium on September 5, 1901, the day before the shooting. (McClure, Alexander K. & Morris, Charles. *The Authentic Life of William McKinley: Our Third Martyr President.* Washington, DC: Act of Congress, 1901, pg. 77.)

President McKinley and his entourage leaving the New York State Building. . (*Harper's Weekly*, 14 September 1901, pg 912).

The Temple of Music where the President was shot. (McClure, Alexander K. & Morris, Charles. *The Authentic Life of William McKinley: Our Third Martyr President.* Washington, DC: Act of Congress, 1901, pg. 108).

The Temple of Music with a crowd in front during the height of the Pan American Exposition. (*Harper's Weekly*, 14 September 1901, pg. 912).

The electric ambulance that took the President to the Exposition Hospital. (*Leslie's Illustrated Weekly*, 14 September 1901).

The Exposition Hospital where the President was taken and where the operation occurred. (*Harper's Weekly*, 14 September 1901, pg. 942).

The President is carried into the Exposition Hospital as a crowd gathers. (*Leslie's Illustrated Weekly*, 9 September 1901).

Chapter 3

Leon Czolgosz – Buffalo Police photos of the President's assassin. (Channing, Walter. "The Mental Status of Czolgosz, the Assassin of President McKinley." American Journal of Insanity 59 (October 1902) 233-278.)

Another earlier photo of Leon Czolgosz. (Channing, Walter. "The Mental Status of Czolgosz, the Assassin of President McKinley." American Journal of Insanity 59 (October 1902) 233-278.)

Paul Czolgosz – father of the assassin. (Channing, Walter. "The Mental Status of Czolgosz, the Assassin of President McKinley." American Journal of Insanity 59 (October 1902) 233-278.)

Another photo of Paul Czolgosz. (Channing, Walter. "The Mental Status of Czolgosz, the Assassin of President McKinley." American Journal of Insanity 59 (October 1902) 233-278.)

A letter penned by the assassin to a friend. This is one of the few examples of the signature of Leon F. Czolgosz. (Channing, Walter. "The Mental Status of Czolgosz, the Assassin of President McKinley." American Journal of Insanity 59 (October 1902) 233-278.)

Jacob Czolgosz, brother of the assassin. (Channing, Walter. "The Mental Status of Czolgosz, the Assassin of President McKinley." American Journal of Insanity 59 (October 1902) 233-278.)

Letter sent to lodge brother John Grinder by Czolgosz while he was staying in West Seneca, using his alias of Fred C. Nieman. Most co-workers and casual acquaintances knew Czolgosz by his alias, which he said he used to prevent discrimination. (Channing, Walter. "The Mental Status of Czolgosz, the Assassin of President McKinley." American Journal of Insanity 59 (October 1902) 233-278.

Chapter 4

Dr. Presley M. Rixey, the President's loyal personal physician. (Halstead, Murat. *The Illustrious Life of William McKinley: Our Martyred President*. Privately Published, 1901.)

Dr. Roswell Park, who was put in charge of the President's treatment. A famous surgeon, he was performing an operation in Niagara Falls when the President was shot. He was rushed to Buffalo on a special train, but arrived just as the operation on the President was ending. (Halstead, Murat. *The Illustrious Life of William McKinley: Our Martyred President*. Privately Published, 1901.)

Dr. Matthew D. Mann, who performed the operation on the President. (*Harper's Weekly*, 14 September 1901).

Dr. Charles McBurney, specialist from New York who assisted in the care of the President. (*Harper's Weekly*, 14 September 1901.)

Dr. Herman Mynter, who also assisted in the President's care. (*Harper's Weekly*, 14 September 1901)

The Milburn house under guard as the wounded President fights for his life. (McClure, Alexander K. & Morris, Charles. *The Authentic Life of William McKinley: Our Third Martyr President.* Washington, DC: Act of Congress, 1901, pg. 399.)

The press tents which were set up across the street from the Milburn house. (McClure, Alexander K. & Morris, Charles. *The Authentic Life of William McKinley: Our Third Martyr President.* Washington, DC: Act of Congress, 1901, pg. 400.)

Press along the ropes near the press tents. (McClure, Alexander K. & Morris, Charles. *The Authentic Life of William McKinley: Our Third Martyr President.* Washington, DC: Act of Congress, 1901, pg. 189.)

The rear of the Milburn house. Shown is the addition that had recently been built. The x's mark the President's sick room and death chamber. (*Leslie's Illustrated Weekly*, 14 September 1901).

George Cortelyou gives the press a bulletin from the porch of the Milburn house. (*Leslie's Illustrated Weekly*, 14 September 1901).

Vice President Roosevelt talks with Senator Mark Hanna near the Milburn House. (*Harper's Weekly*, 21 September 1901, pg. 942.)

The Milburn house under guard. (*Harper's Weekly*, 21 September 1901, pg. 943.)

Organizing guards at the Milburn house. (*Harper's Weekly*, 21 September 1901, pg. 942.)

Doctor Eugene Wasdin (center) and Dr. Herman Mynter (left) in a lighter moment when it was thought that the President would recover. (*Leslie's Illustrated Weekly*, 14 September 1901).

Senator Hanna and Secretary Hitchcock show the optimism of the moment before the President's fatal downturn. (*Leslie's Illustrated Weekly*, 14 September 1901).

Dr. Charles McBurney outside the Milburn house. (*Leslie's Illustrated Weekly*, 14 September 1901).

The x-ray machine sent by Thomas Edison that was never used to locate the bullet lodged in the President. (*Harper's Weekly*, 21 September 1901, pg. 944.)

Senator Mark Hanna talking with reporters in front of the Milburn house. (*Harper's Weekly*, 21 September 1901, pg. 944.)

The Glenny House, next door to the Milburn house on Delaware Avenue. In this house, the cabinet and other dignitaries met during the President's convalescence. (*Leslie's Illustrated Weekly*, 14 September 1901).

The Buffalo Club, about two miles from the Milburn house on Delaware Avenue. The Cabinet also met here during the week long ordeal. The building still stands. (*Leslie's Illustrated Weekly*, 14 September 1901).

Chapter 6

Leon Czolgosz's signed confession.

The gun, handkerchief, and cuffs on display during the 100th Anniversary of the Pan American Exposition at the Buffalo, NY Historical Society. (Photo taken by author)

Original Buffalo, NY Police Photo of the Murder Weapon and Handkerchief.

The interior of the Temple of Music. (*Leslie's Illustrated Weekly*, 14 September 1901).

The spot where the President was shot. . (*Leslie's Illustrated Weekly*, 9 September 1901).

Buffalo City Hall, where the President lay in state and where the Czolgosz trial was held. (*Leslie's Illustrated Weekly*, 28 September 1901).

Erie County Jail, where Czolgosz was held before his trial and before his transfer to Auburn Prison. He was led from this building, through the "Tunnel of Sobs," to his trial in City Hall. (*Leslie's Illustrated Weekly*, 28 September 1901).

Auburn Prison, where Czolgosz was held and executed. Czolgosz's cell is marked with an 'x' (*Leslie's Illustrated Weekly*, 28 September 1901).

The execution room at Auburn Prison. (*Leslie's Illustrated Weekly*, 28 September 1901).

The Supreme Court courtroom where Leon Czologosz was tried for the murder of the President of the United States. (*Harper's Weekly*, 5 October 1901, pg. 1014.)

Warren Mead, the Warden of Auburn Prison, where Czolgosz was held and executed. (*Leslie's Illustrated Weekly*, 12 October 1901).

Francis P. O'Brien, the artilleryman who recovered the gun at the scene of the shooting. (*Leslie's Illustrated Weekly*, 12 October 1901).

Thomas Penney, Buffalo District Attorney who was the prosecutor at the Czolgosz trail. (Halstead, Murat. *The Illustrious Life of William McKinley: Our Martyred President*. Privately Published, 1901.)

James B. Parker, a by-stander who jumped on Czolgosz immediately after the shots. (Halstead, Murat. *The Illustrious Life of William McKinley: Our Martyred President*. Privately Published, 1901.)

Secret Service Agents Samuel Ireland (left) and George Foster. (Halstead, Murat. *The Illustrious Life of William McKinley: Our Martyred President*. Privately Published, 1901.)

James B. Parker, who assisted in apprehending the assassin. (Halstead, Murat. *The Illustrious Life of William McKinley: Our Martyred President*. Privately Published, 1901.)

Emma Goldman, who was harassed by authorities after the assassination. (Halstead, Murat. *The Illustrious Life of William McKinley: Our Martyred President*. Privately Published, 1901.)

Judge Truman C. White, who presided over the Czolgosz trial. (*Harper's Weekly*, 5 October 1901, pg. 1014.)

Loran L. Lewis, who served on the Czolgosz defense team. (*Harper's Weekly*, 5 October 1901, pg. 1014.)

Thomas Penney, the prosecutor of Leon Czolgosz. (*Harper's Weekly*, 5 October 1901, pg. 1014.)

Robert C. Titus, Czolgosz defense attorney. (*Harper's Weekly*, 5 October 1901, pg. 1014.)

An artist's illustration of Leon Czolgosz in prison, which appeared on the cover of *Leslie's Illustrated Weekly*. (*Leslie's Illustrated Weekly*, 31 October 1901).

Illustration showing Czolgosz being led to the death chamber. (*Leslie's Illustrated Weekly*, 9 September 1901).

Chapter 7

Vice President Roosevelt talks with reporters. (*Leslie's Illustrated Weekly*, 14 September 1901).

Vice President Roosevelt speaks with Senator Hanna near the Milburn house. (*Leslie's Illustrated Weekly*, 14 September 1901).

The Wilcox Mansion on Delaware Avenue where Theodore Roosevelt stayed and where he was sworn in as President of the United States. (*Leslie's Illustrated Weekly*, 14 September 1901).

Chapter 9

Leaving the Milburn house. (*Harper's Weekly*, 28 September 1901, pg. 966.)

Taking the Casket into Buffalo City Hall. (*Harper's Weekly*, 28 September 1901, pg. 966.)

Removing the casket from the hearse at Buffalo City Hall. (*Harper's Weekly*, 28 September 1901, pg. 966.)

McKinley casket taken into Buffalo City Hall. (Everett, Marshall. *The Complete Life of William McKinley and the Story of His Assassination*. Privately Published, 1901, p. 247.)

McKinley funeral procession in Buffalo passing St. Paul's Cathedral en route to funeral train. (Everett, Marshall. *The Complete Life of William McKinley and the Story of His Assassination*. Privately Published, 1901, pg. 248.)

Lying in state in the Buffalo City Hall. (*Harper's Weekly*, 28 September 1901, pg. 966.)

The line of mourners waiting to see the President in Buffalo City Hall. (*Harper's Weekly*, 28 September 1901, pg. 966.)

The train tracks near East Palestine, Ohio, where people waited for the funeral train to pass. Many put coins on the tracks to be smashed by the train to keep as souvenirs. (*Harper's Weekly*, 28 September 1901, pg. 988.)

The casket on the way to the funeral train in Buffalo. (*Harper's Weekly*, 28 September 1901, pg. 967.)

Independence Hall in Philadelphia decked out in mourning. (*Harper's Weekly*, 28 September 1901, pg. 976.)

Lying in state at the White House. (McClure, Alexander K. & Morris, Charles. *The Authentic Life of William McKinley: Our Third Martyr President.* Washington, DC: Act of Congress, 1901, pg. 318)

Members of Congress in the McKinley funeral procession pass the Treasury Building from the White House to the Capital. (McClure, Alexander K. & Morris, Charles. *The Authentic Life of William McKinley: Our Third Martyr President.* Washington, DC: Act of Congress, 1901, pg. 354.)

The President's Casket is born up the steps of the Capital. (McClure, Alexander K. & Morris, Charles. *The Authentic Life of William McKinley: Our Third Martyr President.* Washington, DC: Act of Congress, 1901, pg. 327.)

The casket being taken into the Rotunda of the Capital. (*Harper's Weekly*, 28 September 1901, pg. 969.)

The east front of the Capital as the casket enters. Note the umbrellas due to the rainy weather. (*Harper's Weekly*, 28 September 1901, pg. 970.)

Another view of the umbrellas in the plaza near the Capital. (*Harper's Weekly*, 28 September 1901, pg. 970.)

The Rotunda of the Capital ready for the President's funeral service. (McClure, Alexander K. & Morris, Charles. *The Authentic Life of William McKinley: Our Third Martyr President.* Washington, DC: Act of Congress, 1901, pg. 271).

Rev. Dr. Manchester, who delivered the funeral address in Canton. (*Harper's Weekly*, 28 September 1901, pg. 977.)

Bishop Andrews, who delivered the funeral oration at the Capital. (*Harper's Weekly*, 28 September 1901, pg. 977.)

Reverend Locke. (*Leslie's Illustrated Weekly*, 14 September 1901).

Arrival of the funeral train in Canton. (*Harper's Weekly*, 28 September 1901, pg. 973.)

McKinley home under military guard in Canton. (*Harper's Weekly*, 28 September 1901, pg. 973.)

The funeral train at Canton. (*Harper's Weekly*, 28 September 1901, pg. 988.)

One of the specialty constructed funeral arches in Canton. (*Harper's Weekly*, 28 September 1901, pg. 972.)

Taking the casket into the church in Canton. (Everett, Marshall. *The Complete Life of William McKinley and the Story of His Assassination.* Privately Published, 1901, pg. 356.)

McKinley funeral procession moves through Canton. Everett, Marshall. *The Complete Life of William McKinley and the Story of His Assassination.* Privately Published, 1901, p. 273.)

Stark County Courthouse in Canton. (*Harper's Weekly*, 28 September 1901, pg. 973.)

Taking the casket from the church in Canton. (*Harper's Weekly*, 28 September 1901, pg. 973.)

Casket in Canton. President Roosevelt can be seen, second from left with the hat. (McClure, Alexander K. & Morris, Charles. *The Authentic Life of William McKinley: Our Third Martyr President.* Washington, DC: Act of Congress, 1901, pg. 435).

Canton City Hall at the time of the McKinley funeral. (Halstead, Murat. *The Illustrious Life of William McKinley: Our Martyred President.* Privately Published, 1901, pg. 389.)

McKinley casket being placed into the vault at burial site in Canton. (Everett, Marshall. *The Complete Life of William McKinley and the Story of His Assassination.* Privately Published, 1901, pg. 374.)

Photograph showing floral arrangements at burial site in Canton. (Everett, Marshall. *The Complete Life of William McKinley and the Story of His Assassination.* Privately Published, 1901, pg. 391.)

The McKinley monument in Canton. (Picture taken by author.)

The caskets inside the monument. (Picture taken by author.)

The marker that stands in place where the Temple of Music once stood. (Picture taken by author.)

Parking lot where the Milburn house once stood. (Picture taken by author.)

INDEX

MCKINLEY (cont.)
318 356-359 361-363 366-
367 370 372 374-375 377-
379 381-382 396-397
Nancy Allison 1 President 1
21-23 25-29 31 34-36 39 41
46-47 49-50 55 63 68 78 80
82-83 101 118 127 131 134
139-140 147 152 156 162
165 167 182 187-188 197
204 211 216 218 220-221
227-228 239-240 243-245
273 278 296 315-317 319
321-323 331 331 333 344
355 358 360-362 366-367
372-373 375-377 379 381
383 385 387 398-399
William 1-4 9-10 13 15 20
23 26 192 194 212 244 262
281-282 330 336 338 360
362 385 398 William Sr 1
MCWILLIAMS, Lafayette Mrs
357 Mary 152 152 Mrs 190
Mrs Lafayette 160 172
MEAD, 307 J Warren 297 312
Warden 298-299 301 304
306 308-309 311-312
Warren J 303
MECHTLANIC, Julia 212
MERKLE, Officer 248
MERTENS, Joachim H 261
METZFALTR, Catarina 85
Katren 85
MEYER, Dr Edward J 133
MILBURN, 34 39-41 47 50 56-
57 61 63 74 139 145 145
147 151-153 158 162 166-
167 170 173 180 188 317-
318 383 John 35 135 148
154 160 185 319-320 357
370 394 399 John G 33 386

MILBURN (cont.)
Mr 51 62 149 183 189 268
271 277 Mrs 76 319
MILLER, 297 391 C W 247
MINCEL, Mrs 85
MINTZ, Jacob 286
MISGALSKI, Valentine 87
MITCHELL, 256 285 293-294
George N 261 292 Sheriff
296
MOHN, Miss 170
MOLITER, 86 Henry 85
MONTGOMERY, 67 Benjamin
F 66 Col 181
MOORIS, Gouverneur 328
MOOT, Adelbert 250 342
MORGAN, J P 337-338 359
MORRIS, Miss 138 Miss M C
137 Nurse 137-139
MORSE, Mrs 3
MORTON, Levi 18 Rev A D 4
MOST, 217 Johann 216 218
MULLER, Henry 41
MUNN, 119 R L 118
MURPHY, 42 213
Commissioner 41 Frank 298
MYNTER, 136 265 392 Dr 135
137-138 142-144 148 155-
156 160 163 170-171 173
175-176 178 181 184 193
196 198-199 203 248 258
266-267 Dr Herman 134
264 391 Herman 83
NAYLER, Rev H R 375
NEBOCK, 298
NEBROCK, 91
NEFF, Louis 58 275-276
Private 59 Pvt 272
NEIMAN, Fred C 212
NIEMAN, 102 104-106 109
228 236 Fred 101 103 209
Fred C 77 91 111 113

428

About the Author

Jeff Seibert is a 1979 graduate of Morehead State University with a B.A. in Communications and a double major in Radio-Television & Journalism. This is his first book. He has been a history enthusiast since college, with a particular interest in political assassinations, the American Revolution, the Civil War, the 1960's and Russian history. He has worked in broadcasting and written briefly for newspapers, before being employed by the Internal Revenue Service in 1988. He collects sports memorabilia and autographs. He currently is serving as President of the National Treasury Employees Union at the Cincinnati IRS Service Center. He resides in Batavia, Ohio.